THE SCHOOL FIX, NYC, USA

MIRIAM WASSERMAN

OUTERBRIDGE & DIENSTFREY

DISTRIBUTED BY E.P. DUTTON & COMPANY

Grateful acknowledgment is made for permission to reprint excerpts from *The Sociology of Teaching,* Willard Waller, 1967 edition (New York: John Wiley & Sons, Inc.); *Culture Against Man,* Jules Henry, 1963 (New York: Random House, Inc.); and *Leviathan,* Vol. 1, No. 3, June 1969.

Library of Congress number 78-110139
First published in the United States of America in 1970

Manufactured in the United States of America
First Printing

Outerbridge & Dienstfrey
200 West 72nd Street, New York, 10023

TO JOSEPH I. AND ANNA WOLF WEBER,
MY OWN FIRST AND MOST IMPORTANT TEACHERS

Part I. Power and Status in the Schools

Part II.
The Struggle for Power and Status

Part III. The Struggle against Power and Status

Postlude: The School Fix, USA 513

PREFACE

My aim in writing this book has been to discover and explain how American public education works—what functions it performs and by what processes. I have also wanted to tell some stories about events and people whose drama, or fates, or significance touched me.

As a matter of fact, when I first thought about writing the book, I mainly wanted to tell the stories. Like several other teacher-writers of the last few years, my relationships with the students I taught—as it happened, in New York City—had stirred such deep feelings in me that when I began to write, it was about them that I wanted to tell the world. Then when I came to it, in 1967, it was apparent that a great and exciting challenge to the New York public school system was in the process of fermenting, to which I should have to attend if I wanted to write about the New York schools and the people in them. So events pushed me from the grateful task of telling about the personal situations and struggles of people I very much cared for to the equally grateful task of telling about a movement and a conflict that might be productive of social change. The movement was the community-control movement, and the conflict was between it and the various groups in the school system that were resisting social change.

But sitting down to write, I found that I couldn't tell the stories of either the people or the conflict without understanding what they meant. There is a kind of idiocy to the tales of public education in New York (and the whole nation) which makes them incredible, except if one appreciates that idiocy, too, has a core of meaning.

Recently I drove across the country and talked with people on the way—in New Jersey, in New Mexico, in California—about the schools in their towns, and sometimes they'd say, "Did you read that book about the terrible things that go on in the Boston schools?" (Jonathan Kozol's *Death at an Early Age,* dramatizing the schools' brutality), or, "You know that book by . . . what's his name . . . Kohl?" (Herbert Kohl's *Thirty-Six Children,* dramatizing their indifference), or "I read Herndon's hilarious book about teaching in a California school," (James Herndon's *The Way It Spozed to Be,* dramatizing their lunacy). "Tell me," they'd go on, "do you think that's really true—Kozol, Kohl, Herndon? Is it really that bad—in Boston, New York, California?" The skepticism is natural enough in the face of arrangements and behavior so blatantly antipathetic not only to the schools' apparent aims but to all we know about how children grow and to all we are as human beings and nurturing animals.

The knowledge that learning is something people do, not something they receive, is part of the wisdom of the race, shared by mothers, piano teachers, and trainers of prizefighters and articulated by the writers and thinkers of almost every age, from Rabelais to John Dewey to John Holt. Nevertheless, the public schools of the nation typically enforce on their pupils an onerous passivity and silence which make the teacher's task difficult and the students' lives wretched. Among the young of every species but our own, learning (growing) is endowed with the spontaneity that accompanies the fulfillment of biologic imperatives, but the learning that the schoolchild experiences is typically received with the loathing one feels for that which is foreign and compelled. And among the adults in the school, engaged in the human pursuit of rearing the young, which more than any other human activity except conceiving them has its meaning in the warmth one gives to it and the satisfaction one derives from it, there is less warmth and less satisfaction than there is between the fisherman and the trout.

The persistence and prevalence of our schools' antieducational, antihuman, and antibiological ways suggest that not merely chance or teachers' perversity or children's nastiness is the source. Something must be going on here. Some function is being performed which society and the schoolpeople themselves may disclaim, or not recognise, or dislike, but which they nevertheless continue to tolerate on a wide scale and over a long time. And perhaps not only to tolerate but in some covert, unacknowledged way, to welcome.

I felt I had to discover for myself and my readers what is going on.

Both the stories I tell and the interpretations I offer by way of explaining what is going on focus on one city, and on that city in a time of vicious, but also in a way exhilarating, crisis. Moreover, both stories and interpretations lean heavily, although not exclusively, on the school experiences of the most oppressed and least respected subgroup—namely, the nonwhite and poor—of a generally oppressed and unrespected group of people, namely schoolchildren. (I think that if I had had the perceptions about the school processes when I began the book that I have now as I finish it, I would have investigated more fully the modes and effects of oppression and lack of respect on white and middle-class schoolchildren.) But even the distorted processes of the malfunctioning school system of one unusual city move within the bounding needs and injunctions of public schooling in the whole nation. Freud taught us how to use an examination of the abnormal to achieve insights into the functioning of the normal. From the agonies of New York we should be able to better understand the quieter miserableness of Denver, Colorado, or Little Rock, Arkansas, or Lincoln County, Maine. And from the nasty battles of New York perhaps we will learn to devise more effective strategies of change in Washington, Atlanta, Detroit, and maybe even some day again in New York. In a way, then, this book is an exercise in synecdoche, with the New York school system representing the American school system, Miss Jersild's or Miss White's classroom representing the processes of American education, and Miles Randolph or the students, representing its products.

I don't want to carry the symbolism too far, however Denver and Little Rock and Lincoln County don't have to go the road New York has gone—any more than a fellow with a mild mother-fixation has to end up in the psychopathic ward. And the lessons to be drawn from New York's struggles may help parents and students in Washington, Atlanta, and Detroit to avoid the stinging defeats that New York's parents and students experienced. (There are some additional comments on this matter in the concluding section.)

More important, no individual, or school, or classroom that I have described is "typical." I chose my examples in a terribly unscientific way. Of the people, some I had known previously, others I encountered by chance. Of the schools, again chance, or an invitation, or some public event brought me to visit. Of the classrooms, a principal's selection or a teacher's invitation determined where I went. Usually when I began a series of conversations, I wouldn't know except in a very general way what stories the subject would have to tell, or when I would enter a classroom, I wouldn't know what specific interactions would be going on there (although, of course, I could sometimes make pretty shrewd guesses). But always, when I listened to people and watched them, they were first of all individuals for me, and I hope I have been a skillful enough writer so that the reader, even while appraising the general significance of their stories, will also appreciate the subjects as individuals.

The reader may be interested to know that I used a tape recorder for the personal conversations on which I report, written notes made at the time or immediately afterwards for the classroom observations, and one or the other or both for the meetings and interviews with public figures. I, or my collaborating interviewer, had many meetings, usually over a period of weeks or even months, with individuals, who told about extended experiences—like Willie or Miles or Miss Allbright. But we had only one or two with Mrs. Dalton and her son Brad, who told about a suspension experience; with Miss Jersild, who was a very open person and good talker and with whom I also spent a day in school; and with Benny, with whose family I stayed intermittently for some months, during most of which time he was away in the service. I never disbelieved anybody's account of any experience, but I did try when there was time to get people to go over incidents that seemed extreme or bizarre (for example, the report from Miles that one of his teachers changed her underwear in class or the statement by Miss Jersild that her students had to slide down the bench at lunch to keep making room for other children). I don't think anybody was ever deliberately putting me on. But if they were, the way they chose to do it is also part of their story. Also, while I used only a fraction of the accounts I had, I didn't make it a point either to include or exclude the extreme and the bizarre. I think I tended to select those data that helped me to understand an individual's overall school experience and those that were most significant to him; the criteria tended to merge.

As the reader will see, the subjects—teachers and pupils both—are all very different, in their personalities, backgrounds, and responses to school. What they had in common was a willingness, often an eagerness, to talk about their school experiences, and the fact that I liked them. (I have not described in depth any teacher or pupil whom I personally disliked.) I don't know if these attributes bias the sample or not.

While all the teachers and pupils are real people (with the exception of Miss White, who is a composite of real people), all, except a few whose names were in the newspapers, have been given, or gave themselves, pseudonyms. The same is true of the individual schools.

My accounts of the struggles for and against community control and student freedom draw on both public information and personal investigation. While the latter did not produce any startling inside secrets, it did sharpen my insights into how the school system and the people in it work, and especially into how the echoing and re-echoing of hostility, suspiciousness, hypocrisy, and personal ego needs help to provoke and aggravate social and political crises. Again, while most of the people I associated with in respect to this aspect of the book were daily involved in the struggle, and while a few were publicly prominent, I did not look for "typical" leaders, and I did not even meet some of the best known of the protagonists, for example, Rhody

McCoy, unit administrator of Ocean Hill-Brownsville, or John Doar, chairmen of the board of education.

What I have done, then, in this book is to try to describe the dynamics and the current crisis of public education in the United States, offering in evidence of my generalizations a fcw schools, a fcw classrooms, and a few individuals of one city, none of which pretend to be typical. I hope that the examples will better commend themselves to the reader as "real" just because they are individuals and not norms. But any individual–city or school or human being–can tell us something about the class of which he is a single item. As New York's schools *in extremis* can, I believe, inform us about schools throughout the nation, so can Jerry and Kenny and Loretta, and Mrs. Harris and Miss Truman inform us about the fix in which most of the nation's pupils and teachers are caught. And so, I hope, can the fierce struggles of I.S. 201, the United Federation of Teachers, the student rebels, and the high school principals inform us of the intent and strategies of the revolt against and the defense of the schools' ways.

All the people in my life who personally or through their writings taught me how to think and feel about people and issues helped to make this book. I thank them.

I thank, too, the hundreds of people who contributed specifically to the creation of the book. I regret that I cannot mention by name all the teachers, students, parents, rebels, functionaries, administrators, and other citizens who shared their perceptions and knowledge and feelings with me. I remember them all, for even while as a writer I was serving as a vehicle for their experiences, as a person I was enriched by my encounters with them.

From the young men and women with whom I shared hundreds of classroom hours apparently in pursuit of knowledge of poetry or punctuation, I learned to appreciate style and nerve and a special kind of graciousness. Three of them appear as subjects of this book. I thank through them all those others whom I, and I believe the three I present, sense to be standing behind them. All the subjects whose personal stories are told gave up time and privacy. They created this book as much as I did, and I think they did so with the hope, like mine, that it might benefit other pupils and teachers and parents. If it does, that is their return, to which I add my thanks for their confidence and trust in me.

It was much harder for the people who were engaged in the bitter public struggle for community control to trust and confide in me. My "outsideness," both to the struggle and to their racial experience, added to the difficulty. Nevertheless, throughout the city, people who were living in the twenty-four-hour-a-day travail of trying to defend what seemed to them the first faint chance for change in the ways of the school world, generously gave me time and audaciously told me what they were thinking and doing. Especially people around the 201 Complex did this. Ronald Briggs and Joyce Arnold, administrative personnel in the complex, were courteous and meticulous in providing information and documents and arranging appointments. Florence Thau added hours weekly to her arduous round of teaching, meeting, and telephoning, to keep me accurately informed. Charles Wilson, the administrative head of the complex, suffered my nagging presence and dogging footsteps over a period of many months, only once putting me down, and probably not too many times putting me on, always, however, with wit and charm. Several members of the Planning Board and Governing Board provided documents and reminiscences, and many children and teachers and a number of principals hospitably accepted my visiting.

Many people at the offices of the United Federation of Teachers were generous with time, information, and explanations, and access to their files and their meetings. A number were friends or acquaintances of many years, but their openness was such that I felt it would have been extended also were I a stranger. There is much that I would have understood only much more dimly if it had not been for their help, and I thank them. Among them are John and Vivian O'Neill, who talked with me at length both before and after John and the UFT parted.

Edward Gottlieb talked with me over the years for a total of scores of hours, about schools, children, education, and about the absurdities and sweetnesses of his own long history as an anarchist-pacifist school principal. Bertha Gruner gave me a view of school from the school secretary's side of the office barriers and a view of the young teachers whom I call rebels from an old radical's side of the political barriers. Frances O'Brien kept me generally informed about events in a part of the city I did not often visit and at echelons to which I had no access.

Some of the above read and commented to its profit on all or parts of the manuscript, as did: Marilyn Gittell, James Horelick, Bernice Kornyetz, Deborah Meier, Robert Nichol, Rosalie Stutz, and several of the student subjects. Peggy Creider's full reading led to several improvements in style, logic, and clarity.

The publication of several sections of the book during its early stages by *The Urban Review* provided both monetary and morale-building support. I thank both the Center for Urban Education, publisher, and Joseph Lederer, editor of the *Review*.

Conversations and correspondence over a period of years with Chet Creider provided insights and bibliographic suggestions without which I might never have clarified some of the fundamental ideas of the book.

John Reimann's gifts in human relations produced what I believe are among the book's most useful and sensitive extended-interview portraits, and gained entry into the student movement without which I could not have written an authentic account of it.

Harris Dienstfrey helped me figure out what was wrong when we both knew something was wrong and was quiet when I was agitated; he and his editing strengthened me and the book.

My husband Jac gave me the courage to undertake this book and the time, support, and love to go on with it. I thank him the most.

San Francisco, California
January 1970

Part I.
Power and Status in the Schools

I thought I was nobody and only knew how to obey, and here I am, able to give orders. What is this principle which bestows a value on a man who had no value before? The principle of hierarchy.

—Victor Serge, *The Case of Comrade Tuleyev*

1. THE APPETITE FOR ADVANTAGEOUS EDUCATION

For nearly ten years after the justices of the United States Supreme Court innocently initiated the second Reconstruction by ordering equal education for black and white children, the Board of Education of the City of New York made haste slowly by issuing pronouncements and plans. Also, here and there throughout the city, they allowed a few black children to attend nearby white children's schools under a program called Open Enrollment. (Open enrollment plans have at various times also served as a poor excuse for integration in the Deep South.)

Then the events of the new Reconstruction began to unfold: as the nation watched in horror, nonviolent street demonstrators in Birmingham, Alabama, were set upon by policemen and policedogs, and at the same time four black Sunday school children were murdered; in Oxford, Mississippi, the admission by force of one Negro student to Ole Miss' produced a white riot; in New York City aroused black groups increased their agitation for compliance by the city school system with the law of the land; New York State Commissioner of Education James Allen began to ask what New York City was doing to improve racial balance in its schools; and 100,000 people, spurred by hoopla and hopes, marched on Washington, to demand Jobs and Freedom. And the Board of Education of the City of New York was moved to act.

In September, 1963, it proposed to "pair" two of the city's more than six hundred elementary schools. The schools were in Jackson Heights-Corona, a growing and changing section of the borough of Queens, which lies both geographically and sociologically between the older and poorer borough of Brooklyn and the newer and wealthier Long Island suburbs. One of the schools (in the Jackson Heights portion of the area) was about 87 percent middle- and lower-middle-class white, and the other (in the Corona portion) about 99 percent, largely middle-class, Negro and Puerto Rican. According to the proposed pairing, all the first- and second-grade children, black and white, would attend one school, and all the third- through sixth-grade children the other. Being housed under the same roof, black and white children would presumably be subjected to the same educational process and so would all emerge at the end of the sixth grade indistinguishable except for color.

A year after the plan was announced, the schools were paired, but pairing as a large citywide program has been aborted in the convulsions experienced by many of the parents of the Jackson Heights school and by other parents throughout the city. Some Jackson Heights parents and their allies elsewhere organized into groups called Parents and Taxpayers (PAT) and rallied to the defense of a new symbol, the "neighborhood school," being threatened, they claimed, by a new and terrifying danger, "forced busing." "Forced busing" referred to the possibility that children who were to attend school more than a few blocks from their homes might be carried there in board of education buses. PAT members tended to be lower-middle class and/or second- or third-generation immigrants and their slogan "neighborhood schools," as well as the spectre they raised, "forced busing," was commonly understood to represent anti-Negro, anti-integrationist sentiment: *what the PAT parents were fighting was having their children "force-bused" into "inferior" neighboring schools and having the "inferior" children "force-bused" into their "better schools."* [1]

Four years later, in 1968, when the movement to improve minority children's schooling through integration had become hardly more than a memory, a dispute in another part of the city between two other groups of people again agitated the Jackson Heights and other PAT parents, this time to a condition resembling panic. The advocates of adequate schooling for minority children had shifted ground, demanding now not that the dark children be allowed to go to the academically better schools along with the light children but that the dark children's parents be empowered to make their children's schools into better schools.

In the borough of Brooklyn, in a poor section known as Ocean Hill-Brownsville, a group of neighborhood people who were seeking to control and improve their schools became embroiled in a controversy with the trade union representing the teachers when the local school board, representing the residents, terminated the services of nineteen teachers in their schools. In response to this action, the teachers union called a strike which closed all the city's schools for two and a half months, a disaster for the city's grownups equivalent to, although the opposite of, Pied Piper's exploit. The community group said they had merely "transferred" the teachers out of their schools to board of education central headquarters, while the teachers union said the group had "fired" the teachers without a fair hearing—or as it soon came to be called, "due process"; and the war that waged between those who said "transfer" and those who said "fire" was not less bitter than the controversy between Gregory and Henry over the investiture of bishops—and apparently not less frivolous, except to those who understood that in both cases not the symbols but the status and power symbolized were the objects of the struggle and that the union's real objection was to allowing parents, especially of poor dark children, to control their schools.

It is interesting that the phrase "due process," which seems to embody all that is fair and open and regularized in Anglo-American jurisprudence has, in addition, a long history in America as a legal instrument for protecting vested interests against the demands of the poor and the declassed. Passing into the Fifth Amendment to the Constitution of the United States from English common law, where the phrase protected free individuals from arbitrary action of the Crown, it was intended to protect citizens against arbitrary action by the federal government, reflecting the anxieties along these lines of the Founding Fathers. The clause was little used until after the Civil War when it was embodied in the Fourteenth Amendment with the ostensible purpose of protecting the freedmen against denial of their rights by the governments of the former slave states: "Nor shall any state deprive any person of life, liberty or property without due process of law." It was after this that "due process" became an instrument for the protection of emerging power groups. From about 1890 to well into this century, with a corporation being considered a person under law, the phrase was widely used to prevent state governments from regulating or controlling various corporate functions, or depriving corporations of "property without due process." Thus, in this period, not only was public utility rate control severely impeded, but so also was much humanitarian legislation, such as control of child labor, minimum wages, maximum hours for women, etc.

The revival of "due process" again during the teachers strike of 1968 is more than a historical curiosity. It suggests that power comes to be institutionalized in certain social, legal, and political procedures, which the powerless must either ignore or deliberately challenge when they are trying to wrest power for themselves. When they do this, the beneficiaries of the procedures are likely to rally around a phrase which suggests that the procedures are somehow expressions not of immediate power relationships but of eternal justice.

If the union had used as its slogan a more general term, such as "justice" or "fair treatment," it might have been even more apparent to many people than it was that in the long run, for the children and adults of Ocean Hill-Brownsville there was even less justice and fair treatment than for the nineteen teachers. "Due process," as it referred to the specific grievance of the teachers in that situation and the specific remedy they sought, generally evoked no sense of the wider injustices experienced by the black children and parents.

The union's controversy with the representatives of that little community in Brooklyn, Ocean Hill-Brownsville, caught on like a barroom brawl throughout the entire city, and in no time at all everyone was in there throwing chairs, including the parents from Jackson Heights and the other

PAT groups. They took the side of the teachers in opposition to the black parents, apparently executing a flip-flop on the issues. Originally, they had opposed the entrance of their Negro neighbors into "their" schools, and now they were opposing their Negro neighbors' taking control of their own schools and remaining segregated.

The apparent flip-flop was not a real flip-flop. The fact is that we are unfair to the Queens parents when we accuse them of having acted in the first instance merely to defend themselves against integration. And we only contribute to the confusion if in the second instance we use the catch-all term "racism" to describe their reaction, and the teachers'. In both cases what was under attack, what the parents and the teachers were defending, was nothing less than the public school system as they knew it and wanted it to be and, beyond that, in effect, the entire social system and their children's and their own places in those systems. And by their lights they were quite correct to feel as threatened as they did.

White parents' "insatiable appetite for advantageous segregated education" was a phrase used in a public meeting by a representative of the National Association for the Advancement of Colored People. The meeting, held in February, 1968, before the Ocean Hill-Brownsville imbroglio, was a public hearing on a miniscule board of education plan to improve the racial balance in some Queens high schools. At the meeting a teacher who supported the board's plan, but probably not because it would "advance colored people," also testified:

> Something subtle begins to happen in a de facto segregated school after the school's Negro population passes the 40 percent mark. Normal trends become irreversible and the pace is accelerated. Early symptoms of a fatal illness appear. The building becomes underutilized. The departments cut back on their courses, the brightest pupils go elsewhere. Teachers are excessed [a procedure for transferring out extra teachers when the student population declines, according to a complex formula involving seniority]. Academic departments decline and a form of rigor mortis begins to set in.[2]

The argument that it is the black students who degrade the school, rather than the school which degrades the black students, is a relatively common one. For example, in the following year student strife in a neighboring high school was ascribed by its principal and many of its teachers to too many Negro students. A letter to State Commissioner of Education James Allen by the union's chapter chairman at that school said that the school was "about to enter the last phase of an academic deterioration that began four years ago when the student population began to shift from predominantly white to predominantly black."[3]

The teachers' reasons for supporting integration in the Queens high schools were not the same as the NAACP spokesman's, but, on the contrary and surprisingly, were based on the same value judgements as those underlying the Jackson Heights parents' opposition to integration. The NAACP spokesman sought simply an end to the insult of segregated education and thereby, it was hoped, an end to the injury of inferior education. The reasoning was the same as the Court's in 1954: send them to the white schools and there they will get as good an education as the white children. But the teachers and the PAT parents regarded the black children themselves as the bearers of the seeds of educational inferiority: where there are black students, or "too many" black students, the school is, or quickly becomes, inferior. More than educational considerations are involved in such an argument. For teachers, the inferiority of a too-heavily black student body devalues their professional status. For white parents, too many black students devalue both the education and the status of their children. It produces this dual effect, presumably, by "lowering the school's educational standards." It was the fear of such a lowering that provoked the PAT parents' panic of 1963 and 1964, as it is this fear that annually drives hundreds of thousands of young white families from the central city's schools to the "better schools" in the suburbs.

What the PAT parents envisioned when they had to confront integration was the shattering of the aspirations for their children that had driven them to compete strenuously (and sometimes ruthlessly) for better housing in better neighborhoods, so that they could send their children to better schools. In an analysis of the original Jackson Heights-Corona controversy, two sociologists (Kurt Lang and Gladys Engel Lang) found that opponents of the integration plan tended to be of lower socio-economic status than supporters, and to have fewer years of education.[4] We may infer then that the opponents felt less secure in their own status. Similarly, what the high school teachers saw with dismay and despair as their students turned darker year by year, was that after striving and maneuvering to move out of the worse schools in which many had probably started their teaching careers into better schools with better students and better courses, they were going to find themselves in schools turning black with the "fatal illness" of academic deterioration for all and loss of status for themselves.

And when they fought the Ocean Hill-Brownsville parents' demand to take over and improve their own inferior, segregated schools, the teachers and the Jackson Heights parents were fighting the very same threat. What they and white parents throughout the city dimly sensed, and the teachers clearly saw, was an upsetting of the status and power arrangements that made the 87 percent white Jackson Heights school, for example, better than the 99 percent black Corona school, suburban schools better than city schools, white students better than black students. To send one's child to a "better" school has become as essential to the comfort and the self-image of white America as inside plumbing and a two-week summer vacation. The better school is essential not only to enhance the parents' self-esteem during the school years but also to ensure the child an edge as he moves through school competition toward occupational and social competition. But there is no competition without losers. And "better," of course, is a comparative term, not an absolute: where there is a better, there has to be a worse. It would serve neither the self-esteem needs of the white parents nor the competitive occupational needs of the children if all schools were "better." Just as it would not serve the gamblers if all the horses ran first place.

The positions that various white groups have taken for or against integration, and for or against community control, have to do not only with their subjective feelings about race but also with the kind of social system the schools are; the ways they serve society; and the groups' sense of their status and power positions within the school social system and the larger social system. The schools of

New York City—like schools throughout the nation—perform many functions besides the obvious one of training the young in a few rudimentary skills and conveying to them a smattering of superficial and frequently false information. Primarily they serve as a status-reinforcing institution. This is so at every level and in all their respects. It is true as between the children and their teacher, the teachers and their principal, the principals and their district superintendent, and the district superintendents and the superintendent of schools. At each level the inferiors, literally as well as figuratively, sit quietly in rows before their superior and raise their hands when they want to speak. It is also true as between "good" children and "bad" children, "good" classes and "bad" classes, "good" schools and "bad" schools. These designations describe an individual's or a group of individuals' status within a particular category; thus a good class is higher than a bad class, and a teacher in a good school higher than a teacher in a bad school.

The ways in which the school as a status-reinforcing institution serves the larger society is the subject of another book, although I hope that the reader will join me in occasionally thinking about this relationship. What are some of the instruments that schools use to reinforce status; how the institution of school as a status-reinforcer serves individuals and groups in it, with great damage to all but compensating gains to some; how those who are most damaged have sought either to acquire gains for themselves or to destroy the school as a status-reinforcer (which leads defenders to accuse them rightly of trying to destroy the school system); how some of those who profit from the system as it is are seeking to protect their profits; and how others are renouncing the little gains of the system to go after larger human gains—these are the concerns of this book.

2. EDUCATIONAL INPUTS AND OUTPUTS— CONVENTIONAL MEASURES

During America's first century and a half as a nation, education was one means of economic mobility. More common ones were business and politics. But the sons of those who moved along in business and politics customarily received, as they still do, more and/or better schooling than did the sons of those who were left behind. Advocates of public education believed that the poor needed enough education, especially moral, to fit them for society's needs: "As [Henry] Barnard told the Rhode Island legislature in 1845, civilized men had to decide for the urban poor how best to raise them from barbarism."[1] And the sons of the nouveaux riches needed education not so much for occupational advancement as to polish up the roughnesses left by their humble origins. Nowadays, even for the well-to-do and the wealthy, education has become a prerequisite to merely staying in the same place. (Among some groups, indeed, the higher the original status, the more education the scions must undergo. In a private school in New York patronized by the excessively wealthy and powerful, three year olds are expected to learn to read. Not only are the rich no longer idle, but their children no longer experience childhood.)

In those early years, there was a myth and also a reality that poor children who could manage to stay in school would have advantages over those who couldn't. The poor boy who studied hard might become a doctor or an accountant, and the poor girl a teacher or a nurse, perhaps giving them an advantage over their peers who left school for mine or shop or clerk's desk at age twelve or fourteen. With the enactment of child labor laws in the early twentieth century (which coincided with the economy's declining need to exploit the young in that particular way), school-leaving age was gradually raised in one state after another, and poor children were no longer leaving school at age twelve or fourteen.

Unlike the practice in many European societies, American society with its centuries of considerable social fluidity has had the tradition of sending middle-class children and poor children alike to public, state-supported schools. Thus, the poor children who stayed in school for increasing numbers of years attended the same school systems and frequently the same schools as their middle-class age mates. In the case of Negro children there is the minor variation that in the southern states there have always been, as in the Deep South there continue to be, separate school *systems* for Negroes and for whites, and in the northern cities not separate systems but, as a matter of convention, separate schools. (Northerners have regularly protected themselves against the charge of discrimination for maintaining separate schools by explaining that not the will of school officials and parents but housing segregation has created school segregation. This argument is an evasion. Separate housing arrangements for Negroes and whites are dictated not by laws of the natural universe but largely by white families' desire not to live in proximity with Negroes. This is especially so among white families with schoolchildren, for whom the color of the neighborhood school's population is a primary consideration in choosing a living place. Where overlapping black and white neighborhoods have forced whites to send their children to school with blacks, the schools have frequently managed to segregate the two groups within the school building. Thus, what southern communities achieved simply and thoroughly by state law and honest custom, northern communities achieve covertly and not quite so thoroughly by means of the free housing market and administrative arrangements within schools.)

But the means used to separate black from white pupils are not crucial. For the fact is, whether the systems were separate, the schools were separate, or only the children were separate, well-to-do children and poor children—and, of course, cutting partly across class lines, white children and black children—have for many decades now received *unequal* education in America. And because all persons are now required to attend school until early adulthood, the inequality of the educational experience has become a way of reinforcing inequality of economic and/or racial status. Compulsory schooling has thus become another way of keeping the down down. As the situation now is, it might be plausibly argued, for example, that if the children of some Negro families were allowed to leave school at an early age, or never had to attend school at all and were entirely under their parents' tutelage, and if school credentials were not required to enter the work world (but simply training, ability, and performance levels), those children would have a clear advantage not only over their brothers but also over many white children who attend "better" schools. A fifteen year old that I know who was suspended from a Louisiana school for refusing to salute the flag was set to reading and studying four hours a day by her father. Both child and parent were delighted by how much more she had learned after six months than she would have in the eight hours she would have spent attending school and doing homework. But she missed her friends.

The Educational Dollar Rewards Status

The South's dual school system has for long been the most dramatic exemplification of honest inequality of education—and the most distressing to many northern whites, including northern educators and teachers.[2] Northerners and southerners, black and white, have all understood that the South's dual school system fitted functionally into the South's entire social-racial-class system. But only black northerners and unreconstructed white southerners have understood what obtains throughout the nation: *that human and material resources are apportioned among students in accordance with the educational outcome to which their social class is believed to entitle them.* The noted spokesman for continuously accelerating competition in schooling, James Bryant Conant, pointed out in *Slums and Suburbs* that wealthy suburban schools spend as much as $1,000 per child per year, while big city public schools, which serve large numbers of the very poor, typically spend less than half that, and that the suburban pupil-teacher ratio is about 1 to 14 while the big city ratio is about 1 to 25. Recognizing the existence of such differences, the white Queens parents we met above, not content with better urban schools, typically move on to still better suburban schools when family circumstances permit, "better" being measured not only by dollars spent on education but also by levels of academic expertise expected of the students.

The differences between suburban and urban schools, like the differences between the northern cities' separate schools for blacks and whites, are achieved not by a simple stroke of legislators' or administrators' pens but by a complex interlocking of many social factors. First, public school systems in America are financed largely by local taxes on real property. With migration from urban centers of well-to-do families and of industry and business, the tax base of most large cities is declining rapidly and so their capacity to finance public services, including schools, for those who do not move to the suburbs—which means, more and more, the poor. In addition, suburban property owners, many of whom are parents of schoolchildren or are engaged in business enterprises that are dependent on a white, middle-income, family-man work force, are more likely to exert political pressures to keep tax rates high enough to finance expensive public schools than are urban property owners who have little interest in better schools for the children of the urban poor.[3]

Further, the power of cities and counties to tax and to operate schools is granted by state governments, and states regularly make financial contributions, called "state aid," to local school districts. The states could redress the inequality of the financial inputs of the various local districts, and it has been argued that the inequality of financial support for schools between school districts within a state is a violation of the Fourteenth Amendment to the Constitution which forbids the states to deny "equal protection of the laws" to any person. (In the case of *McInnis* v. *Ogilvie* in 1969 the U.S. Supreme Court sustained a lower court ruling which rejected this argument.)[4]

While some apologists ascribe the unequal financial support of poor urban versus well-to-do suburban schools to impersonal demographic and economic trends beyond the control of man, James Conant (in *Slums and Suburbs*) has neatly summed up the human basis of the inequality: ". . . to a considerable extent what a school should do and can do is determined by the status and ambitions of the families being served." A sentiment similar to Conant's was expressed as humanitarian tenderness by an elderly resident of the midwestern town that August Hollingshead studied some twenty years ago and reported on in *Elmtown's Youth*. The resident said of a teacher much admired in the community: "She is such a wonderful teacher. She teaches every child in a different way; she knows each one's background and treats it accordingly."*

That Conant is right and that human decisions lie behind the unequal education of the urban poor is demonstrated by differences in conditions of schools *within* cities. One documented example of such differences, from Patricia Cayo Sexton's study of a half dozen years ago, *Education and Income*, is of a large industrial midwestern city where, as between schools for the middle class and schools for the poor, there were considerable differences in favor of the former in respect to school overcrowding, age and condition of buildings, assignment of experienced teachers, and the granting by teachers of favors and prizes. In this city many of the low-income children were Negro.

The evidence of the Coleman Report that there is little significant difference nationwide in the financial inputs of schools for whites and schools for other racial groups does

* *Hollingshead's book is worth looking at again for a description of how a previous generation of middle-class Americans reinforced status by means of slightly different institutions than ours.*

not conflict with the general experience that within any given area (state, city, or locality), the schools for the poor tend to be less well endowed financially than the schools for the middle class, and that in the urban-suburban contrast this difference frequently coincides with the black-white difference. In addition, the report's nationwide figures tend to mask the race factor by the inclusion of poor white schools from such specific areas as Appalachia or the state of Maine as well as from the entire Deep South, where white as well as black schools are generally the poorest in the nation. But, as one might expect, the black school/white school differences that the report did observe favored the white schools.

In New York City, the tendency to neglect the schools and the children of the poor has existed at least for several decades. In the 1930s, the WPA Writers Project amassed a series of documents and reports entitled "Negroes in the New York City Public Schools," which rings all the changes on the tune "the problems of educating underprivileged children" that we sometimes consider a brand-new hit of the late 1960s: neglected, overcrowded buildings; inadequate outdoor playgrounds; inhumanly overcrowded lunchrooms; weak administrators covering up for one another; parents associations controlled by the schools' principals; demands by advocates of the community for strong, responsible principals; and an investigation by the mayor into the causes of civil disorders in Harlem. And the explanation that the children don't learn because they come from deprived environments and families without fathers.

In the face of firm data to the contrary, an assistant school superintendent wrote to one of the WPA investigators:

All the schools in the city are treated alike in regard to the money appropriated for their use. It is on a per capita basis, regardless of the place in which the school happens to be located.

But a witness before a commission to investigate the causes of the 1935 Harlem disorders (appointed by Mayor Fiorello La Guardia, like another, more recent, New York mayor, considered a liberal defender of the underdog) complained of the familiar frayed excuse for poor schools, already fraying in the 1930s:

I think that the reports that have been given before the commission are just not exactly right. It was pointed out that home conditions, the poverty and unemployment, affected children in the school and that this is the reason for the poor scholarship. I think that the commission must not make that mistake. I think that we should state definitely that discrimination is the practice and policy of the Board of Education and this means it is the policy of the city government. *[Emphasis supplied.]*

The documents collected by the WPA investigators lie in the files of a great and neglected library, part of the Schomburg Collection, in central Harlem, crumbling to dust. (To my knowledge they have never been published.) At the time of their gathering, many of the parents of the children now daily being taught the lessons that New York City schools teach to Harlem children were not yet of school age, some not yet born. They came into the world, grew to school age, and learned how to be a child in Harlem in preparation for being an adult in Harlem, and they brought their children into that same world after many more reports and commissions and fires next time, and their children were another day's children to whose "home conditions and poverty" the shapers of that world continued to ascribe their poor school performance and their parents' despair.

Thirty years after the WPA investigations, organizations concerned with the schooling of poor New York City children were still pointing to evidences of financial inequities. The United Bronx Parents, an action-oriented group organized in 1965 to exert pressures to improve individual schools in low-income neighborhoods in the Bronx, compared the academically elite, 93 percent "Other" Bronx High School of Science and the 3.8 "Other" Morris High School. (Until 1969, New York City school ethnic surveys classified students as Negro, Puerto Rican, and Other. "Other" comprised about 98 percent Caucasian, and the remainder Oriental. Beginning in 1969, ethic surveys used the classifications Negroes, American Indians, Orientals, Puerto Ricans, Other Spanish Surnamed Americans, and Others–i.e, Caucasians.)

The study found that in the school year 1966-67, the 15-year-old building that houses Bronx Science was utilized to 100 percent while the 65-year-old Morris High School was utilized to 177 percent. (Utilization, the degree of "crowdedness," is the ratio of enrollment to building capacity.) Bronx Science had a student-teacher ratio of 18.9 to 1, Morris, slightly higher, 20.7 to 1. At Science, 78 percent of the teachers had five or more years of experience, at Morris, 49 percent.* If the educational inputs at Bronx Science exceeded those at Morris High, so, by standard categories, did the educational product. In June, 1967, 92.8 percent of the students who had entered Bronx Science as freshmen or sophomores three or four years earlier received Academic diplomas, that is, certificates that would permit them to enter college and, economically speaking, American mainstream society; 2.9 percent of the Morris entering class did.[5]

This last datum raises the crucial question of how nonschool environment, school environment, and academic performance are related, causally or fortuitously, to the utter failure of Morris High to process its students for entrance into American mainstream society.

Looking at the pupils rather than at the schools, the Coleman Report found that very little of the variance in pupil performance could be ascribed to differences in the schools' financial inputs. A statistical study of specifically New York City schools for the academic year 1967-68 made the same finding—that conventional measures, such as per capita pupil expenditure, number of experienced teachers, and size of class, apparently have no relationship to academic performance.[6] But most Americans believe

* *An item not recorded in the study but a matter of common knowledge among faculty and students of many of the city's non-Other high schools is that numbers of discarded texts from the better high schools regularly turn up in the book rooms and classroms of the worse high schools, where, though they may be last year's or last decade's style and not quite the right fit, like Miss Anne's old clothes, they can be made do. Further, even within the predominantly dark high schools, many department chairmen habitually allot their annual textbook allowances to new books for the more or less Other "top" classes, from which the books eventually get handed down to the less-favored classes at the bottom.*

that there is a direct and important relationship between dollar inputs and educational product. And the inequitous expenditures on middle-class over poor schoolchildren, and on white over nonwhite, whatever their educational significance, reflect our judgment of the worth of those children. Similarly, an Academic diploma from a high school may be no real evidence of knowledge, skill, or wisdom, as over no diploma. But our society believes that it is, and we accord higher status to those who have such a diploma than to those who do not and award such a diploma to the children of higher-status parents in far greater numbers than to the children of lower-status parents.

Another study by the United Bronx Parents for the academic years 1965-67, examined twenty-four Bronx elementary schools, from among whose graduates a few were destined for Bronx Science, many for Morris High.[7] In twelve of the schools, referred to as "top schools," the students' average reading level, as scored on the Metropolitan Reading Achievement Tests, was above the norm, and in ten of these, the schools' average was more than one year above the norm. Of the other twelve schools, called the "bottom schools," all averaged not only below the national norm but more than a full year below. Of the top twelve schools, all in middle-class neighborhoods, eleven were 60 percent or more white; of the bottom twelve, all were located in poverty areas, and all were 20 percent or less white.

These differences were paralleled by wide discrepancies between the material resources provided the mainly white, mainly middle-class good readers and those provided the mainly black and Puerto Rican, mainly lower-class slow readers. Ten of the twelve top schools were less than forty years old; ten of the bottom twelve more than forty years old. All the top schools were less than 110 percent utilized; ten of the bottom schools were more than 110 percent utilized. Therefore no classes in the top schools were on double session or short time, while 18 percent of the classes in the bottom schools were, even though there seemed to be enough underutilized buildings within the district so that redistribution of students could have alleviated or eliminated all short-time sessions.

Average annual expenditure per pupil was $574 for the

bottom schools, $724 for the top schools–or if one averages out three special schools among them, $635 for the top schools. This difference existed despite the fact that all the bottom schools, because they were located in poverty areas, qualified for $150 to $200 more per pupil as Special Service schools. (Observation and firsthand experience also suggest that similar disparities are likely to occur *within* each school, especially within the more racially mixed top schools, with top classes being serviced with the newer books and the older more experienced teachers.)

The greater part of the disparity in per capita expenditures derived from the higher salaries paid for the greater professional experience of the teachers and administrators serving the top group. Variations in salaries for teachers and administrators are a measure mainly of their years of experience in the system. In the top schools in this study, 50 percent of the tenured staff were earning $10,000 or more, while only 26 percent of those in the bottom schools were; among the administrative staff of the top schools, 63 percent of the principals had served the same school for six or more years as compared with 34 percent in the bottom group. The responsible official for each thirty to forty schools in New York City is the district superintendent; in 1966-67, ten of the district superintendents serving the top group had at least five years experience in that position, but only one of those serving the bottom group.

I do not believe that the higher cost of experienced educational personnel, any more than the higher cost of new buildings and books, is necessarily transmuted into a better educational product. It is true that where a school regularly experiences high turnover of personnel and a predominance of new and newly assigned teachers, its whole social system–administrators, teachers, and students–is likely to be beset by anxiety, insecurity, confusion, and attendant group tensions and hostilities (as in the schools and classes described below as "chaotic"). On the other hand, given a stable social system to support them, young and inexperienced (and therefore cheaper) teachers and administrators are not per se less capable than older, more expensive ones. On the contrary, having more energy and hope, they may be more effective.

But the clustering of more experienced, and more

expensive, personnel in middle-class ("better") schools, like the allocation to middle-class schools of more funds, newer books, and less-crowded, better-kept buildings, is further evidence of our society's judgment of what the children there are worth. And again, regardless of the extent to which staff differences determine educational outputs, they most assuredly evidence status judgments. Except for that small proportion of teachers who move up the career ladder into administrative positions, horizontal mobility, from lower-class to higher-class schools, characterizes most long-term teachers' careers. One pair of researchers, working in the 1940s and '50s and examining nationwide data, reports that "because of problems of teaching, discipline, and of *pupils with unacceptable morale* [italics supplied], most teachers eventually transferred away from the lower-class school in which their careers typically began." In general, the study found that teachers in low-socio-economic schools were found to be least satisfied and least experienced, and they most wanted to get into better schools.[8] We shall look at this critical feature of a teacher's professional life in more detail later on.

In the absence of systemwide data, we cannot say definitively that in New York City at the time of writing, there is a significant positive correlation between per capita school expenditures and the incomes of the families being served. There are conflicting tendencies. Title I money (federal funds for schools serving low-income children) and city special programs provide extra funds for schools with low-income clientele. On the other hand, almost 90 percent of the school budget goes to personnel service (salaries), and for status reasons (discussed more fully below), salary costs are significantly lower in poor children's schools than in middle-class children's schools.

The Reading Score Accords Status

If, judged by the conventional measure—money—there is considerable disparity of input into the schooling of middle class and poor (also white and nonwhite), likewise, by the conventional measure—reading scores—there is a disparity in the output, or educational product. Eliminating race as a factor, middle-class children produce higher reading scores than poor children, and eliminating class as a factor, white children produce higher scores than black children.

Scores on nationally standardized reading tests have become so popular a measure of educational attainment that they must now be referred to in almost any discussion of the human condition. I refer to them here and elsewhere not, as even some critics of them claim, because, inadequate as they are, they are the best measure of educational achievement that we have, but because they are the measure the system uses to determine not only an individual's educability but also his importance. (Thus it comes about, paradoxically, that there are vast numbers of students who are not being taught to read primarily because they can't read—and are therefore judged not worth teaching to read.) Indeed, the standardized reading tests are an unreliable measure of reading skill, and moreover they are, along with the "readers" on which they are based, grossly inappropriate for use with urban minority children (I have defended this position elsewhere[9]). Further, with the widespread use of the media for conveying public information and the possibility of using the media far more extensively for vocational training, the demand for great skill in interpreting the printed word can only be ascribed to cultural lag. The ability to read traffic signs, advertising blurbs, and directions for opening or operating simple household and office or shop appliances—in other words, the equivalent of about a fourth-grade reading level—serves most adults quite adequately, and reading for pleasure, personal fulfillment, or learning, or reading out of habit is becoming a rarer and rarer pursuit among the educated as well as among the uneducated. Except for those in the highly literate professions, we require most jobholders to be overqualified in reading skill.[10]

But if the level of education and reading skill we require for entrance into American mainstream society is not essential to the operation of our technological and distributive plant and if it goes largely unused by most individuals who attain to it, it does serve an important sociological function. It serves as a way of distinguishing the ins from the outs.

In New York City the schools begin to separate the ins and outs at very tender ages, in many schools as early as kindergarten and first grade, and the sorting becomes ever more refined and rigid and the cleavage between the ins and the outs ever wider as the children grow older. Much of this sorting is based on reading scores. Throughout the city the discrepancy between the reading skills of poor (mainly Puerto Rican and black) children and the reading skills of middle-class (mainly Other) children grows larger from grade to grade, like a spreading malignancy. Thus, whereas for the city as a whole, the average reading scores fall well within the national norms, schools and districts embracing mainly poor children show progressive retardation. As the pupil population is over 50 percent black and Puerto Rican, this suggests that the Others are experiencing progressive acceleration.* Thus, a study of youth in Harlem for the school year 1960-61 found 30 percent of the third-grade students in twenty central Harlem schools to be reading below grade level, and 80.9 percent of those in the sixth grade; 21.6 percent of the third graders reading above grade level, but only 11.7 percent of the sixth graders.[11] In 1967-68, the Metropolitan Applied Research Center analysis of the most recently administered series of reading tests suggested that "critical" reading retardation was on the increase in the city, it being generally acknowledged, in the opinion of this analysis, that the bulk of the critically retarded readers were poor black and Puerto Rican students.[12] In a study of an experiment in improved schooling for poor children, reading scores for the control group (poor children not receiving any special treatment) showed the following retardation in terms of national norms: at second grade, –0.5; at third grade, –0.6; at fourth grade, –1.1; at fifth grade, –1.5; and at sixth grade,

* *The annual reports of the Office of Educational Research, Board of Education of the City of New York are the best source for this information. School by school and district by district comparisons are not published by the board of education, but must be laboriously amassed by individual research. To date, such research has been conducted almost entirely by understaffed and underfinanced groups and individuals whose primary area of concentration is educational improvement rather than educational research. The findings of even these investigators, however, have not to my knowledge been challenged as generalizations, although, of course, the critics and the defenders of the school system have different explanations for the stipulated findings.*

−1.3.[13] Other sources show greater discrepancies. Thus, *Youth in the Ghetto*, the HARYOU study, shows a retardation of −1.2 at third grade, −2.1 at sixth grade, and −2.5 at eighth grade. Performance on standardized arithmetic tests demonstrated similar although somewhat less severe trends.

The ever-lowering school status that is the fate of the students who produced these ever-lowering scores is shown in the data covering the awarding of junior high school and high school diplomas. In New York, a ninth grader (in some cases an eighth grader) receives a junior high school diploma if he has passed four majors, three minors, and has a reading level of at least 7.0 (two years retarded); he receives a lesser document, a certificate, if he has passed two majors, two minors, and has a reading score of 6.0 (three years retarded). To receive either credential, he must also have a record of "satisfactory attendance and behavior." If he is very much overage, he may go on to high school with neither a certificate nor a diploma, even if he is unable to read a single word. (Functional and absolute illiterates are regularly encountered in New York City high schools. The educational career of one of them, Willie Gallagher, is recounted below.) About 50 percent of the graduates of central Harlem's junior high schools (95.7 percent Negro, 3.7 percent Puerto Rican, and 0.6 percent Other) receive diplomas. In high school, about 60 percent of them drop out or are put out, and of those who graduate, 77.5 percent receive what is called a General diploma, a piece of paper about as negotiable in the job and college markets as an old trolley transfer.[14] In the borough of the Bronx the percentage of high school graduates in a given year receiving Academic diplomas (qualifying them for but not at all guaranteeing them admission to college) was as follows:

High School	*Percent Black and PR*	*Percent Receiving Academic Diplomas*
1	96	2.9
2	92	1.8
3	92	8.3
4	82	8.3
5	81	8.4
6	65	14.2
7	54	33.0

An overwhelming proportion of those receiving Academic diplomas were members of the schools' minority Other group.[15]

Whether, other things being equal, more money could actually produce better urban schools and better urban scholars we cannot know. Because without equalization of expenditures we cannot hold other things equal. Our society conventionally attaches status awards to money as well as money awards to status. Thus, poor buildings, cheap teachers, old books, crowded lunchrooms, while they may not in theory be impediments to quality education, are so in actuality because they are symbols of low esteem and low status. The teachers, the administrators, and the pupils who are undersupported know that society doesn't value them and they tend not to value themselves, one another, or the process of education in which they are supposed to be engaged.

Regardless of relative status, however, decent schooling in rich America demands a certain absolute minimum school standard of living-space, cleanliness, books, and relief from a trying parsimoniousness that makes a stick of chalk or a paper clip in an urban school an item worth stealing (and often stolen). If all the nation's educational resources—local, state, and national—were to be allocated equally among all income groups (or fairly, which would mean allocating more to those who have less), I believe that public pressures would then squeeze out more public monies for education—that is, the inadequacy of the current monies would have become visible. At present, one way inadequate educational budgets are made publicly tolerable is by skimping on the portions handed out at the foot of the table. In New York, for example, this skimping helps to account for the differences on the money issue between the United Federation of Teachers (major organizational spokesman for New York City's teachers) and the advocates of community control (spearhead of the revolt against New York's school system). The former has argued for an increased educational budget as the primary weapon of reform, the latter for equal distribution, dollar by dollar, of educational funds.* The difference is

* *Dr. Kenneth Clark, member of the New York State Board of Regents, director of the Metropolitan Applied Research Center, and*

analogous to the difference between alleviating poverty by business subsidies, a few drops of which are supposed to "trickle down" to the poor, and ending poverty by guaranteeing every family a minimum annual income.

However, I do not believe that a complete reapportionment of educational resources throughout the country, even amounting to a complete reversal of the present biased distribution so as to favor poor children, would substantially alter present school perfomances unless such a reapportionment were to symbolize and be reinforced by new standards, expectations, and ways of relating among the adults and the children who attend the schools. For, in their present structure and dynamics, the schools' failure in some areas is the price paid for its success in others. There ought to be more money for urban education, and the money there is—more or less—ought to be apportioned among schoolchildren according to need or at least equally. But money alone will not overcome.

We have to be skeptical of money as a measure of educational inputs. We also have to be skeptical of reading scores, diplomas, and examination results as measures of the educational product. But whether the high scorer is or is not wiser and more informed than the low scorer, he does have the status attributes (for example, speech habits) and the kinds of skills that our society values, and he is therefore accorded a place nearer the top. Meanwhile the no scorer (the dropout, the illiterate) struggles to keep his place on the welfare rolls.

Whether poor children are bad school learners is the subject of national debate. The poor child and the nonwhite child may or may not come to school with home-derived impediments to acquiring the socially valued

for many years a leading advocate of improved educational opportunities for black and Puerto Rican children, has gone so far as to propose a moratorium on any *additional amounts of educational expenditures until the schools can show improvements within the present budget. See the symposium "Ghetto Education," a supplement to the* Center Magazine *[Center for the Study of Democratic Institutions], November, 1968. Such a moratorium would freeze educational salaries and likely prevent even mandated salary increases, and can thus be considered to be as politically unrealistic as the demand for a just distribution of resources between schools for the poor and schools for the well-to-do.*

school skills. But there is no doubt at all that the school itself puts very great impediments in his way as he tries to acquire these skills. Schools, as we conceive them and run them, make it hard for poor children and nonwhite children to learn what you have to learn to get along well in American society. The school system is so arranged that, generally speaking, the low-status first grader will be a low-status tenth grader and eventually a low-status adult.

In New York City formal arrangements and subjective attitudes combine to produce this effect. We can view the process by cutting a segment at any level of the system. I shall begin by offering for examination the administrative arrangements and status distinctions among the adults in the school system.

3. ORDERING THE ADULTS

Once, having been away from New York City and from conventional schools for several years, I paid a visit to the "bad" high school where I had once been a teacher. The school was housed in a new building, and students and teachers expressed pleasure at the clean floors and walls, unbroken windows, modern equipment, expanded library. Federal funds for education were beginning to flow, and an energetic and optimistic administrator told me about all the new programs: "advancement placement" courses for the college-bound, remedial reading courses at two levels for the "culturally disadvantaged," "work-study" programs for the potential dropouts. "We have something for everybody," she said brightly, like a smart department-store buyer. The civil rights movement was beginning to shed drops of dew even in New York City public schools, and in the English department a new chairman had instituted a paperback buying program and prepared an anthology of Afro-American poetry. But late in the afternoon, looking in through a windowed door on a departmental meeting in progress, I knew that the new building and the new money and the new programs were thin-coated over the old school, which was still there. Twenty professional adult men and women were seated neatly at the students' desks looking up at their departmental chairman, who was conducting the meeting, pointing with a ruler to indicate that this one or that one might speak next. And there came flooding back remembrances of all those little status games that made one behave like a good little girl toward one's "superiors" and like a kindly, or cruel, despot toward one's "inferiors": the apologies and excuses and lies proffered and accepted, or rejected; the humiliations endured and imposed; the failure to accord respect to those below or to demand it from those above; the cheap ego gratifications bought at the expense of others' dignity.

Throughout the school system, the interpersonal relations are such that each individual, beginning with the actual children, is a child to the person above him and a despot to the people below him (except, of course, for the children, who have beneath them only the most despised of themselves). I suspect that for many people, including even visiting parents, the social and physical atmosphere of a school alone stimulates these ways of relating by returning them to the childhood state of impotence and anxiety which they experienced in their earliest school days. The infantilization of the teacher, which began years earlier when she surrendered her childhood self in the interests of learning to be a pupil, is reinforced at every phase and in every aspect of her training and professionalization until she surrenders her adult self in the interests of being a teacher. Then, if either vertically or horizontally mobile—moving either to "better classes" and "better schools," or up the administrative ladder to supervisory positions—she retains and strengthens the personality and behavioral characteristics that she may have first discovered in herself when she was pencil monitor in first grade. The status premise is manifested at the interpersonal level by humiliation and manipulation, and at the institutional level by organized mistrust, usually in respect to petty details of little or no educational significance. Institutionalized mistrust is unashamedly acknowledged as between each adult and the "children" under him. But the return flow of mistrust by the children in respect to the grownups is likely to be denied to consciousness. Most teachers don't acknowledge, for example, that the children they teach are continuously watchful and suspicious of them.

The decision about which is the child and which the despot between any two people is based almost entirely on their place in the bureaucratic hierarchy. Although status differences may sometimes be aggravated by race differences and are undoubtedly experienced as primarily racial by many nonwhites in a system in which they are in the minority and clustered toward the bottom, the interpersonal games of one-upmanship are played with little distinction as to race or social class. Place in the bureaucratic hierarchy also ordinarily supersedes such other status determinants as professional qualifications (degrees), wealth, social class, and age. Even the commonplace ritualistic deferences that men customarily accord to women in our society (opening doors, carrying heavy objects, and so on) frequently go unobserved where the man is of a higher rank than the woman, although they are likely to be played to the hilt where the status is reversed. Upon the school system as a whole, the effect of the primacy of bureaucratic place as a determinant of status is to elevate administrators (clerks) over educators as persons of consequence and power, and administration over all other pursuits, including education, as the system's primary concern.

The customary status criteria of the larger society may also be ignored in respect to volunteers who are not full-time members of the bureaucracy. I once watched a conference of local school board members, almost all of them middle class, a majority of them white, many of them doctors, lawyers, business executives, or wives of same, allow a representative of the city board of education take their meeting away from them and turn it over to the then president of the board, who proceeded to one-up them in classic middle-class parent or kindly-schoolteacherish style. For a whole long morning, local board members from throughout the city had been recounting to one another their frustrations at having to deal with professionals who would have liked to will them into nonexistence and who generally treated them as if they had already done that. At a plenary session after lunch, they passed a motion that the agenda prepared by the board of education official be put aside and that the little time remaining before they would have to leave the building be given to trying to set up a citywide council of local school boards, which might better enable them to cope with their common problems. The board-appointed chairman of the meeting immediately restated the passed motion so as to make an affirmative vote one that would restore the original agenda, put it to a voice vote, which probably did not carry, and proceeded with the board agenda, which consisted of an address by the then president of the board (Alfred Giardino). The chairman announced that after the address there would still remain ten minutes before the building must be vacated when the meeting could take up the business the members had in mind. The president then addressed the meeting in kindly and cultured tones, concluding:

> There should be and must be more consultation [between the local school boards and the supervisors and bureaucrats]. I have noted, as I'm sure all of you have noted, a substantial difference in the development and activity and interest and *maturity* of the local school boards over the last several years. When you realize that we can have, that we are having, the kind of serious, mature, equal discussion and sharing of views and sharing of frustration, then when you realize that there is the possibility for more power and responsibility with legislative change, it's because the organism has *grown.* The local school board system has grown. And I must say that I am extremely proud, as I know our board is extremely proud, of the high calibre of the local school board members, of their dedication, of their zeal, their sitting here on this Saturday, all for the same cause as we are all trying to serve. If I may, prior to your own little [*sic*] vote and discussion, suggest three areas where we can continue to make progress . . .[1]

The local board members of whom the president was so proud had been appointed by the board of education. So he spoke as a father whose pride in his son is elicited by the father's success in making the son into his own image. It is the pride of the maker plus self-pride. "Maturity," a favorite word with educators, signifies an underling's (child's) willingness to be manipulated rather than forced into surrendering his will. As in this instance, educators commonly promise increased "responsibility" to those who demonstrate increased "maturity." The exchange is no more than an understanding to the effect that "we will let you into our game when you agree to play by our rules."

The manipulative ploys which Giardino practiced on a group of concerned adults serving the schools many hours weekly without compensation, and which, moreover, the adults tolerated almost without a grumble, are practiced up and down the entire school hierarchy, from the superintendent through the district superintendents, principals, teachers, and parents—with occasional detours en route to allow entry of headquarters personnel, building custodians, assistant principals, department chairmen, paraprofessional aides, and so on.

Not all personnel are capable of performing the relatively sophisticated ploy demonstrated here, the ploy that seems to be according respect and approval while actually conveying the speaker's superiority to and power over the listener. Crass and open reminders of the inferior's child-status are relatively common, especially scoldings, threats, and "talkings to," all officially called "conferences." A teacher reported to me observing a corridor encounter between a supervisor and a paraprofessional aide in which the aide was hanging her head in the face of a tongue lashing. The supervisor reached out and lifted the offender's head with a movement under the chin, ordering, "You look at me when I talk to you!" "I'm not a child, don't touch me." "I don't care if you're a child or not, you look at me when I talk to you." The entire encounter was conducted in the presence of the group of children of whom the aide was in charge. It is not at all uncommon for supervisors to interrupt a teacher's lesson to deliver a scolding or a reprimand. Other forms of what teachers call "supervisory harassment" include excessive visits to "observe" the teacher, piling on of extra chores, regular assignment of "bad" classes and failure ever to assign "good" classes, slowness in providing necessary supplies (chalk, paper, books, etc.), extra inspection of teachers' records and lesson plans, veiled or open accusations of dishonesty, complaints about bad housekeeping, sudden interruptions of teachers' classroom routines for lessons delivered by the supervisor, terrorizing and discomfiting the children, and simple nastiness and discourtesy.

The reduction of teachers to the status of children in this wise aggravates considerably the siblinglike rivalries, backbiting, tattling, and complaining that characterize the relationships of many groups of peer-workers under a common authority. I suspect also that teachers who are victims of these vulgar status ploys are more likely to be harsh, sarcastic, and possibly brutal with their pupils than are teachers who are themselves treated with respect. I myself as a teacher would find that after even less galling putdowns than most of those I have listed, I would tend to be irritated and impatient with my students and that they would seem to me on such days to be provocative, stupid, and unattractive people. I think that all the little ways which teachers habitually use to keep students low status are continually reinforced by all the little ways in which teachers themselves are kept low status.*

Where supervisors play these nasty games, as well as in many schools where they behave more decently, teachers almost never receive and would certainly never request serious educational guidance from their supervisors. Supervisors who are or are felt to be primarily operative as critics cannot also play the role of trusted colleagues and consultants in the common task of educating children. And teachers, even beginning teachers, are likely to feel that a request for help or advice will be taken as a sign of weakness and incompetence which may immediately or some day be used against them. (When one teacher, whose story is told later, asked her supervisor for help, she was told to "put it in writing"; she knew by this that the principal and her assistants were preparing a case against her.)

These harsh kinds of status games, while not uncommon, are considered crude by decent and cultivated supervisors, many of whom are fastidious about observing the common canons of courtesy and respect, and schools run by such supervisors are likely to be better schools with higher staff morale. Even in the best-run schools, however, there is an institutionalization of adult-child relationships which is

* *An example of the kind of ego- and group-bolstering scorn usually reserved for the privacy of teachers' lounges was printed in the* New York Times *(August 31) just before school opened in September, 1969. An article listed some of the amusing little student "boners" which teachers in a Brooklyn high school annually collect for their principal's delectation. The tastelessness of the display was aggravated by the fact that a number of the "boners" were actually quite perceptive comments on the human condition.*

expressed in the prevailing rules, the mores, and the postures. Teachers punch a time clock, bring a note from the doctor when they are sick, and when they are performing tasks other than classroom assignments are customarily required to be present at a given place rather than to perform a given piece of work. For example, high school teachers regularly perform "building assignments" (patrolling the corridors, supervising study halls, and so on), and I once heard a teacher whose building assignment was to be present in the department chairman's office in case he had things for her to do ask for permission to "leave the room" at a time when there was no work to be done. The chairman, a civilized supervisor, of course granted it, but I think it would never have occurred to him to declare the request superfluous.

On another occasion, at another school, during a teachers meeting, the teachers requested some rearrangement of the faculty parking lot. The principal thought it was a good idea but explained that he was about to leave on a six-month sabbatical and would take care of the matter on his return. "Can you imagine!" exclaimed the unusual schoolman who was telling the story to me and another unusual schoolman. "He has to be king of the parking lot. Why couldn't the teachers work it out themselves? No! He has to be king of the parking lot!"[2] The common procedure in such a case would be for the principal ultimately to appoint a committee, which would be empowered to issue regulations subject to his approval. Appointment to such a committee would convey status and authority. To neither the principal nor his teachers would it be likely to occur that the teachers simply choose two or three of themselves to take care of the parking lot arrangements.

Status and the Primacy of Administration

In the hierarchy of the individual school, the principal, at the top, is *responsible to* the higher administrative personnel above him and *responsible for* the running of the school. Lines of authority pass from him through his subordinates (assistant principals, department chairmen, grade supervisors, and so on) down to the teacher at the bottom. While the teacher is *responsible for* the child and the class, and for most of the actual process of education, she is *responsible to* a supervisor whose major concern is with administration (clerical tasks). A natural concomitant of this authority arrangement is that the entire adult school population tends to be preoccupied with administration. This preoccupation is undoubtedly reinforced by the supervisors' schoolteacherish fussiness about niggling details which derives from their personalities, from their original professional training as classroom teachers, and from the demands made on them by their supervisors. A high employee of the United Federation of Teachers, a gifted explicator of the ways of the system, once told me: "Up to now the New York City schools were run for administrative convenience. Headquarters had to get certain papers and records in to the state, mainly attendance records, and headquarters was satisfied if the district superintendent got his reports in on time. The district superintendent was satisfied if the principals got their reports to him in on time, and the principal was satisfied with the teachers if they got their records in on time."

Critics of the New York school system, from David Rogers, author of *110 Livingston Street*, to the average classroom teacher, commonly lament both the system's inefficiency and its colossal bureaucratic, record-keeping labors. It is true that the multiplicity and inefficiency of administrative and clerical tasks tend to interfere with good school performance, even of the administrative tasks themselves, not to speak of the school's educational tasks. Everything is organized at the top and recourse must often be had to busy and unavailable supervisors for the smallest matters, e.g., procuring copies of forms required to be completed by a given date. Detailed records must be made out by teachers in many copies sometimes with no carbon paper available. The cheap labor of students and teachers eager to please their supervisors and at the same time escape from the tedium of the classroom obviates the need to rationalize and/or computerize these operations. All this is standard. Nevertheless my own experiences lead me to believe that it is not the amount or even the inefficiency of nonteaching paperwork but its primacy that produces the feelings of burdensome distress.

The first week of a new teacher's orientation into a new school, or into her first school, is customarily given to gaining familiarity with nonteaching rituals and routines. (Real mastery takes six months to a year and involves learning where, when, and how to short-cut, evade, swindle, make friends, and risk making enemies.) Supervisors customarily aid and support the new teacher in this area, to ensure that, if she is going to take a long time learning how to teach, at least her paperwork should be well accomplished.

Staff meetings customarily concern administrative or clerical matters, sometimes procedures involving the children, such as manner of entry into the building, behavior in corridors, assembly procedures, administration of standardized tests, and so on. Those principals who do occasionally take up substantive educational matters are likely simply to lecture, and there is little of that free exchange of opinions and ideas necessary to professional growth. The level of professionalism of school personnel is revealed by the reading matter commonly found in teachers' lounges, usually women's magazines and perhaps an occasional copy of *Look* or *Life*. Departmental offices in high schools will contain copies of the texts being used in the department, and the very parochial, amateurish board of education publication for teachers, *High Points*. Serious pedagogical or scholarly literature in the disciplines of the department's concern or new texts to be evaluated are rarely found. Material of this kind which comes to the principal or the department chairman is almost never distributed among staff for evaluation. Even the lively and relevant *Urban Review*, a periodical on education distributed free to every school in the city (it is published by the Center for Urban Education, a regional educational laboratory), is never seen by most teachers.

An important example of the primacy of administration over education is the way that teachers gain status and the attention that leads to promotion—precisely through administrative-type, nonteaching activities. The larger the school and the higher its level (i.e., elementary, junior high, etc.), the greater the number of special administrative and paperwork jobs that must be performed outside of the classroom. The following are some of the "in charge of" positions listed in a recent study of personnel practices in

New York City schools (*Teacher Mobility in New York City* by Daniel Griffiths and others): field trips; assembly program on elections; student government; purchase of craft and garden supplies; school color guard; lost and found service. The high school where I taught also had positions "in charge of" the lunchroom patrol-force of aides and teachers; dispensing bus passes; dispensing free lunch tickets for the children of welfare clients; and collecting fines for lost textbooks. Besides the "in charge of" jobs, teachers also served as head and subsidiary attendance clerks, and as "grade advisors" (making up the programs for several hundred students, most of whom the "advisors" did not know personally). Many of these jobs confer status on their holders not only by putting them into positions where they can give orders and perhaps dispense or refuse to dispense favors to students and possibly one's colleagues but also by relieving them from some hours of classroom teaching. As administrators have higher status than teachers, classroom teaching comes to be considered a low-status pursuit, and escape from it a promotion of sorts. (One of the last official acts performed by the retiring superintendent, Bernard Donovan, in September, 1969, was to punish a teacher, Leslie Campbell, for misbehavior of various sorts during the previous academic year by assigning him "for the 1969-70 school year . . . to classroom teaching duties only."[3]) Thus, despite the fact that almost no skill, initiative, or discretionary powers are involved, these out-of-teaching assignments are considered desirable plums, and the union contract provides that they must be rotated among qualified candidates.

The Griffiths study suggests that the desirability of these jobs stems from their being on the route to advancement, as a first way in which an ambitious teacher gets attention from her superiors, rather than from their being a relief from teaching. "It is assumed," Griffiths writes, "that if remaining in the classroom were the road to higher rank, the vertically mobile teachers . . . would remain 'with the children.' " But the point is that that is not the way the system works. (I tend to believe that given the primacy of administrative concern which is characteristic of a bureaucratic status system, remaining "with the children" could not be a road to promotion and that only a complete upsetting of all present status arrangements could make it so.

The adult system's emphasis on administration is mirrored in the management of the classroom, where the children are taught that it is more important to come on time, not talk, and line up nicely than it is to learn to read and reckon. Thus the obsessions with the minutiae of discipline which we will observe below are not odd teacherish idiocyncrasies but relevant patterns in a consistently styled overall design.

The Merit System

In the power struggles which rocked the New York City school system beginning in 1966, the first and always a conspicuous target was the school principal.

Actually and legally, the principal has considerable powers over the educational processes in his school. Trained, raised, and appointed by the bureaucracy and responsible to it for further favors, he nevertheless has quite a free hand in respect to education. Because of the system's primary concern with administrative detail and because the immediate supervisor of the principal (the district supervisor) customarily has twenty to thirty schools to supervise and so cannot seriously concentrate on more than a few at most, the principal to a large extent has no one to answer to in regard to educational matters. (In the years of the integration struggle, what Charles Wilson—who became the administrator of one of the city's three "experiments" in community control—calls the power vacuum between the district superintendent and the principals made it possible for the latter to sabotage official board of education integration directives.)[4] Likewise the teacher who faithfully fulfills her clerical obligations and whose classes do not appear to be completely out of hand may have considerable autonomy in respect to her educational program. This is especially so in respect to strong and experienced teachers. Unfortunately, the obverse also obtains: principals and teachers who fulfill their clerical obligations may have little or no educational program at all and not be held responsible by their superiors.

That, despite far more freedom than obtains in many other parts of the country, few teachers and few principals are in fact bold and innovative is closely related to the system's prevailing values and personnel practices. Throughout the nation, the concept of school and the place of school in society mean that in most school systems timidity, conservatism, and preciseness tend to be selected as characteristics of school personnel over courage, imagination, creativity, boldness. In New York City, over and above the personality preferences and college training courses that, like the preferences and courses elsewhere in the nation, help to determine which adults shall man and lead our public schools, there also operates a selecting process known as the merit system. Intended to serves as a restraint on arbitrariness and favoritism in respect to individuals, the merit system has come to express a systemic favoritism in respect to racial groups and to strengthen the preference for cautious, administrative-oriented personalities over bold, education-oriented personalities.

New York State, like most states in the Union, prescribes the educational requirements for certification as a public school teacher, including degrees, subject matter courses, and "education" courses. Most New York State school districts, including the "better" school districts serving the state's well-to-do suburbs, accept the state's minimum standards as their own and select qualified candidates by interview. But New York City adds to the state's minimum standards a complex examination system—including written, oral, medical, and classroom practice examinations—both for appointment of teachers and for promotion up the administrative ladder, indeed for about 1,000 separate positions within the school system. This examination system is administered by a semiautonomous adjunct of the board of education known as the board of examiners. In an earlier period when college graduates languished for jobs and when the number of teacher candidates in New York City far exceeded the number of teacher openings, this system was supposed to eliminate rank favoritism, including ethnic favoritism, in handing out jobs and promotions, and so came to be called the "merit system." My UFT informant, the gifted explicator, once described the system so: "The board of examiners and the examination system were established to prevent the various ethnic groups in the city from battling over jobs. After establishing basic literacy [which the state minimum requirements take care of] it wouldn't matter what the test was. It could be a test for standing on your head, just so long as it was fair. The tests don't select good teachers or bad teachers, they're just objective."

This is a slight exaggeration. The tests do test the subject matter the candidate will be teaching, as well as a kind of rock-bottom literacy, and perhaps serve to screen out the few illiterates and ignoramuses who might have survived the college credentialing process. (Most candidates, however, are graduates of academically competent New York City or nearby colleges, so that this problem is actually very rare.) At the same time, however, the elaborate, arduous, humiliating, and often foolish testing procedures of which each written test is merely a single element also serve to screen out people who are too impatient, too independent of spirit, or too intellectual to be willing to tolerate these procedures at a time when there are relatively abundant job openings in nearby and often "better" school districts. The merit system in times of a tight labor market thus tends to choke off the stream of candidates without in any way raising its quality. It is this factor that has led a number of academic researchers and policymakers in the last decades to suggest that the board of examiners be abolished. Its survival in the face of these many attacks from high quarters can probably be ascribed to the self-perpetuating powers of status institutions and to the support of personnel in the system who, having laboriously achieved the insignia of status that the board of examiners confers, are likely to imagine that the insignia are relevant to the job they are doing.

Besides making it more difficult for New York City to recruit teachers, the merit system as administered by the board of examiners tends to screen out certain personality types which are not congenial to the needs of the system. This was demonstrated during the years beginning about 1966 and 1967 when a teaching job in New York City was accepted by many draft boards as a basis for draft deferment and many non-teacher-type young men became available to teach in the city's schools. To be able to exploit this new pool of candidates, the system's licensing procedures, as well as the colleges' also often silly and irrelevant qualifying procedures, had to be modified and simplified. Interestingly, the efficacy of the system's normally stringent licensing procedures in producing teachers who would fit into its orthodox status system was demonstrated when many of the products of the relaxed procedures joined the revolt against the school status system beginning in 1968-69.

Not only the complexity of the testing procedures, and the status-conscious arrogance of most personnel at the board of examiners, but also the tests' actual contents discourage certain personality types. In the practical classroom examinations, for example, the teacher candidate is expected to perform correctly certain highly stylized, ritualistic classroom minutiae involving prescribed use of the blackboard, manner of calling on students, procedures for passing out books or supplies, written form and order of development of the lesson, form of opening and closing the lesson, and so on. While at least some of these ceremonies are helpful props for an insecure beginning teacher, the ability to memorize and perform them is within the medium-grade-moron range, and the merit system's insistence on this kind of ceremony and rote turns off many better than average candidates.

Procedures include an interview whose subject matter pertains to curriculum, class management (discipline), and relations with other school personnel, the occasion is also used to evaluate the candidate's speech habits, one of the three examiners being a speech specialist. Non-New York regionalisms, either black dialectal colloquialisms or pronunciations, and foreign (e.g., Spanish) accents were until very recently considered unacceptable speech patterns. (In addition, the special snobbery of old-fashioned speech specialists may be evidenced in the rejection of candidates with slight lisps, dental t's, lateral s's, and so on, although in recent years these defects have been dealt with at the municipal college level where teacher candidates may be required to take special "remedial speech" courses.) In former decades, speech betraying "Jewish" accents, "Brooklynese," and so on might disqualify a candidate, but more recently almost any non-Negro, nonforeign speech is likely to pass.* So it is that many school people who themselves scorn the "bad English" of their black and Puerto Rican students speak in patterns that in other parts of the country and especially in certain Waspish circles are scorned as "New York Jewish" (although they are not necessarily Jewish, as in the case of a recent superintendent of schools with marked New York speech patterns).

The speech test, an evidence of the kind of social-class speech snobbery about which Americans like to tease the British, has the perhaps unintended consequence of further downgrading black and Puerto Rican pupils. Teachers who pass the speech test, especially those to whom their "acceptable" speech patterns are an important status badge, are likely to equate speech patterns with intelligence, or at least with educability, and to look down on parents and children who do not attain to "acceptable" speech. I once heard a teacher in a community-control school say of black parents and colleagues on the school's governing board, "They want to run a school, and they don't even know how to talk English." In addition, the gap in speech patterns between the teachers and the students actually interferes with communication, and so with the instructional program. (We shall see one example in the case of Miss White.) Recent studies by linguists also suggest that Negro children's reading ability and ability to understand classroom directions are interfered with by the differences between their dialect and the dialect of the teachers and the schoolbooks, so that a teacher with command of her students' dialect, even though she might retain some traces of it in her own speech, is probably more effective than a teacher for whom the students' speech is both foreign and contemptible.[5] Most teachers, like most other speakers of the standard dialect, are unaware that their students' speech is not "bad" or "sloppy" English, the product of "lazy tongues and undeveloped minds," but an internally consistent system with its own syntactical regularities and distinctions. Further, their belief that their students "don't know how to speak in sentences" betrays a failure to recognize that most of us don't

* *In the last year or two some speech examiners have been passing candidates whose speech betrays Negro and Spanish traces, and this trend will probably continue.*

employ the complex speech structures of formal language for everyday conversational use.* Some of the same problems exist of course in respect to the instruction of Puerto Rican students.

Criteria for promotion up the school administrative ladder serve the same function as those for original appointment as a teacher. Additional courses and degrees plus written and practical examinations serve to infantilize the candidates and trivialize their perceptions of the educational process, in addition to rewarding the kind of mentality and industry that can lead an adult to devote himself to memorizing minute rules of English usage, long outdated grammatical terminology, details of grade-school geography, and some miscellaneous nuts and bolts of general information that are useful only to show off in drawing room conversation, or to pass New York City school promotion examinations. For example, an examination for junior high school principal queries the candidate on the differences between a ripsaw, a crosscut handsaw, a hack saw, and a backsaw and on identifying the period—Jacobean, late Georgian, Regency, or early Georgian—of the designers Adam, Hepplewhite, and Sheraton. Candidates are also tested on administrative procedures, handling of disciplinary and personnel problems, and supervision of personnel. To help them pass both the general information and the so-called professional parts of the examinations, most candidates take intensive coaching courses, usually given by persons in supervisory positions and often by supervisors who at one time or another served as examiners in such tests. A recent instructor in one such course regularly gave his students two sets of answers to some of the questions about

* *Teacher training seems to reinforce rather than help overcome the linguistic ignorance of most college students and teachers. For example, a text used in a required course in one of the colleges of the City University of New York contains, along with a lot of other rather alarming nonsense about lower-class and minority children, the following: "Vocabulary and general adequacy of speech vary by socioeconomic class. Speech is poorer in form and articulation, less in amount, more restrictive and less precise for children at lower socioeconomic levels than for those at higher social levels." Boyd R. McCandless,* Children: Behavior and Development *(Holt, Rinehart & Winston, 1967).*

discipline and personnel, one set for practical use and the other labeled "FEP" (for examination purposes). It may be observed that as most professionally ambitious teachers and supervisors are engaged in taking the courses or preparing for the examinations necessary for promotion throughout several decades of their careers,[6] it is likely that the merit system as it functions reduces considerably the amount of work energy available for the jobs for which they are being paid. (And perhaps also the time and energy of other personnel: one administrator had his secretary type thousands of American history questions and answers on index cards, which he sat shuffling in his office for several hours each day.) Likewise, beginning teachers, who often lack all the course credits and examination successes necessary for obtaining a regular license, are likely to be busy about these distracting matters during the very years when merely getting through the school day and the school week drains their emotional and intellectual energy almost to exhaustion.

The merit system for selection and promotion of educational personnel, as it operates in New York City, tends to choose bookish (not necessarily or even probably intellectual), cautious, conforming, detail-loving individuals (something like what the Freudians would call anal types). It may or may not be historical accident that at this time in the city's ethnic history, the Jewish population produces so many individuals with these status-serving characteristics, and the Negro and Puerto Rican population so few. About 90 percent of the teachers of New York City are white, and about 42 percent of the pupils are, while about 35 percent are black and about 23 percent Puerto Rican. There are fewer than 200 professional educators of Puerto Rican background, less than 1 percent of the professional staff. Of 55 superintendents, 2 are black; of 1,438 elementary school principals, 67 are black, only 2 of them regularly licensed and appointed; there are only 3 black high school principals, and only 1 of them is regularly licensed and appointed; of 1,498 clerks, 346 are black.[7] Of the black principals, as of November, 1969, only 4 were regularly licensed and appointed; the remainder were "acting."

It is not the merit system alone, of course, that selects out nonwhites, but the whole school-accrediting road from kindergarten through college, a system that reinforces the low status of nonwhite children in such a way as more or less to ensure that few representatives of nonwhite groups will be sufficiently raised in status to be able to become the teachers of the next generation of low-status, nonwhite children. The merit system merely strengthens and adds one more step to the long process and also precludes the possibility of such a dual status system, one black and one white, as characterizes many other heavily nonwhite urban centers as well as the entire Deep South.

The justification for the merit system is a dual one: it eliminates or reduces favoritism in appointments and promotions; and it provides the best candidates for the positions. The first is largely true, even though there is some evidence that apple-polishing is a customary first step in teacher promotion. As a step leading to promotion, teachers are likely to be chosen by their supervisors for various out-of-teaching positions and responsibilities first and then to be given positions as "acting" supervisors, i.e., supervisors in fact but without the license and therefore without the salary. An "acting" is sometimes kept in his post until he is licensed as a regular by means of a device called "plugging," whereby the regular supervisor is held on sabbatical or terminal leave until the acting fulfills the license requirements to be appointed as a regular, whereupon the supervisor "on leave" can formally retire.[8] This device, like "deals" for getting teachers out of a school (described below), makes the "merit" system a little more flexible than it appears to be. It also exemplifies the way in which the appearance of a strictly objective merit system conceals arrangements that meet the needs of the individuals involved. But by and large, individual favoritism is probably less significant in formal promotion in the school system than in most other hierarchical career arrangements (in the business world, for example). However, the system reduces individual favoritism only at the expense of encouraging a kind of mass group favoritism, in that the nature of the examinations and qualifications discourage those very candidates, members of the nonwhite population, for whom special encouragement rather than discouragement would be most necessary to ensure fairness. (While the idea of providing special encouragement or advantages to black and Puerto Rican candidates, whose entrance into the system is educationally desirable, is frowned upon as "condescending" or "racism in reverse," I have never heard a word of complaint about the 5 and 10 point advantages in examination scores given to veterans, whose entrance, as veterans, is educationally irrelevant.)

In respect to the second justification, that the system selects the best qualified candidates for the jobs, its truth depends on how one conceives of the job. The board of examiners has never "validated" its examinations, i.e., determined that the tests do indeed measure those qualities and capabilities that are deemed necessary to successful functioning in the specified positions. Nor have they established the "reliability" of the tests, i.e., their ability to produce consistent scores from similarly qualified candidates or from the same candidate in successive trials at a test. In the survey on personnel practice by Griffiths, the question "Do the promotional tests help retain good people in New York City schools?" produced a heavily negative response from teachers, with only a third responding "yes," although older teachers had significantly more faith in the tests than younger ones. Only a little over half the teachers believed the tests are "fair," and of those who believed they are not fair, 33 percent gave as their reason "ethnic discrimination." The ethnic breakdown of responses to the question of fairness shows that 56 percent of the whites, but only 40 percent of the Negroes and *none* of the Puerto Ricans felt that the tests are fair. Similarly, 73 percent of the whites, but only 58 percent of the Negroes and 50 percent of the Puerto Ricans thought that promotional opportunities are open to all. (Unfortunately, questions about the tests' fairness and the openness of promotional opportunities were not asked of licensed supervisors, those who had been appointed through the merit system of promotion. It is likely that, like the survey's older teachers and white teachers, and probably more than either of them, the chosen supervisors would believe in the tests and in the openness of promotional opportunities.)

The extent to which minority group candidates, or would-be candidates, for promotion were blaming their failure on the system's prejudice rather than on their own personal difficulties with the system cannot be judged. But it should be noted that anonymity in the written examinations is well protected, and, of late, minority group membership may sometimes be an asset in the oral examinations. The racial bias of the promotion system lies in its entire orientation, not in vulgar, small-time swindling.

More generally, if one formulates the system's primary dynamic as being status-reinforcing, then one must say that the tests are valid, that they are fair, and that they do keep "good" people in the system. The kind of people who are chosen or the kind of person a candidate must learn to become if he is to be chosen is a "good" person to implement the system's status-reinforcing function. In addition, the promotion and examination system confers its own special status insignia. Passing an examination gives one status, passing it well (grades and relative position on the list of successful candidates are public information) gives one special status. This status is believed to be related to one's general competence as a professional and general level of culture as a person, and persons who have passed examinations become very distressed at suggestions that persons who have not even presented themselves to the examiners should hold the same title or receive the same salary that they do, even though for long periods in the intervals between examinations, unlicensed persons actually do the jobs as "actings" and not necessarily with less competence than those formally pronounced fit and paid to do the jobs. The following letter forwarded (in March, 1969) by the school secretaries chapter of the UFT to their union representative illustrates some of the ego investment people have in the examination system:

Please be advised that although I am not able to attend the U.F.T. meetings because of other commitments I am very aware of the issues at stake.

The workload has increased tremendously in the last few years and is still expanding. We need additional School Secretaries, NOT ParaProfessionals, as I understand the Board is considering. We need qualified help with all the necessary skills and educational background. *The School Secretaries have to meet the public in an intelligent and refined manner and be able to cope with all the problems that arise in these troubled times.* [Italics supplied.]

I wish to bring to your attention the fact that the Local School Boards have been given permission to hire secretaries without any qualifying examination and without any credits above high school diploma. Their *starting* salary is $8500! Isn't that shameful considering that a School Secretary in the school system has to work at least 12 years with 60 credits above high school and three years of business experience and still only gets $8210 maximum. How can they answer to this great injustice?

I expect my union to make a very strong effort on behalf of all the School Secretaries. I have been in touch with many of my colleagues and they all agree with me and are pretty sick and tired of the inadequate settlements the union has made for us. Please show this letter to Mr. Shanker and let him know how I feel about this so when he enters into negotiations he will keep us in mind and DO RIGHT BY THE SCHOOL SECRETARIES!

The basis for the passionate defense of the merit system put up by opponents of community control during the great battles of 1968-69 are well illustrated by this letter. What was at stake was not only the ego's investment in status made during the examination rites of passage but also the time and money invested in preparation for and successful completion of the examination or examinations, all adding up to a vested interest not only in the job but also in the system by which the job was awarded and by which subsequent openings are to be filled. To many people, their own and their colleagues' actual job security or tenure also appeared to be at stake. Union leaders repeatedly advanced the proposition that the triumph of community control would threaten the job of every teacher in the system, while the teachers sensed that community control actually threatened their status in the system and the established promotional arrangements. This sense of things was justified. Community control threatened the promotional arrangements by proposing to revise the merit system so that supervisory openings should quickly be made available to black and Puerto Rican candidates. And it threatened status by proposing that to some extent teachers and certainly principals should be made responsible to the community (parents) rather than to an administrative hierarchy. It is less certain that community control constituted an immediate threat to most teachers' actual jobs; in the face of a continuing teacher shortage, replacement of large numbers of teachers would have been difficult to effect. But of course, in the long run, community control did threaten the rationale of many teachers' entire careers—whether that rationale was babysitting or playing missionary. And community control would probably have gradually eased out those teachers who could not learn to play new and more productive roles.

The Security Syndrome

For most school personnel, as for most other civil servants, job tenure is probably the dearest held of their career perquisites, becoming dearer as each year they make an additional investment in the pension fund, in the ascent toward maximum salary, and in the life and beliefs of the school world. Most teachers will endure considerable physical discomfort, bad working conditions, disrespect of person, relatively low status in the outside professional world, relatively low salary by comparison with other professions, and sometimes, as in the case of the worst "bad" schools, complete job demoralization, rather than risk or give up their tenure. The whole battle for trade union recognition has been aimed at reducing this enormous human price that teachers have to pay for security.

Elaborate arrangements in respect to performance, evaluation, charges of incompetence, and grievance procedures protect the security of most school personnel. Regular teachers serve a three-year probationary period, after which they are granted tenure. Licensed supervisors likewise have tenure in their positions after a period of probation. Tenure is accorded even for jobs at a level of responsibility and salary that in the business world would be classed as top executive and so subject to a certain amount of risk.

Employees are given annual ratings by their supervisors of "satisfactory" and "unsatisfactory"; for probationers, "doubtful" may be used. In addition, the principal may bring a teacher up on charges for behavior or performance so egregious that it seems to demand immediate punishment.

As the formal, stylized teacher-made "test" is the

primary basis for evaluating a child's learning, so the formal, stylized classroom observation is the primary basis for evaluating the teacher's performance. The supervisor (who may be the assistant principal, department chairman, or principal) comes into the teacher's room, sometimes with, sometimes without, prior notice and "observes" her lesson. He may observe for ten minutes or for an hour. He will customarily request that she provide him with a copy of her written "lesson plan," a very precise and rigidly outlined mode of annotating the intended procedure for a given lesson. His written report on his observation may then include comments on the following kinds of matters: appearance of the room; teacher's preparation; aim of the lesson as written on the blackboard; "motivation" of the lesson; behavior of children; kinds and number of questions asked; number of children called on; manner (posture, voice, etc.) in which children recited—all matters that can be evaluated by more or less objective standards. (The expression "motivating a lesson" actually means "motivating" the children by introducing the lesson with a tricky little device supposedly related to the children's lives. If a teacher talks about spring, for example, he should "motivate" the "discussions" by bringing in a twig of leaves, or a picture somehow showing spring. The emphasis on "motivating the lesson"—in addition to the linguistic atrocity committed by the phrase—is an evidence of educational bankruptcy. Having first choked off the child's natural wellsprings of desire for learning, growth, and mastery, the teacher must then think up a trick to catch his unwilling attention.)

Failure to motivate a lesson effectively, failure to write the "aim" on the blackboard, failure of children to face the class when they stand to recite, failure of children to pay attention, failure to produce a properly designed lesson plan, asking questions that can be answered "yes" or "no," may each or all be evidences of an unsuccessful lesson.* Unsatisfactory lessons, conduct unbecoming a teacher, excessive latenesses or absences, bad relations with one's colleagues, and insubordination may lead to a general rating

**One teacher was given a "U" rating for general untidiness of her room, specifically "excessive rubber erasure leavings on the teachers desk." Reported in the* United Teacher, *February 4, 1965.*

of "unsatisfactory." But any generalization must be backed up with specific instances recorded in writing and included in the teacher's file. "Bad attitude towards students," "is racially prejudiced," "is lazy," "hates children," and so on are surely characteristics that appear among teachers and that make a teacher *in fact unsatisfactory.* But they are too general to be considered valid grounds for an *unsatisfactory rating.* However, "children didn't line up before lunch," "didn't give Zachary a reader," or "floor littered with paper" might be contributory evidence for an unsatisfactory rating. A union spokesman explained to me that the union's insistence on concrete evidence is largely responsible for the trivial grounds for many "U" ratings, but I think he was giving the union too much credit.

The consequences of receiving a "U" rating vary. The teacher may lose her license, be transferred to another (possibly easier) school, or lose certain subsidiary rights, such as a scheduled salary increment. Teachers are entitled to appeal a "U" rating, and also any alleged violation of the union contract or of customary procedures, and in fact a good deal of the work of the union consists of helping teachers with such appeals, called grievances. The steps for appealing a "U" rating, like the steps for bringing a grievance, are carefully spelled out in the union contract and in board of education procedures and constitute the procedures which the union, in the strike of 1968, came to call "due process" (a term which, as we have seen, has had a long and sometimes respected career in Anglo-American jurisprudence and which, as we shall see, also has a quite specific content). The process consists of administrative hearings in three steps: first before the principal of the school (in other words before the author of the grievance being appealed); second, before the district superintendent, the principal's immediate superior; and third, before the superintendent of schools or his representatives, usually three persons of assistant superintendent rank. A teacher with a regular license may finally carry an appeal to the courts, but a teacher with a substitute license may not. The hearing officers at every level are in positions where their concern must be more with administrative smoothness than with fairness to one teacher. A few days before the famous firing/transfer of the Ocean Hill-Brownsville nineteen in April, 1968, A union spokesman explained the actuality of the grievance and hearings procedures to me in some detail, saying:

> Grievance hearings are not trials by your peers, but a kangaroo court. In a hearing on a "U" rating, you have to show why the adverse judgment of a trained supervisor is *not* accurate. [That is, the teacher is presumed guilty unless she can prove her innocence.] You may not bring in evidence of or even mention a supervisor's prejudice against you. They say, "We are not hearing your complaint against the supervisor, but his against you."

A few months later, when it was already apparent that a bad brew was bubbling up in Ocean Hill-Brownsville, the same spokesman explained that the union did indeed, despite the unfairness of the kind of hearing provided, win a certain number of "U" rating appeals, he thought maybe 20 percent of the cases. The hearings are a way, he explained, in which "the irrationalities of local management, mainly the principal, can be corrected by central management."

In fact the system is both more and less rigid than it might seem. More rigid, because even the possibility that a tenured teacher might eventually have a fair court hearing in respect to a dispute with her principal usually does not reduce the insecurity that makes her seek to avoid such a dispute—or the peer pressures that enforce conformity even where the rules do not. And less rigid, because anyway the game is not played strictly according to the written rules. A teacher who is deemed unsatisfactory by her supervisor—or whom her supervisor doesn't like, has a grudge against, can't get along with, or wants to get out of the way to make a place for someone else—may be asked to find an opening in another school or advised to give up teaching as an inappropriate career. Depending on his professionalism, decency as a human being, and relations with the teacher, the principal may or may not precede such a suggestion or request with general harassments, excessive observation visits, demands that the teacher undergo a medical examination (for emotional instability, faulty hearing or sight, or other ailments that might interfere with her teaching), or an open or veiled suggestion that if she does not agree he will give her a "U" rating, but that if she does he will give her an "S" rating and she may go in peace. Most principals prefer to avoid both putting the blot of a "U" rating on a teacher's record and having to go through lengthy hearings if the "U" rating is appealed. A deal that gets an unsatisfactory teacher out of his school suits the principal's needs, and if she goes on teaching in another school that's none of his business. Only the strongest and most principled teachers are likely to be able to resist such a deal. Why go on teaching in a terribly distressing interpersonal situation when one can get out? And even the strong and principled are likely to yield because they know they can find another post rather easily and moreover will be able to be a more effective teacher in a school whose principal is sympathetic. Principals sometimes even help the rejected teacher to find a new post and almost always provide an adequate informal reference when asked for one by an accepting principal of another school. The frequent classroom observations that are likely to precede the confrontation are not necessarily intended as harassments. The principal (or his delegate, an assistant principal) is simply gathering evidence to be used in defense of a "U" rating if it becomes necessary to go that far. The triviality of the grounds for such a rating is such that it is a rare teacher against whom a case cannot be built (although not necessarily sustained). Even the strongest and most effective teacher will probably begin to crumble in the face of a concerted campaign against her.

The union's role in "U" rating hearings and other grievances is to advise and support the teacher, urging her to bring a case if her case seems strong or to back down and accept a deal if it doesn't. (James Horelick, whose story is told in Part III, is an example of a young teacher who accepted a deal on the advice, actually the insistence, of his chapter chairman, and much against his own wishes.) The union cannot move in and make an issue unless the aggrieved teacher is willing for an issue to be made, and there must be thousands of deals of one kind or another made every year that the union doesn't know about. Where a case seems important to the union, of course, it will try to make the teacher see its importance. This happened in the 1968 strike.

A fairly typical "U" rating case in which the teacher had a good case and appealed successfully was that of Miss

Truman, a biology teacher with a substitute's license. (Miss Truman's case comes from the UFT grievance file. The names are falsified.) She had taught in the same school for two years and was therefore entitled to her place there unless a teacher with a regular license should be appointed. A reading of the record suggests that at one point in what must have formerly been a satisfactory relationship and a more than satisfactory teaching record, Miss Truman offended her department head deeply enough to make him decide he wanted to get rid of her. (The pettiness of the concerns of the bureaucracy is often accompanied by a pettiness of interpersonal behavior.) The department head began a series of observations and reports which culminated in a "U" rating. Miss Truman did not receive, as procedures required, a copy of the fifty-page complaint that was made against her. According to her, the department head, Mr. Spinoza said, "It was lost in the mail. I don't have the time to make another copy for you since it is over 50 pages. You can come to the office and read it there. I certainly would not make additional copies. I have no time. I'm busy." The record of the appeal reports such charges and responses as the following:

Charge: The pupils at the front of the room always face you when reciting, and since many of the students mumble, the rest of the class cannot hear.

Response: As a whole, the pupils spoke quite clearly, but did begin to hesitate when a visitor stepped into the room. They said Mr. Spinoza [the chairman] frightened them, and they could not respond the way they wished to. I have explained to the students that they should not feel this way, but since they are so frightened, I did not insist that they face the class when Mr. Spinoza was sitting in the back of the room.

Charge: Miss Truman used only one microscope for the class. She should have used one for each row.

Response: When I observed Mr. Spinoza giving the same lesson, he only used one microscope, and I was following his procedure.

Charge: Although the bell [to begin the period] had rung, the students were noisy.

Response: The students were distributing homework

papers, writing on the board, and so on. The students who were moving about may have been a distracting factor to Mr. Spinoza, but they were constructively occupied.

Charge: The room was unsightly. There were papers scattered about the floor.

Response: Mr. Spinoza on several occasions reproved me in front of the class because there were papers on the floor. This was at the beginning of my first period in that room. His bias was so apparent and the reproof so obviously unjust that one of my pupils one day got up and said, "Miss Truman doesn't speak up for herself, so I'll speak for her. We just came into this room."

Charge: Miss Truman clocked in but did not remain in the building on the day before graduation. [This would be a nonteaching day when teachers would be required to be in attendance to complete their end-of-semester clerical tasks. Teachers who have completed their chores often leave the building for some hours between clocking in and clocking out, although they are not supposed to do this. It is one of the little degrading deceptions common to the profession.]

Response: I was in the building. Instead of remaining in the classroom, I took my record cards to the women teachers lounge to work on them there.

This was one of the 20 percent of the cases in which the "U" rating was overturned. I should think that Mr. Spinoza's failure to have his rating sustained may be ascribed to his sloppiness in the handling of the complaint procedures. There is nothing unusual in the nature of the charges and also nothing that might help us to know whether Miss Truman in fact was an able or an incompetent teacher, except the slight evidence that there was good rapport between her and her students in the face of the common enemy.

Just as, according to the majority of teachers questioned in the Griffiths study, the merit system does not seem to help retain good people in the system, so the evaluation proceeding probably relates only very loosely to teaching effectiveness. As the apparently objective criteria are in reality only critical hooks on which the evaluator hangs his subjective response to a given teacher, it is in reality the principal's personality and subjective responses that determine whether a given teacher will be retained and how she will be rated. This will vary to some extent as different teachers and principals interact.

While most supervisors stress control and routines, some tend to tolerate a little less rigid control on the part of a teacher who is strong on academics or in group projects for assembly programs and so on. Most principals recognize as an asset the few really strong teachers that turn up in almost every school and are likely to reward them with "positions of responsibility"–which accounts for the frequent complaint among children and parents that the best teachers simply don't stay at teaching. (A few really remarkable persons among this little group of top teachers value themselves at their true worth and refuse to leave the classroom, but most of them accept the systems evaluation of administration over teaching.)

Occasionally weak or insecure supervisors feel threatened by strong and creative teachers and try to get rid of them. This peculiar but normally rare disease of the merit system appeared as an epidemic during the academic year after the 1968 strike, aggravating the miserable symptoms that the system was already experiencing. At that time, what was generally known to insiders, including many students, was made apparent to many outsiders: that while classroom effectiveness may have some bearing in evaluating a teacher, the most important consideration is her willingness and ability to fit into a status system in which the principal of the school is the key figure of the school community, the child is an object to be manipulated according to prescribed rites and ceremonies, and the parent is a remote figure in the child's life whose sole function, from the point of view of the school, is to serve as an instrument in the manipulation of the child.

Even within the ranges of abilities and personality types selected by the accrediting and examination systems to be teachers, there is still, as in any large population, a considerable variety of abilities and aptitudes. There are a few people who, as one strong supervisor once described them to me, "can teach anybody, any place, under any circumstances." There are another few (or perhaps more than a few) for whom teaching is pure torture (or torturing). There are a good number who can teach under some circumstances but not under others, some kinds of children but not others, in some kinds of schools but not in others. And there are the many who are more or less effective as teachers depending on what their supervisors, their colleagues, their pupils expect of them, and what they expect of themselves.

The rigid protective system which can be made to bend only by deals fails to adjust to or even acknowledge these variables. Further, by allowing no open and legitimate way for the school system to relieve itself of teachers who perform all the correct rituals but fail to teach, or for a particular school to relieve itself of teachers who cannot adapt to its children's needs, the rules aggravate hypocritical formalism and diminish the schools' credit as a public institution.

Depersonalizing the Parents

As the child, theoretically the most important person in an institution created by society to fulfill some of his needs, is actually the least person in the school's status system, so his parent, the one who is most concerned about and most influential in his education and also the one on whose behalf society assumes some nurturing and socializing functions, is the least adult in the school's status system. His concerns for and observations about the child are matters of small consequence to the participants in this system; his physical presence in the school building is likely to be considered a nuisance and an interference; and his existence as the central adult in the child's life and a possible ally in the child's struggles with the school is felt as a vague threat.

The school typically seeks to neutralize the threat by keeping parents at arms' length, by limiting severely and rendering highly impersonal encounters between them and school personnel, and by coming down hard on those parents whose children seriously misbehave. It is rare for public school personnel to send for the parent of a child who appears to *have* trouble—the child who is withdrawn or frightened, fails to socialize, or doesn't learn. But they will relatively quickly send for the parent of the child who *makes* trouble—interferes with the smooth functioning of the classroom. The typical parent conference about a discipline problem consists of scolding the parent for the sins of his child, with overtones of warning that the child may be suspended, sent to a special school for bad children, and so on. The parent is likely to respond to this unpleasant experience with fury, often directed against the child who has thus exposed him to humiliation and shame. The beating or other punishment that the furious parent may then administer is justified as necessary discipline. For many children, "I'm going to call your mother" is the worst threat the school can make, and almost any school punishment seems preferable. (Loretta, below, rather than have her parent sent for, accepted demotion to a lower-track class.) So the school uses shaming the parent in respect to his child, or merely threatening to do so, as a way of keeping the child in his place.

Removing the parent from the status system and according him full respect as the most rather than the least important adult in the school system would also involve upsetting the child's relative place on the ladder. School personnel's complaints that they had difficulty controlling the children of community-control advocates and other rebellious parents were probably well founded. As these parents were demanding revision of the school's priorities to give greater emphasis to education and revision of the school's status ladder to accord more respect to themselves and the children, the children surely became more uppity and less inclined to submit to despotic authority. (Many of these students participated in the rebellions against school authorities, treated in Part III.)

Parents of children who are not disciplinary problems are expected to attend school on specific formal occasions: parents visiting day, conference night, perhaps a special assembly performance, and "Teacher Recognition Day." Except for parents association functionaries, who play a role in the adult hierarchy analogous to the role played in the classroom by the pupil monitors, many parents find even these encounters ego-damaging and/or hypocritical. The official visiting days and five-minute conferences between teacher and parent are highly formalized rituals, gratifying only to those parents whose exceptionally good or exceptionally achieving children have commended themselves to the teacher's attention. Parents of "average" children and of low-status black and Puerto Rican parents are made to sense their children's low status and are likely to feel put down and embarrassed on these occasions.

Richard's mother comes to meet the teacher who rules over ten or twenty or thirty hours weekly of Richard's life. For Mother, Richard is strong, quick tempered, funny, a good athlete. He's lazy when it comes to doing errands but very good with the baby. He has a cute double cowlick and when he frowns looks exactly like his Uncle David. In short, Richard is the sum of all the qualities that make him uniquely Richard, and infinitely precious. Richard's teacher greets Richard's mother with a prepared smile, perhaps fumbling in the back of her mind for an image of Richard, consults her grade book, and ticks off mechanically his spelling grade, his attendance record, his good behavior except for—now she remembers something—the time Richard and three other boys stole Madeleine's notebook and made her cry. "But he's fine, he's getting along all right." And the conference is over. The sense of Richard's insignificance is, of course, far more distressing if Richard happens to be, not "getting along all right," but a loser, in which case the teacher's disapproval of him will surely be conveyed.

Middle-class parents of high-status children (students in various sorts of academically advanced classes) who are made to feel good about their children when they attend school functions are far more likely to attend school functions than poor and nonwhite parents of low-status children, who are made to feel uncomfortable about their children when they attend school functions. School officials and teachers often say that the fact that black and Puerto Rican parents, for example, don't come to school for visiting day, assemblies, and so on, proves that these parents don't care about their children and don't care about how their children do in school. I should think it quite likely that many stay away because they care very much and seek to protect themselves against shame in respect to their own and their children's low status.

The community-control movement, which began around 1965, sought in effect to reverse the relationship of parents to school. Where the parents had been at the bottom of the status ladder, sometimes a scapegoat for the school's failures, sometimes an instrument of the school's control system, community control sought to put the parents in a position of power and influence and *to make the school an instrument of their goals*—educational and social success for their children. To the extent that the school is a more or less self-contained and consistent system, such reversals would undermine its entire way of being, rationale, and authority arrangements. How the system mobilized to defend itself against this subversion is the subject of Parts II and III of this book.

4. GROUPING PUPILS TO SERVE THE STATUS SYSTEM

One important way in which schools in New York City (like schools in many cities throughout the country) signify and reinforce the relative status of various groups of students, and especially of white students relative to black and Puerto Rican students, is by homogeneous grouping, or tracking. Almost all teachers and administrators and many parents believe that homogeneous class grouping, supposedly based on academic potential and/or achievement, facilitates *teaching*. To the extent that teaching is synonymous with keeping order, this may be so. But both extensive evidence and the experiences of individuals suggest that homogeneous grouping does not facilitate *learning*, if by learning we mean learning school skills. Further, in New York, many factors other than academic ability serve as criteria for assigning children to higher- or lower-level classes. Moreover, homogeneous grouping institutionalizes status judgments, including self-judgments, about the pupils, and about their mentors.

By the time a New York City child has completed kindergarten, he will very likely already have been selected as one of the ins or one of the outs in the continuous series of selections to which he is to be subjected throughout his school career. A 1966 board of education circular to district superintendents and principals stated: "For the purposes of proper classification and placement in grade one, teachers and supervisors should make every effort to identify intellectually gifted children by the end of the kindergarten year. The judgment of teachers and supervisors should be the basis of such identification."[1]

Oversimplifying, the five-year-old child who was selected to be out will drop out before high school graduation or at best receive a General diploma ten or twelve years after the initial designation, while the five-year-old selected to be in will graduate with an Academic diploma from one of the "good" schools.

The mechanics are simple.

Throughout elementary school children are grouped ostensibly in accordance with academic ability, with scores earned on standardized reading tests as the primary criterion. In most schools, the classes are designated by numbers, the lower the number, the higher the reading scores; thus 1-1 is the "smartest" first-grade class, 1-14 the "dumbest." In other schools, in a vain effort to prevent the children from knowing whether they are the elect, the average, or the damned, names are used, or an elaborate rearrangement of the number system; for example, highest to lowest might be 1-2, 1-4, 1-6, 1-1, 1-3, 1-5, and so on. I have yet to meet a child (even one of the supposedly stupid 1-14s) who did not know pretty well where he stood in the grade hierarchy. At the top of the hierarchy are the classes for the intellectually gifted (I.G.C.). To be intellectually gifted in the New York City school system, you have to score about one year over the norm in reading—which is what a large proportion of white, middle-class, metropolitan-area children do score—and meet some additional more subjective criteria, including among others "initiative and desire to participate," "interest in a variety of things," "emotional stability," "good character," and "sensitivity to feelings and needs of others." At the bottom of the hierarchy are the classes for children with retarded mental development (C.R.M.D.). I know a perfectly normal young man, Georgie, whose learning to read English was interrupted about second or third grade by his going to Puerto Rico for two years and who after his return spent his remaining school years in a C.R.M.D. class until at age seventeen he was asked to leave school because he was a chronic cutter. He never did learn to read.*

In between the "gifted" and the "retarded" are what we might call the "commoners," looking up with envious distaste at their academic superiors and down with self-sustaining contempt at their inferiors. Benny Wilkinson, who transferred from predominantly black and Puerto Rican Harriet Tubman Elementary School in Spanish Harlem to nearby predominantly white Thoreau Junior High School, under the board of education's Open Enrollment Plan, tells what it's like to be a commoner: "[At Tubman] I was usually in the top four classes. [At Thoreau] I thought I was bad because I got put in 7-6, because the dumbest classes we had over here at Tubman was in the 9 and 10 category. And I seen that 7-6 and all that, and oh, man, I was in a dumb class! . . . But then I saw this thing way down to 7-29. . . and it *kept* going down. I looked and I realized that I wasn't in as bad shape as I thought I was. I didn't feel so bad."

While theoretically no formal arrangements prevent an elementary school child from moving from one level or track to another, and students may be moved from a 4 class, say, to a 6, or 10 to a 9, or a 2 to a 1, a pupil's relative position in the entire grade tends to become more and more fixed as the years go by, so that what we have is a kind of schoolboy's miniature caste system with extremely limited mobility. (And this caste system eventually feeds into the larger society's modified caste system.) The relative inflexibility of the system is upheld by the students', the teachers', and the board of education's belief in the transcendent validity of the implied placement criteria. Students more or less assume that the adults are making correct judgments about whether they are smart or dumb. "What class is this?" I once asked a student in a class I was observing; I meant what grade. "Seven-fourteen, the dumb

* *The concept that having another language than English makes a child a mental retardate is not limited to schoolmen in New York. In San Francisco, the retesting, in Spanish, of all Spanish-surnamed children in classes for mental retardates produced the finding that 45 percent were of average or better than average intelligence. The school official who defended the testing program suggested that it was the children's fault that they didn't fit the tests: "I don't think it was as much the fault of the test as it was the cultural deprivation of the child," he said.* San Francisco Chronicle, *January 24, 1970.*

class," he said. Teachers are reluctant to trust their own perceptions when they contradict official arrangements. A teacher whom I questioned about illiterate Georgie said first, "Oh, yes, I know him, that C.R.M.D. boy," and then in response to evidence I offered of his ability to function astonishingly well in the face of complete illiteracy, said, doubtfully, "Well, maybe we ought to have the bureau of child guidance test him again." (But why should Georgie, for his part, agree to undergo another confrontation with assured failure?) The board of education assumes that the criteria are objective and that almost all first judgments about a child's placement are accurate. I.G.C. classes begin in fourth grade, and if one is to be judged intellectually gifted, that is pretty much when he must win that judgment. "Initial placement in an I.G.C. class in Grade 5 or Grade 6," the board circular reads, "should be considered only in special cases."[2] Further, I.G.C. reading requirements demand increasing advancement year by year, assured to the children already in I.G.C. classes by the intensified reading program to which they are subjected there, but not likely to be achieved by most children (especially children from nonreading families) who are in ordinary classes, where little is demanded of them.

What movement up and down within the grade level there is, is likely to have a different character for white and nonwhite children. A black or Puerto Rican child in a top grade who misbehaves or is considered troublesome can easily be "busted" in rank, and by the time the next class reorganization comes about, no one—perhaps not even the child—knows that he was put in a bad class not because he was dumb but because he was naughty. And by this time he might even have accommodated and become dumb. His parents usually don't know how the system works, are afraid to challenge the experts' decisions, or both. A white child in a racially mixed "dumb" class, on the other hand, may be examined closely by the teacher for signs of academic potential and be moved up if possible. If the child is bad or he fights (less likely among middle-class white children than among poor children), so he was bad—any kid is bad once in awhile—that doesn't mean he's stupid, does it? If a white middle-class child really has difficulty making it academically, his parents are likely to provide outside support or withdraw him from the public schools altogether in favor of a private school "where he can get personal attention and a better education."

In elementary school, all classes within a given grade theoretically cover the same material, so there is no formal impediment to a child's moving up within the grade. But in junior high school and high school, moving to a higher track is impeded not only by what the child hasn't learned (achieved) but also by what he hasn't "taken"—that is, the courses that the school administrators didn't program him for. It is in junior high school that the courses in foreign language and elementary algebra required for an Academic diploma from high school are begun, and those children who come into junior high school in the middle to bottom classes are automatically not programed for these courses thus making them candidates for a General diploma or for dropping out. The children who come from the I.G.C and other top classes almost automatically move on to the junior high schools' Special Progress (S.P.) classes. There they receive not only the beginning courses for an Academic high school curriculum, including a foreign language and beginning algebra, but also either an accelerated program which achieves grades 7, 8, and 9 in two years instead of three, or an "enriched" program which involves a good deal of outside reading and report writing. (Because the entrance requirements for S.P. are fairly rigidly prescribed by the board of education, some junior high schools also offer special orchestra or band classes, the entrance barriers to which are a little lower than those for the S.P., as a kind of consolation prize. Thus, in racially and socially mixed school districts, like those found in many parts of Manhattan outside of Harlem proper, white middle-class children who cannot quite make the S.P. standards, plus a few nonwhites, are accommodated in other semi-prestige and semi-segregated classes.)

Graduates of the junior highs' S.P. classes, particularly in those districts that do not have a predominantly Other well-reputed Academic high school, typically compete by examination for entrance into the city's few specialized high schools. Among these are: the Bronx High School of Science, probably the most prestigous and therefore the most sought after by ambitious students whether or not they are primarily interested in science; Stuyvesant High School, also specializing in science and, until one girl was admitted by court order in 1969, all-male; and the High School of Music and Art, offering special majors in either music or art, for either of which entering applicants must pass a qualifying examination in aptitude and skill. Because Music and Art has lower academic entrance requirements than either Science or Stuyvesant (but higher than can be met by most nonwhite students), many Other students whose neighborhood high schools are "bad" schools and who believe that they can't make Stuyvesant or Science (or who don't want to because these schools are by reputation fiercely competitive) are coached by private art or music teachers for two or three years or longer, to prepare them for taking the Music and Art examinations. There is also one extremely competitive and academically very high level all-girls high school, Hunter High School, administered not by the board of education but by the board of higher education in conjunction with Hunter College, a branch of the City University.

Scattered throughout the city, except in Manhattan, there also are some predominantly white middle-class high schools which are considered by the populations they serve and the city at large to be good schools. Among the populations to which these schools are accessible, only the especially ambitious students seek to enter the specialized high schools; a few genuinely gifted ones may attend Music and Art. The rest attend their neighborhood high schools, where they are programed for Academic diplomas, many in special "Honors" or "advanced placement" courses. In areas where there are no nearby "good" high schools, special Honors tracks have been created in the regular high schools to accommodate the white underachievers, "misfits," and recent arrivals in the city, as well as the few nonwhites who have miraculously survived as "ins." The customary practice in most nonspecialized high schools is to "block track" all or almost all students; thus most students are likely to be programed for all Honors, all Academic, or all General courses. Further the "official rooms" (home rooms) are organized by tracks and numbered in accordance with their place on the grade ladder. So, except for physical education and, in some schools, required art and music, students are grouped throughout the day in accordance with their school status, always readily identified by their "official room" designation. While block tracking may occasionally involve academic misplacement of a student, it has the advantage for school personnel of facilitating administration.

Up and down the ranks of the adults and of the children, almost all individuals learn to adapt not only their behavior but also their beliefs to the needs of the status system and the roles they are assigned to play in it. Those few individuals who failed to learn these most important lessons were for many years the system's "misfits," until more recently they became its rebels. Among the misfits were the occasional brilliant or creative but erratic students whose oddness no amount of indoctrination in uniformity could convert into failure; the students destined for success who yet continually, and more or less successfully, avoided their destiny (called "underachievers"); and the poor dark-skinned students who somehow resisted all the system's pressures to turn "poor and black" into "dumb." Some of the misfit children had misfit parents—middle-class whites more concerned with their children's spiritual and intellectual soundness than with their academic achievement, or lower-class or middle-class nonwhites who refused to adopt a head-scratching posture in respect to school personnel. Also among the misfits were the gifted teachers and unusual administrators who acted as if schools' and their major function was to meet the children's not the system's needs. Many children of the poor—and likely many middle-class children, too—experience one beautiful, beloved teacher during the course of their school careers and remember her all their lives, often recalling her with the words, "She really cared. She really made you learn." The one shining teacher seems especially to be the experience of the Harlem children who succeeded in school—overcame the school's program for their failure. (Both Miles Randolph and Loretta Tubman, whose tales are told below, are examples.) Misfit supervisors were more scarce than misfit teachers for obvious reasons. Teachers who "really cared" were more likely to want to stay close to the children about whom they cared than were those teachers whose personal values, premises, and personalities meshed smoothly into the system's gears, and they were less likely to want or perhaps be able, to take advantage of the system's status-reinforcing ladder of promotion. The very rare misfit supervisors would thus shine out from among the expected shabbiness like precious jewels, and people would have to write books and articles about them to prove that they existed.*

How Tracking Helps Teach Children (Their Place)

Wherever shifting populations or white preference for urban over suburban living gather together blacks, Puerto Ricans, and Others, homogeneous grouping serves as a quite precise instrument of socio-economic and race grading. This may be confirmed by simple observation in almost any mixed school.

Theoretically the basic school tracking arrangements set up or authorized by the board of education are uniform throughout the city. But grading in elementary school and junior high school for classes below the top rung of I.G.C. or S.P. are relative within each school. The situation with I.G.C. and S.P. classes is more complex. Having uniform admission requirements, they supposedly provide the same educational experiences regardless of whether the classes are in a school in poor black Harlem or Bedford-Stuyvesant or in middle-class white Forest Hills. Indeed, the necessity for "upholding standards" is considered so grave by the board of education that many if not most elementary schools in poor nonwhite neighborhoods have no I.G.C. class at any grade level, because not enough children in the schools meet the standards. Sometimes one central I.G.C. class will be created in one school to serve several nearby schools. In a predominantly white middle-class school, on the other hand, there may be two or even three I.G.C.s on a grade, and two or three S.P.s in the junior high schools, with the members of these classes as well as the faculty aware of which class is the very best of the best—the very summit of Mount Everest.

* *See, for example, Nat Hentoff,* Our Children Are Dying *(Viking, 1966), about principal Elliott Shapiro, or my own remarks elsewhere in this book about principal Edward Gottlieb, both men with a more than normal endowment of human decency and lovingness, not unworthy of the public praise educational writers have lavished on them but worthy of it largely because these qualities are so rare in the educational universe. It is as if books would need to be written and plaques put up for every doctor who gave not only his skill but his devotion to his patients. Is it not sufficient that his patients love and appreciate him?*

Actually the experience, academically speaking, of an I.G.C. or an S.P. in a predominantly nonwhite or even partly nonwhite school may be substantially below the experience of an I.G.C. or S.P. in a predominantly white school, although there are always certain status advantages to being in an S.P. class in a mixed or "bad" neighborhood, an unearned increment, as it were. An example is provided by the Oppenheimer family which moved from a predominantly white neighborhood in Brooklyn to the very mixed (white, black, Puerto Rican, and Chinese) Lower East Side of Manhattan when Janet was in the seventh grade. She explained:

We were looking around to find a school that gave the stuff I had been taking. In Brooklyn the three-year S.P. class was a good class, and it is supposed to be enriched. But here the three-year S.P. is absolutely nothing. The S.P. just means you behave better because you're an S.P. class. The work is generally the same [as] the regular classes. The kids just get better grades. While the S.P. class is better and five other classes [just below the S.P.] are better than the rest of the classes in the junior high school, the rest of the classes are terrible, while the S.P. classes are no better than the regular classes in Brooklyn. In Brooklyn just about everyone got a language all three years, and everybody got it in the ninth grade. [In the Manhattan school only the top classes studied a foreign language.*] But for the S.P. classes it was less oppressive because you're special and you get special privileges. The teachers treat you better than the other kids.

**A foreign language is customarily offered only to those students whose reading score is on grade level, which provides the formal reason for not programing most nonwhites for a foreign language. If foreign languages were taught by the oral-aural method, instead of primarily as reading-and-grammar languages, there would be no need for this English-reading prerequisite. Most foreign language teachers, however, are not native speakers of the language they teach and many do not even have good command of the spoken language. Until the late '50s, or early '60s, in fact, native speakers of the tongue with traces of their native accent in their spoken English found it almost impossible to pass the English "speech test" required to become licensed teachers. Thus, the frequent anomoly of thousands of Puerto Rican and other Latin American students being "taught" Spanish by teachers who could not understand their students when they talked Spanish among themselves. The English-reading requirement serves primarily to accommodate the teachers.*

In other mixed neighborhoods and schools, the I.G.C. and the S.P. do in fact receive as demanding a curriculum as they would in an all-white neighborhood. But in either case and in general, students are aware that race and background determine their class placement. Where occasionally class and race lines are crossed, as in the placement of a high-achieving black or Puerto Rican student in a top white class, the children nevertheless continue to observe social and racial distinctions.

Kenny Fields, a white, middle-class, extremely gifted and high-achieving student, describes a fellow student, Stephan, who may have been either Greek or Puerto Rican (the difference to Kenny was not significant), who made a very brief appearance in his S.P. class:

I was assigned to tutor him—and that's how I discovered how really bright he was. But he really didn't . . . he didn't have a strong inward . . . my impression was that he didn't have a strong desire in himself to learn—he kind of accepted it if it was forced on him.

You mean he didn't work hard?

He didn't work at all. But it's a question of, say, like paying attention to what's being said. He would talk to other people, he would talk to me.

You were fairly friendly with him?

Yeah.

And how about the rest of the class?

I'd say they were kind of friendly to him—actually fairly friendly. None of us felt towards him like we did to our personal friends.

How would you explain that?

One thing is, like I said, he was only in the class for a very short time [before] he was put out into I guess one of the slow classes. And another thing is that he came from a different background and it was much harder for us to accept him. For instance, the fact that he took school so seriously.

In other words, part of your acceptance of your fellow students was based on their attitude towards school?

Their attitudes towards everything, actually. We would brag to each other that it [school] was overdisciplined and everything.

Kenny's apparent contradiction—that Stephan didn't

work hard, didn't seem to want to learn, but that he "took school so seriously"—can be understood in terms of his own attitudes and experiences, and those of many others like him. "By the time I was in sixth grade," he once said, "I knew perfectly well that I wasn't going to learn anything at school—ever. It turned out not to be true, but that was still my idea of what school would be." And again: "There are all kinds of ways, you know, to sit in class: You can sit just out of everything. Or you can sit like, if the teacher asks you a question, you answer it; you can hear everything and be able to repeat it. Or you can understand things." Mostly Kenny went through classes in what he called the "hearing-and-repeating stage." In other words, he recognized that his school experiences were ritual rather than learning, but was willing to perform the ritual even while scorning it among his friends. Stephan, on the other hand, apparently believed that the ritual *was* learning, but, for reasons we cannot know but can suspect, seemed to need to interrelate more with his fellow students than with the teacher. We also cannot know, but can suspect, why Stephan, whom Kenny knew to be very bright (as the teacher could have known), was "busted" from the S.P. Kenny, so educated outside of school as virtually to put him beyond the school's power to educate, attended school then mainly to associate with his status peers and to learn to perform certain socially required rituals. Stephan, who needed the school to provide a kind of education that his out-of-school life did not provide and who could have acquired it from better-educated fellow students, was removed from their presence in order that he might observe his own worth in the company of his status peers and, together with them, share the rituals appropriate to their common status.

Ishmael Raymond, another bright but underachieving white middle-class boy, was moved from a middling class to an I.G.C. class. "In the I.G.C. class, as I recall, there was about maybe three, four kids who were not Jewish middle-class. There might have been a Negro kid in the class, but I'm not sure—I just have the feeling that, when I think back about the class, there was like three outsiders." In response to a series of questions about what made them outsiders—their dress, their names, their color?—he said: "Not their names. See, like when I was in that other class [the one from which he moved], which was not Jewish middle-class, I didn't feel apart from those kids. I felt perfectly comfortable with those kids, who would have been outsiders in an I.G.C. class. So what I think it was, was something in the way that the rest of the class treated them."

That teachers more or less conform to and even enforce judgments about who belongs where was evidenced by another incident told by Ishmael. He was playing in the yard during recess with a group of Puerto Rican boys, and the teacher on duty came to break up a small dispute. She then said to him, "Why don't you go play with your own friends?" Her judgment about who was friends with whom had to have been made on the basis of social discrimination, because none of the boys were known to her as individuals.*

While we know very little about these group-school interactions, the generalization seems warranted that in New York, tracking at once adapts to and reinforces student ranking practices which originate in the larger society.

Homogeneous grouping, first developed during the 1920s along with the educational testing movement and theoretically for the purpose of improving instruction of slow as well as fast achievers, has caught on or languished at various times and in response to various historical events and trends, of which the panic and shame induced in the American educational universe by Sputnick I was one.[3] Whatever functions an institution or practice is at first

* *Although ethnically an "in," Ishmael hung on the fringes of the in-group throughout his school career, something in his evaluation of himself and of the school situation influencing his own judgments of his fellow students and his teachers' judgments of him. "I felt the regular* I.G.C. *kids were like selling out. I didn't feel they had a basic self-respect, which I felt the other kids had. I've always respected more the not Jewish middle-class kids. And I think that the teacher [of the* I.G.C. *class] felt that I didn't really fit in that class, [although] I ended up, as did 90 percent of the class, getting all 'Excellents' on my report card." These remarks, and also Kenny's, open up a crucial and so far as I know largely unexplored area of educational research: how educators respond to and interact with students' social systems and how, in turn, such interaction affects learning. This question is raised again in the study of Miles Randolph below and in a general way in section 6 of this Part, "Blowing the Curve at the Bottom."*

designed to fulfill, if it survives it comes to fit into the dominant needs of the system of which it is a part—or into the needs of the dominant members of the system. Patricia Sexton, from whose detailed study on the unequal apportionment of educational resources in one big city I quoted above, wrote in a later work, *The American School*: "Stratification has increased in American schools. The 'tightening of standards' following Sputnick moved homogeneous grouping into early grades in a presumed effort to isolate the scientifically gifted. [One might write a book entitled *The Effect of the Cold War on the Life of American Six Year Olds.*] Transfer of Negroes out of segregated schools also pushed ability grouping downward into early grades as a means of separating the newcomers."

Tracking or homogeneous grouping—whatever may be its effect on students, slow or fast—dovetails into the needs of teachers and administrators and of middle-class, status-oriented parents (and children). I do not mean to say by this that only white middle-class parents (and children) are status-oriented, or that lower-class, white or nonwhite, parents would not be status-oriented if they had a better chance to achieve status. Many if not most of the participants (parents, career educators, and community leaders) of New York's community-control movement, described in Part II, were status-oriented but simply felt that the status system as it then functioned did not allow black and Puerto Rican children a fair chance to compete. (We will see the same attitude in the story of Miles Randolph, a black student.) But the fact is that the middle-class white parents are in a status-position through which they can exploit to the full the status possibilities of school arrangements. In this they are likely to receive the cooperation of teachers and school administrators as a matter of course.

The cooperation between status-oriented school personnel and status-oriented middle-class families sometimes amounts to what would be called collusion were it not so unselfconscious and without guile—and without awareness of the long-term consequence for the outs of special favors granted to the ins. For example, the rules of admission to I.G.C. and S.P. classes allow retesting where candidates fall slightly below required reading or math requirements. Normally, it is the province of the teacher to make use of this option (though few of them do). But when the children of white parents, especially those living in "high-mix" neighborhoods, do not meet the standards the first time, the parents often request that their children be retested either immediately or after a period of special coaching. Every time a favor is granted to an "in," on such matters as retesting or by arranging for exceptional admission to a good class or a good school or by yielding on a point of school discipline, the distinction between ins and outs is reinforced and all participants are helped to recall that individual worth is determined largely by (racial) group membership. And every individual favor that reinforces the status system serves to damage those who are automatically assigned low status.

And most favors do reinforce rather than blur the status system. While white parents whose children fail to achieve I.G.C. or S.P. frequently request exceptional assignments or retesting, very few black and Puerto Rican parents do. An analysis of grouping by Christina Tree reports that principals are more likely to be questioned about why a child is not in a top class (i.e., questioned by a white parent whose child is in a middling class) than about why he is in a bottom one (i.e., questioned by a black parent).[4] Black parents are generally uninformed about the criteria and the significance of grouping. And they do not know what is the almost assured academic fate of children assigned early on to low groups. What they know is what their children's report cards tell them. And by and large the "Excellents," "Goods," "Outstandings," "Needs Improvements," and "Unsatisfactories" that the child carries home on his report card are an evaluation of his performance *by comparison with the other children in his class.* If a child is not learning to read or cannot perform in math, the teacher, comparing him with all the others in his class, not to speak of the school or the entire racial group, who have the same deficiency, is not likely to inform the parent of this. She will likely inscribe alarming marks or comments on the child's report card only if he is behaving so badly that she needs the parent's help to bring him in line. Also, the parents of automatically low-status children are likely not to know and/or not to understand if their children are programed in junior high school in such wise as to preclude their being able to pursue an Academic program in high school.

The children themselves, however, do develop very early in their school careers a pretty good sense of how the system works, but for obvious reasons they don't question the judgment of their teachers. As Benny explained when asked whether he thought predominantly white Thoreau Junior High School to which he transferred from black Harriet Tubman Elementary School had made a mistake in moving him down several notches: "No. You know, when they program you for something like that, you don't think about mistakes or nothing like that. All you think about is that I am in a dumb class or I am in a smart class or something like that. You know, you can just leave it up to them. Everybody does that." Benny took it for granted that the complicated rating procedures would be competently and fairly performed to determine his precisely correct niche in the school world.

Actually, leaving aside the question of the validity of the entire system as a way of determining learning potential, there are occasional cases of gross error even on the system's own terms. These may be corrected when brought to administrators' attention. But for a number of reasons they often are not brought to the administrators' attention. The teacher of a slow class will be understandably reluctant to give up the one misplaced fast-learning child who turns up in her classroom. Again, teachers tend not to trust their subjective perceptions of students' abilities in the face of "scientific evidence" or supervisors' judgments to the contrary. And at the high school and to some extent at the junior high school level, the depersonalization of teacher-student relationships has often gone so far that teachers simply don't want to go through an administrative hassle on behalf of a student with whom they will have contact for only forty minutes a day for less than five months and then will never see again. On the other hand, concerned teachers sometimes report that their requests for a transfer upward of a clearly misclassified child have been ignored for one reason or another by the school administrators. To a large extent, as should be clear from section 3 of this Part, "Ordering the Adults," the retention of a student in a given track once he has been assigned to it is a matter simply of massive administrative inertia.

Tracking and the Needs of the Adults

Homogeneous grouping serves not only to reinforce status among various groups of pupils, but also to reinforce status as between the teacher and the children and between one teacher and another.

In the classroom the uniform children can be assigned uniform lessons (in reading, "readers") with the teacher as the constant center of attention. Thus what such grouping actually facilitates is not so much individual learning as a particular conception of classroom order. An artistic seven year old of my acquaintance refused to draw in school because, he said, "The teacher always has to conduct my drawings." The role of conductor of the group, rather than instructor of individuals or organizer of individual learning, reinforces the teacher's own status vis à vis "her" children—and confirms and strengthens for her and for them their prescribed status among the classes of the school.

I once spent a morning with a lower-track all-black fifth-grade class, many of whose members were "holdovers." Mrs. Chestnut, the teacher, treated the childen in all respects as if they were mental defectives and conducted her lessons at an agonizing snail's pace. The children drooped like sad unwatered house plants and I myself shared their, and relived my own childhood, sick feeling of the eternity of an hour. A school administrator, who considered this particular teacher somewhat rigid but declared "she gets results" (what results?), asked my impressions at the end of the day. I offered what favorable ones I could and then suggested that I thought that this class might progress a little faster. The administrator's face shed its friendliness as she said, "No. You're absolutely wrong. I know those children." My suggestion that children whom she considered "slow" might not in fact be slow offended that administrator's sense of the rightness of things.

When the United Federation of Teachers, the teachers union in New York City, proposed their More Effective Schools programs in 1966, they had as hard a time selling the program's plan for heterogeneous grouping to their own members as they did selling the $500 added annual cost per child to the board of education.*

In the school and in the school system, homogeneous grouping and tracking serve to provide status symbols and goals for status striving among a group of professionals who are considered relatively low-status in the larger society.

Albert Shanker, president of the United Federation of Teachers, is concerned with how school arrangements affect teachers. He likes to discuss with interviewers the real problem of competing interests in the school system, often using medicine as an analogy. He points out that teachers, like doctors and waitresses, serve not only their primary function—teaching, healing, or serving—but also their own sometimes conflicting private and group interests. He said in an interview with me: "Any person who studies systems and organizations . . . will admit that . . . every system serves a heck of a lot of needs and a heck of a lot of purposes; there is never a single purpose for which something operates. The school system is going to operate to satisfy political needs of board members, it's going to satisfy certain administrative needs of supervisors, it's going to satisfy the economic and psychological and status and all sorts of needs of teachers." In the case of tracking, there is considerable evidence that the interests of teachers (as a class, not necessarily so for each individual) are better served by the institution than are the interests of children, certainly those of the "dumb" children.

Good and bad schools and classes are incorporated into the seniority and status system of both teachers and administrators. Good classes and bad classes serve teachers as status symbols, and administrators as instruments for rewarding or punishing teachers. Getting into a good school early in one's teaching career confers the kind of worth that is conferred, for example, by picking up a cashmere sweater or a piece of genuine Wedgewood for a song; that is, it

* *Throughout the academic year 1964-65,* The United Teacher, *organ of the* UFT, *ran recruitment appeals to persuade teachers to volunteer to teach in* M.E. *schools, which were going to provide all the conditions that teachers had been begging for—smaller classes, more space, much more equipment—and one thing they did not want: heterogeneous classes. The teachers held back. One of the* UFT's *appeals suggests why. "I do hope that the teachers in the* MES *program will not give way to their anxieties, study the problem of classroom techniques with small heterogeneous class groups, give the practice a fair trial."* The United Teacher, *March 22, 1965.*

derives from a combination of luck and astuteness. But there is no particular ignominy attached to having to wait the normal three to four years to find a place in a good school. Being assigned to teach a good class, on the other hand, is a recognition of special professional competance. The board of education recognizes that special qualifications are required to teach I.G.C. classes, for example. It lists eight requirements for such a teacher, only one of which is an objective item—"having taken a course in teaching the intellectually gifted child."[5] The others are the usual schoolish things (good attendance, working well with other teachers, good classroom management, etc.) with a heavy emphasis on personality and cultural background (the former should be "warm and stable," and the latter "fine"). It may surprise some that these qualities, plus such others as evidence of "creative teaching" and of "ability to cope with a challenging and demanding program," are not thought to be especially necessary to teach the children of the poor, that while special qualifications are thought to be required to teach those who are most likely to get most of their education outside of school ("I never learned anything in elementary school that I didn't already know," said Kenny,) no special qualifications are thought to be needed to teach those, who must learn school things in school or not at all. The United Federation of Teachers, which throughout the years has fought invidious and salary distinctions among classes of teachers (high school versus elementary school; English versus physical education, etc.), has embodied the special requirements for teaching "intellectually gifted" children in its contract with the board, specifying only that I.G.C. classes should be rotated every three years among "qualified teachers."

Being assigned to teach an I.G.C. class in elementary school, an S.P. class in junior high school, or an Honors class in high school, by conferring high status within the rank, compensates a teacher for the profession's low status, and for her very one-down position in relation to her supervisors. Meanwhile teachers not so chosen tend to focus their *ressentiment*—a kind of unfocused, generalized, free-floating grouch[6]—as simple resentment against the administrator for overlooking their talents or against the not smart children they teach for not being smart.

Teachers chosen for a school's academically top classes

are known by the children and parents to be the school's "best" teachers, and (as we shall see in the career of Miles below) they compete with one another, or set their classes to compete with one another. Ishmael explains: "Well, in the first place everyone knew that Dr. . . . whatever the hell his name was, who was the teacher of the other I.G.C. class, that he was the best teacher in the school and he always had the I.G.C. classes . . . I mean, I don't know how we knew this but by the best teacher, I mean he had the biggest reputation and I suppose that all the teachers knew that he was going to be a principal some day." So a mutually reinforcing status system operates, in which the children's brightness confers status on the teacher and the teacher's professional reputation confers prestige on the children.

Miss Weber, a misfit teacher in predominantly black and Puerto Rican Norman Thomas High School, reports as follows:

In our school the non-English-speaking classes were the bottom classes because nobody knew how to teach them—or make them behave. I liked those classes, and I also liked the General classes, which were considered dull. The kids were fresher and more fun than the middling Academic classes. Those Academic kids were just grinds. The middle Academic classes I didn't care about one way or another, but it was fun to have one Honors class. Everybody wanted the Honors, but my chairman would always give me one Honors even if I didn't ask for it, kind of as a reward for taking all those other classes that nobody else wanted. I remember one teacher, a kind of slow-moving and very pedestrian black teacher, the chairman would *never* give her an Honors class. And she was very bitter about that. Of course, the Honors classes hardly had any black kids in them. I don't know if that had something to do with it.

As Miss Weber suggests, there is likely to be a difference in style, as well perhaps as in diligence and ability, of teachers of top classes (at least so far as I have been able to observe; I know of no objective study that has been made of this matter). Administrators seem to favor teachers who are or seem to be more than normally assiduous, or perhaps more than normally ambitious, somewhat free in style rather than rigid, and perhaps a higher than average cultural or intellectual background and interests. But what we cannot know about several of these qualities is the extent to which they would have been manifested if the individuals chosen had remained teachers of middle- or low-ranking (i.e., of lower-status) classes and the extent to which they were stimulated by both the status award and the teacher's interaction with brighter, more ambitious, or more school-oriented children. It may be that not only can a good teacher make a class brighter but that a bright class can make a teacher better.

There are safeguards in the teacher-status system to help preserve the self-respect of teachers of both the middling and the bottom classes. In the case of the former, the teachers, like the whole system, conventionally ascribe the school's failure to the children, thus preserving the teacher's worth at the expense of the children's. Clearly this is more necessary in mixed and all-minority schools than in mainly white middle-class schools, where merely teaching in a "good" school confers worth on the teacher, even if she does not teach a top class. At the very bottom of the teaching status system, there is an institutionalized safeguard. Teachers of the mentally retarded are specially licensed, thus being recognized as possessors of special skills and training. And teachers in the schools for the system's most severe "disciplinary problems" (for many years designated by numbers in the 600s, and so called "600 schools"), receive special battle pay—or a consolation prize. Even so, there is likely to be a serious morale problem among teachers of middling and bad classes in bad schools, as we see a little further on in the case of Miss Jersild in Harlem.

Effects of Tracking on Learning

Most school people and school-oriented parents are so committed to the official rationale of homogeneous grouping—that it provides the conditions for more effective teaching of slow and fast learners alike—that they tend to believe that without homogeneous grouping there would be almost no teaching (learning) whatsoever. Actually, though ability grouping serves the status needs of already advantaged children and of teachers, there is no firm evidence that, other conditions being equal, it improves learning for children at any ability level. And ability grouping, like segregated schools, does make it easier to make other conditions unequal—in other words, to preserve status differences. Teaching materials and perhaps teaching ability are conditions that are unequally apportioned as between "good" and "bad" classes.

Perhaps more important even than these inequalities is the matter of teacher attitudes toward and expectations of their classes. In a recent series of studies on teacher expectations, two psychologists, Robert Rosenthal and Lenore Jacobson, who had discovered that experimenters' expectations about the learning performance of experimental animals significantly affected the animals' performance, set out to determine whether this might not also be true of teachers' expectations of students' performance. Ostensibly on the basis of standardized relatively nonverbal intelligence tests administered to all the children in a test school, certain teachers were given the names of children in their classes who, the teachers were told, were "late bloomers" and were about to experience a sudden learning spurt. Actually the names, about 20 percent of the student body, were chosen at random. Tests administered both a year and two years later showed that by comparison with a control group of children equal in other respects to the supposed bloomers but not so designated to the teachers, the selected students showed considerable gains in I.Q., with more dramatic gains among the younger than among the older children.[7] The students also showed significantly greater gains in reading, as shown by report card marks.

Rosenthal and Jacobson, though they speculated about the process, did not specifically hypothesize concerning the dynamics of the results they observed. Also they did not try the obverse experiment—telling the teachers that a certain group of children could be expected to show retardation—because that might have been damaging to the subjects. But if the implications of these studies are sustained by further research, educators and parents will want to ask what the teacher *does* to make the children she thinks are smart *be* smart.[8] It may be supposed that whatever subtle messages the teachers of the supposed bloomers sent to those children to influence their self-image and their relation to school learning, teachers of slow, middling, and fast classes also send to their classes.

But in addition to these sorts of cues and influences, tracked children daily receive very unsubtle messages regarding their abilities and the school's expectations of them. "We're 7-14, the dumb class," the student told me. Moreover, different books, easier and fewer homework assignments, less outside reading and research, and (as we saw above with Mrs. Chestnut's class) slower-paced lessons, all clearly reduce the rate of learning. A young teacher once told me about an older experienced teacher in a Harlem school under whom she had done her practice teaching. For three days one March, the experienced teacher "instructed" a slow second-grade class in the symptoms of spring. "What month is it?" "What day of the month is it?" "What season begins in this month?" "What happens to the trees when spring begins?" Etc., etc. On the first day, the children raised eager hands to answer. On the second day, they answered politely. On the third day, they had to be prodded to answer. And on the fourth, putting them on the rack wouldn't have got answers out of them. Whereupon the old teacher turned to the young one, and said, "You see what you have to contend with? They don't remember from one minute to the next."

One justification for ability grouping by concerned parents and teachers is that it is unfair to the brighter children to hold them back to the rate of learning of the slower children. Over the decades, studies made under controlled conditions concerning the effects of ability grouping on learning fail to demonstrate that fast learners learn less in the presence of slow learners, and there is some evidence that slow learners learn more in the presence of fast learners.[9]

In a school district in Westchester County, New York, composed of about 65 percent white children and 35 percent Negro children, almost all living in racially segregated neighborhoods, classes were deliberately mixed to reflect all variations in race, achievement, socio-economic background, and emotional adjustment. In one year, in one school, slow readers (children reading a year or more below grade level) improved their reading an average of from 0.7 to 1.8 and fast readers (children reading a year or more above grade level) improved an average of from 1.0 to 2.6. Further, although the Negro slow readers outnumbered the white slow readers by about 2 to 1, the number of Negro fast readers was proportionate to their number in the whole group.[10]

Thus, while the good readers do not seem to have experienced a *learning* disadvantage by attending classes with slower readers, the white fast readers would seem to have suffered a *competitive* disadvantage as compared with a situation in which there is a built-in tendency to place white students in superior groups, where they will progress rapidly, and black (poor, Puerto Rican, Mexican, etc.) students in inferior groups, where they will progress less rapidly or not at all. In this case of desegregation to overcome racially derived status differences, the "smart" white children remained as "smart" in absolute terms, but they lost some of the status advantage of their smartness because the "smart" black children kept up with them.

Our primary concern in this book is not with possible school and classroom arrangements for maximizing learning and minimizing status differences but with the ways in which the New York City school system, and many other American school systems, do actually minimize learning and maximize status differences. What is happening with ability grouping and tracking in the New York City school system, and in systems elsewhere, is that the children called smart and put in smart classes are learning more (or at least something), and the children called dumb and put in dumb classes are learning less (or close to nothing). What is expected to result results. The constituent elements in the educational universe, ordered in accordance with some people's view of that universe, spin in the orbits into which they are thrown—some as suns, some as planets, and some as satellites. And whether a given child is destined to be sun, planet, or satellite is heavily influenced, if not determined, by his skin color, his parents' income, the block he lives on, or the universe-orderers' perceptions of these. Given the relative status of rich and poor, and white and nonwhite in the larger society, we should not be shocked that this should be so—that the ones who take the most luminous place in this kind of system are the white and the well-to-do, and the ones who are cast in a shadow, the poor and the dark.

5. MISS WHITE'S SECOND GRADE

Inside the classroom the interaction between the teacher and the children continues the process that began for each child with his assignment to a top, middle, or bottom class—the process of teaching the children their relative place in the world. For all children in conventional schools, regardless of class and race, schooling is learning to submit to authority, procedures, rituals as much as it is learning skills and acquiring information. Also, schooling is learning that many of their natural social, physical, and emotional impulses are either nasty or irrelevant to the teacher's needs and so must be denied, repressed, or perverted. For non-middle-class children and nonwhite children sitting under middle-class or would-be middle-class teachers, whether white or nonwhite, such lessons are likely to be even more pronounced. The teacher's anxieties about the children's strange or despised family origins, their low-status speech habits, and their unfamiliarity with typical middle-class physical and emotional repressions—anxieties often related to vague, implicit sexual fears—may lead her to concentrate almost one hundred percent of her teaching energies on trying to socialize her pupils according to middle-class criteria rather than on simply imparting the academic skills and information that are supposed to comprise the curriculum. And as she concentrates on socializing, she is likely to convey to the children, perhaps even without so intending, the inappropriateness of their group and individual life styles. Depending on the teacher's personality, her degree of distaste for the attitudes, speech, and habits of which she is seeking to cure her pupils, and her sensitivity to the children's reactions to her, she may also convey quite explicitly her disapproval of her pupils as representatives of a low-status social group.

This kind of communication, where nonwhite children are involved, is called racism by those of the children's advocates who disapprove of it. It is, in fact, a complex cultural and social process, in which white pupils may sometimes be the objects or Negro teachers the actors. So, although the phenomenon overlaps racism, it is not identical with the kind of racism that derives from a conscious belief in the inferiority of nonwhites and an explicit wish to keep them unequal and inferior. Indeed, it often parades under a sentiment that is quite the opposite of conventional racism. Thus: "These are poor children who have none of the advantages children ought to have—not even parents who can teach them right from wrong. And I am doing everything I can to make up for some of these terrible deficiencies in their sad little lives."

Miss White's second grade is an illustration of the way in which classroom organization and teacher messages convey a sense of the children's worth and interfere with teaching the academic skills. The teacher and the events are a composite of several elementary school classes that I visited in predominantly nonwhite areas. But all the incidents and behavior patterns actually occurred. I should record that I also observed a number of classes in which there was much more teaching of skills and subject matter and much less teaching of manners and place. On the other hand, as permission to observe had always to be obtained both from the principal and the teacher herself, I did not observe at the elementary school level classes in which the teachers' naked racism, extreme hostility, or utter indifference set the tone—classes that student and parent informants frequently report. I believe, while the style may vary from teacher to teacher, the kinds of messages conveyed by Miss White, described here, represent a very common experience for nonwhite (perhaps also white) lower-class children in New York City elementary schools.

In rereading my own notes on my visits, I am most struck by the way in which the teacher (the classroom situation), in teaching the child how to be a pupil, alienates him from his fellows, from his body, from his feelings and impulses, from his immediate physical surroundings, from his opinions, from his language and thoughts, from his community and daily experiences—in other words, from all that he is as a human organism living and growing in a nourishing, sustaining environment. He is denied access to the very biologic and human wellsprings whose flow is necessary to learning and growing, and converted into a little automaton who makes gestures and repeats answers to please an adult to whose signals of pleasure and displeasure he must become almost pathologically sensitized. So he sustains her status as the central figure in the social situation and gratifies her ego's demand for attention, while she downgrades his status by remaining more or less insensitive to his satisfactions or dissatisfactions except insofar as they interfere with the classroom routine (her needs).

The whole school is assembled in the great dreary inside yard. The children in straight lines by size places, the teacher at the head of each line sh-sh-shing, frowning, prodding. One alert young teacher walks up and down her line arranging her children. She pulls a boy's hands out of his pockets, grabs a hand that is scratching a head and sets it down neatly along the side of the body, mutters a scold at a girl whose finger is near a nostril. Another, looking hardly more than a college girl, with twitching mouth and haunted eyes, can't manage her line at all; as fast as she pops two in, squeezing and hissing, three more pop out. What is going to happen among these thirty people when they are alone behind the closed classroom doors? The principal never once looks in her direction. I think she must be among the already condemned. The principal is walking about like Elizabeth reviewing the troops; where a line is crooked or whispering, she frowns at the teacher, who jabs a word or a hand at a child. Finally she dismisses the lines to their rooms in the order of the quietest and straightest. On the way up the stairs the teachers recite sharply, "Don't run, you'll fall." "Which way are you walking? Then LOOK that way." "One step at a time, Roger, one step at a time, you'll trip." "Sh-sh-sh. Sh-sh-sh. Sh-sh-sh."

I come to Miss White's room where the principal has arranged that I am to visit.

Miss White is fortyish, tall, thin, pale, stiff in her movements, very hard-working, very energetic. Indeed, she seems to me to expend at each turn an amount of energy quite out of proportion to the task being performed. At lunch she told me that she uses herself up trying to help those children but that their home backgrounds are so poor she feels she is hardly making a dent. I suspect that if she were able to relax and forget about their unfavorable home backgrounds, both she and the children would accomplish a hundred times more than they do. She seems to be fighting herself and the children every moment.

Her room, like her person, is aseptic. It is a small class, and the children's movable chairs and desks are spread about the room as far from one another as possible, as if some centrifugal force had flung them apart, each child to be suspended alone in his allotted space. On the side bulletin board, arranged with infinite precision under a frill of yellow and green construction paper, are arithmetic and spelling exercises, with the examples and the words identically positioned on each paper. On the back bulletin board, under a frill of red and blue construction paper, are the results of an art lesson, rexographed outlines of an Easter bunny bearing a basket of flowers colored in with crayons. The bunnies are all white and the baskets all blue, but there is some variation in the colors of the flowers. The children must have spent hours producing these pictures in which the colors remain so obediently within the bounding outlines. Only the irregularly printed names announce them to be products of individual, real-life children.

Miss White introduces me to the children. "This is Mrs. Wasserman, children, a very distinguished writer. Say 'Good morning, Mrs. Wasserman.'" "Good morning, Mrs. Wasserman." "Good morning, children." "This is a very s-l-o-w class, h-o-l-d-o-v-e-r-s," she spells, trying to enlist my gaze in an understanding complicity. I look away, ashamed.

The well-trained children stand neatly behind their chairs. At a signal, first the girls sit, then the boys. Miss White says, "Feet flat on the floor, heads up, sit straight, hands clasped on desk." I think that some kind of posture exercise is about to begin, but it turns out to be the required position of the morning except when the class or a child is ordered to stand, go to the board, etc. If occasionally a child slumps, scratches, bends down to retrieve an object he has cleverly managed to drop, or turns his head to look at another child, the whole lesson comes to a grinding halt as Miss White announces, "Just one minute, Alette [or whoever is reciting], Julio isn't listening." Or, really angered, "Franklin, you look at ME! You listen to ME!" During the hours of tutelage, the children must give over to her keeping their bodies as well as their souls. One ingenious boy, held immobile, has learned to ripple his abdominal muscles behind the desk. He does this on and off throughout the morning, looking down surreptitiously at his jiggling belt buckle.

Only Beryl is excepted. Small, light-brown, quiet, almost always faintly smiling, Beryl comes in late, sits when and as she wishes, picks up a book from the book table and reads if she wishes, plays with her fingers if she wishes. She is quiet and alone with herself. She is never called on in the way the other children are. When the homework assignment is to be copied, Beryl and Alonzo turn out to have left their notebooks home. Miss White gives Alonzo a sheet of paper, but ignores Beryl. She later explained to me that it would have been pointless to have had Beryl copy the assignment as she wouldn't have done the homework anyway, why waste a sheet of paper. One example of a teacher's expectations reinforcing a child's deviant ways. While the children are writing, Beryl helps herself to a book and reads. I invite her to my back corner to read to me, which she does willingly and well. Although the other children ignore her, and she them, every twenty minutes or so, with no external stimulus that I can see, Miss White turns on Beryl her own and the entire class's disapproving attention. "Beryl, don't you want to learn? Do you want to be left back? If you don't pay attention, you won't go on to third grade. Don't you want to go on to third grade with the other children?" Beryl only sustains her thin smile. But Jewell manages to catch my eye in a gaze of disapproving complicity that is a replica of Miss White's.

To the extent that they respond overtly to one another at all, the children do so entirely in accordance with the teacher's needs. So, when Miss White has three or four times downgraded one boy for giving a series of wrong answers, the children finally all laugh aloud at him. Then she transmits a signal quite opposite to the one she had been transmitting, saying, "You mustn't make fun of Collins. That's unkind."

The opening lesson is to read from the blackboard a list of twenty words. It seems to me that the children already know these words (i.e., can read them), but with scoldings about hands beneath the desk and Beryl's diversions, frequent reminders that these words "might, ju-u-ust might" turn up on next week's Metropolitan Reading Tests, and somewhat meandering discussions after each word, the lesson takes thirty-five minutes. The discussions, which Miss White later explained to me are a way of lightening the lesson by letting the children tell about "their own little experiences," are actually explicit reminders of the rules of middle-class morality and the irrelevance and unworthiness of their own impulses, opinions, and experiences, for which reminders the bodily regimentation serves as unremitting practice.

A child is called on, and reads, "Sling shot." Miss White, "That's right, 'sling shot.' Does anyone know what a sling shot is?" A chorus of responses, "When you take a rubber band. . . ." "You go like this with a paperclip." Etc. "Hands, hands." Silence. Hands are raised. A child is called on and explains. Miss White, "Do you think it's a good idea to use a sling shot?" Chorus of disapproving "No-o-o's," and one unwary, "Yes." Miss White is very angry. "Who said 'yes'?" "Not me. . ." "It was Josie." "Josie did." "Josie, you ought to know better than that. Don't you know somebody can get hurt? You could hit a person's eye and blind him." She enlists the whole class's dismay and disapproval of naughty (too honest) Josie.

A hand is raised, "My uncle he blind, and. . ."

"My uncle is blind."

"My uncle he is blind, and one day when I be walking with him . . ."

"One day when I was *walking with him."*

A few tales of the blind and the halt are told. Miss White sometimes but not always interrupts to correct the storyteller's speech. The child dutifully parrots the revised sentence, and then like a rubber band, his tongue snaps back into the speech he first heard from his mother's lips and hears (and uses) all his waking hours except from his alien teachers or TV*). He will be corrected five or ten times a day every day he is in school, for ten or twelve years, but will remain loyal all that time to his mother tongue.*

Miss White points to the next word and calls on a child. It is "plow," which the child pronounces to rhyme with "snow." A chorus of spontaneous corrections. Miss White draws herself up menacingly, scolding, "Excuse me!" *Silence.* She *corrects the mispronunciation. As in every instance when the children move or call out, they are required to suppress their natural impulse to set aright what is wrong, to respond verbally to the written symbol, to essay an answer and see if it goes ("If you don't know, don't guess.")–in other words to learn.*

If the children cannot (or do not) adopt the teacher's speech as their own, she sometimes does not even understand theirs, or the ideas they seek to convey by means of it.

"What is a plow?" she asks.

"Like a trapter," Alonzo responds confidently.

"Like a what?" *less confused than angry.*

"Like a trapter," somewhat less confidently.

"Speak up, Alonzo. What are you trying to say? Talk more carefully. Now once more. What is a plow?"

"Trapter?"

Miss White is by now very annoyed and disapproving. "Trapter? Trapter? I don't know what you're saying." She makes a kind of shrug of hopelessness. Alonzo is expressionless.

"Now, somebody else. What is a plow?"

"A snowplow?" Jewell asks hopefully.

"Well. Not exactly. Look." Miss White gets out a book, and shows a picture of a farmer in overalls and straw hat walking behind a plow being pulled by a drayhorse. "That's a plow. Now I want you to remember what a plow is. You might, you just might, meet it on the reading test." She sighs.

Now Miss White points to "flower." A child reads it. Then, "Who sees a flower in the room?" Josie, straining out of his seat and grunting as if he were on the toilet, is called on and rushes toward the Easter baskets. "JOSIE! Did I tell you to get up? Go Back To Your Seat. . . . Now, can someone tell me where there is a flower, without getting out of your seat." (Ah, Josie, Josie, you have a lot to learn.)

"Flower" is followed by a long hassle in which the children describe a "trunk" (also from the Metropolitan Reading Tests, where it is illustrated by a picture of a footlocker) as "where you put the suitcases."

"Why in the world"—trying to imagine perhaps the homes they come from—"would you want to put a suitcase in a trunk? Unless," speculating, "there isn't room in the closet."

"You know, like to go on a picnic."

Outraged, "Who would take a trunk *on a picnic?"*

All of them, teacher and children, are now utterly bewildered, caught in a kind of entanglement of confusion, and helpless to extricate themselves. I think if a visitor were not present someone would have some kind of a temper tantrum, out of the fury of impotence. I violate a cardinal rule for observers and break in to say that maybe the children are referring to the trunk of a car. I shouldn't have done it; of course Miss White is embarrassed. "Oh," explaining, "it is some years since I've had a car." Then disapprovingly, "You know they *all have cars"—one-upping after having been one-upped.*

Alonzo meanwhile has fallen out of position and is languishing. "Alonzo, sit up. What did you have for breakfast, Alonzo?"

"Crackles and peanut butter-and-jelly sandwich."

"Who gave you your breakfast, Alonzo?"

"Me myself."

"Tell your grandmother she *should give you breakfast." To me, "He's terribly n-e-g-l-e-c-t-e-d." To Alonzo, "You make sure your grandmother gives you supper tonight, Alonzo."*

"She always do."

To me, "You can see what the trouble is. . . ." Then, "Alonzo draws very well. Show Mrs. Wasserman your picture, Alonzo." I tell Alonzo it is a beautiful picture. (It is not a coloring in, but a genuine creation.) "But that's all he wants to do," she says, negating the effects of her and my praise.

Now a relief teacher comes in and Miss White sits down with me at the back of the room to perform some clerical chores and brief me on what I have observed. This one hasn't even seen *Mary Poppins* because his mother won't take him to the movies, and that one has had three "fathers" already. What can you expect when they come from homes like that? They don't even know how to talk in sentences. They have to be stimulated to think, they don't have an idea in their heads. They look around them and they don't know what they see. *But they know that a snowplow is a kind of plow, that a plow is related to a tractor, and that you put the picnic things in the trunk. And one too-brave soul knows that he likes to use a sling shot. But what they see is declared to be not there and what they think to be wicked. "Beryl just came to us from Ocean Hill-Brownsville. It's no wonder she's so bad and doesn't know anything." I said I thought she read very well. "Yes," sighing, "but that's all she wants to do."*

The relief teacher is distributing some construction paper buckets that the children had made on a previous day. They are different colors and on each is written the name of the child who made it. But they are passed out at random, and the children begin to demand to receive their own with their own names. The teacher says it doesn't matter who gets which one. (That is, it doesn't matter to her.) The children have had empty hands and empty desks since the morning began and many grasp at the little pieces of colored paper like a hungry infant at the breast. The teacher says they mustn't touch them until she tells them what to do with them, they are only paper and they can tear, if they tear then they won't have them for what they need them for, and on and on. Miss White several times nervously interrupts her conversation with me to jump up and remove one child's hands from the paper or rearrange another's limbs. Most of the children refrain from touching and content themselves with looking. It is said that slum children are not good learners because they are incapable of delayed gratification. I find my stomach in knots until finally the signal is given that the pathetic little papers may be touched. I suspect that slum children are bad learners because they are denied the gratification of being allowed to learn.

The buckets are finally employed in a mass enactment of Jack and Jill. Miss White explains that this way the children have an opportunity to "experience some freedom and new experiences" and the teacher can "get into the children's world." Next comes Humpty Dumpty, which is an occasion for some cultural background. It is elicited that Humpty Dumpty is an egg. "What happens when you drop an egg?" "It breaks." "What comes out when an egg breaks?" There is some hesitation. Finally a girl who has learned to read the teacher's mind faster than I says, "The yolk." No one asks what happens to the white, but "yolk" is written on the board. Then they go on to Little Miss Muffet. One boy, enacting the spider, so far departs from the script as to snarl at Miss Muffet with clawed hands and bared teeth. The class cracks up, in the first spontaneous interaction among themselves I have seen. Miss White drops her pen and hurries to the front of the room, saying, "No, no, you must do it on the word 'frighten,' not before. Like this. Now class, recite it again and watch how I do it."

Dutifully, they recite it again, and Miss White acts the spider, while the boy spider returns quietly to his seat.

Now they copy their homework assignment and finish just in time before the bell rings for lunch.

This is a holdover class of slow readers. Except for Beryl, who will certainly get a bad report card, during the entire morning's instruction, they have read all of twenty words, plus "yolk." And the educators are trying to understand why year by year the children of the poor show progressive reading retardation.

6. BLOWING THE CURVE AT THE BOTTOM

HOW TO TURN YOUR CHILD INTO A CLASSROOM WIZARD

215,000 Copies Sold in America Alone!

Speed-reading is a trick! Problem solving is a trick! Burning facts, figures, whole lessons into your child's mind is a trick! And, above all, taking the sting out of tests and making them half-answer themselves IS A TRICK! . . . DOUBLE YOUR CHILD'S GRADES IN SCHOOL! . . . PUT HIM ON THE ROAD TO THE COLLEGE AND FUTURE OF HIS CHOICE–TODAY!

–advertisement in Parade, *November, 1968*

HOW TO MAKE THE RIGHT MOVE IN THE PUBLIC SCHOOL GAME

"For people looking for a new place to live," says the head of a local [Washington, D.C.] real estate firm, "the most important consideration–bar none–is schools. Will our children get a good education? Will the school system help keep property values up? These are the questions my salesmen get every day."

Racial integration remains the touchiest issue in the public schools around Washington . . In the District a few schools in upper Northwest continue to have a majority of white children, but the rest of the D.C. schools are almost all black . . . Normally you send your child to a school in the district in which you live, but area school systems do allow nonresidents to enroll their children on a tuition basis in schools where there is classroom space available. . . .

The District school system is in trouble. Most middle-class parents have either fled to suburbia or enrolled their children in private schools. Over ninety percent of the children in the District schools are black. . . . Many parents are contributing time and effort to help the system but until there are really massive infusions of money for new buildings and more teaching resources, color the District school outlook bleak.

—The Washingtonian, *June, 1969*

STUDENTS AWAIT WORD FROM COLLEGES

The days of torment are upon the city's high school seniors as they await the letters that open or shut the gates of college education and its prerogatives to them.

Anxiety taints their laughter as they spill out of their schools in noisy clusters. It spoils their tidbits in candy store and lunchonette hangouts. It haunts them on dates and on after-school jobs. It lingers as they work out for sports events or rehearsal for plays.

"We're really sweating this year," Lawrence Abramson of Stuyvesant High School said. "It's almost like a panic situation."

—New York Times, *April 21, 1969*

JERRY RUBIN: PORTRAIT OF A LEADER IN THE FREAK REVOLUTION

When Jerry grew up in the Avondale section of Cincinnati, it was the goal of Jewish mothers that had sixth-graders sweating to get into Walnut Hills [admission-by-examination only, elite high school]. Now, thanks to urban renewal and other facts, the temples [Jewish synagogues] have become A.M.E. Zion and Southern

Baptist churches. The school is surrounded by black families, few of whom send sons and daughters to Walnut Hills.

"At Walnut Hills, I was so bottled up, just working for grades, competing with other kids, being nice to teachers I didn't like," [Jerry] told the present generation at his alma mater. "When it was over, I was perverted."

—Washington Post, *April 27, 1969*

LETTER TO THE EDITOR

[We are seeking] an end to the rat-race competition of the classroom, an end to the many subtle humiliations and degradations foisted upon [our children] in the name of "keeping up with the rest of the kids." . . . It saddens me to watch my daughter—no genius but bright and eager for someone to excite and respect her intellect—return from school these last months distraught in her innocence over invidious intimidations to achieve, achieve . . .

—Beverly Waite and Sandra Barnard,
Amsterdam News, *July 20, 1968*

Formal education in America, long conceived as a kind of race as well as a way of personal and social fulfillment, has in the last decade been wound up to such a pitch that for most contestants personal and social fulfillment has been almost squeezed out by the exigencies of ensuring one's place at the finish line. It is likely that the pace of the race will quicken, as lead runners are spurred on by the hot breath of new entrants and by the managers' imprecations to succeed, succeed, succeed. One prominent educator recently lamented that the nationally standardized average reading scores had remained stationary for several years in a row. Apparently, like the Gross National Product, whose annual increase is an evidence of the nation's economic health, the nation's educational well-being depends on an annual increase in the Gross National Reading Score.

But like economic inflation, which may benefit those in a position to take advantage of it but leaves whole groups of citizens languishing half-starved in the economic backwaters, educational inflation, too, may enrich the advantageously situated while depressing still further the relative educational standard of living of the disadvantaged.* In a serious inflation, no amount of cost-of-living increases is going to maintain the relative position of the pensioners, the widows, and the orphans. And in a serious race, in which the runners with the big money on their backs are mandated to come in ahead, no piling on of little handicap advantages is going to turn the losers into winners.

To reduce the metaphor to the actuality: middle-class parents manifestly would not tolerate an educational arrangement in which their children of average endowment would end up with the postmen's, bus drivers', gas station attendants', and receptionists' jobs, or their children of less than average endowment with the charwomen's, porters', supermarket clerks', and messengers' jobs, if not on the welfare rolls. (Although those scions of the middle class, like Jerry Rubin, who have decided to kiss the whole thing goodby are doing just that—by their own choice.) Nor would they tolerate an educational arrangement that produced twice or three times as many qualified candidates for medical school, computer programer jobs, and army officers as there were places, all the less so while not enough people were left to clean the hospital floors, wash the restaurant dishes, and wear the enlisted man's uniform. The notion, espoused by most advocates for black and Puerto Rican schoolchildren and by many white educators, that "quality education," meaning "superior" education or "the best" education, must be made available to *all* the nation's schoolchildren would, if effectuated, produce just such an intolerable situation. And so it is absurd, in the sense of both illogical and utopian. Of course, it is quite conceivable that reading instruction for the present population of failures might be so improved that their level, as a group, would be raised by, let us say, three years, and

* *How educational inflation, exported along with Coca-Cola and other North American goodies to underdeveloped countries within the United States sphere of influence, corrupts and undermines the societies there, and sharpens class differences, is analyzed with brilliant lucidity in "Outwitting the 'Developed' Countries" by Ivan Illich, in* The New York Review of Books, *November 6, 1969. "As the mind of society is progressively schooled," Illich writes, "step by step its individuals lose their sense that it might be possible to live without being inferior to others."*

there would be no more absolute illiterates. But statistical norms are created not only by the middle and the right side of the bell-shaped curve but also by the left side, and the consequence of such an improvement in reading would be the calculation of new norms and a demand for still greater achievement by those at the top. There would be little alteration in the relative position of those at the bottom, although perhaps some improvement in their exploitability.

The relation of the school race to the college and the career races is more apparent perhaps to those who are running along nearer the stragglers and the potential dropouts than to those running well in the lead. Families whose sons are likely to attend Exeter or Groton and Yale or Princeton often have no serious objection to evening up opportunities in public high schools and municipal universities. But at one of the colleges of the City University of New York, grumblings were heard among the white students about the general unfairness of the very small-scale special program that admitted low-achieving black and Puerto Rican high school graduates and dropouts—despite the fact that after a year of special coaching the special students were performing up to level in regular college classes. The white students seemed to feel that all their years of striving in school were made meaningless by the presence in college with them of students whom they had already bested in a previous encounter. And who is to say they were wrong?

Education in New York and elsewhere is a jockeying for status from the time the child enters kindergarten until he leaves high school (through the front or back door), but at each turn in the course and each moment in time the middle-class competitor is so involved in his immediate position and closest competitors that he cannot in fact know about or care about the fate of the losers. Nevertheless it must be observed that a necessary, although remote, consequence of the frenzy among the winners is a trampling under foot of the losers. And it is the poor blacks and Puerto Ricans who are picked to be the losers by the betters and the managers—and by the other contestants. "I knew I was supposed to succeed," said Ishmael, whose spirit was troubled by a vast distaste for the competitive success he knew he was destined for. "I knew I was supposed to succeed, because I am white."

The price of Ishmael's success was another child's failure. A competitor gets ahead only by getting ahead *of someone.*

Explaining Failures

When (some decades ago) it became unfashionable to ascribe Negro and other poor children's failure to learn school things to their lower native intelligence, other ways of disclaiming school responsibility for school failure were proposed. Three popular explanations for black (and Puerto Rican) children's failure to perform according to school standards of white middle-class performance are: (1) that these children, like many children of the poor, experience the grave learning difficulties associated with poor physical and mental health; (2) that their cultural differences, commonly called "cultural deprivation"–especially the absence of the father from the home, underexposure to printed matter, educational toys, and "cultural" trips (to zoos and so on), and the absence of language stimulation –prevent these children from learning; and, related to this second explanation, (3) that the influence of the peer group is to downgrade school achievement. I have stated these in what I consider their inverse order of importance as explanations of mass failure.

The first explanation gives rise to what we might call the guidance-oriented educator, the educator whose profound concern for the personal difficulties of the student tend to reduce the expectation and the insistence that the child learn. That the intention of the guidance-oriented educator may, as in the case of Elliott Shapiro,[1] be a legitimate concern for the child's welfare does not preclude possible damaging effects. A terrible and emotionally self-serving corruption of guidance-education has been occurring more and more often in the schools of many "enlightened" principals. (We shall examine an example of one, John Brown Junior High School, in some detail.) Now, in respect to physical ailments, bad hearing, poor eyesight, and less easily remediable ailments, the health explanation is valid, but only for those children who experience actual physical defects. Even if these mount to 30 or 40 percent of the children in a given class or given school, there is no reason why the other 60 or 70 percent should not be learning normally.

The same applies to the "mental health" explanation, of which perhaps the most central example (also part of the cultural deprivation persuasion) is the argument that the want of a father in the home (a situation with a very high rate of occurrence in black, and especially poor black families) imposes a psychological barrier to learning. Kenneth Clark, himself relatively conservative and status-oriented in respect to educational matters, once said of the social-work-psychology-oriented educators who take this and similar positions: "I'm glad that when I went to P.S. 5 in Harlem it wasn't this progressive. No teacher ever asked me whether I was from a broken home. I was. Teachers in those days were concerned with whether I did my homework, not whether my mother got tired of my father and left him in Panama."[2] For my own part, I suspect that a teacher's concern with the sex life of the mothers of their pupils is as much an evidence of their own middle-class prurience as of anything else. In any case, there is more systematic evidence to doubt the absent-father contention. "Contrary to much that has been written," says the famous Coleman Report, "the structural integrity of the home (principally the father's presence or absence) shows very little relation to achievement for Negroes."[3]

Among large populations of poor urban Negroes, the mother-centered home is the norm and apparently neither embarrassing (except financially) nor emotionally disturbing to the children. Indeed, the mother-centered home may provide some strengths to the children that middle-class people are unaware of, as it seemed to have done in the case of Miles Randolph whose story is told below. So, while there may very well be a higher incidence of home-related learning problems among the poor than among the well-to-do, it seems equally likely that there are also learning strengths among the poor that our present educational system not only does not exploit but does not even recognize.[4]

Middle-class children who fall below their parents' and society's expectations for them in respect to school performance are likely to be supported by one or several helping persons—private tutors, child psychologists, learning clinics, and so on. And this support is customarily given when difficulties begin to appear, rather than five years later when the child has been classed, and has classed himself, as a loser. Further, there is so great a discrepancy between society's expectations for the middle-class (Other) child and for the poor (dark) child that what would be regarded as a falling off of performance and need for support in the former is regarded as normal in the latter. Thus the free, too scarce, and not always concerned or capable assistance provided for disturbed or nonlearning poor children (learning and psychological clinics, school remedial reading, and so on) are provided only for those who are in a much worse state than most white children considered to need help, and usually at a much later, more hopeless stage in their development.

The second explanation for the low academic standing of black students is their "culture." The cultural differences—variations in life style, in language, and in kinds of social and personal experiences—between nonwhite and white children, and to some extent between poor and middle-class children, are now taken to signify a state of "cultural deprivation" among the former, which interpretation has been achieved by reducing the word "culture" from its anthropological to its popular sense and reducing the quality "different" to the quality "inferior."[5] The way in which cultural differences are considered by the system to represent a state of cultural inferiority and so a barrier preventing the teacher from understanding and from teaching is exemplified in the description of Miss White's second grade. There is no reason—except the system's failure to recognize their validity as experiences on which to build—why the popular songs or counting out rhymes that the children know should not serve as classroom diversions, rather than the alien and perhaps more childish nursery rhymes which they are taught and which therefore because of their strangeness lose their recreational quality. There is no reason—except that the teachers scorn them—why the children's language and experiences, rather than the teacher's, should not be the basis for learning literacy, for further development of the spoken language, and for learning about the world.*

* *Of course, I am playing innocent. There is a very good reason, indeed. More than any other attribute, their language fixes people in*

The failure of the school system to recognize the reality of the poor nonwhite child's life, language, and history appears not only in the all-white courses in American history given at the secondary level. The failure is present from the very first years of the child's school life, and it is especially apparent in the teaching of reading and in the testing of reading skills, on which, as we have seen, so much of the child's school career depends.

The first grader, poor or middle class, arrives in school already master of a considerable body of language-learning which derives from, and which he uses to cope with, his quite complex life experiences. The speaking vocabulary of this first grader, poor or middle class, "serves as the basis of [his] reading vocabulary. He cannot be expected to read words he does not know how to use. Through a series of experiences with visual symbols, the child learns that [written] words represent experience."[6]

The "essence of language," says Edward Sapir, "consists in the assigning of conventional, voluntarily articulated sounds, or of their equivalent, to the diverse elements of experience."[7] He goes on to explain that the word "house," for example, represents not a single phenomenon but a generalization or a concept "house." Thus, words, "the significant elements of speech," are "the symbols of concepts." The written language is secondary to the spoken language, "symbols of symbols," says Sapir. The configuration *h-o-u-s-e* appearing in ink on paper or chalk on blackboard has most meaning for an individual who understands the significance of the sound *howss.*

Now, it is not at all uncommon for a reader or a reading test to ask a young urban child to relate a primary symbol (picture) of a phenomenon he may never have encountered—a goat, for example—to a secondary symbol, a representative in letters, *g-o-a-t*, of a sound he may never have used in a real life situation (although he may have heard the teacher say it in a reading lesson).[8]

The reading comprehension paragraphs in the reading tests are probably more culturally biased than the vocabulary items (any normal child who is familiar with

their socio-economic place. A beautiful perception of this and some shrewd comments on speech, school, and society are exemplified by "Stokely's Speech Class," This Magazine is About Schools, *Spring, 1970.*

dogs, cats, and rats, can learn to conceptualize a goat or a cow even if he never gets to see one). But some of the difficulties with the paragraphs are subtle in ways that neither the test makers nor many teachers perceive. These were revealed to me one day by a group of children with whom I went through a test that was for a lower grade than was the test they had taken several days previously.

In one very short and easy passage which the children had no difficulty reading aloud, they flubbed a question the answer to which depended on familiarity with the diversion of throwing a stick into a body of water for a dog to retrieve. In another passage which they read with facility, only one child in a group of four knew what a "cookout" was; the others correctly inferred the meaning from the context, but the inferring took more time and introduced more doubt and insecurity than was warranted by the elementary level of the passage. In a third passage, a boy and his sister plant a garden of pansies in a box on their roof. In addition to the absurd improbability of a nice boy and girl going up to a filthy and suspect place like a roof to plant a garden (!), the children knew only one meaning for "pansy," which they delicately refused to divulge, smiling faintly with heads hung to the side.

The makers of the reading achievement tests—authors and publishers—do not invent the contents of these tests out of thin air in order to confuse the children of the slums. The vocabulary and subject matter of the tests are based upon a consensus of the leading school readers in use throughout the country.

The reading testing program, along with the readers on which they are based, are not alone at fault. They are woven into the fabric of predictions and the means of fulfilling predictions in such a way that whole groups of children are shrouded in defeat before they ever enter school. The explanation of cultural deprivation (in respect to language and social experience) becomes a rationale for ignoring (devaluing) the reality of the children's lives, from which skill and subject matter learning could proceed far better than it does from the unreal world of most schoolbooks, and a rationale for maintaining a school status system in which poor and nonwhite children are from the beginning at a disadvantage.

It may also be observed, although in terms of total effect

I consider individuals a less significant factor than the overall school orientation, that the status of the individual teacher vis-à-vis her class is also maintained by the cultural-deprivation explanation, in respect not only to language differences but also to experiential differences and communication failures. It was certainly a derogation of Miss White's status in the classroom when it appeared at the time of the "trunk" hassle that not the children but she didn't know what was going on.

That cultural *differences* (perhaps primarily child-rearing and child-relating patterns) rather than biological-race differences, economic-status differences, so called "cultural deprivation," or family pathology, are a primary cause of school-learning and also of I.Q. differentials between different groups is suggested by a very interesting study made by Morris Gross.[9] He reports on differences between two middle-class, American-born Jewish groups, one of European and the other of North African origin. Equated for almost all factors except cultural background (in the anthropological sense), the former group were all-around better school performers. Gross concludes from his study of these two groups that "cultural deprivation" is an inadequate construct, and that competitive academic drive is not necessarily an attribute of a "higher" culture.

Likely the factors that must be sought in explaining the different school performance among the children of these two groups are in the areas of life styles and group and family values. These are differences that relate to the third and I believe most valid of the explanations commonly given for the poor school performance of black and Puerto Rican children as a group—the influence of one's peers. The Coleman Report's observation that regardless of a black child's own individual background, the educational background and interests of his fellow students seem to have more effect on his performance than any other factor, including school expenditure and teacher effectiveness, tends to confirm this explanation, as does the experience of individual black or Puerto Rican children who attend predominantly white schools and/or who reside in predominantly white communities. From this evidence, integrationists, black and white, draw the inference that the solution to the problem of inferior school performance by black children is to put them to school with white children.

Without passing judgment on that inference, I think it is necessary to try to understand what happens between school and children in the many predominantly black schools that do exist and, barring the intervention of heaven, will continue to exist for some time. I suspect that the attitude toward school of the community of black children, in distinction to the attitude toward school of the community of white children, is not a function of black genes or even of "soul" but rather of the manner of socializing the black child from his earliest years and of the manner in which the black child is received in school.

White middle-class children appear in their interactions with parents, siblings, teachers, and fellow students to be oriented more strongly toward the adult in whatever kind of group than toward the other children, black and Puerto Rican and poor children to be oriented more strongly toward the other children. This conclusion, which I draw from observations of children's play groups and from the comments and attitudes of the young people whom I interviewed for this study, is reinforced to some extent by the Coleman Report's finding that white students' school performance was far less affected by the attitudes and quality of their fellow students than was Negro students' performance, and that this difference between the two groups' responses to their fellow students increased with age. School personnel typically respond to black students' peer-group orientation by treating individual black children who are achievers as deviants, "not like the other children from around here at all." (The comments of several black radical students about the common school process of picking off, distinguishing, separating successful black students from their brothers are quoted in Part III.)

A classroom social structure arranged, even as to the placement of the furniture, so as to atomize the children, downgrade the group, and orient each child solely toward the teacher draws on the strength of the adult-oriented middle-class child and destroys the strength of the peer-oriented minority child. Miss Jersild, whose school tribulations are reported below, was continually distressed by the way in which her lower-grade students (in the "bad" classes) "helped" each other in ways that teachers consider cheating; she had to watch them like a hawk, she said, to keep them apart. And one bedevilled teacher, Miss

Allbright, whom we shall meet later, had to separate two little boys in her successful remedial reading group because they talked:

I found out that when this one little boy and this other boy, who was very slow, were together, they really both opened up. The slow one was supposed to be a behavior problem in class, which I couldn't understand because when he first came to me he was just so quiet. But the other boy really opened him up, and they could just talk and talk and talk, and we would have great conversations. But they wouldn't want to read, so I finally had to split them up. And the kid just went silent again. Like he couldn't talk to an adult. The other kid was like a catalyst for him.

(Paradoxically, black children are considered at once nonverbal and a behavior problem if they talk. The stereotype "nonverbal" is undoubtedly based on their reluctance to respond to the half-foreign teacher talk in stylized unnatural sentences with alien or irrelevant content: "Today is March 21st." "March 21st is the first day of spring." "Children should not use a sling shot." Etc.) As the teacher-centered classroom and stress on individual competition devalue and undercut the children's natural lines and modes of communication and their social system, so the individual child whose ties to the native, peer social system are stronger than to the alien, adult system turns his back on the school.

The common observation of educators of black and Puerto Rican children that the school seems to be able to maintain the flow of education during the first two or three years but that thereafter there is a rushing out of the tides, suggests that it is at about age nine or ten that the peer group clearly asserts itself as the enemy of the child's enemy. The successful educational programs of the Freedom Schools of the Deep South during the years of the civil rights movement (and even of some more conventional tutoring programs there), of the Urban League street academies in New York, and of the phenomenally successful Workers Defense League-A. Philip Randolph Institute apprenticeship training programs suggest that the strengths of the black and Puerto Rican youth community can be mobilized to produce school success rather than school failure in programs where school success is relevant to the needs of the community (whether political, educational, or economic), where the teachers expect success rather than failure, and where success does not alienate the individual from his brothers and is not counted in terms of their failures.[10]

Creating Failures

A beautiful contrast between schooling that uses noncompetitive group mores and schooling that proceeds by destroying them, occurs in the native and the imposed education of American Indians. Referring to a white-run reservation school for the Sioux, anthropologist Rosalie Wax writes:

On the Pine Ridge reservation, a majority of the young men arrive at adolescence valuing élan, *bravery, generosity, passion, and luck, and admiring outstanding talent in athletics, singing and dancing. While capable of wider relations and reciprocities, they function at their social best as members of small groups of peers or relatives. Yet . . . in order to graduate from high school, they are told that they must develop exactly opposite qualities to those they possess: a respect for humdrum diligence and routine, for "discipline" (in the sense of not smoking in toilets, not cutting classes, and not getting drunk), and for government property. In addition, they are expected to compete scholastically on a highly privatized and individualistic level, while living in large dormitories, surrounded by strangers who make privacy of any type impossible.*[11]

And Wilfred Pelletier, an Odawa Indian from Ontario, writes of his education:

If you beat someone by pulling a bow and arrow and shooting the arrow further, it only meant that you shot the arrow further at that moment. That's all it lasted. It didn't mean you were better in any way whatsoever. . . . I will never forget the kinds of things we learned, because to me it all belongs to me. It isn't something that someone says is so; it's mine.[12]

Murray Wax and Rosalie Wax concluded from their studies of the Sioux that the "vacuum" ideology (the notion that other-culture children arrive at school empty of all cultural content) and the goal of individualist achievement are an attack on the self-respect and the very existence of ethnic and lower-class communities.[13] But this is the basic premise of education in America: individualist achievement at the expense of other individuals.

In the competitive conventions of our school system learning is measured by comparative grades or scores; brightness is a matter of triumphing over (someone else's) stupidness; good classes, good schools, good colleges, good careers are scarcity priced; and self-esteem if not contentment is bought by access to the restricted suburban neighborhood and the fiercely fought-over letter of admission to the prestige college. We do not conceive of schools as institutions in which everyone learns more or less what he is expected to learn, and thus in which everyone succeeds, as in an Army or a vocational training program. It is clear that this system is one which requires failures. This was demonstrated when the accreditation of San Francisco State College was called into question, in 1969, not because of the student and faculty turmoil which had disrupted normal educational processes during the entire previous academic year, but because the professors gave out too many A's and B's.[14] A poet college teacher friend of mine says, "If we didn't have some people blowing the curve at the bottom, we'd all be getting C's." In a system that requires failures, if some groups (the children of the social, or economic, or racial outcasts) are marked by their origins to be the ones who will blow the curve at the bottom, individuals in the groups not so marked experience throughout a systematic advantage. In this sense every National Merit scholar has his foot on the neck of a tenth-grade dropout.

The institutionalizing of success by failure begins, innocently perhaps, in the classroom. Anthropologist Jules Henry records a classroom example:

AT THE BLACKBOARD

Boris had trouble reducing "12/16" to the lowest terms, and could only get as far as "6/8." The teacher asked him quietly if that was as far as he could reduce it. She suggested he "think." Much heaving up and down and waving of hands by the other children, all frantic to correct him. Boris pretty unhappy, probably mentally paralyzed. The teacher, quiet, patient, ignores the others and concentrates with look and voice on Boris. She says, "Is there a bigger number than two you can divide into the two parts of the fraction?" After a minute or two, she becomes more urgent, but there is no response from Boris. She then turns to the class and says, "Well, who can tell Boris what the number is?" A forest of hands appears, and the teacher calls Peggy. Peggy says that four may be divided into the numerator and the denominator.

Thus Boris' failure has made it possible for Peggy to succeed; his depression is the price of her exhilaration; his misery the occasion for her rejoicing. This is the standard condition of the American elementary school, and is why so many of us feel a contraction of the heart even if someone we never knew succeeds merely at garnering plankton in the Thames: because so often somebody's success has been bought at the cost of our failure. To a Zuñi, Hopi, or Dakota Indian, Peggy's performance would seem cruel beyond belief, for competition, the wringing of success from somebody's failure, is a form of torture foreign to those noncompetitive redskins. Yet Peggy's action seems natural to us; and so it is. How else would you run our world?

Looked at from Boris' point of view, the nightmare at the blackboard was, perhaps, a lesson in controlling himself so that he would not fly shrieking from the room under the enormous public pressure.

From the point of view of the other children, of course, they were learning to yap at the heels of a failure. And why not?[15]

The classroom is a little mirror for the entire system. While an occasional teacher misfit may be more interested in teaching children fractions than in teaching them who is smart and who is dumb, for most teachers, teaching means ranking and being ranked not only in respect to one's inferiors and superiors in the status hierarchy but also in respect to one's peers. For some pupils to get *A's*, others must get *F's*. For some children to attend the elite Bronx High School of Science, others must attend the nearby custodial center for, mainly black, outcasts. And so for some teachers and administrators to be rewarded with the better schools and the nice children, others have to put up with the worse schools and the not nice children.

The various individuals—teachers, administrators, and students—who function relatively smoothly within this system are geared in their most profound beliefs and most spontaneous behavior to reinforce social status. Which doesn't mean at all that they are happy about the way their gears mesh. On the contrary, many—teachers and students, successes and failures—are very discontent indeed about the roles they have chosen or have been chosen to play. (Students and failures are more likely to be discontent than teachers and successes.) But what the discontented are likely to want is to change their roles in the system, not to change the system in which their role is one of the roles that has to be played.*

Thus, teachers of bad classes are likely to hate the unlovable children who have turned them into unloving adults—or the unteachable children who have turned them into teachers who do not teach. It hardly occurs to them that they have been assigned precisely the role of the unloving adult and nonteaching teacher who helps to produce the bad classes and the unteachable children that are as integral a part of the system as are the good classes and the smart children. Miss Allbright, a teacher we shall meet below, hated herself for yelling at and hitting the

* *Late in 1969, however, some public figures began to express uneasiness about the whole system, and especially the effects of the educational inflation. History offered up one of its occasional tasty tidbits of irony when Vice President Spiro Agnew appeared, in one of his "radical" speeches, as an ally of the antischooling "radical" youth. He inveighed against the emphasis on college degrees, saying it has "prolonged the period of dependency . . . discriminated against noncollege youth, and directed others, in disregard of their desires, into higher education . . ." And in California, a state legislator proposed that admission to the state university, where limited, be determined by lottery rather than by competitive class standing. It would seem a reasonable and fair way of taking the pressure off the kids and equalizing scarce educational resources, but about as unrealistic a proposal, given the rationale of our school system, as quality education for all. I suspect that, led by good instincts as they probably were, neither of these gentlemen quite realized the subversive implications of their remarks. See San Francisco* Chronicle, *December 11, 1969, and December 22, 1969, respectively, for the two statements.*

hateful children who were making *her* hateful. But in a system in which administration is more important than education, in which the adults are more important than the children, in which the experienced teachers get the "better" classes in the "better" schools and the inexperienced teachers the "worst" classes in the "worst" schools, and in which the "advantaged" children have higher status than the "disadvantaged," there will be, every year, in every "bad" school a certain number of Miss Allbrights, whom some principals will regularly fire under the illusion that it is they, such teachers, who produce the failure–rather than recognize that it is the necessity for failure that produces them.

The most common and, from the school system's point of view, the preferred alternative to the Miss Allbrights are the Miss Whites, who produce failure without so much disorder, but, locked as they are into their distrust and disapproval and communication distortions, hardly less discontent.

If the teachers of the failures are discontent, so are the failures themselves, many of whom take the school's failure on themselves with heavy accompanying guilt, as we will observe in the case of Benny Wilkinson below. Likewise the teachers of the successes, and even the successes themselves. The teachers, exemplified by Miss Jersild with her 8-1s, are distressed with their students' frantic grabbing for grades. And the students, exemplified by Temma Fields below, children who must strive mightily for twelve years in order to meet their parents', their teachers', and their own expectations of themselves–in order to be and become the successes against whom all others are measured–know that they are never going to be able to stop running and look around at the scenery.

In the next sections we will move about among some of the classrooms and people whose experiences led me to develop the schema developed here, focusing on two apparently different but closely related kinds of low-status schools and on some people in them.

7. A WELL-ORDERED SCHOOL: JOHN BROWN JUNIOR HIGH

I sometimes come away from a day-long visit to a school with the feeling of having been in an insane asylum in which the deranged are the keepers and the sane the kept. I felt this the day I spent at the John Brown Junior High School. To the lunatic unreality of the textbooks and curriculum was added a system of communication in which the teachers continually misheard the messages the students were sending, while themselves sending both contradictory and manifestly untrue messages. Because this was a well-controlled school, there was none of the chaos which we will see later in other schools, but most students were in either Kenny's "listening-and-repeating stage" or in a kind of sullen "completely out-of-it stage." In two top classes that I observed, a few students might have been in the "understanding-it stage" if the subject matter had made any demands on the normal faculty of understanding. As for the staff, its members spoke among themselves with a mixture of almost prurient fascination with their students' out-of-school lives and frank contempt and dislike for all but the few chosen to make it. Students and classes were never referred to without the track designation which signals the expected feeling-tone response to any information conveyed. A teacher would never say "my seventh-grade English class" or "my ninth-grade guidance class" but always "my 7-14s" or "my 9-1s"—that is, my dumb class or my smart class.

The ordering of children into good and bad classes is, as I have noted, one of the many messages that tell children whether they are good people or bad people, i.e., people destined to make it or to not make it. But perhaps even more critical is the overwhelming importance of such designations to the teachers, for whom "7-14" or "9-1" is a more signifying tag than "Maria" or "Belle" or "Leroy." Value systems carried over from their own childhood, plus a kind of ideological claptrap now widely peddled by honkytonk psycho-sociological defenders of the system, lock teachers into insensitive, judgmental categorizing of their students as potential successes or failures. To these judgments, the successes-to-be respond with ingratiating courtesies and the already condemned with misanthropic sullenness—so reinforcing the judgments. Closing the circle, the teachers among themselves gravely ascribe the misanthropic sullenness to the children's unhappy home lives.

In the teachers lunchroom at Brown Junior High I asked the homeroom teacher of an 8-8 (low-middle) class I had observed in English earlier in the morning (and had found at worst somewhat bored and somewhat boring) how he liked that class. He responded with the kind of sniff expressing the necessity to endure the distasteful with which I had become familiar over the years and which I have several times seen directed toward, rather than merely expressed in reference to, students. After lunch I accompanied the particular teacher I was visiting and her 8-2 class to the school library, where the hospitable librarian, upon being introduced to me, gave me a tour of the library along with the customary complaint about how much longer it took to get books now that the board of education had computerized their book ordering. Then she served up an instant analysis of the problem of the New York City schools, and in so doing manifested one aspect of the madness and arrogance of the system: "The problem of the New York City schools is to civilize children in whose lives there are absolutely no civilizing influences. They are victims of the madness of the slums. That's it in a nutshell.

Only no one understands this. The way to solve it is simple—use federal money to do two things: Drop all the fancy special programs and simply reduce class size, so the children will have more exposure to the civilizing influence of the teachers. And send people into the homes to teach the parents to send their children into school ready and willing to learn. It's as simple as that."

She saw the madness in the slums. I saw it in the school. And I saw the teachers victimized by it as much as the students.

Miss Jersild, the teacher I was visiting, was a child of lower-middle-class immigrant parents, brought up in semi-suburban Long Island. She had originally planned to be a dietician, but was unhappy in her first job in that profession. Thereupon she entered a nearby junior college as an English major, but dropped that when she got halfway through, as she "couldn't stand reading" and "hated books." She finally did very well as a home economics and education student and was licensed as a home economics teacher. Her first year of teaching (described later) in a chaotic Harlem school had been a traumatic nightmare. She escaped from that school, she felt, by the skin of her teeth, just before wholly surrendering her soul. In John Brown, she now primarily taught English. She also had one guidance class. Yet for all her prying into her guidance students' private lives, she had almost no perception of how *they* reacted to either their out-of-school or their in-school experiences but thought only of how *she* as a child would have reacted or how *she* as a teacher believed they ought to react.

Miss Jersild had four English classes, 8-2, 8-3, 8-7, and 8-8; her guidance class, whose members she met as a group once a week and at intervals for individual conferences, was 8-15. She had told me when I first met her that she had been having a good deal of trouble with her English 8-7s and 8-8s—that is, the two lowest English classes. And the guidance class, lowest of all, she felt to be a complete disaster. But she thought she was doing well with her 8-2s and 8-3s, despite not having been trained as an English teacher.

She was a concerned teacher, in the sense that she thought about her school experiences, tried to understand them, and even acted with some independence toward her supervisor. For example, believing that the sixth-grade textbooks that her supervisor had given her for the 8-7 and 8-8 English classes were too easy for them, she persuaded him to give those classes the same books as her top classes had. But the English books that Miss Jersild was using were not, as might be supposed, books to be read or even so-called readers. They were a kind of pudding composed of bits of stale grammar, usage, and teenage morality, and published under the title *English in Action*. The 8-7s and 8-8s had no difficulty whatsoever with the books and could do quite as well as the 8-2s and 8-3s. Having made this discovery, she began also to assign outside reading to the 8-7s and 8-8s, requiring them to read a book every two weeks; the 8-2s and 8-3s, on the other hand, being better readers, were assigned a book a week. She did this so that the children would get into the habit of enjoying reading, and, much to her delight, they did. (It is to this teacher's credit that although she herself did not enjoy reading, she wanted her students to.)

Talking about the two top classes and all the other classes, she said:

It's like teaching in two different schools. You have the children whom you can teach and speak with and be normal towards, and then you have children whom you have to sell yourself to in the most dramatic way. They [the children in 8-2 and 8-3] are a pleasure to teach. These children, they will respond to anything. It's just like teaching in the suburbs. [But] as soon as you go to your other classes, it is not just a matter of teaching a subject, but it is a matter of getting the children interested and that is a different problem altogether.

The difficulties which she encountered were not only in the way the different groups responded to learning but in the way they interrelated with one another.

In 8-2 when I give them a test, they will hide their papers from each other, and I don't ever have to worry about cheating. In 8-7 I have to sit there like a hawk because they will just. . . well they are very communal, they like to socialize, they like to talk and help their neighbor with anything they can give. "Here is my paper." "Here is my book." They are concerned about each other's welfare more. That is probably the largest thing in the community; it is socializing rather than academic. But with the 8-2s and 8-3s. . . the children who are competitive are much easier to teach. I can go into a class and have the children respond exactly as I want them to. They really sense how a classroom can and should be run. It really flatters me how they are responding to me this way, and it makes me feel successful as a teacher.

"The children who are competitive," these are the children, according to Miss Jersild, who "really sense how a classroom can and should be run," the children who make her "feel successful as a teacher." What Miss Jersild experienced as success was what little Marya Jersild had experienced as success fifteen years before, as she herself recognized. She said, "I can look at myself at age 12. Not only myself, my little sister now age 12. I look at her by comparison. She is very much like the 8-3s. The whole class is very much like her."

One difference for Miss Jersild between the 8-2s and the 8-3s was that the 8-2s were enormously competitive for grades, some of them already having their eyes on Bronx Science, Stuyvesant, and so on. Miss Jersild was somewhat distressed by a kind of fierceness she felt in their determination to succeed. The 8-3s, on the other hand, seemed to have more fun with learning, to be more relaxed, and she liked that. ("I love this class!" she said as we left them. "I can really relate to them.") She scolded the 8-2s for not wanting to do well in a test just for the sake of doing well rather than for the sake of the grade. But even while she was scolding them, she was dangling before them shiny little merits, "excellents" on the section sheet, rewards in the form of special privileges. These children could thus grow up to be college students and adults who would at once reach out with all their beings for the golden prizes and condemn heartily the outclassed who did not value Education.

If Miss Jersild loved 8-3 and approved of 8-2, although feeling that they overdid the success bit, there was almost nothing about 8-7 and 8-8 that pleased her, and 8-15 filled her heart with anxiety, disapproval, and self-dislike (feelings and assessments that all in all exhibit very nicely the way in which a class fulfills a teacher's status and ego needs). She saw the students in these classes as prone to violence, disorder, hostility to her and to one another. If they responded by playing the role in which she had cast them, she was immeasurably distressed and became harsh and joyless, a role in which she hated herself. Naturally she put the blame for this on the students. And naturally, one may suppose, they put it on her.

Speaking of the black students versus the Puerto Rican students, two down groups which play the one-upmanship game with each other, she said: "They don't know how to be liked. They do things that cause them to be disliked. They are really cruel to each other. They are hurting each other's feelings. They are mocking each other because they don't understand each other."

She assigned her 8-8s a lesson from *English in Action* (J. C. Tressler and Marguerite B. Shelmadine) entitled "Making Friends." The selection reads:

> *Pleasant conversation will make friends for you; rude, thoughtless remarks will drive your friends away. If you interrupt or embarrass others and if you disagree rudely, people will not enjoy talking with you. If you are courteous, listen attentively, and talk on topics of interest, you will find yourself making friends easily. . . Avoid bragging about how much faster you can run than anyone else, how much you paid for your bicycle, how much money your father makes a year.* [Certainly a highly appropriate warning for a child whose fatherless family is on welfare].

The 8-8s told her that that isn't the way you make friends at all—the way you make friends is by accepting a challenge to fight. She was surprised and upset. "I just simply don't like violence, it frightens me. People with people, the only happiness you get out of life is people with other people, with social beings. How can these people ever be happy, afraid of being hurt? Or always being hurt?"

She thought a lot about their home lives and about how unhappy they were, and that made her unhappy.

The principal of John Brown was a guidance-oriented educator, and the school, like many other "progressive" junior high schools and intermediate schools, had instituted a fairly extensive guidance program. In some cases, guidance teachers function like Army chaplains, giving the kids a chance to blow off steam, without fear of reprisal, about school things they don't like. But in John Brown, guidance was the institutionalization in the curriculum of the deprived-child theory, namely, that poor children don't learn because they have barren and/or oppressive home lives. At Brown the guidance teachers, Miss Jersild among them, concentrated on the students' home problems which were thought to be—and some of which may actually have been—interfering with school performance.

Miss Jersild thought that the Puerto Rican girls were sulky in school because their fathers were too strict with them (not because their teachers were hostile or contemptuous), that a girl who was afraid to answer questions in class was responding to a mother who beat her (not to a teacher who humiliated children when they gave wrong answers), and that the fighting in which the children sometimes engaged, derived wholly from hatred for one another (not from the game get-the-teacher or from those teenagers' mode of awarding status). She said: "It is almost like a plea for help when they talk. 'My mother hates me, and she picks on me.' 'I have no father at home and my mother has to go to work.' 'We have somebody in the house all day who hits us, and everybody is picking on me at home.' They are really depressing. Every time I go into it, I generally wind up feeling very depressed. And then there is nothing I can do."

Some students at Brown had learned to play upon the teachers' proneness to weep with them. An obese, acne-marked teenager whom I had seen hanging around the guidance office for two successive periods was described to me as a chronic guidance-office visitor and complainer about his unhappy home life. He cut out of class especially when tests were being given and carried his sadness from one guidance counselor to another. The bleeding heart game was thus played not only by staff as a way of looking away from their failure to teach but by students as a way of escaping from learning.

This game can also be played by clever upper-class students as a way of stroking the teacher's ego in exchange for being released from customary disciplinary routines. For example, one high school student who had previously attended John Brown said she cultivated the role of eccentric, unhappy genius. "They all expect you to cry on their shoulders," she said. "They tell you you're unhappy. That is what they want to hear. They want you to confide in them. You find that *they* end up crying on *your* shoulder."

That many of the students do have pressing out-of-school problems, and in some cases problems that interfere with learning, is undoubtedly so. (As, indeed, do many middle-class teenagers whose mothers have jobs, or lovers; whose fathers spend twelve or thirteen hours a day working and commuting and the remainder drinking in front of the TV; and whose mothers or fathers may not beat them but do manipulate and manage them. But middle-class teenagers are expected to succeed in their teenage life tasks despite their problems.) And a sympathetic counselor might very well prove helpful to them. But the counseling role can be filled only by an individual with a sense of and *respect for* the elements in the students' culture that the students themselves accept as given and only in an institutional setting in which the students feel welcome. (Again, as in section 6, I use "culture" to mean a group's peculiar interlocking mosaic of behavior, language, values, pleasures, and dislikes; their ways of interrelating and of using time, space, and things; and the value judgments they attach to those ways.) Guidance, as it is practiced at John Brown Junior High School, downgrades the students' culture and is simply another way in which the school reinforces status, not as the hidden message in the reading or arithmetic or history lesson but as the direct and explicit message of the guidance class or conference.

Guidance reinforces the teachers' statement as well as the students'. The depression, or pity, which Miss Jersild experienced in respect to her students' sad home experiences is an unpleasant but nevertheless sustaining emotion. Being cut off from the rationale, from the very meaning of one's associates' lives produces feelings of distress and uneasiness. Translating these feelings into pity, as in Miss Jersild's case, or into contempt in others', helps turn one from being the member of the group who is down and out of it into the one who is on top of it. What the students encountered at every turn was a reminder of the vast difference between their way of being and the school's, or the right, way of being.

In 8-2 were three boys, whom Miss Jersild described as "very bright but from poor families." She said of them, "They are a different status, not the status of their culture. They would like to stay in a little group and chatter, but by separating them, they accept it [the separation] and are used to it and do what they should." These boys must have occupied a position in the class similar to that of the three outsider children in Ishmael's I.G.C. class. They could not be allowed to be an enclave but must be atomized. Eventually, they would learn to be deviant to their peers so that they might succeed. Or they would refuse to be deviant, refuse to "accept it and do what they should," in which case, like Kenny's very bright Greek or Puerto Rican classmate, Stephan, they would one day be made to disappear from the class of successes. Or a third possibility, they would turn from misfits into rebels: acquire the school skills and turn them against the oppressing institution.

That Miss Jersild's continuous meta-message "be like I was when I was twelve—be like my little sister in the suburbs" interfered with her relations with the students and so with the inculcation of the school's manifest curriculum, was bewildering and distressing to her. She wanted to be a successful teacher. "Honestly, when I began the year, I was absolutely determined that the children [i.e., the different level classes] would be the same. I would give them equal opportunity in learning and knowledge and time and tolerance."

But the 8-7s and 8-8s took advantage of the privilege she granted of going to the bathroom whenever they wished; she felt they were making a sucker of her, and resented it. (In a situation structured to make emptying one's bladder a privilege, self-respect would seem to require taking every possible advantage of the privilege. Miss Jersild's only recourse would seem to have been to accept philosophically the role of sucker unless she could provide, in the classroom, some more exciting activity than peeing.)

In the weekly guidance class which made a nightmare of all her Tuesdays, she tried to have discussions but gave up in despair when the students all shouted out at once instead of raising their hands neatly and waiting to be called on. They "made" her "put down charges and threaten [them] with discipline" and tried to make her scream at them like all their other teachers did, but she refused to be a screaming teacher. In the end she gave up having discussions because she so feared their getting out of hand. She also gave up trying to have fun with those classes, because she found they couldn't take a joke. And she resented them for this. She told me one example of how they couldn't take a joke:

I had a little set of compositions about when they were happy. I took the time to put little personal messages on them. This again hurts me, this is another thing that angers me. I spent a long time putting on each of these papers a little personal remark because they have told me something about themselves. All their papers talked about wanting to do something . . . having a nice apartment. One boy talked about having an insurance agency. And I wrote, "You have very, very good ambitions. Think about how you can get these things . . . the importance of studying and learning . . . Study, study, study." Things like that. When I gave the papers back, instead of reading their own messages, they exchanged papers and mocked them. Just to be cute, one girl said she was very happy when a boy was kicking her foot in the movies, and I put, "Kicking your foot in the movies! Shame on you! Young girls shouldn't be doing that!" Just very humorous. One girl said she was happy when she had somebody come over and watch TV, and again I said, humorously, "Aha. Now I know why you don't study for your tests. I bet if I gave you a test on 'I Love Lucy' you would get an 'A' on it." They thought it was absolutely hysterically funny, but not in a funny sense, they scorned it. This really bothered me. I put comments on my papers in the other classes, and I don't get that response. The number of children that enjoy it is worth it for me. In 8-3, I will write things about not being in the movies—that they are too young—on their papers. They delight in that. They really delight in it. I kind of feel that someone in eighth grade is like an inbetween—they like to be treated like babies and be told they're too young. One girl, I spent five lines lecturing her about being with a boy. She is going with a boy whom she has had for a year. And she was so delightful about the whole thing. [But with the 8-8s] I, as a person, I don't want to put myself in a situation again and again before a firing line where children are going to make fun and mock. I would love to have fun with the classes and make them laugh. But if they are going to mock me, I won't do it.

Miss Jersild also lectured the boys, especially the Puerto Rican boys, about the inappropriateness of their staying out late at night, and one of the Puerto Rican girls, whose whole joy in life was her attendance at a revivalist church, on not giving up so much time to an activity that could do her no good in school. Reflecting on the fact that among the "children" whom Miss Jersild scolded for their dating behavior were undoubtedly some who were already having sexual relations, I suspect that some of their harsh laughter must have been in embarrassment at their teacher's innocence.

What was fun teasing for this conscientious and troubled teacher, or reminders of what she considered age-appropriate behavior, or attempts to teach the children how to have an orderly discussion, must have been for the students continuous reminders of their generally unacceptable life style, snubs in response to their honestly expressed joys and wishes, and repression of their undoubtedly noisy and undisciplined expressions of opinions and feelings. (What would they have thought if they could have heard some of the hollering-and-screaming "discussions" about them that their teachers were having around New York during that school year of 1968-69?) In any case, school for them had become a place where they masked their normal teenage ebullience (which might be observed in any nearby candy store after three o'clock) with the kind of dull, bored, sullen tone that made their homeroom teacher sniff with distaste and the librarian want to send missionaries into their homes to proselytize their parents.

That the 8-2s and 8-3s responded with "delight" to the little teases, rather than with scorn, can perhaps be explained by something Kenny Fields once said: "I really was in general exceptionally well-behaved, maybe servile, because I was in general wanting to please my teacher, even if she was a bad teacher. Which is kind of what she is expecting, too. She wants to be pleased in exactly, you know, this sort of way." Kenny was an extraordinarily self-critical and self-perceptive person; I should judge that a good deal of pleasing-the-teacher kind of behavior is thoughtless and habitual rather than deliberate.

A dull tone—likely betokening a kind of low-key mutual hostility between teacher and class—characterized Miss Jersild's meetings with 8-7, 8-8, and 8-15, all of which occurred in the morning. The disorder, walking around the room, insolence, shouting out, overturning furniture, and fighting which her previously expressed anxiety about those classes had led me to expect—there was none of that. Only a kind of collective sniff of mutual distaste. Miss Jersild herself was somewhat tense, but no more than anyone would have been who was a young teacher in a new school teaching a subject she didn't know—and in the presence of a visitor for the day. The English lesson was "How To Be a Good Listener," and she interrupted the proceedings frequently with reminders not to speak without raising your hand ("We have a class of talkers, not listeners."), as well as reprimands for coming to class "without your book two days this week," and scolds and little punishments for not following directions. The lesson itself was intended by Miss Jersild as a kind of elaborate joke-test in following directions, but the students didn't get the joke, which made Miss Jersild later declare to me in exasperation that they had no sense of humor. Actually there was in that room not the littlest spark of that spontaneous unguarded opening of one's self to another that is the essence of humorous exchange. But the students were "good" in the sense that they obeyed the teacher and did what they had to do with only occasional muttered grumblings. And the teacher was good in the sense that she had a well-prepared lesson, called on many different students by name, and was not either harsh or openly derisive in her dealings with any of them. If I had been her supervisor, I should have given a good report of her.

But still if I had been asked if learning was going on, I should have recalled the remark misfit Ishmael Raymond once made about a second-grade teacher whose style was very similar to Miss Jersild's and in whose class he was not, as the term has it, performing at all (actually he was putting on all kinds of performances, but he was not learning to read): "I was feeling desperate. I don't know what I mean by that . . . I was fighting for my life. I was fighting her. I think I couldn't let myself learn to read from her—that's kind of the theme that has run through my whole school career—I would have sold out if I had learned to read from her. Because I didn't like her. And I didn't respect her. And I was going to be God-damned if I'd give her the pleasure [of knowing she had taught him something]."

I did not speak with Miss Jersild's students. But knowing how little she respected them as they were and for what they were, I can see little possibility that they might have respected her—although, because this was a well-ordered school, they in fact "gave her the respect," as Loretta Tubman, one of the students whose story is to follow, would say.*

That Miss Jersild was a teacher whom students could like and respect she demonstrated in the afternoon with her 8-2s and 8-3s, whom she liked and respected as approximations of the all-American suburban prototype. With these children she was a different person. Her eyes shone and her cheeks were pink. She sat on the desk swinging her legs instead of stalking nervously back and forth. She made spontaneous jokes, sometimes to the whole class, sometimes to an individual student here or there. She ignored, because she literally did not see, the children who had to double up with books because some had forgotton to bring theirs. She was undisturbed by and even shared in the students' somewhat disorderly talking out without raising their hands, their talking to neighbors, the laughter, and the general noisiness which made of that classroom a gathering of living teenagers not sullen zombies. At intervals the students would come back together again as a group with either some students hollering out "shut up" or hissing "sshh" or the teacher herself recalling them.

* *Most of the Negro children who broke through into white schools in the South and encountered there the open hostility of teachers and students generally responded differently. They worked very hard and they did learn. See Robert Coles,* Children of Crisis *(Little, Brown, 1967). I suspect that the difference is the difference between masked and open hostility. If the teacher sends the message, "I am doing my best—despite obstacles—to try to make you learn," the student refuses to collaborate with a teacher whom he senses to be his enemy. If the teacher sends the message, "You don't belong here. I don't want to teach you. And I'm sure you can't learn," the student learns, in order to prove himself and to spite the teacher. The former regards learning as an abdication of self-respect, the latter as an affirmation of it.*

When later that day I called to Miss Jersild's attention the difference in her responses to the two groups, she said she couldn't let go like that with the 8-7s and 8-8s, and especially not with the 8-15s, as they would take advantage of her, they would be so noisy she would never be able to get them together again, they would throw paper around, they would kick somebody's chair. "The class cannot handle it, they take it as a sign of weakness," she said.

Likely she was right. They would take it as a sign of weakness, they would take advantage of her, as they did when she let them go to the toilet at will–against the school rules. And instead of her being the one to put them down with gentle little jokes, teacherish moralisms, and scolds about books and talking, they would be continually humiliating and discomfiting her. She would be seen as a weak teacher, not only by her students but also by her supervisors.

If school is going to be structured as a social system of control and one-upmanship, then the party that is usually one-down (here the bottom-class students) is always going to be looking for opportunities to get one-up. The 8-2s and 8-3s of the school world are those who have learned to play the school game: in exchange for not seriously challenging their one-down position in respect to teacher, they are allowed to proceed through the years of elementary school, high school, college, and beyond in a one-up position over many or most of their age-mates. The economy of their egos, reinforced by respect paid to their dignity and humanity in regard to their state of being outside of their role as students, can afford the payments they have to make to the teacher's one-up position. The 8-7s and 8-8s are those who between the ages of six and eighteen progressively withdraw from the school's one-upmanship game as they struggle to defend their inner selves against the world's attacks. If they are black or Puerto Rican, they are likely to sense that their vulnerability and defeats derive not only from their youth (for so many adults a condition that evokes tolerant condescension) but also from their particular color, language, and social class (for so many Americans, characteristics that evoke contempt, anxiety, or distaste). The 8-15s are those who tend to fight the game at every turn and in every way they know how. Ishmael "fought for his life" by refusing to learn. The 8-15s are all Ishmaels in one way or another. And they fight by refusing to learn, to the point where any teacher who would expect them to learn would be considered out of her mind, both by them and by her colleagues. They also fight by breaking not only the school rules, including those made for their own protection, but even ordinary, generally observed social conventions. As long as they are fighting, they know that they are still alive. And when they are fighting, they are always fighting *back*.

Almost every New York City school with any substantial numbers of black and/or Puerto Rican students has at least a couple of classes of fighting Ishmaels—usually one or two to a grade. Perhaps it is not too much to say that throughout the slum areas, whole schools—children and adults—are engaged every single day in a battle for survival.

But even many of those low-status children who do not fight—the low-status children in nonwhite high-status classes, the 8-2s and 8-3s—nevertheless do not succeed by white middle-class standards. Drawing on a reserve of confidence that enables them to compromise, without abdicating, their dignity, in order to learn school things and to please the people who must be pleased if a black student is to "make it," they grow up to be the "credit to their race," the "successful Negroes" whose presence among us fills us with pride and hope, but whose professional status would be counted very mediocre indeed by white middle-class standards. The reasons for the limits to their success are suggested by the stories of two such students told below. The first of them succeeded precisely to the extent that the system intended her to succeed. The second, riding the crest of the education-for-deserving-Negroes wave, managed in effect to outwit the system and when I saw him last was on his way to a far better than mediocre status.

8. LORETTA TUBMAN: "BEING A SECRETARY JUST ISN'T ME."

The most popular contemporary explanation for the schools' failure with poor and nonwhite children is that they are "culturally deprived." The cliché "culturally deprived" in its various uses includes all or some of these: low income, slum housing, fatherless family, (southern) rural origin, nonconcern for school success, want of parental discipline, unfamiliarity with the written word, and lack of exposure to zoos, museums, etc. For example, shortly after the strike of 1968, the New York City controller, Mario Procaccino (a subsequent candidate for the mayoralty), was quoted in the UFT organ, *The United Teacher*, as having said that "many underprivileged children were coming to school from homes where they had never seen a newspaper, a book, or even a pen or pencil, where there was little or no drive to learn. In many cases, children were sent to school to keep warm, to get a hot lunch, the only meal of the day for them, or to be in a safe place while the mother worked."[1]

It was precisely the view of schools as a custodial institution, here ascribed with a touch of scorn by Procaccino to the poor parents, that many poor parents ascribed, with rage, to the schools' personnel and defenders.

A half-dozen years ago, Kenneth Clark reported that more than half of the white New York City teachers interviewed in a large-scale survey, expressing essentially racist opinions about Negro children, believed that they were inferior in intelligence and that the "humanitarian thing to do for these children is to provide school essentially as custodial institutions."[2] While the cliché "culturally deprived" may accurately characterize an indeterminate minority of "underprivileged children," most slum children, however poor and black, have certainly seen, and even own a few, books, pens, and pencils, and many have a very strong drive to learn. (Indeed the controller's hyperbole is so gross that, despite the sociological, "liberal" cant, it has the ring of "nigger.")

Loretta Tubman was one of many Harlem schoolchildren who, although she did not as an individual fit the cliché "culturally deprived," was—as one of the *class* considered "culturally deprived"—denied educational opportunities commensurate with her and her family's motivations and goals. She had absorbed from her family all the middle-class virtues that should have made her a school success—morality, cleanliness, honesty, brightness, school ambition, respect for her elders. If she had been white, she would have been programed, like other whites with those qualities, for a medium- to high-status college, and perhaps would have become a teacher or social worker. Even black as she was, if she hadn't made primarily one misstep such as would have earned a white child a mere sharp reprimand, she might well have found her way into one of New York City's community colleges. But as she was black, and as she did make this misstep, she graduated from high school with a General diploma and moved on to a respectable, but humdrum, job as "the lovely black secretary in our office."

Loretta's family lived in a railroad apartment in a decaying building on a sad yet resilient street in west Harlem where the addicts who hung out on the stoops knew her and sometimes walked her to the busstop to protect her against molestation by other addicts who didn't know her. She loved her family, and they loved her. Among her older siblings were a stenographer, a welfare case worker, a registered nurse, and a brother who worked for General Motors. Her younger brother, who had all Loretta's charm and a mite more luck, was studying to become an opera singer, working at an unskilled full-time job and also taking evening courses at the City University in case he didn't make it as a singer. Loretta loved and admired all her brothers and sisters and her mother, but she especially loved and admired her father, and even her resentment at his having left the family when she was twelve didn't diminish her love for him. She told me:

My father should have been a doctor. Because people really had faith and trust in him. He was quick to catch on, he was responsible, he was very smart in school. My mother said they used to call him teacher. He was *very*, *very* smart. My mother was very smart in school [too]. He had the opportunity to become a doctor if he had pursued it. But his mother didn't have the money. He started working on the railroad, the Penn Central. He would have been a very good doctor. He had a lot of kids, he just didn't—not that he didn't love them—he just couldn't afford them. And that's very depressing and that's probably one of the reasons why he left . . . I missed him. We didn't have any money and stuff like that, but my mother always found a way through. She did good as a mother and father. We sort of took a lot. But we still walk out there with our heads up.

Almost every time she talked about her father, she would tell about the ways they loved each other. I suspect she may have been his favorite child. She once said:

He spoiled me. He used to love me to death. I used to cry, and say something was in my eye, and he'd say, "Will a quarter take it out?" And whatever was in my eye was gone. When he used to come home from work at four o'clock in the morning, you know, cold and everything, I used to jump out of bed, you know, and then I'd ask, "Do you have any socks to be washed?" and stuff like that, and jump on his lap and eat half of his food. And, oh, he spoiled me when I was a kid. But as a matter of fact, he's very, very proud of all his children. Every time I walk up and get a diploma or something, he's running around with his baby daughter's diploma.

Loretta's father may have "spoiled" her, as she claimed,

but, along with his love, he and her mother provided a disciplined, purposeful home atmosphere which Loretta carried with her into her school life. Once, when she was telling me about how many kids on her block had "messed up, made one mistake and then instead of profiting by it had gone on to make another," I asked her how she explained that no one in her family had messed up. She said:

Well, I'd say it was the way we were brought up. My mother's special interest, my father's special interest, too. Each of us had to be in the house at a certain time, you know, used to have to be home from school, do our homework. We had a sort of like schedule. My father was fussy about everything. We had to keep a clean house. We had to be in bed at ten o'clock. The house had to be cleaned up. Our homework had to be done. Everything had to be put away. And, ah, my mother was the same way, but she was a little more lenient than he was. He was really interested in us trying to make it. And so was my mother. My father had this budgeting system, he used to give us an allowance, and we had to budget our money, stuff like that. One thing he told us not to do was to steal, or to tell a lie. He used to get very upset if he heard that one of us was lying about something, or stole something from somebody. We used to be a family that—we went to church together. My mother, she didn't go, but she got the rest of us all dressed up Sunday mornings. She used to have the white shoes all lined up along the window sill, and send off all of us to church on Sunday. And the dresses ironed nicely. And she used to put those "balooky" curls on us, you know, with the hot comb. And we used to be the prettiest things out! And we used to enjoy all this, too. I don't think there's anyone in my family who objected to going to church. I think that the parents play a very important role. They can't *make* you go to college, you know, and they can't *make* you finish school, but they can influence you to the point that you would want to do it yourself.

By her account, Loretta received from her parents as much love, as much discipline, as much guidance, as much of a sense of purpose as any middle-class child—and probably more than many. All of these gifts were incorporated into her personality and her relationship to school. Chunky, dark-brown, dimpled, pretty, she had an engaging giggle and could produce pools of merriment in a classroom. Fundamentally she was a good girl, as that term is understood in school circles. In the same way as she wanted to please her beloved but strict father and her good, not-so-strict mother, she wanted to please her teachers. And she was certainly not stupid. How was it then that Loretta failed to achieve the academic skills and status that would have merited her an Academic diploma and admission to college? Mainly because her teachers, with one exception whom she will never forget, demanded very little of her in the way of school learning.

According to Loretta, some of her teachers were openly contemptuous of almost all their pupils. I opened the first interview with Loretta by asking her to tell me about the first teacher that came to her mind. She answered unhesitatingly:

> I remember. . . Miss Stein. . . She was a very, very disgusting teacher because she didn't seem to care about the students that were in the classroom. She just seemed to remind us of the fact that she has hers and we have to get ours. She didn't, you know, try to make us do anything. If we couldn't read up to a certain level, she'd just put us in this group and just forget about us, and work with the girls that, you know, that did read well. She cared about those who were already ahead, not those who were trying to get in and [who] she was supposed to teach. I didn't like her. And. . . but. . . she did do something good for me. She made me a monitor. And then we had this dance, and the class messed up; they got out of step, and I was the only one who brought them back into step. She was pretty happy about that. That's what made her put me on patrol, as a matter of fact. I didn't like her that much though, because she didn't seem like she was "involved" like she should have been. . . . I always disliked her, but I gave her the respect, you know, she deserved. After all, she did have hers. . . .

Almost all of Loretta's teachers from elementary school on through high school did what Miss Stein did: In exchange for the kind of charm that many schoolchildren early learn to use to advantage, Loretta's teachers rewarded her with merits, stars, monitorships—those tinny school trinkets given out as compensation for the want of solid nutrients in the educational cereal box.

The next teacher she remembered without prompting was Mr. Gold, her fifth-grade teacher who played favorites. Loretta, who may very well have been a classroom favorite at various times in her school career, was not Mr. Gold's favorite, possibly because she was dark-skinned. His favorites, as Loretta described them, were two very light girls with "curly hair, not kinky, curly." They sat in the front of the room one on either side of his desk and were chosen to do all the little special chores and errands, and also to play the lead roles in class plays. Loretta must have been very jealous: "In as far as intelligence is concerned," she said, "neither one of them was as smart as I was. I believe that. Neither one of them was. He had some reason for liking them."

One day during recess Loretta got into a fight with Priscilla, the prettier of the two light-skinned girls. Perhaps Loretta provoked the fight. She told Priscilla she'd leave her two blocks behind running. And Priscilla answered, "You can't do nothing, black stuff." Loretta didn't like that but she managed to contain the insult until the other girls started agitating. They said, "Loretta, I wouldn't take that if I was you." So Loretta, who from having been carrier of the records knew more than she should have known about the other pupils' personal histories, snapped back cruelly, "I may be black, Priscilla, but I was not *adopted*." Priscilla went crying to Mr. Gold, who comforted her and kept Loretta after school. Being scolded by Mr. Gold, she made the mistake of losing her control a second time that day:

I said, "You're just pickin' on me, because she's about your complexion." Something else I said, "She's almost as white as you are." And, oh, Mrs. Wasserman, he turned so red, looked like he was gonna grab me. He [Loretta imitated a shocked gasp] . . . he did just like that. He was sort of strange-looking anyway. Then another teacher came in, and he was saying something I think in another language. That's when he said, "Well, you, ah, you go along home." And everybody was downstairs waitin' for me.

When I came home from school, I told my mother about it and she said it wasn't right—for me to tell—you know, after we found out that the child was adopted, she didn't know about it, she [my mother] said it wasn't right for me to tell her. But she said it wasn't my fault, if she said what she said to me. Two wrongs don't make a right, and she always was sort of philosophical about everything. My father was annoyed. "Who was she, who was she? She had no business saying that to you, you're just as good as she is."

And she went home and her mother found out and they didn't invite me to her birthday party. All the boys and girls were invited. And I got left out. But there was about twelve who didn't go, they said that they thought she was wrong, you know . . . And the hungry ones went.

And Mr. Gold gave me a "D" in conduct. Circled in red. And he gave her an "A."

Loretta's interpretation of the reason for Mr. Gold's preferring Priscilla and her friend seems plausible. Miss Jersild once reported, unsolicited, that she preferred light-skinned to dark-skinned Negro children, and those with Caucasian to those with Negroid features. That many Negro people themselves, even in the present upsurge of black pride, also have such preferences, especially in respect to hair quality, is no mitigation of the racist judgments that whites express in this aesthetic. On the contrary, Negroes' preferences for light skin and "good" hair, insofar as these preferences are the result of prevailing white standards, are clearly a corruption of self. That Mr. Gold allowed these feelings (perhaps unacknowledged and therefore irrepressible) to drag him into a mean and petty schoolgirls' spat as a participant is, of course, especially reprehensible, but it must be recalled how often nasty little feelings of just this kind are elicited by the petty atmosphere of the school's adult status system. A teacher's role in a children's spat ought to be to try to contain the hostilities in time and effect. Mr. Gold's involvement did just the opposite.

In sixth grade Loretta hit the jackpot: A real teacher! Miss Brodley, who expected her students to learn, gave a gold star every time a child finished reading a library book, and because Loretta liked gold stars, she read a book every week, sometimes two.

This was a very good teacher, Miss Brodley. You could tell that not only did she love her work, but she loved to see somebody else learn it. . . you know, [learn] what she knew. She would do anything just to make you learn. She used to say, if you don't understand this. . . you know, she'd go over it, three times maybe. Then she'd say, "Well stay after class, and I can help you." She'd take some of her own time, you know, to help individuals. The sixth grade is where I learned practically everything. I learned about fractions, about math, you know, a little bit about history, and reading, new words, and you know, a whole lot of things. She was the best teacher in the elementary school, I think. She's one I'd fully recommend to teach in our community.

Loretta described her, recalling with delight both how attractive and how tough Miss Brodley was.

[She was] real short, she had very keen features, very long nose, and she used to wear her hair in a pony-tail. As a matter of fact, I found her quite. . . quite attractive. She wasn't that attractive, it was her way. She had a way that was, that made her look beautiful. To me. And if she got angry, you knew it. WHOOEE! "If you don't stop that talking I'll move you out of that seat!" And I'll always remember, she wrote something very, very sweet in my autograph book, too. She said that, "I know you will be successful in whatever you do." . . . [She paused and lovingly savored the name.] "Miss Brodley. . . . M. Brodley."

After a year of getting gold stars for reading books rather than for being on patrol or correcting the other children's mistakes in the dance performance, Loretta's reading score soared, and she came into junior high school in one of the top seventh-grade classes. If she had managed to stay there, she might have found her way into the Academic track in high school and with a little luck into college. But once again, as in the incident with Priscilla, Loretta's refusal to sacrifice her self-respect or the respect of her peers led to her downfall, this time with serious, long-lasting consequences. She got into a fight with a tough girl, named Red, who must have been testing her courage and her position of leadership among the boys and girls:

We were in front of the library. She called me. . . said she wanted to fight me. So I said, "For what?" She said she didn't have to have a reason, she just wanted to fight me. So I said "OK." So she said, "Well, I'll see you at three o'clock." . . . You know, outside of school. So three o'clock came, and I met her outside. I kept on my gym suit. So then I squared off, you know, and scared as I was, I wasn't going to let her know it. So she walked up to me and I stood there, you know, ready. And she said to me, she said, "I like you," she said. "Even though you were scared, I know you were scared, you was going to fight me anyway. I admire you for that. Therefore, you're one of my friends." And inside I said, "Phwew!" Because I was scared!

So we left, and she went her way and I went mine.

Then two days later something must have changed her opinion, because she got mad at me in class, and she started pinching me, and I told her to stop. And then you know, I'm mostly smiling all the time, and the expression on my face changed and she said, "Watcha gonna do, watcha gonna do?" So I showed her. The teacher, Miss Levitt, was out of the room, first of all. And we were fighting when she came back in. I had to get out of [Red's] way. So I was pushing the chairs around, you know, and stuff like that [because] once she got me cornered, that's when you could find out how strong she was. The class was hollering. Everybody was hollering: "Get 'er, Red" and "Get 'er, Loretta." We're fighting. And then Miss Levitt walks in. She was the type who became emotionally upset, she gets nervous when something like that happens in their classroom. As a matter of fact she [later] left the school. There was another fight in her classroom, and she left the school. She ran out crying and she never came back.

[When Miss Levitt found Loretta and Red fighting, she sent both down to the dean of girls. The dean questioned Loretta.] "Did you hit her back? Who hit first?" I told her that Red hit first, that I hit her back. The dean said that she *should* request that our mothers come in. And I started crying, because I knew that, you know, if she sent for my mother, that I was going to get it when I went home. And I started crying and crying, and I begged, and I said that I would never fight again, and stuff like that, you know. I said, "Oh, give me one more chance, please, I won't fight any more." And she said, "Apologize to her." And I apologized. And Red wouldn't apologize back to me, so I guess that's why I got a luckier break than she did. They moved both of us. But she was put in a dumber class, she was put in an all-girls class, which was the dumbest class in that particular grade. But I was put in like the middle, 7-6.

Loretta must have counted herself lucky to have got off without her mother being called in. But what actually happened was far more consequential. As a result of her misbehavior, she was put into a lower-track class at a critical point in her academic career. Still, programed for a secretarial course, she was better off than Red, who, because she refused to apologize was put into the dumbest class in the school, in other words, programed to drop out. All, so far as we can tell, for a breach of *discipline*, for behavior that had nothing to do with the intellectual capabilities, or even the academic standing, of the two girls. What fighting is in the peer-group ethics of many black children of this age, talking or perhaps passing notes in class is in the white peer-group ethics. For such a "white" offense, such a retribution as Loretta received would clearly be outrageous.

The 7-6 to which Loretta was sent was not assigned outside reading, did not get programed for the math and foreign language that would be required for an Academic course in high school, and behaved very badly.

That class was so bad! As a matter of fact [the teacher's] main purpose in that class I think was trying to keep the class quiet. That was a bad class. We had a party . . . popcorn . . . we didn't have a party like everybody else . . . we had popcorn all over the floor! We were the only class that messed up like that. See, like, this class was uncontrollable. They used to make noise [even] during the silent change. They did so many things. Actually, I didn't think I belonged there, but since I was in there, I was enjoying myself. I guess I was just too young and wild [to know any better].

I still used to do all of my homework. I just didn't do any extra reading. And my teacher was very fond of me. As a matter of fact she put me back on patrol. I had a half a page full of "charges" [demerits]. But I had my way about it. Like, after she'd finish writing the work over the board and everything, then I'd say, "Miss Barnes, would you like me to erase the board?" She'd say yes, and then she used to give me a "special." [A "special" negates a "charge".] So I got on patrol with her recommendation.

Loretta said "of course" she stopped doing the outside reading she'd been doing for Miss Brodley, and I asked "Why 'of course'?" She said:

> Ah, I guess it was the change in the type of people, really that I was with. But I still got good marks in English and stuff. It's just that I was with a type of people . . . we used to joke around in English class. When I'd see somebody in the classroom that was doing better than I was, then I tried that much harder. And in that [top] class, it seemed that everybody was trying, and that made me try hard. But I didn't get a chance to really, you know, stay with them, because I was out of the class before I knew it. And then when I got in that other [bad] class, it changed my attitude.

She continued on into a middling eighth-grade class, and as she never read books, her reading score fell further and further below grade level. Eventually she was programed for a remedial reading class. The class used the "SRA reading lab," a pseudo-scientific apparatus of graded short reading passages printed on cards with accompanying questions. Students are taught to keep individual score cards on their reading progress. The lab, designed as a remedial tool to allow students in slow classes to progress at their own rate and "motivate" them (presumably more than a book would), is produced by Science Research Associates, an affiliate of IBM.*

* *The elaborate madness of the whole maneuver with Loretta—in effect removing her from an association with books and with other students who liked to read books and then subjecting her to a phony "scientific" reading program—was recalled to me when I read in April, 1969, that in the midst of the bad publicity the country's managers were getting because millions of Americans were on starvation diets, President Nixon "put off indefinitely plans for a comprehensive attack on hunger in America," but proposed to enlist citizen volunteers in an "attack on social and economic ills." (*New York Times, *May 1, 1969). President Nixon could be an educator, Loretta's teacher could be President: the kind of mind that will cure illiteracy without books will also cure starvation without bread. It only remains for SRA, or IBM, to provide the scientific apparatus for the foodless program against starvation.*

Loretta went on to high school as a Commercial student and continued to charm her teachers, especially the men. She didn't learn enough to pass the history Regents (state examination required for an Academic diploma), but, as in elementary school, her classroom manner got her through:

For history I had Mr. Goodman. He was the sweetest teacher. But he should only teach Honor class students, because you have to know what he is talking about in order to keep up. And a lot of times I didn't know what he was talking about because I hadn't any past [background]. I got a 65. He was too nice to fail you. If he saw you was trying and everything . . .

Then she added: "I think that if he would have failed me once, that would have did me some good."

A guidance counselor signed her up for a "college discovery" program intended to prepare "deprived" students for special entry into the City University. This meant that Loretta spent her lunch hours in a special "college prep" class, where the students studied how to take the College Board Scholastic Aptitude Tests and "learned different words, discussed different things, different issues." College prep was synthetic vitamins for a patient who would have flourished on meat and bread and spinach. Not only did Loretta not learn enough to pass the history Regents, but she was never programed for the math and language that she would have needed for an Academic program.

It wasn't until the latter part of the eleventh grade that I was told that I didn't have any math. That's when I started changing, when I was almost ready to graduate that year. That's when I really thought that I should go [to college]. And then certain people told me that I had the qualities to be a teacher. And then again, I felt . . . I loved kids. And I felt I had the potential to be a teacher. Anyway for primary students. I feel I could teach them something. If I became a teacher and I came back into this community, I feel a lot can be done because sometimes, you know, from my experience, I don't think the teachers *care* very much about the students, because they feel that they have theirs and everything. But I feel that I would not only be involved with the students individually because I like, you know, I like children. And I'd also participate in the community.

I applied for an Academic program to two community colleges. If I'd applied for Commercial I think I would have made it. But I applied for Academic, so I could be a teacher. And the only reason I thought that I didn't make it was the fact that I didn't have enough academic background. [The guidance counselor] explained it to me, I . . . I kind of understood . . . that I didn't have enough math and language, and I didn't have any Regents.

As a matter of fact, I think that I'm more suitable for teaching than I am for secretarial work. I've been on my job for two years now, and . . . well, I just don't think secretarial work is me. I do my work and all that. I do my very best. But I don't think it's me, truthfully.

9. MILES RANDOLPH: "I COULD PLAY BASKETBALL. I COULD STUDY. I WAS A JIVE CAT."

Directly over his desk in his comfortable dormitory room, conspicuously tiny among the blownup photographs and posters—of Malcolm X pointing, of pinup girls, of Reuben's "Head of a Negro"—Miles Randolph had stuck up a photograph of a mountain climber and the quotation from Saint Exupéry, "L'homme se découvre quand il se mesure avec l'obstacle." The wall decorations nicely defined the room's occupant. The new motel-like dormitory was in a small, liberal arts, Ivy League college in New England which I shall call Winchester College. Having come all the way up in central Harlem without ever having been arrested, Miles was arrested once in his junior year at Winchester for his part in a black students' sit-in in the administration building. He was majoring in Afro-American culture and history, and by his sophomore year had probably read more Negro-American literature and history than, ten years before, had anybody in America but a handful of scholars. He was both reflective and opinionated and would discuss with serious devotion Langston Hughes, soul music, the causes of poverty, his conception of his role as a dorm counselor for the lower classmen, Huey Newton as a black leader, the New York City public schools, the removal of poor peoples' homes for urban renewal projects, and Marcus Garvey's Universal Negro Improvement Association. The summer after his sophomore year at Winchester, he had gone to Jamaica for a couple of weeks on a research grant and had had a series of talks with Amy Jacques Garvey, Marcus Garvey's widow. The trip had been both a study trip and vacation after a two-month job as administrative director of a teacher-training program. Though low-key in voice and manner, Miles always had a couple of things going simultaneously.

He was apparently relaxed and comfortable with the younger Ivy League-type boys who wandered in and out of his room with the excuse that they needed to use his private phone. He liked making jokes about his white friends, saying of a fellow student, "He's a good white man. A credit to his race."

Miles was short, stocky, dark-brown, and he spoke quietly and with a trace of a lisp. At a time in high school when he had had hopes of becoming a teacher I had thought that the lisp would probably disqualify him in the speech test which is part of the merit system—if indeed he could ever overcome all the other barriers a dirt-poor black boy from central Harlem was likely to face. In college he was still dirt poor. Even with a full tuition and room-and-board scholarship, he juggled two jobs during the school year and three in the summer, so he could help his widowed mother, a domestic, support herself and his seven younger brothers and sisters. But his fortunes looked bright. With black scholars at a premium, he was about to become the success that nothing in the system had meant him to be, thanks largely to two misfit teachers, and a brother, now dead, who had taught him as a child to love poetry. And some rare quality in himself which made him a misfit in the street and a misfit in school—but "jive."

If Loretta, in her background, represented a negation of the deprived-child thesis in all its absurd patness, Miles represented its opposite. From his infancy on, he had experienced almost every one of the environmental conditions that the psychosociological educators tell us make a shambles of a child's life, and he had emerged with a sound inner strength that carried him through a healthy boyhood to a healthy manhood. He drew his strengths from what to the middle-class observer were adversities, and he looked back on the adversities with a kind of serene unconcern. Only when he told about the occasions on which a teacher or the "system" had refused to recognize him for what he was did he look as if the words tasted sour. If Loretta should have succeeded because she knew so well how to please the people a child has to please to succeed, Miles did succeed because he knew what he wanted and how to go after it. He knew how to please himself.

Miles's mother came north when Miles was three and Major, his brother, was five. His father was not with them, and Miles hardly ever spoke of his natural father at all. His mother found an apartment in a slum neighborhood; they moved once during Miles' boyhood, to another slum neighborhood:

The buildings are rundown. They have always been rundown, for let us say the last twenty years. There are no effective building codes. We had to ignore that. It was there. It was there wherever we moved. There was no getting away from it. We couldn't move away from it to a better building. It was always there—at all times—no matter where we moved—anywhere in the ghetto.

Mrs. Randolph went to work as a five-day-a-week domestic. The little boys were on their own, but were not completely unsupervised, while their mother was at work:

There was a neighbor who used to take care of us. When we were living across from 177th Street, my grandmother kept us till Mother got home. There was always somebody to look in on us. They kept an eye on us, and if we wanted to go downstairs, we had to ask their permission and all that kind of stuff. Like they would be right across the hall. Mother didn't get home until five o'clock. She always brought stuff home. She worked for a Jewish lady who made Jewish pastry. She'd always have something for us.

Without a father, mother away all day, Miles and his brother had none of the equipment and experiences considered necessary by middle-class America to prepare the young child for school entry.

Did your mother read to you in the years before you could read yourself?

No.

Did you have picture books as a preschool child?

No, but I had a lot of picture games.

What kinds of toys did you have as a preschool child?

Basically a bicycle, cowboy things, baseball glove.

Did you have educational toys?

You mean blocks and all that?

Yes.

No. [Much laughter at the ridiculousness of the question.]

Did you get taken to zoos or museums? So-called cultural excursions?

Those were school trips.

By the time he started school, there was a stepfather in the house, whom he didn't like, whom he never came to like. Psychologists say that a boy needs to have a strong father figure to love and admire, and that the mother-centered family characteristic of a good portion of America's black population is a pathological family whose offspring are emotionally crippled and socially defective. I wondered how Miles had become so apparently healthy a young man in spite of this "pathology," and I asked him in what way first not having a father and then having a stepfather whom he intensely disliked was a deprivation for him.

The deprivation was an asset because that may have been one of the reasons why I felt so strongly about being independent. I didn't want to accept anything from anyone. I just wanted to do everything myself. It just developed that way. I kept doing things myself. Rather than having anyone do anything for me, I'd do it myself. My mother liked [his independence]. If she hadn't liked it, it probably would never have developed. My mother always sort of regretted that she couldn't give me very much—in the way of things. Sometimes I'd go out and work and I'd bring money home and I'd give it to her. She was . . . I was the baby and she was the central thing. I was always very close to my mother. In a way I miss her now, for we are on a different level. But the distance is the distance of me leaving her and becoming my own man, and then returning to her. But she and I were very close. We were very much alike. She was both a mother and a friend. I really can't tell . . . I know she and my brother were . . . . Anything beyond them just wasn't family. They were just the central focus of my growing up. And I guess a great many things revolved around my pleasing her. I knew she would be pleased if I did well in school.

At our first interview, after Miles had told for the first of several times about a deep grievance he bore the school system from his high school days, I asked him two questions on matters I was curious about. I wanted to know, in consideration of his almost prototypal underprivileged background, how he explained his success as a student. And then, knowing he had long been hooked on books, I wanted to know if he remembered learning to read and learning to love to read.

Well, in a very real sense, I'm a conceited person. If the teacher gave me something, you know, I would try very hard to get it out. I enjoyed reading [as a child]. I didn't like many people so I wasn't . . . I was playful, but I wasn't . . . I didn't fool around too much. I was always sort of staunch and a little more disciplined, I think. You know, I would read or I would sit there. If I had a problem and the teacher says, "Well, this is this," and I wouldn't understand, and then he would say, "This is this and so," if I could, I would figure out a way to do it so that it would come out right.

I really learned to read from comic books. I'd go through the Dick and Jane job in school—but comic books . . . like I would go out one night and buy five comic books and read them all night. And then trade them and read six more. I just read it through and once in a while I would smile and throw it down and read the next one and that's how I learned to read. I got acquainted with new words, and I guess maybe the drawings sort of associated me with the meaning of the words. I figured them out. I did that all the way through the sixth grade and then I sort of lost interest in comic books and once in awhile I would pick up a comic book, but my interest had turned to science. [The comic books] had these lurid science facts in the back. So I would get a book on magnetism or something and read that.

I usually went to the library a lot, you know Countee

Cullen [a branch of the New York Public Library located in central Harlem].

The "staunch" independence that drove Miles to conduct his own reading instruction program also provided him with the pocket money he needed. From his early elementary school years he had Saturday jobs—"I always had some hustle going," he said, "first on a fruit wagon, then on a watermelon wagon, then for a grocery store." His earnings went into comics, clothing, some for Mother, and a Sunday movie to which he and Major took two little girls. (He would have been amused at Miss Jersild's scolding fourteen year olds for dating.)

Until, as Loretta found Miss Brodley, Miles found two devoted teachers in junior high school, school was to be endured. Also like Loretta, he remembered first the teacher he hated most, Mrs. Harris in sixth grade. One behavioral habit which he reported about her seems incredible to me, but as he insisted on several occasions even ten years later that his recollection was accurate, I include it in his account.

She was a weird broad really. She used to change her underwear in class. She would have the boys turn their heads. I don't know why, but she did it. Also she always favored girls over boys. I mean, you could be sitting together, a boy and a girl in the front, talking and she always punished the guy. Everybody in the class knew this. She would always punish the guy. And all the boys sort of banded together, because we concluded she hated boys. She was a stern disciplinarian and she insisted upon silence—all that kind of thing. Everything was "Peace, children." "Hello, Mrs. Harris." "Peace, children," she would say. And she liked to berate. If you didn't get the right answer, she would berate you. I know I disliked her intensely. I remember making mistakes in her class, and I disliked her for that.

When teachers scold or make fun of a child who can't answer, or for something else, what is the reaction of the other children?

Laughter. A majority of teachers use that technique at one time or another. You do something wrong and the teacher makes some crack, and everybody laughs.

What did the laughter mean?

Sometimes it meant that the guy was stupid because he didn't know the answer.

When the teachers made fun of you personally because you didn't know the answer, how did you react?

She is trying to make me look like I was stupid. You feel mad. You sort of feel you are pierced. You have been humiliated. I felt angry with the teacher because she was trying to make me look stupid. *I* didn't think I was stupid. When you shoot your hand up and you don't have the right answer, you are disappointed even if she doesn't berate you. But when a teacher berates you, what is on her damned mind? Who is she to know if you are stupid or not stupid?

Humiliation as a pedagogical technique is officially frowned upon by educational authorities; yet almost all schoolchildren report humiliation as an everyday expected cruelty, sometimes by reporting the exception: "She was a really nice teacher. She would never make fun of you in front of the class." One must conclude that there is something in the relations of teachers to children, something in the system, that nurtures the need to humiliate. My guess is that it is the teacher's constant feeling of being humiliated. In the case of nonwhite children in a bad school, the teachers' low status in respect to better placed colleagues would further encourage both the feeling of humiliation and its projection onto the children. I should think, further, that open and deliberate shaming is a natural extension of the customary school process of accounting the achievements of the successful in terms of the failures of the unsuccessful, as we saw in Jules Henry's account of Boris at the blackboard. Part of the school curriculum is "character training," one element of which is to learn to swallow humiliation without grumbling. (White children, and even academically successful white children, also report being shamed in class, and while it is difficult to say how one gets the resources to repair the damage of such shame, it seems clear that the lives of white children offer many more possibilities for at least papering over the damage than do most poor black children's lives.) Miles was probably exceptional in that, although he writhed under the shaming process, he knew it was not justified.

In seventh grade, the spring that had been trickling quietly through Miles' personal life was brought bubbling to the surface by a teacher who expected even poor black children in central Harlem to read books.

Whatever I learned in school I learned from Mrs. Penman in seventh grade. That's when I learned to read—really learned to read. I read more in seventh grade than I did at any other time. We had to do weekly reports for her class. What I would do is I would read a science book in Penman's class and do a report on a science book and at the same time be learning more science. She impressed us with the importance of reading. She was my English teacher and my home room teacher and she just kept up the pressure on us. But when I got through that experience, my reading experience was considerably strengthened because I had transferred from comic books to actual books. And so I got used to different types of stories. And my brother who was in the ninth grade at that time had about a 10.8 reading average and I had a 10.9 and I used to tease him.

When you didn't bring the report in on time, do something else out of the rules, you hit yourself. You punished yourself. If you didn't hit yourself hard enough, she hit you. Once she broke the ruler over a guy's leg. It was like this stern power, but it was very flexible, and you worked in that sphere. I learned to work in that sphere and I had to hit myself maybe twice because you know—I read the books. Mrs. Penman. I loved that woman. I went back there once and she wasn't there, but I hear she is there now. I plan to go see her. I have never forgotten her and she. . . well, she just kept us reading.

I should like to comment on two contradictory ideologies about corporal punishment in the light of Miles's response to Mrs. Penman's "stern power" and Loretta's response to Miss Brodley's strictness. One is a dictum commonly uttered by both black and white educators of slum children: "You have to hit them, that's all they understand." The other, more common among "progressive" whites, is that corporal punishment destroys the child's trust in the teacher and brutalizes him in such a way as to prevent sound emotional development. Miss Brodley apparently did not hit, but used anger as an instrument of control. Mrs. Penman, apparently keeping her cool, either hit or made the child hit himself. In both cases, the punishment was in the service of a higher goal which the children clearly recognized and remembered as valid and desirable, while recalling the teacher's strength with something like awe. By comparison, the shaming device is recalled with fury and not seen as contributing to learning. I should think that it is not the form of the punishment (hitting or not hitting) that is significant to the teacher-pupil relationship and the child's development but the consequence of the punishment in terms of learning and its source, that is, whether it proceeds from teacher weakness or from teacher strength.

Perhaps the most significant pedagogical quality that both Mrs. Penman and Miss Brodley had was their determination that the children should learn. They must have been the kind of businesslike, hard-working, demanding teachers whose classes I sometimes observed with delight, because the classes had moved from an imposed and empty order to an internalized order filled with purpose and with learning. Mrs. Penman and Miss Brodley knew that children learn to read by reading, not by moralizing about words, and that the best source of the printed word is books. What made these teachers loveable and beautiful to their pupils was their educational purposefulness. While such teachers are tragically rare in a system in which educational purposefulness is buried beneath administrative concern and pseudo-psychology, it is a common enough human quality and most teachers would be quite capable of being educationally purposeful in a system in which they would be expected to be so.

Miles's next teacher, Mr. Kenny, also had that quality:

After I got out of Penman's class I went to Kenny's class; he was the science teacher. He was [also] my home room teacher. I was also on monitor duty out in the halls. So I got a chance to talk to him during lunch periods. And all we talked was science. Then, like, I learned so much from that guy those lunch periods that when I went to Paine [High School] the first year. . . . Biology, I never studied it. I only studied fifteen minutes for the biology Regents. [His mark was] 85, 89—something like that. We talked about cells and cell structure, about the atom. Like he would mention something in class and during the lunch hour I would pick his brains clean.

[Once, Miles got into a fight in class.] He was going to hit me on the hand with two rulers tied together. So I said, "No, you're not, because [the other guy] hit me first." So he said, "OK, bring your mother to school." Well, I brought my mother to school, and I sort of collared the [other] guy in the corridors and he told the truth. So my mother made Kenny apologize to me, rather than me to him. Mother had a rule, like, she, you know, she let a teacher chastise the child if it don't get out of hand. [Kenny] was like a friend. He was my main man.

At that point, age thirteen, Miles hung between two worlds. In school, he was a success, learning and loving to learn, and even achieving a certain notoriety among his fellow students. Besides science, he read and wrote poetry. He was led into poetry by Major, his older brother. ("He read poetry; I read poetry. He wrote poetry; I wrote poetry.") He was known as "sort of a minor expert on Poe," and was nicknamed Anabelle Lee because he had recited the whole poem from memory in an oratory contest. But along with the respect his achievements earned him from his peers, there seemed to accrue something of the scorn that lower-class schoolboys express, only half out of envy, for their academically successful schoolmates. Miles must have felt himself to be a candidate for the weak, out-of-it, deviant role of "Peter Prep," a role that would have alienated him from the guys in the street, perhaps temporarily, perhaps for life. Once during a long talk at Winchester, he reflected in a general way on his feelings during those adolescent years:

The one thing about aspiring to college, you have to be a deviant. You have to make a choice between being one of the guys and being a Peter Prep . . . . The value system at home—in the context of your contemporaries—is a different system [than the one at school]. [It] makes of the pimp and the hustler cultural heroes. In the teenage years the guy you look up to is the guy with the $75 shoes and the $30 shirt. The pimp and hustler was a high class guy. The games you play as far as interpersonal relations were concerned are the games of either physical or mental superiority. You know, you're more together than this guy. So you use him and take advantage of him. You have your relations with a girl, you use the girl, she's a bitch. The thing is to see who's slicker. Is she slicker than you? Is she going to be going with you and two other guys? Or are you going to be going with her and three other girls?

Certain things the guys do. They smoke cigarettes, drink wine, and smoke pot. They *could* buy liquor—but they prefer wine. It's their thing. The hours are irregular. You might cut out of school and go steal some stuff—or go up to the coop on the roof, fly pigeons. You might come out on the block at night, start playing games, play ring o' livio, sit around and talk about the good old times.[1]

Miles pretty much stayed away from the gang, without however rejecting their values, in this way slipping through the narrow place between two worlds, helping himself to what he wanted in the world of the good guys while not condemning—and pretty much not being condemned by—the world of the bad guys.

Being black is a conglomeration of things, it's not a monolithic culture. There is a whole mixture of values. I was never really permanently in one group. I sort of interacted between the two [the good guys and the bad guys]. They called me "Peter Prep"—in the negative sense. But in a way they looked up to me. They say, "That guy's going to make it."

I was a loner, and I had a small circle of friends . . . a lot of friends in school. In a way I enjoyed going to school. There was nothing much else to do. I guess it gave me a chance to excel. There was nothing much to excel at at home, though I knew how to cook, I could iron and all that. So I was enjoying going to school, which means I never played hooky. I'd always be in class getting what little there was to get. There weren't that many [teachers] that I learned a lot from. And when I was interested, I paid attention, and when I wasn't, I talked. I never really studied. If I'm particularly interested in something, I read the material concerning that something in a very keen manner. Those facts stick in my mind. After that, I can do a lot with it. As I increase knowledge around that one particular theme, I can make variations around that one particular theme, because that central theme is there and it ain't going no place. In reality the whole school system is that, constantly going over the same thing and then making a little extension, going over that, then going on to the next grade, going over that, then making another extension. Like American history. Just keep going over it. You just keep going on the colonial period, colonial period, colonial period, Jacksonian period, Age of Reform. You were given objective tests and there wasn't very much more to learn. There was always a way of being slick. American history tests I could do in ten minutes, then I would help all the other kids to make sure they passed the test.

When I wasn't interested in class, I started talking and playing—you'd be classified in terms of discipline—that was the "bad guys." When you're doing what the teacher wants you to, you're the "good guy."

But I didn't really do anything *very* bad, you know. I never went with a bunch of guys that stole something. I did a little dirty here and there and then there was some things I didn't do. Stole alone—never stole with the group. The thing is I didn't have much time. I'd go home, do whatever homework I had to do—whatever homework I was *going* to do. And I'd go play basketball or I'd go on to the grocery store and hustle.

I just don't like crowds. I don't like crowds at all. If I'm walking . . . there was a time I just wouldn't walk down the crowded side of a street unless I absolutely had to. I wasn't a sissy, I had never lost a fight. Not many people would fight me. I could play basketball. And I could study. I was a jive cat. I was respected because I could hang out if I wanted to and I could fight if I wanted to. I was jive. I did what I wanted to.

The next year, in the ninth grade, the little narrow space between the two worlds through which Miles had been slithering narrowed further. When Miles's self-respect had required that he challenge Mr. Kenny on the issue of the unjust punishment, the challenge had been accepted and fairly disposed by a strong teacher. But when his self-respect and loyalty to the values of his peers required that he challenge his next teacher, by putting his school career on the line, he was dealt a stinging putdown, and only his own strengths pulled his academic career out of the fire three years later.

Rivaling Mrs. Penman and Mr. Kenny as the top-status teachers of Miles's school was a third teacher, Miss Barry, for whom worth was measured not by what her students learned but by what they achieved.

I was in 8-1 [with Mr. Kenny as a home room teacher], and Miss Barry was the home room teacher of 8-2. She pushed her class into competition with us—strong competition. There was a general assumption made around school that she was a bitch. She was just, you know, a nasty person. Well, anyway, one Christmas [her class] gave her a Christmas tree to put presents under, and she ran in to tell Mr. Kenny. She ran in all excited, "Mr. Kenny! Mr. Kenny! Come, come quick!" [mimicking in an affected falsetto]. And in unison the entire 8-1 class says, "Oh, Mr. Kenny! Mr. Kenny! Come, come quick!" [same tone]. She laughed a little while, too, but in a sort of mocking voice. Then she said, "Let's stop this petty feud between us." Because actually, you see, the feud was between 8-1 and Barry, not between 8-1 and 8-2. Barry [not her class] was the object of any abuse toward 8-2 from 8-1.

Then one time we went to Stratford to see a Shakespeare play. I guess there were too many people in one bus, so she had to sit in the bus with our class, and our class insulted her at such a sturdy rate so when she got off the bus she was in tears. You know, the feud between the opposing class and the teacher was rather biting. Well, anyway, she said, "Let's forget this feud." And then she made the remark, "Some of you will be in my English class next year." And [two fellows] and myself *were* in her English class [the next year]. And the first thing in the English class, after assigning us to seats, she called us up and said, "You gentlemen were in Mr. Kenny's class last year." And we said, "Yes, Miss Barry." And we knew what was coming. She said, "Well, you're going to fail." And that was it.

When she said you were going to fail, did she just say it, just like that? Or did she say something like "If you don't watch out?"

She just said it: "You're going to fail." That's what she said. Those were her words: "You're going to fail." We just a little bit laughed. We didn't give a damn. We just walked away and we forgot about it. In a way forgot about it. I thought about it, I know.

[The other two did not fail.] And they should have. I did. I did all the reading . . . I did all the work . . . and

I kept a passing average in the class—somewhere in the 80's—something like that. I knew, because I'd kept all the tests.

Probably all three "thought about it." Indeed, Miles thought about it so much that he virtually pushed Miss Barry to fulfill the threat.

I was on the G.O. Council [a student government status position]. The members of the G.O. Council got to go to all the G.O. dances with our sister school. I think we had a dance every two weeks or something. Each time a different class went, but the representatives could go to every one of them. This was considered civic work, and the teacher whose class he would be missing had no say, and couldn't do anything about it. And so every time a dance came up, I went . . . and missed her class. And so finally she called me in one day when I was getting ready to go to the dance, and she said, "Well, Mr. Randolph, which is more important to you, my class or the dance?" And I said, "The dance." I believed she was going to fail me, and I said [to myself], "Well, if she's going to fail me, she's going to fail me."

The self-fulfilling prophecy came about. There was a big "F" on my card, so I took home all my tests and my mother brought them to the assistant principal's office, and he said there wasn't anything he could do about it. And I went to summer school. Got a 90 on the English in summer school. I didn't have to study for that. I'd done it.

Miles probably knew, when he flung "the dance" in Miss Barry's face, that that was a showdown moment between them. Perhaps he had been taunted by "the guys" with being a "Peter Prep" one more time than he could tolerate and what he had to do was save his self-respect—and status with his peers—at the expense of his school career. Miss Barry too probably knew that it was a showdown moment and perhaps even wished that, by humbling himself, he would save her from committing a nasty vengeance against a child who had joined in humbling her. But if he was going to refuse to play the school game as it is supposed to be played, he must take the consequences.

The conflict with Miss Barry seems to have had one more consequence than the necessity of spending a summer taking English. Miles, after failing the tests for the two competitive high schools to which he applied, went to his third choice, Thomas Paine High School, where his brother was a student in the Honors course. Now, students entering a non-elite high school which has a special Honors track or department are recommended by their junior high schools for that track on the basis of school grades plus reading and math achievement scores. Perhaps because the one flunk pulled down his average, perhaps by oversight, perhaps by intention, Miles's junior high school did not recommend him for the Honors track, although his academic record was likely high enough to qualify him for it. Certainly, as Miles says below, he thought it was. Still, he came in as a regular Academic student. Once, in high school, a teacher suggested that he be transferred to the Honors track, but he refused:

I couldn't be bothered. Because I knew I deserved it, but if they were going to wait till now . . . I mean they knew what my average was. They knew I should have been in the Honors class before. And if they were going to wait till now, and finally review my records, so they could put me in the Honors class, I didn't want to go in the Honors class. What big deal is it anyway?

Actually, it was a pretty big deal, although at the time he refused the change in track, Miles probably didn't know it.

When I had first asked Miles if he would tell me about his school career for this book, he had said, "Sure, as long as your book is going to be against the system as it stands." At our first interview I asked him what he most objected to in "the system as it stands," and he explained his remark:

Well, any system has a natural sense of stratification. But the most visible thing that I noticed—well, an experience that points it out best is: My brother, the older brother that died, was in the Honors section, but when I came into the school I was in a regular section.

I . . . the people in my section were never told about the PSATs [Preliminary Scholastic Aptitude Test, taken in the junior year by college-bound students as practice for the Scholastic Aptitude Test, which is taken in the senior year, sometimes several times, and on which many colleges place heavy emphasis in decisions about admission and placement of candidates]. The kids in the Honor sections took those PSATs as a matter of course. In fact, the teachers strongly urged that they take those PSATs in order to get some practice for the next year's SATs. And I didn't take a PSAT until I got into my senior year, and then I found out I had to take an SAT.

That sticks in my craw. We were all students and we supposedly were all aspiring to college. Why weren't we all told about these things? Just as simple as that.

The majority of the kids in the Honors class were given the chance to go to private schools [colleges]. [The college guidance counselor] didn't just write them off to city schools, which were over-crowded and not that good anyway. If you were on the track team [like I was] you were stamped as stupid. So you go to Bronx Community [a two-year junior college] or wherever like that you can get them in. She [the counselor] didn't know anything about me. All she knew was what she saw on her little record of everything I did from elementary school on up. She didn't know me, she couldn't know me, I never interacted with her. Except when I wanted to go to college. My high school average wasn't high enough to get in [to the free City University]. During that four-year period the [required average] was raised to 85. I said that I wanted to go to college and I didn't want to go to night school. [Students with lower than the minimum high school average required for entrance as matriculated day students may be admitted as special students into the night school of the City University.] But that is what they push—the city colleges and the community colleges. We didn't have any information on the different colleges South and North.

(Another black student said of this same school four years later: "The school does everything in its power to encourage Honor students to go to college, but the regular Academic and the General, they do as much as possible to steer them away from college. We have a black-skin, white-mask teacher for a guidance counselor and college advisor, Miss Davis. She is one of the greatest Uncle Toms you'll ever find. She'll treat a white kid better than she will her own. When a black kid goes up to her, she has this attitude she's superior to us because she's made it and we're lazy and we're no good. My friend Ford, he was *very* smart, but he started to rebel. He wanted to go to college, and she said, 'You! There isn't a college in the country that'll take you.' So he said, 'Up yours.' ")

Miles went on:

Well, I got lucky. I was working with [a tutoring organization in Harlem], and I met this guy whose father used to teach at Winchester, and he said, "Why don't you apply there?" I didn't have a cent, but I just didn't want to go to night school. I wanted to go to a daytime college and if I had to go 300 miles away to do it, I was going to do it.

To appreciate the emotional and financial cost to Miles and to his mother of his going away to college, even with all expenses paid, one must know that while he was in high school his stepfather died in a mysterious accident on the roof of the tenement where the family lived, and that two years later, his brother Major, always sickly and probably a tardily diagnosed cardiac case, also died. So Miles was the only man left to help his mother support his seven half brothers and sisters, a responsibility he took very seriously. For his mother to have accepted his leaving New York after the two deaths must have taken considerable courage, as well as faith in him and in the importance of education.

I filled out my own application. And I went to get letters of recommendation from teachers—whatever they wanted to say about me. I had to go to Miss Davis for my transcript. She gave me some static then, said, "You know what kind of school Winchester is? You can't get in there." I had a 'tude [negative attitude] when I walked in there because I didn't like the woman. I said, "Look lady. Don't worry about it, just send my transcript. If I have to pay $2.00, ok, but just send my records."

I finally obtained a four-year scholarship to Winchester College.

I meant to go back and tease her about it after I got accepted, but I never did.

A year after he had told me about these events, and four years after the events themselves, he did go back to Paine High, and to Miss Davis. Not, however, to tease her, but in a role that would have been even more gratifying to him, if it had worked. He went back as part of a Winchester recruiting team composed of black undergraduates to find among the next generation of black students at Paine just such hidden misfits as he himself had been and to persuade them to come to Winchester. But even after years of agitation on behalf of blackness and black students in New York, Miss Davis was no more "together" than she had ever been. She questioned Miles skeptically about how he, an "average" student, was getting along at Winchester, but she did not send for any potential candidates for the recruiters to meet.

So the recruiters went out of the building and did their recruiting in the street, which is where the black boys are at anyway.

10. CHAOS SCHOOLS AND THREE VETERANS

"Chaos" was the word most often used by the school system's defenders to describe both the community-control advocates' struggle to achieve power and status in the schools and the students' struggle, which began shortly thereafter, to destroy power and status in the schools. Close behind in frequency of usage were: "maelstrom," "incite," "vigilantism," "melee," "rampage," "menace," "apartheid," "stalk," and "violence." And, surprisingly, "racism"—in reference only to black demands and black anger (as if when the God of the people of Israel called down ten plagues on the land of the Pharaohs, that were to be called "racism").

"CHAOS" reads the headline of one paragraph in a UFT advertisement opposing pending decentralization legislation: "Our schools will be transformed from centers of learning into maelstroms of ideological and emotional conflict." "NEW YORK SCHOOLS IN CHAOS AS RACISM SPREADS," read a headline in the radical-right *The Jewish Press*. "Disorders and fears of new and frightening dimensions stalk the corridors of many of our schools," declared the High School Principals Association. And, more quietly, John Doar, then president of the board of education, said: "The Board of Education is determined to see that the New York Public Schools are places where children can learn and teachers can teach *without disruption, disorder, or violence.* We intend to reaffirm . . . the school's disciplinary policies . . . to be certain that the range of penalties is relevant to . . . the necessity of *maintaining an atmosphere in the schools conducive to learning and to insure the safety and welfare of students and teachers* [italics supplied]."[1]

But "chaos," "maelstrom," "fears," "violence"—and "racism"—were precisely what many children and teachers of New York's "bad" schools had been living with for decades.

John Brown Junior High School was a good lower-class school. There was courtesy, if little goodwill; quiet, if little communication; and control, if little learning. Attendance was taken, cutters reported, flags saluted, records kept, and textbooks given out and returned. The hallways were kept clean, and the students went to the bathroom only when the teachers gave them permission. With all the school ceremonies properly performed, the principal and the president of the parents association could congratulate each other that they had a well-run school.

When a school functions as John Brown was functioning, most parents are satisfied. That is, most poor parents. Middle-class parents are likely to have higher expectations, that is, to expect learning as well as observation of the ceremonies. In studies of parents' attitudes toward schools, poor parents typically report less dissatisfaction with school and with teachers than do middle-class parents. In one study, 29 percent of those earning $10,000 or more rated their neighborhood schools as poor, contrasted with only 16 percent of those earning under $3,000.[2]

But even the least sophisticated and most undemanding poor parents recognize chaos as complete school bankruptcy. And chaos has traditionally been the condition of many schools throughout the city's black and Puerto Rican neighborhoods and of many bottom classes in even the well-run schools in these neighborhoods. "An atmosphere conducive to learning" and schools that might be "centers of learning" were precisely what the rebels accused of making chaos were seeking the power to create. The board of education could hardly "maintain" what for tens of thousands of schoolchildren had never existed. For the schools the children were attending were not "centers of learning" but systems of chaos, chaos sustained by career-minded administrators maintaining custodial institutions and looking for a way to move on to white schools, meanwhile blaming this teacher or that child for the systemic violence; by frightened or indifferent or hostile teachers, here today and gone tomorrow, or even here this morning and gone this afternoon; by parents who didn't know what went on in school on all the days that weren't visiting day, or thought it must be the children's fault if they did know; and by children who responded to indifference with indifference, to violence with insolence or cynicism, and to weakness with license.

Many teachers and administrators, like the librarian at John Brown, assumed that the children brought the "chaos of the ghetto" into the school. But the "ghetto" has its own order and the school its own chaos, as one might observe who walked from the lunatic atmosphere of some chaos classrooms and corridors to the school play yard, where hundreds of children, unsupervised, divide up space and make and administer their own rules in intricate and mutually accepted social systems. There are, of course, occasional disputes, but nothing by comparison with what goes on as soon as the bell rings and the children are subjected to the supervision of their mentors inside the schoolhouse. And the fact that in adjacent and sociologically like areas, there may be two schools, one chaotic and one orderly, bespeaks the contribution of each school's adult society to the attitudes and behavior patterns that the children manifest in the school. In most cases, it is assumed to be the principal whose style and strength or weakness determine how orderly or chaotic a school will be. This assumption is the reason that the community-control movement from the beginning emphasized the need for community control over appointment of principals, and that, as the movement accelerated, principals throughout the city were especial objects of community and parent attack. Actually, in some schools, like P.S. 39, discussed below, a happy combination of staff produces a well-functioning social system regardless of who the principal happens to be, while in others the intergroup hostilities deriving from the larger school struggle become so harsh that Solomon himself could not reconcile the battling parties.

There have been descriptions galore of the "chaos" schools, with the children who light fires, turn off all the lights, break furniture, pull the fire alarm, throw things out of windows, sass the teacher, and most terrible of all molest one another; the teachers who hit, pinch, name-call, and scream; the substitutes who come for a day or an hour and rush crying from the classroom, never to return; the classes that go through a whole year with never the same teacher for more than a week or two; the principals who barricade themselves in their offices never to be seen, or those who storm about chastising or suspending this child and tongue-lashing or firing that teacher, as if the child and the teacher were the doers of evil rather than its victims. It is in these chaos schools that both racism and violence are most prevalent. If the word "nigger" is not used by the adults, then "jungle," "animals," "ape," or simply "they" and "them" are. And everyone in the schools is quite aware of the words' significance.*

The New York City school system does not allow corporal punishment, but it is widely practiced, usually in elementary schools, in many cases with parents' approval. In almost every largely or wholly black and Puerto Rican elementary school that I have heard of, hitting on the knuckles is a common practice; this is less likely to be so in junior and senior high schools. In orderly schools like John Brown, or orderly classes like the ones Miles was in or others I personally have observed, the hit on the knuckles is likely to be a regularized punishment for a specified offense. It may be one in a graded series of punishments: verbal reprimand, charge (demerit), one or more raps, going to the principal's office, sending for mother, suspension, transfer to another school. Each child more or less knows what the next item in the series is and is less and less likely to risk it.

* *To be fair, it should be pointed out that not only white teachers use these terms. To be sensitive, it should also be pointed out that minority group members generally tolerate ethnic or racial epithets from their own far better than from others. "Yid," "mick," "nigger," as used by people who are "yids," "micks," and "niggers," can be imbued with a mixture of affection, humor, and self-deprecation that takes some of the sting out of the insult.*

But in the chaos schools, hitting and violence are widespread, accompanied by the philosophy "I'd like to see anyone control these kids without hitting." Hitting is not only common but also random. Any order whatsoever, like "Come on, let's get going there," is likely to be accompanied by a rap on the buttocks or back of the legs. Many teachers go out in the corridors only with a yardstick or blackboard pointer in their hands. Raps on the skull with a ruler or pencil, pinching, and grinding into the instep with a spike heel (as a way of informing a child, for example, that he is out of place in what is supposed to be a straight line) are also common. These tactics I know from personal observation and teachers' reports. Children also report beatings in a dean's or administrator's office. Reports of interviews by the staff of a Harlem tutoring organization in 1963-64 with young children in one Harlem elementary school is strewn with complaints of physical punishment, including smacks for giving wrong answers: "The teacher should not take the children in the bathroom to spank them." "My teacher be hollering at them; hit them across the head with a ruler." "When they don't know a thing, she get at them." "Mr. G. [a supervisor] was pushing and pulling him and the teacher said that's good for him and the mother came and was fussing with the teachers." (These children also complained that the teachers "shouldn't all the time be talking about their families" in class.)[3]

The frequency or infrequency of deliberate, premeditated beatings by supervisors or teachers is a matter of dispute. They do occur, arising out of the unremitting abrasive interchange between children and adults and the adults' feeling reaction of impotence and rage. Miss Allbright, who, as will be seen, had reason to feel both impotent and enraged, explained her feelings when she began to follow her supervisor's suggestion that she "hit them a little bit": "I think what happens with the hitting is that you just get so frustrated when the kids aren't doing what you are saying, that you just do anything that comes into your head. Of course it doesn't do any good . . . Well, sometimes it does, like to get the kid to sit down or something. But you just don't know what to do. You're just hitting the kid—it's like banging the wall. I think it's just the frustration coming out, that's all it is."

In such a social system, there is no longer a question of teaching and learning. The central dialogue is about survival. The teachers hit, pinch, scream, push, grab. The children squirm, fight, hide, run, destroy, or—among those who for one reason or another have no heart for that game—seek to escape the notice alike of their violent teachers and their violent classmates. Considering the general level of violence, the incidence of pupils' hitting teachers is remarkably low. Any teacher who explicitly rejects the terms of the struggle as they are defined by her colleagues is likely to be looked upon by them as a fool—or a traitor. I worked as a per diem substitute in a chaos school over a period of a few months during the school year 1967–68. By the end of the first day I found myself upholding, with some diffidence, the position that it is unfair to hit children with a hard object in the hand. I didn't dare risk the old-timers' scorn by saying one shouldn't hit one's pupils at all. They assured me that if I were there every day I would very quickly come to understand about hitting. Perhaps.

Aside from the brutalization of adults and children alike by a system of violence that none of them as individuals can escape and aside from the racism apparent to all in a system of brutality in which a large majority of the adults are white and almost all the children are dark (so that racial epithets need not even be used; the situation is racially structured), the chaos schools (or chaos classes in other schools) nakedly reveal the aim to subdue, not to educate.

The immediate and central anxiety of the community-control movement was in respect of the chaos schools. Not only the children's futures, their careers, and their spirits, but their physical well-being were daily endangered. In many chaos schools, the dilapidated condition of the buildings also contributed to the danger. (One local school board had to sue the board of education to get maintenance of a neglected old building.) The children's advocates were begging for order, as were the children themselves in their own way. At the same time, most of those active in the community-control movement knew very well that the system would have to move beyond externally imposed order, beyond the John Brown junior highs, to achieve education.

For demanding both order and education, for insisting

that the children be made to behave but that discipline not be the central concern of the educational process, the community-control advocates were sometimes accused of being contradictory in their educational philosophy. But they were right in perceiving that both the kind of order and the violent chaos to which their children were being subjected were destroying the children, that the school dialogue ought to be neither about order nor about survival, but about education.

Miss Allbright: A "U" (Unsatisfactory) Teacher

What a chaos school is like for a new teacher and how the system chooses to see her difficulties are seen in the story of Miss Allbright. A child of middle-class professional parents, Miss Allbright herself attended a "good" school in middle-class Queens, where, she reports, she was a good but always anxious pupil. She graduated from one of the colleges of the City University one June, and from September to January served her practice-teaching apprenticeship, half of it in the kind of school she had herself attended and half in a bad Harlem school. In February she received her license and was taken on by the second school, in accordance with the practice of giving new teachers their first assignments in the most difficult schools. (The most badly run nonwhite schools have the highest turnover rates and therefore the greatest demand for new teachers.)

Her first class was a fifth grade whose beginning-of-term teacher had left in December. Between then and the time the class was assigned to Miss Allbright, it first had been taught by a man substitute for a week and a half, and then he had left. Then it had had a young woman substitute and when she left after a week, it was split up and dispersed to various other classrooms, despite the fact that the school was a Special Service school and so had a large number of supervisory personnel, special reading teachers, and other "cluster" teachers all of whom had no regular assignments. When Miss Allbright first took over the class, there weren't enough books to go around, and she didn't know the procedure for getting more books in the middle of the year.

(She later discovered a lot of books stashed away by one of the previous teachers who had taken them from children for being bad.) One of the critical reports later filed against her by the supervisor referred to the fact that some of the children didn't have books during a reading lesson. The children, undoubtedly recognizing her inexperience and confusion, had a wild time at her expense for about two weeks until one day a newly assigned young man substitute was sent in to help her. He was tough and kept order while Miss Allbright taught, and for a few days matters improved. The children said Miss Allbright became stricter while he was there. Then one day, with no explanation, the young man was pulled out of her room and assigned elsewhere, and chaos was restored.

Miss Allbright went to her district superintendent to say she considered herself a failure and was going to quit teaching. He persuaded her to stay, saying he would ask her principal to assign her to a younger and easier class. For two weeks while she waited for a first grade to become available, she was assigned to remedial reading with individuals and small groups. (What happened to the four-times orphaned fifth grade she never knew.) She liked the remedial reading assignment and experienced the satisfaction of seeing a number of children make remarkable progress in a very short time.

Finally she was given her first grade—a bad first grade which became available when the principal sent away the substitute who had been teaching it because she couldn't keep order. The first grade's previous teacher, before the substitute, had gone on maternity leave. Miss Allbright couldn't keep order with that first grade either. The children tormented her and one another, ran around, refused to stay in line, cried, hid in the closet, and rushed out of the room. She went to her supervisor to ask for help, but when the supervisor said, "Put the request in writing," she stalked out in tears. (Miss Allbright, the teacher mentioned above, now realized that a case was being prepared against her.) Finally the supervisor began to pay attention to her plight—but a curious sort of attention. Five, six, eight, ten times a day, she would burst into Miss Allbright's room, imperiously create order, and then exit, whereupon the subservient bodies so neatly put in place would again be transformed into autonomous human beings whirling about in chaos. A half-hour later the same supervisor, or another, would enter to find that in her absence Miss Allbright had again allowed the madness to resume, and would again quiet the throng. Clearly the disorder was Miss Allbright's doing.

One day, Miss Allbright was peremptorily ordered out of her class, as her "inability to control her class created hazardous conditions for her pupils," and was assigned to the district superintendent's office pending a decision to take away her teachers license. Her supervisor's reports on her case indicate that she received help from her supervisors over a period of months but was unable to benefit from this help. According to her own report, the help she received consisted primarily of: the supervisor's almost hourly invasions; advice to walk behind a line of children instead of in front of it, to line the children up *before* taking them from the room, and to "hit them a little and see if that wouldn't help"; and warnings that she would "just have to improve her classroom management."

Miss Allbright received a "U" (Unsatisfactory) rating and lost her teachers license, a victim of a weak, malfunctioning system which somehow believes it can gain strength by purging itself of, rather than supporting or calming, its weakest or most disruptive members.

Miss Jersild in Harlem: "I was almost in a total state of shock the whole time I was there."

Miss Jersild, whom we met, during her second year of teaching, at orderly John Brown Junior High School, had started her career, as did Miss Allbright, in a chaos school. But, unlike Miss Allbright, she was not beaten by the system, nor did she join it. Somehow she recognized the system's threat to her humanity, and she managed to escape the chaos school. I think she must have had a kind of tough inner spirit which was struggling to overcome the cultural deprivations of her suburban, middle-class upbringing.*

* *It may be of interest to record that by a year and a half after I had first met her at John Brown, Miss Jersild was interacting with her low-status classes in a way that was giving her warm pleasure. Even the slant of her jokes had changed, from snide digs about moral and mental striving, to cracks about matters closer to the seat of the body and the passions.*

The School Fix, NYC, USA

I applied to the board of education [for a substitute teaching license]. And they send you of course wherever they feel like it. They sent me to this school in Harlem. It was very, very, difficult, and very demeaning in every sense to teach there. You need only to be there to see how the children feel. You know exactly how they feel because you were wearing your junky clothes to school. Nobody would think of wearing anything good to school because the place was filthy. [The men] were sloppy, too; [they'd wear] jeans. I'm serious. It really was a filthy place. You would be just covered with dirt when you got out of there. I would come home with little flakes of dirt on me. We had a custodian who would wear a snorkle at four o'clock when he cleaned up the school because he didn't like germs. A mask. I mean it! It was like a loony bin. It's what the whole situation was like. No place to eat at all, so we had to bring our lunch because there was nothing even we could buy, and there was absolutely no place where the teachers could eat. It was awful.

And the children! There were 1,100 children; all of them had lunch in school. They had a cafeteria the size of this room [her living room, about 18′ by 24′]. It's still there. I'm not saying they *had*. They *have*. There would be a row of tables—two rows of tables in a long line and a bench on either side. When the children get their lunch, they sit down and they *slide*—like this [sliding along the couch where she was sitting] when they eat!

What do you mean they slide *when they eat?*

They slide on the bench when they eat, like this. When they get to the end the tray drops to the floor so they just better bop the food in their mouth or they don't eat. Even with separate sessions for groups to come down and eat, the school cafeteria just couldn't handle them. It's the most depressing thing in the whole wide world! The school was built when it was a Jewish neighborhood, and it didn't need facilities like this. This was *so depressing*. We kept threatening to call the *Amsterdam News* to tell them about this intolerable situation, but no one had enough . . .

The *Amsterdam News* knew about conditions in chaos schools' lunchrooms, as did their readers, city and state officials, and even the president of the board of education. In one tour and school "luncheon" for city officials sponsored by the United Bronx Parents, 53 health violations in lunchrooms were cited. John Doar, then president of the board of education, visited one Harlem school which hadn't been painted for seventeen years (not a record at all), in which purse snatchers, entering through rotted doors, roamed the halls, and in which 900 children were fed in a lunchroom built to accommodate 175.[4]

You leave there [at three o'clock] thinking "Oh, my gosh, I'm not a human being any more!" I was near staircase 9 on which the children urinate—they use it as a toilet. So few toilets in the school they have to stand in line to go urinate. No soap—in the teachers' room or in the children's room. When you'd complain, they'd say "bring your own." They steal it if you put it there—or teachers steal it. No paper towels at all, because the children would stuff up the toilets with them. You just were no longer a human being. You were not a person.

The teachers say they would stay on because after a while you begin to feel you're incapable of teaching. It grabs you and you think that you no longer can teach, that [children in a better school] would overwhelm you—that you can't do anything. You are just—you're not a human being any more.

You have so many failures in your classroom, day after day after day that you think that you can no longer cause achievement. And you think that you are an inferior person. And you're afraid to apply to another school. You're afraid to even look. And then you say to yourself, "Why bother because they're all like this?" Now I was told by teachers who were in the school, "Don't bother changing. All the schools in the city are like this. Except others are even worse because you have the same type student and the administration is on your back. At least here nobody bothers you." Which they don't—no one could care if you were living or dead.

You being new in teaching, you're very insecure. You don't know what kind of teacher you are . . . And then you have one failure after the next. And then you're totally browbeaten. You feel as if you're incapable of doing anything with a class. I've talked to people, and they've told me how a school in Harlem sucks you in. You get sucked into the system. [Another teacher put in an application to transfer but changed her mind.] The principal pleaded with her to stay. Because she was doing such wonders with these children. "Look how your classes manage to stay quiet for one second!" [The friend changed her mind again on the last day of school.] "I'm going to tell him I'm leaving and I'm not going to turn around because I somehow suspect that what these people are saying is true. This will suck me in—the Harlem school—where everybody is very depressed, everybody is very unhappy."

I was there for a year. Just the whole environment is ruinous—it really is. You try to do a good job with the children. You try to teach them things, and yet because no one has any self-respect or any dignity, you just change as a person. I began taking... you know, taking pens is nothing —in Harlem—it's one of the most moderate things. When you need a pen, you just grab one. So I'd never have a pen, I'd just pick up one. I said, "Dammit. Here I am stealing pens! I don't even think twice about it any more." And after this happens to a teacher . . . And then the level at which you think children should be working absolutely changes.

I was almost in a total state of shock the whole time I was there. I can honestly say that. I look back on that now, and I say, "How were you able to stand that?" I think probably I did not know anything else in teaching. I really didn't. I thought that this was the way the city schools were. And, you know, when a principal will tell you that this is all normal, and when teachers are going around accepting it as this is the way things are, you adjust to it.

They have accepted it, and I don't think acceptance of this is the thing to do. And I wish . . . well, every instance I have seen where a teacher is considered a good teacher because he can "handle" the children, he handles them by becoming totally insensitive to their problems and their needs. He handles it with hitting children. And it just goes on and on.

When they say a teacher is "experienced in the ghetto," I honestly think that teacher has given up fighting it.

Willie Gallagher: "You like a baby. You come up, you don't know what's good for you."

Little Willie Gallagher entered into a collusive agreement with his teachers that he wouldn't bother them if they wouldn't bother him. For reasons neither he, nor his friend and tutor who tells his story, nor his good grandmother who adored him, quite understand, but which may have had something to do with an early illness that made him often absent, he did not learn to read at age seven or eight. Therefore, he was in the "real bad" classes. But he arranged with his teachers to be the good boy in the bad classes if they would leave him alone. Willie stuck to his part of the agreement, and the teachers stuck to theirs.

So Willie slid through nine years in central Harlem schools arriving finally in high school, wise, shrewd, and as innocent of the printed word as the day he was born. He had collaborated with his teachers in his own educational destruction (spiritually he was indestructible), and they had collaborated with him in trying to preserve the peace. He guessed what his educational destruction had cost him, and knew what his survival was worth.

In Willie's history we can see how the ways of the black city boys and the ways of their teachers accommodate to each other to produce the illiterate, unemployable black urban men between whom and white America there seems to be no way of accommodating at all.

The "I" of Willie's story is a white friend and occasional tutor who wrote this account of their five years of learning from each other when both men were in their early twenties.

I first met Willie in the summer of 1964, when he was seventeen years old. That was before he dropped out of school. Unlike many ghetto youths, he had a warm, open smile. He used to come up to the basement on 147th Street, where we were running an art workshop, to be tutored in reading.

Willie had managed to get all the way to tenth grade on the slide. His survival in school depended on his ability to fake it. He had one way or another of getting around the fact that he was completely illiterate. It was a pattern that he developed as far back in school as he can remember.

In fourth grade, he recalls, the class used to get a weekly assignment of words to learn to spell. He'd go home, do the assignment, which consisted of looking the words up in the dictionary and copying out dictionary definitions. He knew the alphabet and could do this, sometimes with the help of a younger sister, without knowing at all what he was writing.

The teacher knew he didn't know anything and wasn't learning anything, and conspired with him to help him avoid confronting the problem. The weekly spelling tests were arranged as a contest between one half of the class and the other. [Often called "spelling baseball," this event is for many classes throughout the nation the high point of the week, a joining of the children's Friday afternoon need for a recreational break with the essence of the week's curriculum.] Willie, however, never participated in them. According to him, the teacher and he "worked together" to keep him out of the contest. He wanted to stay out, he says, to avoid the embarrassment in front of his fellow students. God knows why she wanted to keep him out; she probably told herself that she was doing him a favor.

This was typical of Willie's school career. He was always a good boy in class, he says, so the teacher never had it in for him. The way he saw it, the teachers called on—"bothered"—the more unruly students. "You so smart—tell me the answer to this," is the way he describes their attitude. About himself, he says, "I was quiet. I always find out, if you be quiet, since I couldn't read, you could get by. Just lay in the back and be quiet. 'Cause anybody that know they couldn't read would know if you stay in the back and stay quiet, you won't be embarrassed about learning to read. If you be a big mouth—start trouble—you be singled out all the time."

Sometimes, though, when the class was very bad, and the teachers came and went at the rate of several a week, then Willie would get bad too. Willie said: "I went to the fifth grade. That class was bad. Every day for two weeks . . . was it two weeks? I don't know how long it was. It was a period of time. We had a new teacher every day. I was always quiet, but the class was something else. At the time of that class, I started getting bad. It seemed like . . . it was fun.*" But then a new teacher came, a black teacher who smacked their hands with a ruler and got them in line, and Willie became Willie again.*

When they gave tests, sometimes he just didn't take them, sometimes he "just scribbled stuff, and the teacher never picked it up."

"How did that make you feel?" I asked, "That you scribbled something and she didn't even bother to look at it?" I was sure that that would have hurt him.

"I felt all right. Nice. Like, I knew it was wrong. Like I was getting away with something."

In the series of conversations we had, I often returned to that point, because I couldn't believe that somewhere, he didn't feel hurt, neglected. One time when we were talking about ways in which school helps "to keep black people down," I suggested that a teacher's not going out of her way to draw a student out could be one way in which she might be telling him he's not very valuable, that a teacher should make a student work, so he would feel worth something.

"But the kid won't get the idea," he said. "He just be glad that you not bothering him. He'll feel he's getting away with something. 'Cause he's afraid to be embarrassed, and know he don't know it. He just getting away. He feels great about it [not having to work]. Least I did."

I kept coming back to that point in our conversations about being ignored in school. I still couldn't quite believe that he didn't have more mixed feelings, and every time, he insisted that at the time he felt great about "getting away with something." In the absence of any contradictory evidence, I have to take Willie's word for it. Perhaps this attitude is connected with the feeling he had that "if you can't read, you just can't read."

"What do you mean?" I asked him.

"It'll just come later on. You'll learn to read somehow. You'll get it somehow. It's no need to push yourself. It'll come later on."

"Somehow, but you don't have too clear an idea of how," I said.

"It'll work itself out."

"Most of the time does it or doesn't it?"

"Most of the time it doesn't work itself out. That's why people are in a trick bag today—they figure it'll work its way out."

So Willie went through one year after another figuring it would work its way out; he would get it later on. I asked him if he felt his teachers, by their behavior, were telling him he'd get it later on.

"Way I see it, they was telling me you not getting it

now. Don't know when you get it, but you not getting it now."

Twice, once in fifth and once in sixth grade, he got left back. Otherwise, he did fine. He got A's on his report card—for good conduct.

If his teachers weren't pushing him, neither was his grandmother. He says his younger sister's school career was more important to his grandmother than his. She went to a Catholic school and he didn't, though he wanted to. "I come home, they don't say, 'What did you get for homework? How you doing in school?' It was nothing like that. You know, 'Can you read this commercial, or read this paper?' It was nothing like that. Come home and do what I want to do and that was it."

Now he wishes thay had pushed him. "You like a baby. You come up, you know, you don't know what's good for you. This is good for you, this is going to help you, this is vitamins, you know. You don't know if it's going to help you or not."

Still, when I asked, he said he never felt unloved by his grandmother. "I got everything I want in the house, sooner or later . . . If I would see something I want, I would get it . . . I had this room all to myself. I had a box like this here of toy soldiers. A tank . . . And any time I want the front room, it would be all mine. Nobody could come in there." He seemed to recall those days fondly.

This aspect of his home life he relates to his good behavior in school; he says he was good because he was spoiled.

Some time after he began to try to learn to read with me, his attitude towards school changed some. He began to feel that "people jigged me up. Teachers jigged me up. They supposed to help me, they didn't help me. Parents supposed to love me, they didn't help me. Everybody loved me . . . but nobody helped me."

Specifically he began to blame his teachers. I tried to say it wasn't the teachers, it was the whole system. But he argued about that: "Right, but see, what I'm trying to say is how I came all the way up through the system, and I wasn't the only one. And look at me. Why was I all juked up? I wasn't mean. So, I look back, it must have been the teachers. Like I was there. Every day. In the class. All day. And I wasn't mean. So, like, if they was dishing it out, I should have got some of it. Other words, they wasn't dishing it out."

He could not see how his family was responsible for his not learning in school, saying, "I don't see how it could involve my family too much. Because everything I did, it was in school. My work was in school. My family wasn't there."

He would tell me how sometimes in class he'd raise his hand and say, "Teacher, I don't understand that there," and she'd say, "Well, just copy it down and I'll explain it to the whole class later." Once he started to imagine making the teacher teach him. He ran off a little dialogue:

"Well, teacher, I can't really read this here."

"Wait till later on, Gallagher . . ."

"But you said . . . I don't want to wait. I want to learn it now. *Help me with this here."*

"Well I ain't got time."

"Well, what you going to do, then? I'm in your class to learn. I'm not learning anything."

"All right. Go down to the Dean."

"Dean, she not teaching me anything. I'm not learning. I can't read this here. I'm going to fail the test that's coming up."

"All right, I'll talk to the teacher about it."

"Woo-oo! I'd be something else!"

The school year of '64-'65 he was on his way out of school. He couldn't read, and, as it now appears, wasn't really working at it. He occasionally used to say something about killing himself, which it was easy not to take too seriously because it was said so casually.

"I was just tired of my surroundings. Like, you know, what we used to do on the weekends? We'd mug three, four, five people at a time. Every weekend, you know, it was nothing else to do . . .

"It always be Friday or Saturday. Friday, after the center close at ten o'clock. Sit on the stoop, talk, find out where a party is. 'Well, let's go to the party, you-all.' 'All right.' Hang out by the liquor store for a while, get a couple of drinks. On the way to the party we was looking to go down the dark ways. See a guy, you know, somebody would grab him . . . 'Come on, you-all—let's go to the party first.' 'No.' Somebody would grab him. 'All right—you, look out.' I was always looking out. I wouldn't be grabbing nobody.

"It was really funny. It was . . . in a sense it's a serious crime mugging somebody, if you get caught. And you never know what the person have on them. Never know if the person got a gun, is a karate champion, ex-cop, you know. And you grab him, one man here, one man here, and one man there. You know, about twelve of us, nine, eight of us, you know. And most times, they never had no more than fifteen dollars . . . The things we was doing wasn't worth the risks we were taking. I was getting bored. I was there just to be there, nowhere else to go."

He was doing this very shortly after I first began to tutor him, but he never said anything to me about all this at the time. He didn't want me to think he was a bad guy. From my point of view at that time, things looked pretty hopeful for him. Anyway, I was teaching him to read. From his? "Hopeless and helpless," he says. And had I known where he was really at, I might have agreed.

The next year he joined the Muslims, got sent to jail for mugging, came out and went to live with his uncle in Brooklyn. "I got a whole lot out of the Muslims," he says. "They made me realize it was all out there for me to get."

When he first told me the story of his arrest, he said he had had nothing to do with it [the mugging], and I saw no reason to disbelieve him. He said that they were in an integrated neighborhood and that the victim had identified him, probably because all Negroes look alike to whites, and anyway, it was dark.

When he told me again recently about how he used to mug people in Harlem, I asked him if he actually was guilty of the mugging for which he was convicted. He talked around some.

"That robbery, did I have anything to do with that? Can't remember, John, it was so long back. Let me see . . . let me see . . Yeah. It was the night I had left my money at my man's house. Went all the way up in the Bronx. We was going to Topps. Saw this man. They said, 'Come on.' I said, 'Naw.' They said, 'Yeah.' I said, 'Well, why not?' So it just happened.

"Got busted. Paid the cost."

"How come you're telling me now?" I asked him.

"John. You know, who's John? You know, John is John. After you get to know somebody, you feel that you can tell them something, it won't bother them, you know.

'Cause they know that you ain't as bad as you . . . you know . . . Like, if you kill somebody, John, I know that you not a real killer, so I won't be afraid of you or anything like that there. I'd think, 'He's all right,' you know. If you told me why you killed him, I'd understand, you know . . . After a while you feel that you can trust this person and tell them these things, and they would trust you in that way."

After Willie got out of jail, he got married to a girl he had got pregnant. He became, half-seriously, involved in a black militant group. He's had a series of jobs none of which pay enough to keep him up to date with his household bills and also buy him the clothes and partying that he loves. Still, the surprising thing is, he doesn't give up, quit working, go on dope, or anything like that. He was married at twenty, and now he wants out. He runs around with other girls, sometimes falling passionately in love. As a matter of fact, the only thing that keeps him at home is his little daughter whom he really cares for.

One evening recently I came home and put on a tape of what was supposed to be a reading lesson that Willie was to have done. Instead I heard the following:

Wow. Life is a drag. You ain't got money. More likely, you ain't got a chance. Everything's against you—everything. Get ahead—live good. Not knowing how to read, every time you want to eat, that works hand in hand. Can't read, you can't eat what you want to eat. If you can read, that dollar there. All your life is money. You look at yourself -you could be like the man around the corner.

Little old man—twenty-two years old. All your life, been having a dream you was going to make it. And didn't make it nowhere.

The whole world in front of you. Feel like reaching out for it; and you just can't get it. Every time you get up on it, it moves away. You get a job, making some money, but, you still not happy. You want more money! Why you want more money? 'Cause the money you getting—it's going too fast. The Man allows you to make enough money—not enough to get by—enough to strain, to scrape by. He got you straining every week, every year, to get by. It's a thing. A circle.

Supposed to have enjoyment, and, in my position, it's a

survival. Survival. Family. Self. Sweetheart . . . And I had to fall in love. To top off all my problems. Could not be love. Could be a different person. Trying to get away. Tearing me up inside. Picking me apart. Why'd I have to meet her? Why? Destiny. Destiny sure fucked me up, boy.

Look where I am today: Twenty-two. Got a half-assed job. Got a family. And I got bills. Do I deserve all this? . . . Hell no. Didn't do nothing to nobody all my life. Nobody. Maybe a couple of girls when I got older, but they didn't mind.

I am . . . a problem. I have a problem. Let me see. Let me put my finger on my problem. Where does my problem lie at? Does it lie on my wife? Mmmm, yeah. Does it lie on my little girl? No. What is my wife's problem? Well, if she was working, I wouldn't have to bring home so much. Mmm. Yup.

That's it in a nutshell: Money. Ain't enough time to pay all my bills off. 'Cause then, I'm where I was before I paid my bills–back in a rut. Time you pay them all off, something else comes up. Then you back in that circle again. Try to get away; no way out. It'll always be there. If I could read, I'd have nothing to worry about. Reading. Get decent, pretty well-off job, anywhere. I wouldn't be stuck in New York. Go live in Boston, get a job.

Yeah, but then I think about my little girl. If I leave her, what's going to happen to her? Mean, cruel world out there.

Supposing you have a problem–find it, and then deal with it. Problem at home–I'm not ready for it. Not ready for it at all. Can't back out–can't get away from it–so I got to face it. When I face it, I want to run. When I want to run I . . . I *can't* run. So therefore I'm stuck. Stuck in a rut. And trying to get out. Been trying to get out of a rut for twenty-two years. Biggest one I'm in now is reading. Between this girl in Boston. Eating my mind up.

Then looking around you at your problems. How can you do it? If you spend the money, you be sorry later on, 'cause it's going to hurt. Why be sorry? Always have money problems.

But then I think of that circle I'm in, not getting ahead. Making fifty-two hundred a year, still got money problems. That's the trouble.

My life, I'll change with anybody. I don't want it no more.

Did I say I don't want it no more? I wouldn't say that. I've had some good times in my life. Had some good times last weekend! Probably have some good times next weekend! But it's all in the middle of those good times, which you're hurting. And after those, you're hurting. And *before* those good times, you're hurting.

I got to get away. Don't care how I get away, as long as I get away. I want to take my little girl with me. Hate to go alone. My father left me; I used to hate him. Today I know how it was. Probably had it hard just like this. Making a decision. To leave, to stay, be hurt. If he stay, he hate himself. If he left, he be regretting that. I used to say, "Why did he leave me?" Why? He want to be happy. He should have stayed with me and Mommy. But looking at me now I can see why he did it. But then you say, "He should have known what he was doing." I should have known what I was doing, too. Thought I knew. Evidently, I didn't know. Boy, oh boy, oh boy. Feel like killing yourself, but then you say, there's too much fun out there, you going to miss too much if you do . . .

You look down at your little girl. . . She looks up at you and smile. Then you realize that you can't leave. Can't get away. Can't get away at all. Her mother know that she got you around, 'cause she got your daughter. You look at the future for you in your present job, and like it's nowhere. But then you think, if I get down to the books, my job can be somewhere for me. Only if you get down to the books. With the city, it's test after test. Each raise is a test; each test is a raise. The key to getting past the tests is reading. The key to reading is learning to read. The key to learning to to read is finding time to read. The key to finding time . . .

Then you say, well, I better do it 'cause I want to learn and get ahead. But they you find you got struggles in yourself. A house that's divided, it can't stand. If you divided against yourself, you can't function right.

Too many problems. Too many inner struggles . . . to do anything. And it all revolves around money. To live, to eat, to sleep, to enjoy yourself—you must have money. To get money, you must work. To get good money, have a good job. Have a job, have a good education. Have a good education, *study* for it. You must want to study. So it all lies in you again.

Life? Who needs it?

The School Fix, NYC, USA

I do. It's a lot of fun. Lot of enjoyment. Lot of kicks. Lot of headaches. Lot of struggles. Lot of backaches. But then, it's a whole lot of partying.

You party, you party, you party.

You suffer, you suffer, you suffer.

You get older, you get older, you get older.

You find that you through with the party, and you got nowhere to go.

Well, that's the way it is. So why not be that way? Boss if you find it happy.

Part II.
The Struggle for Power and Status

Every organism or group, no matter how corrupt or unsatisfactory, develops ways to protect itself against change. Against the external threat it will use one approach; against another kind of peril, the threatened group will adopt another kind of strategy. But always, no matter how cleverly the strategy is disguised, the group in power will attempt to stop change or, failing all else, limit the degree of change to the least significant area.

—Charles Wilson and David Spencer,
"*The Case for Community Control*"

INTRODUCTION

Some of [the] problems [of American Indian education] . . . arise whenever educators of one cultural tradition confront pupils of another. A key variable in this transaction is the locus of power—the de facto *control of the educational process—which may lie with the educators, the pupils or elsewhere entirely.*

. . . we are accustomed to a tripartite education configuration in which ultimate control rests with a school board derived from the higher reaches of community status and power; day-to-day regulation rests with administrators and teachers of a middle level of status and power; and the parents of the pupils—many of whom represent the lower levels of the community—have little or no voice as to what is taught their children or how it is done. Because we take this configuration so much for granted, it is worthwhile reminding ourselves that, especially in the cross-cultural situation, it is neither natural nor inevitable that the recipients of the education lack control over the school system.[1]

The quotation suggests that when, beginning in 1966, some recipients of education in New York sought to achieve control over the educational process, they did not lack historical precedents. Their demands arose, however, not out of a knowledge of those precedents or out of a developed and coherent ideology but primarily out of the maneuvers and countermaneuvers of a power struggle.

For a decade or more educators and writers had debated politely with one another whether desegregation or compensatory programs would better improve the schooling of poor nonwhite children.[2] At least in respect to the great urban population centers, the argument was frivolous (although those who engaged in it did not and probably could not know this at the time), because the power and status demands of the school system throttled both, in different ways. When in New York, the desegregation battle more or less ended in 1966, there were more black children in segregated "bad" (low-achieving) schools and segregated "bad" classes than there had been in 1954 when it began.[3] It was therefore moot whether desegregation would or would not improve the schooling of poor nonwhite children.[4] In roughly the same period, the board of education had instituted, and in some cases withdrawn, a number of compensatory education programs. From the point of view of those responsible for running the school machine, the sometimes widely heralded "new" and "experimental" programs were intended primarily to compensate for the various breakdowns that the machine keeps experiencing. Thus, however cunningly they may be designed, they must be notched and pared and mutilated so as to mesh into the old gears. Summarizing, I believe it is not unfair to say that one after another these programs kept trying to do what the schools had overwhelmingly demonstrated they could not do: serve the status system and serve black (poor, Puerto Rican) children at the same time.

The demand then arose, not from educators but from the recipients of the schools' services, that the schools, in effect, stop serving the status system either entirely or to the extent that it interfered with serving the black and Puerto Rican children. It was a demand for a shift in the status arrangements and in the locus of power in the educational world, and it was resisted, quite naturally, by those who were more or less privileged in their status and power positions.

The Struggle for Power and Status

The primary participants in the power struggle which ensued were, in Wax's schema, the teachers plus the administrators who were at the middle level of status and power versus the powerless pupils or their advocates, with the representatives of the higher reaches of power throwing their weight now to one side, now to the other, or, to complete the confusion, to both sides at the same time.

1. RATIONAL FOR CHANGE: DECENTRALIZATION AND COMMUNITY CONTROL

Two slogans symbolized the aims of the struggle: "community control" and "decentralization." The content of the terms was elusive, for a number of reasons. In the first place, both terms did mean different things to different individuals and groups who believed in them. In the second place, as the words "community" and "decentralization" came to be equated with "improved education for black and Puerto Rican children," they became "good" words, and so even the plans, proposals, and legislation that were aimed at reinforcing rather than breaking up the old power and status arrangements were labeled with these good words. For example, the act passed by the New York State Legislature in April, 1969, was actually an elaborate legislative shoring up of threatened power and status interests at the middle level (teachers and supervisors), but it was *called* an act "in relation to establishing a community school district system," and was commonly referred to as the Decentralization Act of 1969. Similarly, when the United Federation of Teachers appended to a brief critique of the decentralization proposals contained in the so-called Bundy Plan (see below, section 3) an even briefer set of proposals of its own, it included an item labeled "Decentralization," which reads in its entirety: "The New York school system should be decentralized. The number of local school districts formed should be under 15 [the existing number of districts was 30] in order to insure the possibility of integration within each district and to reduce administrative costs." This proposal was heralded in *The United Teacher* under the front-page headline "EXECUTIVE BOARD ADOPTS OWN DECENTRALIZATION PLAN."[1] And the board of education, which (with the teachers, through the UFT, and the supervisors, through the Council of Supervisory Organizations) put up the strongest possible resistance to both decentralization and community control, issued a "Statement of Policy on Decentralization" on April 19, 1967, which opened, "All members of our Board are committed to the principle of decentralization of operations."

The first level of confusion was between "community control" and "decentralization." The latter, when it was not simply a disingenuous verbal subterfuge, referred mainly to the redistribution of the administrative functions of the central bureaucracy of the board of education in such a way as to reduce inefficiency, waste, and bureaucratic indifference to education. Lifting the dead weight of the central headquarters' bureaucratic procedures from the backs of field personnel, it was argued, would make it possible for field personnel to move about the educational arena a little more freely. In addition, decentralization might allow the intrusion of outside forces into the play of interests affecting the school—including, it was hoped, parents and community leaders. To those rational critics of the school system who saw the educational problem largely in terms of inefficiency, bureaucratic waste and heavy-handedness, anachronistic administrative arrangements, and a closed and tight-fisted hierarchy, decentralization by legislative fiat or by administrative concessions seemed a long step toward a solution. Thus, two popular books published during the early stages of the conflict advocated this way out.

Marilyn Gittell wrote in *Participants and Participation:*

Any effort to change the school system and expand civic participation must face the concentration of power in the professional bureaucracy and the resistance by the bureaucracy to any plan that would erode its power. Thus any plan for change must have as its first objective the diminution of bureaucratic power. Meaningful plans for the reorganization of large city school systems must embody a formula for the decentralization of bureaucratic authority and the expansion of outside nonprofessional influences. Reorganization should also serve the purpose of maximizing public involvement in the schools, and of stimulating the mayor, other officials, civic groups, and a larger public to play more active roles in educational policy.[2]

The inference of the passage, and especially of the concluding sentence, is that administrative reform, initiated *from above*, will somehow eventually affect the relationships of groups closer to the school level.

David Rogers' *110 Livingston Street* similarly concentrates reform proposals on administrative rearrangements at upper levels, effected by decision makers at upper levels, and he expects that from this will flow increased community and parental participation. It is a kind of trickle-down theory of democratic participation: pour in some more democracy at the top and some of it will trickle down to the poor folks at the bottom.

The independent groups supporting decentralization were largely liberal (rarely trade unionist), civic-minded reform groups whose major quarrel was not with the job society had given the school system to do but with the quality of the system's performance.* Decentralization was

* *At the time, groups supporting decentralization were banded together in the Coalition for Community Control (now called the Coalition for an Effective Community School System). The organizations then included: Action for Children Now; Catholic Interracial Council of New York; Citizens Committee for Children; Citizens Committee for Decentralization of the Public Schools; Committee on Public Affairs, Community Service Society; Council of Churches of the City of New York; Interfaith City-wide Coordinating Committee Against Poverty; Interreligious Committee for Community Control; Junior League of Brooklyn, Inc.; Junior League of the City of New York; Manhattan Division, Council of Churches; Metropolitan Applied Research Center; NAACP, New York City Branches; National Conference of Christians and Jews, New York Region; New York City Mission Society; New York State Americans for Democratic Action; New York State Congress of*

also supported by Mayor John Lindsay, the Ford Foundation, the New York State Board of Regents, and, briefly, because it only lived briefly, the lay board of education appointed by Mayor Lindsay.

What these individuals, groups, and organizations sought was not to destroy a status-reinforcing system but merely to ameliorate some of the consequences of the system's internal contradictions. Among these were the contradiction that had arisen through the "professionalizing" of education and of school personnel. "Professionalizing" education is accompanied by the growth of professional bureaucracy whose very numbers give them strength and weight and an immunity to ordinary and necessary political pressures, and so create administrative inertia and inefficiency. The process of "professionalizing" also helps to keep afloat the status-serving myth that education is a pure pursuit remote from the outside world's status marketplace, and it serves to protect not only the status of the school people themselves but also that of a multitude of other groups and institutions: colleg teachers of education courses, boards of examiners, teachers of examination cram courses, textbook authors, textbook publishers, and so on. The decentralizers wished basically to overcome the inertia and inefficiency, but without too rough handling of all the status interests that have a stake in those very administrative arrangements.

Another contradiction arises from the fact that a competitive educational rationale has to produce failures (since whoever comes in last is defined as having failed). And a competitive rationale in a society with a long racist tradition will make the socially inferior race bear an inequitably heavy share of the failure rate. But when people are programed to fall into the lower end of the achievement curve, some of them are going to fail worse than one wants

Parents and Teachers, New York City District; Northside Center for Child Development; Public Education Association; Puerto Rican Community Development Project; Queens Committee for Community Involvement; Rabbis for Community Control; Southern Christian Leadership Conference, New York Chapter; United Automobile Workers 259; Union of Concerned Parents; United Neighborhood Houses; Urban League of Greater New York; Women's City Club; Young Women's Christian Association. New York City. Several additional organizations subsequently affiliated with the Coalition.

them to, and a humanitarian society then has to pay the cost of carrying people who have not attained the minimum skills required for social usefulness. If all those programed for the bottom of the curve would, like Loretta Tubman, achieve a minimum of socially useful skills, then the urban school system would not be seen as faulty. But, as we have seen, the dynamics work out to produce a good number of Willie Gallaghers, and the Willie Gallaghers are experienced as a drag on society. (Conversely, they experience society as a drag on them.) The point was well if unintentionally made in a speech by Marvin J. Feldman, program officer of the Ford Foundation, delivered at the Governor's Conference on Education in New Jersey, in April, 1966, and later printed.

Jobs now require more mental capability, fewer physical skills, a higher educational attainment at the entry level, and greater versatility or adaptability in the worker over his productive lifetime. . . . The primary responsibility for insuring that young people are prepared to function productively in adult life lies with the educational system, from kindergarten through college.

And, under the heading "Better Negro Education":

The kind of educational system I have described has important implications for the relationship between vocational and higher education and the American Negro. It has become commonplace to observe that the United States is faced with a serious shortage of qualified manpower at the technician level *in all professions. . . .*

At the same time vast numbers of the socioeconomically disadvantaged—especially Negroes—are being served by educational programs ill-related to current national occupational demands. Despite many warnings, however, very little has been done, in attacking the problems of status, income, occupation, and living conditions of the Negro, to provide more and better technical education beyond the high school. [Emphasis in the original.][3]

The Ford Foundation was one of the most powerful and helpful of the civic groups that supported decentralization and, to some extent, community control. Whatever may have been their ideological commitment to the democratic element in community control or their humanitarian concern for the struggling individuals involved, it is surely likely that the systemic malfunctioning of the larger society, to which the systemic malfunctioning of the schools makes considerable contribution, augmented their concern with urban education.

There is no doubt that the difficulties the New York City school system faced were aggravated by its bureaucratic centralism, as that centralism functioned. For it was not only colossally inefficient, as so much of the literature on the system demonstrates and as every participant in it knows, but it had the terrible effect, as I have tried to show, of making administrative functioning the primary concern of almost all personnel. If instead of being the superiors of the educators, the administrators were merely their instruments (a kind of staff organization serving the line personnel), it is conceivable that a centralized administration would be more efficient than a decentralized one. But as the situation was, the only way to begin to make education a primary concern of the system seemed to be to take away some of the central bureaucracy's power.

However, fragmenting the administrative functions, whether into 30 or 15 districts, or into five boroughs (as Marilyn Gittell proposed), or up to 60 districts (as the Bundy Plan proposed), would not in itself either weaken or reverse the status arrangements at the individual school level—as between supervisors and teachers, teachers and children, school personnel and parents—or among status-ranked peer categories—as between "good" classes and "bad" classes, "good" schools and "bad" schools, "good" children and "bad" children, and so on. At best, it would allow a point of entry into the system for parents and other citizens *at the district level.* Thus, whereas under bureaucratic centralism, political (that is, public or group interest) pressures could be exerted, if at all, only at the very top through the mayor's appointments to the board of education, decentralizing would presumably open up the professional bureaucracy at a point nearer to the individual school, classroom, and child. District boards would be responsive to public desires and pressures and would presumably have some influence over district superintendents and *through* them over individual principals and schools.

Actually, as we have seen, the usual size of the city's thirty districts, the rigidity of the merit system, and the administrative demands made upon district superintendents and principals tended to make it unlikely that decentralization alone could achieve much in the way of *educational* reform, which was more directly the aim of the community-control advocates. Nevertheless, all those who were defending their own status within the system—even the teachers, who, among the school personnel, had the very lowest status—eventually came together into an alliance of defenders against all those who were proposing any reforms in the system, whether merely administrative and meliorative, as in the case of the decentralization advocates, or educational and radical, as in the case of the community-control advocates. Now, the groups and individuals whose main thrust was for decentralization, legislated administrative reform, the trickle-down kind of democracy sometimes identified themselves as favoring "community control" and did indeed support the community-control groups in their public battles. The more radical community-control advocates, however, generally sought to distinguish themselves from their more conservative some-time defenders. But as the two were sometimes found in bed together it was given out that they must be married.

But the community-control advocates were seeking a point of entry much closer to the educational process. Within this distinction, there were other distinctions among those who, whatever their terminology, were really seeking community control not decentralization. For many, the demand that the recipients of education should control the school system was founded on the black power thesis that blacks (and in New York, Puerto Ricans) constitute a contained colony in America, and that gaining control over their own institutions is a necessary first step in colonial liberation.* For others, the contained-colony theory was rejected, or ignored. Their interest was not in the black-

* *There is a good deal of literature and also a good deal of rhetoric expounding this view. See, for example, Stokely Carmichael and Charles V. Hamilton,* Black Power: The Politics of Liberation in America *(Random House, 1968). To a large extent the theory is an*

white question but in educating their children. They took the position that the educational process which black and Puerto Rican children were experiencing in New York was so evidently bankrupt and the system's managers so evidently unable to restore solvency that, in the interests of their own children, they had to insist on being appointed the receivers.

Both these community-control groups pointed out that all the managers' special attempts to put the operation back on its feet—integration, Higher Horizons, special after-school tutorial programs, remedial reading classes, programed or automated instruction, the UFT-sponsored More Effective Schools, the concept of Special Service Schools—had not been serious and had not been effective.[4] Demanding control by the community of the schools serving black and Puerto Rican children, they said that by the race and class identity of the bureaucracy and the parents, the white middle-class communities already controlled their own schools. (This, of course, is an oversimplification of the actual situation, since there are clearly many conflicts of interest between the white parents and the professionals. But it is correct, as we have seen, in the sense that the dynamics of the system operate to protect the white middle-class families' status interests vis à vis the nonwhite families' status interests.)

For both groups, the crux of the demand for community control was contained in the word "accountability": school personnel should be accountable to the community being served by the school for their performance and their pupils' performance. Thus, from being an outsider to the educational process called in either to be told what the school is doing or to serve as an instrument in the school's control over the child, the parents would become an authority to whom the school personnel would be responsible. And the school personnel would answer for their performance, not at each hierarchical level to the next hierarchical level, each further removed from the child and from the educational process, but at each hierarchical level

adaptation of the theories of colonial liberation of the neo-Marxist Frantz Fanon, who is very influential in the radical black community. See especially his Wretched of the Earth *(Grove Press, 1963).*

to representatives of the parents or community. Such a changed line of responsibility would presumably affect both the relative weight given administrative versus educational considerations and also the status of parents and children vis à vis school personnel. And since schools' evaluation of the worth and the educability of poor nonwhite children seems to underlie their failure in respect to those children, the status shift would presumably affect the schools' performance in respect to the children. (For example, if Miss Jersild's pupils' parents had status in respect to her, then she might not be so quick to substitute her judgment of proper teenage social behavior for theirs. And some forthright confrontations with self-respecting parents would doubtless either diminish the John Brown librarian's missionary zeal and introduce in her some respect for her students or else send her about her business.)

The means to effectuate accountability would be community control over the following areas of school operation:

Personnel hiring. Parents or their representatives should have control over hiring and firing of personnel, especially principals (the key persons, many people thought, in the running of the schools). State minimum personnel standards should apply. One of the three district "experiments" established by the board of education (more about this below) to test the workability and value of community control, the I.S. 201 Complex, stated its personnel needs in these terms: ". . . the pursuit of . . . time-honored routines is not going to help solve complex school problems. Concretely the Governing Board [of the complex] needs the power to recruit, to choose, and to retain the kind of creative, imaginative people the situation seems to dictate."

Relations with personnel. Community-control advocates demanded that each district be empowered to establish fair procedures and negotiate grievances directly with its teachers. The 201 Complex put the demand this way: "The Governing Board will offer the union an opportunity to go forward together to improve conditions within schools. For neither teachers nor parents have the power alone to bring about needed changes. . . . Together they have some chance. If they cannot negotiate *directly*, they have no chance at all."[5] This statement belies the notion, which soon gained currency, that the demonstration districts, or community-control advocates in general, aimed to destroy the rights of teachers. The intent on the contrary was to raise the status of teachers vis à vis administrators. (It should be added, however, that while community-control advocates did not, at the outset of their activities or even in theory, aim to destroy the UFT as the teachers' bargaining agent, they did come to recognize that the union's self-preservation was to be paid for with their extermination. Naturally, they preferred that it should be the other way around.)

Budget. As taxpayer-recipients of the educational services, the community should control the expenditure of funds allotted to its schools so as to be able to purchase the kinds of services it believed would best meet its children's needs. Specifically, the advocates wanted lump-sum rather than item-line appropriations, plus authority to make direct application for state, federal, and foundation funds.

Construction and maintenance of buildings. Schools should be planned, located, and maintained in accordance with the needs and desires of the community. The "201 Story" below (section 2) gives one example of board of education high-handed flaunting of community decision making in respect to planning and location of buildings. Black community-control advocates, continually enraged at seeing public buildings being erected in their communities by virtually all-white construction crews, also intended this demand to be a wedge to effect employment of black construction workers, an intent that was threatening to the building trades unions. (There is no doubt that community-control advocates put a higher priority on the needs of their community than on the needs of, mainly white, trade unionists, and that this factor contributed to the almost solid trade union support of the UFT during the Great Strike of 1968.)

In respect to maintenance, while inadequate resources are responsible for some of the neglect of school buildings, bureaucratic indifference also makes its large contribution. Torn window shades, broken windows, missing toilet seats, and so on go untended for months or forever, contributing naturally to the children's disrespect for school property about which school personnel complain so bitterly. Miss

Jersild's experiences in the Harlem school suggest that physical neglect of building is both a consequence of and contributor to general staff and student demoralization.

Curriculum and textbooks. Curriculum should be determined within state requirements to meet the special needs of black and Puerto Rican children. Experimental programs and methods as well as the teaching of Afro-American, African, and Latin American history should be instituted to reduce some of the unreality of much of the conventional curriculum. (For an extended discussion of high school curriculum and textbooks, see Part III, section 1.) As for texts, the use of "all-white" and/or irrelevent textbooks, readers, and so on in predominantly nonwhite schools was a frequent complaint. The supplies, especially the books, should be selected and ordered at the district level.*

Throughout the city (except, to my knowledge, in the borough of Staten Island, and also to a lesser degree in Queens than in the Bronx, Manhattan, and Brooklyn), various groups of parents and community activists made one or several of these demands, usually in respect to specific issues as they arose. Among the mixture of groups were some parent groups from the Parents Association, others associated with an individual school but not associated with the often system-oriented Parents Association, district boards, districtwide councils of parents and citizens that were not associated with the district board, borough-wide groups of parents and adult and student activists, teachers groups both inside and outside of the United Federation of Teachers, and student groups, some associated with adult groups and some independent. To my knowledge there were no groups of supervisors except for the New York Association of Negro Supervisors and Administrators, but there may have been some

* *The inefficiency of central ordering was glaringly revealed in the fall of 1969 when out of 4 million new books ordered by schools for the opening of the academic year, over 3 million had not turned up in the schools by October. A top board of education official "expressed surprise" at the complaints, and one of the top officials was reported as saying: "I don't think that there's anything massively different than any other year."* New York Times, *September 21, 1969.*

supervisor members of general groups. There were black groups, white groups, Puerto Rican groups, and mixed groups. There were Jewish groups and Christian groups. There were groups with no apparent source of funds at all, and groups who received some funds from OEO, from foundations, or from churches. Some groups limited their activities to distributing informational and polemical material to parents and the public and to making representations to such higher authorities as the board of education, the mayor, the legislature, and so on; most demonstrated inside and outside schools, the board of education, the mayor's office, the UFT office; and one sent picketers to Albert Shanker's home in suburban Westchester County. A few sat-in, disrupted, broke in, and took over, and they did this especially during the period of the Great Strike.

It is probably not inaccurate to say that while the main thrust of the community-control movement came from the black community, the main thrust of the decentralization movement came from the white community. Within the array of groups there was a predominance of blacks at the more radical, activist end and a predominance of whites at the liberal, "persuasionist" end, with a smaller number of each of these groups mixed in at the other end. The Puerto Ricans were in a difficult position. The blacks almost always included them in their rhetoric but sometimes excluded them from their organizations or from leadership therein. Unorganized Puerto Rican parents tended to be less radical and more timid than unorganized black parents, but here too there were exceptions.

Most of the groups supported decentralization legislation in principle, and many of them supported one or another specific plan in particular. But even those that did not, regarded the defeat of decentralization as a defeat for their side. Most of the groups opposed the two pieces of "decentralization" legislation—the Marchi Decentralization Act passed in 1968 and the 1969 Decentralization Act—as sell-outs to the United Federation of Teachers and the Council of Supervisory Associations. That is, they took the position that neither of these acts, but especially not the latter one, made possible the degree of administrative decentralization on which community control could begin to be built.

Except in the three demonstration districts, the "experiments" in community control, there was little development of an educational content to or educational philosophy of community control. Meetings and discussions among groups of community-control advocates were likely to concentrate, for reasons which will become apparent, on the strategy and tactics of the struggle rather than on long-range program. And even in the demonstration districts, planning for educational content and methodology was impeded by the intensity of the struggle for survival.

Occasional group and individual discussions and the programs actually developed in the demonstration districts indicate that different community-control advocates were espousing both positions of the old American educational debate. Thus: should classrooms be quiet, orderly, teacher-controlled, or should they be noisy, busy, inner-controlled? Should the method rely mainly on discussions, library reading, free discovery, trips, or on drill, homework, workbooks, and, latterly, teaching machines and programing? Nor was there agreement in the new American educational debate. Thus: should black children learn Afro-American history and African history or the old "white" American history? Should they be expected to acquire the standard American dialect or should their own dialect be respected? Likewise for Puerto Rican children, what history should they learn? And in what language should they be instructed? In the two debates, there seemed to be no lining up of adherents of one side or the other. Some of the black-content advocates were very conservative in their pedagogical methodology, and so were some of the white-content advocates. Likewise, among those who advocated a freer classroom there were both culture-content and conventional-content adherents.

Many parents and others who had had horrifying experiences of chaos schools and chaos classes were demanding first of all the creation of an order that would make conventional learning possible. Some of these rather simplistically blamed the teachers for not caring, for allowing chaos, for not teaching, for "wanting our children to fail," without recognizing to what extent the teachers themselves were caught in a system that enabled, indeed encouraged, these attitudes and habits to develop and even flourish. Many of the community-control advocates, recognizing the brightness and ambition stifled in their own children, were asking that the schools expect and demand of their children the kind of competitive achievement that is expected of middle-class children. I once heard a Puerto Rican community-control advocate respond to a white lady's challenge to his educational conservatism by saying, "You want to experiment, you experiment with your kids. We just want our kids to learn to read and to go to college and get the jobs your kids are now getting." Like many hard-working Puerto Ricans, he regarded the status system as a viable arrangement within which his people ought to be able to operate successfully.

There were also many black people, especially parents, who took this view. At a meeting in Harlem to discuss the issue of the "disruptive child" (discussed below in section 3), a very ambitious mother (who subsequently sent her children to private school so they should make it) more or less accused the teachers and principals present of making the children disruptive and expressed the aim that her children and their peers should achieve more or less conventional school success. She was determined, indignant, eloquent:

When we send these black children to kindergarten, they're not disruptive. In the first grade, they're not disruptive. Now somewhere along the line someone disrupted these children. These teachers in P.S.–, they expect the children to come to school and fold their hands and not do anything. I know these children aren't disruptive because I see them sitting on my floor, and I know they aren't disruptive. But they're saying to you, "We want to learn." We got a long ways to go and we might as well move because the time is not going to wait for us. Because, you see, I intend for my children to go to Harvard and Yale like the rest of them. When I send them to kindergarten, I intend for you to start building a foundation. I intend to watch. I don't intend to stay out of the school. Because you see we're poor people in Harlem. Sometimes we don't have enough money for shoes. Don't you worry. Because, you see, they might be hungry today–black people been hungry from the beginning of time–but if you teach these children they might not be hungry tomorrow. All you have to do is teach them, so at

21 and 22 they won't be standing on Lenox Avenue without shoes. The whole of black Harlem could lock hands together now and tell the entire world that children are like birds. If you clip their wings before they leave the nest, they won't never leave. And we intend for our black birds to fly. And the sky is the limit![6]

The position of these conventional, achievement-oriented advocates may be compared generally with the "talented tenth" position of W. E. B. Du Bois a half-century ago. Their most prominent spokesman was Dr. Kenneth Clark, who also served as a kind of mediator for the community-control forces on a number of crisis occasions. In general, he opposed the emphasis on cultural-heritage teaching advocated by some black-consciousness educators and advocated that the schools, by emphasizing mainly reading, prepare black children to enter the competitive academic and economic world.[7]

Only one person contributed a somewhat systematic rationale and program for community control, an ideology of community control for its own sake rather than by default of other remedies. He was the Columbia University professor of social work, writer, and activist Preston Wilcox. Perhaps more than any other writer in the field, Wilcox perceived the cultural gap between the children and their teachers in other terms than the stereotype of "cultural deprivation," perceived the black child's environment as having, besides weaknesses, strengths on which education could build, and perceived the possibility that, in respect to the real weaknesses, a community school might serve as a center for helping the whole black community to cope and to change. Wilcox's writings combined many contributions—from John Dewey, in regard to problem-solving, a respect for the child as a self-motivated learner, and involvement of the school with the reality of the child's social experiences; from Leonard Covello, who earlier in the century had sought to use the New York high school of which he was principal as a lever for change in the immigrant Italian community; and a kind of old-fashioned Jeffersonian view of the political intelligence of the average man—to produce a program for not only a community-controlled school but a community school. (This may be the place to say that it seems to me nonsense to assert, as "professional" defenders of the system do, that a man who votes to decide who is going to run the nation is not capable of voting to decide who is going to run his child's school.) Perhaps most influential in his thinking was the Child Development Group in Mississippi (CDGM) which itself had developed out of the Freedom Schools of the civil rights movement, which sprang up throughout the South, but especially in Mississippi, during the summer of 1964 and subsequently. Both the Freedom Schools and CDGM had the aim to organize the community around education for social change.

In Wilcox's first important contribution on the subject, which was published at a critical time in the struggle, he wrote:

If one believes that a segregated white school can be a "good" school, then one must believe that a segregated Negro and Puerto Rican school, . . . can be a "good" school also. We must be concerned with those who are left behind and who will be left behind even if the best conceivable school desegregation program should be implemented. And behind my concern lies the conviction that one can be black (or white or Puerto Rican), reside and attend school in an enforced ghetto, and still be successfully educated to the limits of his potentialities.

He then proposed the establishment of a community school which would function as a community center, offering after-school programs, adult education, tutorial programs for younger children, community projects, discussion of community problems (welfare, police brutality), and presentation of cultural events.

And he concluded by pointing out the implications of his proposal:

. . . the present system has failed, and is failing, in its task of enabling minority group youth to seize the opportunities America holds out to its other citizens. Of course the fault is not entirely the system's. But what this experimental program offers is the possibility that, in at least one school in one community, the school administrators

and teachers will be made accountable to the community, and the community made obligated to them in such a way that responsibility for successes and failures is shared. *In the process, one can expect the school in the ghetto to become what schools in more privileged areas are, a reflection of local interests and resources, instead of a subtle rejection of them. For the operating philosophy of the existing system is too often manifested in a conscious or unconscious belittling of the values and life styles of much of its clientele. By granting that clientele access to the direction of the school, a vicious circle of blame and rejection may be broken. For the students at the school this should mean a significant change in the current pattern of rewards and punishments. Instead of approval being attached almost exclusively to matters of comportment and dress, rewards may come to be derived from one's obligation to his peers and community. We must find a better balance between scholarship and citizenship. Able to bring what is of value to him into the classroom, he may find there the courage to build on it. For the parents (and as many of them as possible should be enlisted in the program) an active participation in positions of influence in the school should help to bring about a change in their positions in the larger community.*

Thus, beside all else, the School-Community Committee represents an effort to activate parents in the ghetto to assume a kind of responsibility which the dominant society has failed to exercise and from which they [the parents] stand to gain the most, the education of their own children. This effort will be wrought with controversy and conflict, but it must be made.[8]

In the attempt that ensued, during the first few years after Wilcox's paper was published, not the educational proposals but only the controversy and the conflict were the instrument of social change. At no time during the struggle for community control did any community in New York City have anything like the control over its schools that would have enabled it to test out new educational and social-change programs in a serious, long-term way. But the struggle itself educated hundreds of thousands of people (professionals and nonprofessionals) to the schools' failures and their indifference to their failures; to what the children (and their teachers) were experiencing in school and what they might hope or expect to experience in school; to the dramatic need for social change and the way in which community and parent involvement in schools might be instruments of social change.

Indeed, only by struggling for power and status in the schools could parents, community members, students, and some teachers come to understand how powerless they were and how their powerlessness was reflected in the children's schooling. "Power concedes nothing without a demand," quotes one of Preston Wilcox's papers from the great American Frederick Douglass. "It never did, and it never will. Find out just what people will submit to, and you have found out the exact amount of injustice and wrong which will be imposed upon them and these will continue till they are resisted with either words or blows, or with both."[9]

The Combatants and the Styles of the Struggle

America's black belt stretches from below Lowndes County, Alabama, to above Madison Avenue and 127th Street, with some uncolored patches in between. And during the summer of 1966, the slogan "black power" and the symbol the black panther ("Move on over or we'll move on over you!") made the trip north as easily as generations of dispossessed black men and women had done. Signifying a disenchantment with the (non)achievements of the integrated black-and-white movement and a development of the concept of the integrated black community ("We've to get ourselves together."), the idea of black power fitted into the bitterness and distrust that Harlem's spokesmen for education were experiencing very intensely at just that time.

The hopes and the disappointments of the movement to integrate New York City's schools were not significantly less intense than those of the movement to integrate the juries and the voter rolls of Lowndes County. I recall standing outside 110 Livingston Street in February, 1964, in what felt to be an immense and immensely powerful body of children and adults in the demonstration that marked the glorious finale to the first boycott for school integration in New York City. We peered over one another's heads to see the singing marchers keep coming from across the Brooklyn Bridge to join us. Beside me a tall young student was jumping up and down shouting, "Look at all those cats coming!" in a kind of ecstasy of solidarity and hope. It wasn't that different, except perhaps more restrained in tone, in Albany, Georgia, or Selma, Alabama, or Greenwood, Mississippi. But as glorious as is the trip into ecstasy, the coming down is bitter.

In Harlem, reality looked different, at least at first, from what it looked like in Selma or Albany or Greenwood. It was less honest and less openly brutal.

Once, when I told a prominent staff member of the United Federation of Teachers that I was writing a book about the power struggle for the New York schools, she opened her eyes very wide and said, "Oh? Do you think there's a power struggle for the schools?" And yet, despite her innocence, she made her own effective contributions to the strategy of the defense. A posture of innocence was perhaps the most striking characteristic of the defenders of the school system throughout the struggle for community control. Each group defending its own status within the system and all together defending a status system dressed out as an educational system directed toward the victims' own good, the defenders succeeded for a time in convincing the "public" that they were conceding when indeed they were hardening; that they were benefactors when indeed they were malefactors; that the system was improving when indeed it had collapsed; that they were defending the common good when what they were defending was a set of exceedingly narrow class and group interests; and that they were struggling among themselves when indeed they were in unacknowledged concordance to defeat what they saw as a common threat. Because the institutions which had to be attacked if power was to change hands were institutions of order—if not of growth or creativity—the defenders could logically appeal to desires for peace and control. And they could speak in the quiet tones appropriate to appeals for order. Because their own resources were stable and considerable, they could advocate patience. And because the public, and the children, would suffer in a power struggle differently, or more visibly, than they already suffered under the established distribution of power, the defenders could counsel limiting the struggle in the interests of the children. The tone which the defenders adopted may well have convinced even some of themselves.

The central bureaucracy, sometimes called simply the board of ed, as the ultimate source of all administrative power in the system, was the first focus of the rebels' attack. For a time, the central bureaucracy defended itself alone, in the way a bureaucracy defends itself: by absorbing criticism and complaint and diffusing them throughout its monstrous spongelike apparatus. It takes years for a large bureaucracy to become supersaturated and start to sweat out drops of criticism. By the time that did happen, around 1966-67, other groups in the system began to react, either by adding to the volume of criticism or by absorbing some of it. While at first one could not be sure what role the others were playing, it gradually became clear that the supervisors and the major weight of the teachers were going to coalesce with the central bureaucracy in such a way as to enable all to absorb far more criticism together than any could absorb alone. The teachers, after having for so long played the role of chief challenger of the bureaucracy and often of the supervisors, could themselves hardly believe that they were playing the role of defenders of the system and protectors of the bureaucracy, and of the supervisors. And they sometimes yapped the old war cries in their perhaps genuine belief that they were still fighting an old trade union battle against the bosses.

To a large extent the press and the media aided the defensive alliance. I suspect that this is partly because journalists, like most people who are accredited by schooling to play the good roles in society, believe that school is a genuine competitive game and not a prescribed ceremony. Therefore the journalists simply could not see what schools do to black children (and more generally, to all those at the bottom). Partly also, the press and the media men were seduced by the defenders' sweet rhetoric of reason and offended by the attackers' raucousness. Lacking any institutional device for registering their dissatisfaction with the role their children were chosen to play, the attackers made frontal assaults. They were not patient, they did not speak of the school system in the kinds of euphemisms press and public were accustomed to hear, and they were not respectful of the kind of order and procedures which they believed were harmful to their children. While they were not, most of them, disruptive for the sake of being disruptive, the logic of the struggle itself pushed them from pleas to demands, from petitions to demonstrations, from courtesy to hostility, from alliances with white liberals to alliances with Black Panthers. And as they moved to these latter positions, the defenders and the press gave it out that community control entailed extremism and violence—when it was precisely the losing battle for community control that was producing extremism and violence. As if the achievements of bourgeois democracy should be judged by the events of the Reign of Terror.

Middle-class America is accustomed to and does not morally condemn evasiveness, contempt of low-status individuals, manipulativeness, disingenuousness, slyness, and institutional (i.e., repressive rather than aggressive) violence. And it is accustomed to and does not recognize race-biased institutions and often even covertly race-biased individuals. But middle-class America is spiritually and morally outraged by overt individual violence, disruption of daily routine, aggressiveness, contempt of institutions, and profanity and vulgarity in public. The former are the styles in which defenders of a system are likely to express hostility and power, the latter the style of balked rebels.

Besides the press and the media, a solid cadre of respected liberals (with whom the United Federation of Teachers had close spiritual and personal ties) and individuals and groups representing the upper reaches of power in the city contributed both to the confusion and to the masking of the terms of the struggle.

In the white liberal community, the smell of black power wafting up from the Mississippi Meredith March in the late spring of 1966 was producing signs of distress that forbode ill. I was living in Atlanta, Georgia, in 1966 and traveling a good deal in the rural South. When I made a visit to New York that autumn, I was struck by how much more distressed white New York was by black power than white Atlanta or white Alabama. For the latter, black power was another slogan for what they had said all along they weren't having any of. But for white New Yorkers, black power seemed to be a black repudiation of all faith and hope in the America which they saw, and in them. It seemed to me that my New York friends were having their feelings hurt. Also that they were angry. Angry at black power. And angry at me because I wasn't angry. The little anger at the idea of black power in Alabama and Mississippi which intruded like a thin chill between me and my liberal friends during that autumn of 1966 eventually blew into a towering rage at the idea of black power in Harlem, and it so tore up the liberal white community that it will probably not mend in this generation. I suspect (along with one of my liberal friends who found her footing somewhere on the same side of the chasm as I) that more than a strategic, political question was involved for the white community, that we were having to confront our whole concept of black and white America and of the role and status therein of liberals and white intellectuals. Two years later when a large segment of the liberal-intellectual community—wholly missing, I believed, the essence of the UFT-community-control dispute—took a stand against the community, I wondered at first why, since they were not involved as the teachers were, they were so blinded. Of course, I was mistaken. They were as deeply involved as the teachers: as intellectuals, their investment in a historical and political weltanschauung was as heavy as the teachers' investment in their job tenure. Through the years of the community-control struggle, the liberal-trade-unionist bloc wove an elaborate rationale of support which clothed the defenders of the system in a mantle of political and intellectual respectability which was ever so much more classy than the vulgar garb of Chief Pritchard or Bull Connor, but looked to the black observers like the same old white man's suit.

At the upper reaches of power, where sat McGeorge Bundy of the Ford Foundation and John Lindsay, Republican mayor of the City of New York, the interest in rationalizing the administrative operation, in making the educational dollar produce, and in reducing discontent among the most discontented resulted in support for decentralization and to some extent for community control. But America is after all a democracy. And when the price of administrative reform and reducing discontent among the most discontented (who were still a minority) turned out to be a mass rage among the only somewhat discontented (who were the majority), those at the upper reaches of power withdrew their support.

These generalizations about the styles and the alliances of the defenders and the rebels are exemplified in the struggle for community control at the I.S. 201 Complex, which began roughly a school year before the board of education was to designate it a demonstration district. Perhaps the telling of the story will throw some light on the ways in which bureaucracies and their challengers interact to produce an impasse, and so, as history, be helpful to groups in other cities where the same problems have still to be confronted. The alliances and the enmities, the strategies and the maneuvers which came to public attention at the time of the Great Strike of 1968 in respect to another demonstration district, Ocean Hill-Brownsville in Brooklyn, had been created and tried out two years earlier in Harlem. So the fate of Ocean Hill-Brownsville and I.S. 201 and of community control in one city were bound up together, and the end was already there in the beginnings. And the story is also told for its own sake. For a few dramatic moments in educational history, public attention had been focused on a "showcase" school that was rejected by the black community whom it was meant to serve and on a principal who was "sacrificed to black power."

2. THE 201 STORY

Trying on Alliances: The Skirmish of 1966

In May, 1964, three months after what then seemed to me the "glorious finale" to the first boycott, which produced some euphoria and no integration, New York State Commissioner of Education Allen proposed in a report for the New York City Board of Education that a series of

* *A good deal of the background information for the early phase of the 201 struggle is taken from a twenty-five page manuscript entitled "Sequence of Events Surrounding Community Involvement with Public School 201," prepared by the 201 Negotiating Committee. It covers the period 1958 to September, 1966. Beginning with early 1966, this account is very detailed, reporting individual meetings, sometimes several in one day, phone calls, and so on. I checked and brought up to date the reporting in the account, referred to in the text as the "chronology," with accounts in the* United Teacher, *and conversations and correspondence with community, teacher, parent, UFT, board of education, and supervisory participants. Other primary sources for the 201 story include notes and minutes of meetings; written proposals, published and unpublished; the 201 newsletter and other releases; board of education releases; Ford Foundation releases; interviews with board of education and Ford Foundation personnel; the vertical file on*

newly formed "middle schools," standing between elementary and high schools, be created in "ghetto fringe areas" to improve ethnic balance in grades five through eight.[1] Fifth-grade children would be moved from segregated neighborhood elementary schools to integrated middle schools drawing on a wider and ethnically more diverse geographic area. "Over the period 1964 to 1970," the report said, "the abolition of junior high schools could make a substantial contribution, particularly to preventing future growth in the number of upper-level ghetto schools. While some segregation will remain in the middle schools, it might be possible to so organize the cluster of primary schools which feed each middle school to increase the racial heterogeneity of most of these middle schools." The writers of the report, who together possessed considerable educational, psychological, and administrative know-how, also thought that shuffling the various ages among different schools would benefit the children. The ninth graders would benefit from moving on one year earlier into high school and the seventh and eighth graders would benefit by not being

201 of the Metropolitan Applied Research Center. Also, beginning in January, 1968, I attended many meetings at 201; served as a substitute teacher in I.S. 201 on a few occasions; observed classes in all the schools in the Complex; talked with teachers, principals, and parents; and spent many hours over a period of more than a year talking with, observing, and generally tagging around after various people on the Governing Board and in the unit director's office, especially the unit director himself.

Besides the New York Times *and the* Amsterdam News, *the following secondary sources were referred to: Dorothy S. Jones, "The Issues at I.S. 201: A View from the Parents' Committee,"* Integrated Education, *October-November 1966; Jeremy Larner, "I.S. 201: Disaster in the Schools,"* Dissent, *January-February 1967;* IRCD Bulletin, *Winter 1966-1967; Thomas K. Minter,* Intermediate School 201, Manhattan: Center of Controversy, *Cambridge, Massachusetts, June 2, 1967;* Report on Three Demonstration Projects in the City Schools, *New York City Commission on Human Rights, February-March 1968;* Final Report of the Advisory Committee on Decentralization *("Niemeyer Report"), July,1968.*

As I found little disagreement among the participants and the accounts in respect to the actual events surrounding the controversy, I have refrained from burdening my account with a multitude of source footnotes. References are given for long quotations and for any details about whose source or authentication I think the reader might be curious.

exposed to the ninth graders' "antagonism and indifference toward school induced by the onset of adolescence."

As so often with experts, they knew their books better than they knew the children. Great numbers of children in poor communities are smoking and dating at ten or eleven and having sexual relations at twelve and thirteen. Only the books could talk about "the *onset* of adolescence" at fourteen or fifteen. What actually happened with the organizing of the middle schools, which came to be called intermediate schools, is that the anarchic ambience of the junior high schools (so many of which fall into the class of chaos schools) was extended downward to include fifth- and sixth-grade children, and the repressive ambience of the high schools was extended downward to include ninth-grade children—and ethnic balance in ghetto areas did not improve one iota. For the experts also failed to take account of the prejudices and pressures to which all previous integration efforts in New York City had succumbed. In the effort to improve the educational experience of poor nonwhite children, the creation of intermediate schools was doomed to fail for the same reason that Higher Horizons, after-school tutoring, programed learning, and legislative decentralization were doomed to fail: neither purely administrative nor purely pedagogical solutions can possibly award the respect and dignity without which there can be no effective teaching and learning. The fact is that top echelon personnel and experts know little of the reality of life in the schoolroom and are thus of all people the least competent to exercise the decision-making power that they are so bitterly reluctant to yield.

One of the schools where the idea of the middle schools was put into effect and exemplified was Intermediate School 201, situated in east Harlem school district 4. The "windowless showcase," as I.S. 201 has been called, was first proposed in 1958 as a junior high school. After the board of education and the architectural firm Curtis and Wright had agreed to plans for the building, the local school board of district 4 was consulted. (Local school boards had been revitalized in 1961 as a way of drawing community groups into school decision making. The local boards were for nine years the unhappy children of the parent board which appointed and then more or less ignored them. The

Decentralization Act of 1969 provided for their election by local parents and citizens, but in respect to power, they continued to be subject to the central board.) Asked by the local board if the community had been consulted about the plans, a board of education spokesman said no but "they were sure the community would be delighted." The board must have reasoned that people who have had to wait so long for any new building at all had better be delighted with whatever you give them, wherever you put it.

At a meeting sponsored by the local school board, people expressed worries about the lack of playground space in the proposed building and the effect on the children's health of the air conditioning that was going to be installed. And, indeed, when the building was erected, the effect of the windowlessness on the children's health, and tempers, was disastrous for two years because blockage of the ventilation ducts prevented almost all ventilation. Only when some prominent members of the larger community holding a meeting in the building experienced the 80° airlessness were engineers finally called in to rectify a situation that had existed from the time the building opened. (It may be recalled that one of the demands of the Harlem spokesmen from the beginning had been for the community to have control over custodial services and repair and construction of buildings. They felt necessary repairs shouldn't have to wait until, say, the president of the Carnegie Corporation chances to be around and says, "It's too hot in here.")

In 1964 construction was begun, spokesmen for the board continuing to allay anxieties about the architectural plan with reassurances that a special curriculum would attract white Queens pupils from across the Triborough Bridge, so that Dr. Allen's integration plan for intermediate schools would be fulfilled. Although the community had been told it would be consulted about the name for the new showcase integrated school, the name "Arthur Schomburg School" was announced in the board of education *Staff Bulletin* while the community was still submitting ideas for a name.

The chronology of events surrounding community involvement in I.S. 201, prepared by the 201 Negotiating Committee, as the group of concerned advocates of a fair deal for the 201 constituency came to be called reports:

Miffed by the breach of trust over the naming of the school, parents began pressing for details on the school's program, the specifics of the zoning, the selection of staff, etc. No satisfactory answers were forthcoming from staff members of the School System . . . The community surrounding 201 became increasingly aroused by the lack of responsible action or even answers *from responsible school officials. Community and Parents' Association meetings were held to discuss the developing crisis. Previous to this time, almost all of the conversations regarding 201 were held* outside *the East Harlem community and did not include parents and community persons who were responsible for the new school.*

The chronology at this point, January, 1966, begins to convey that sense of galling irritation we all experience when the bureaucrat remains persistently incommunicado. While this style of operation is characteristic of many large organizations which have no mechanisms for dealing with a complaining client, the petitioners felt that racist arrogance was involved as well. "Under increasing pressure from the community," reads an entry for February, 1966, "Mr. Schreiber [assistant superintendent for district 4] announced that 201 would be an 'integrated' school. When pressed as to how this was to be achieved, he explained that it would contain 'representative members of Negro and Puerto Rican children.' " The writer adds with neat matter-of-factness, "This had the obvious result of fanning community anger." Later, when, in order to achieve this new idea in integration, the district was gerrymandered eastwards to pick up the Puerto Rican children whom the board was going to integrate with the black children, the Puerto Ricans felt they were being used. If the board had been trying to find a way to exacerbate the hostilities and misunderstandings that so often divide Afro-American and Spanish-American communities, it could not have done better. I suspect, however, that the ploy was produced not by conscious intention to divide and conquer but simply by the bureaucrat's customary colossal insensitivity to people's needs and feelings. Or, as the chronology entry of April 26, 1966, puts it, "By now the school had become a symbol of the bad faith of the public school system and the contempt which its officials held for parents in the ghetto."

Throughout the spring and summer of 1966, the 201 Negotiating Committee expended its greatest energies not negotiating but merely trying to find a responsible official with whom it could negotiate. Representatives of the board of education never spoke with authority for themselves but always for some distant, more highly placed persons. The mayor, the state Commissioner of Education Allen, and the United States Commissioner for Education Harold Howe bounced petitions around among themselves and back to the New York City Board of Education, which was, they all felt, the responsible agent. So that by the time early in the summer a high bureaucrat of the board was proposing "continuing dialogue," the Harlem negotiators were sick of dialoguing without communicating and decided to try some nonverbal communication. They said that unless they had assurances that I.S. 201 would open as a top-quality integrated school they were not going to allow it to open in September at all.

Meanwhile, the board had appointed Stanley Lisser, principal of another Harlem school, as principal of 201, and Lisser had set about to "hand-pick" an integrated staff to serve under him. During the summer the staff underwent ten training sessions for which they were paid by the board of education $30 a session. Three major areas were covered in this training: familiarity with the new curriculum; the philosophy that would underlie the teaching; and orientation to the new building. Lisser also sought to recruit white children for the school, as if single-handedly he could redeem the board's early promises that 201 would be an integrated school. But he did not succeed: the leaflets he prepared to be sent home with eligible white children somehow rarely got as far as the children's hands; and when he tried to arrange for board of education buses to carry into Harlem the few white children he had recruited, he was told that the buses only went in the other direction!

Anyway, it was already too late. Certainly too late for poor Lisser, who was the surf swimmer making all the correct motions to ride the wave in sight (integration), only to see that wave suddenly disappear and to be knocked breathless and have his mouth filled with brine (of which he would never forget the taste) by the powerful unseen wave (community control) behind it. And almost too late for the teachers, conscientiously preparing themselves to teach the children whose parents were preparing not to let them enter school.

Then, out of the cotton fields of Alabama came the black panther—to speak in the voice of the Columbia University professor of social work, Preston Wilcox, who published in July, 1966, in *The Urban Review* the short piece referred to above, "The Controversy Over I.S. 201: One View and a Proposal." Besides roughly sketching out a philosophy for a community-controlled school in a poor black community, the paper made one specific organizational proposal which was then and continued to be a key community-control demand, a demand which again and again was flung against the hardest resistance of one of the most powerful groups in the school system. Wilcox wrote:

Principals in the New York public school system have far more power and independence vis-à-vis the Board than is generally realized or than they generally take advantage of. As such men as Edward Gottlieb and Elliot Shapiro have positively shown, the psychological stance of the principal toward his pupils and their backgrounds is a critical factor in his performance as an educator.

A principal prepared to exploit his position for the benefit of his students is an inestimable asset to the community; such a man is the sine qua non of this experimental program. That the principal should be accountable to the parents of his students will be a new, and probably disagreeable experience for most men who have held this post in the New York system. But the man best suited for the role proposed here would be one whose devotion to education did not depend on his isolation from the community. Instead of being committed to the elimination in his pupils of all that he feels is repulsive in their backgrounds and values, this principal would be committed to utilizing these values as a resource for education.[2]

Although a relative outsider to the school system, Wilcox perceived the extent to which the principal is, educationally though not administratively, a relatively free agent in the system. It was this educational freedom that enabled the principals to scotch whatever small plans for integration the board of education put forth, as demonstrated in Rogers' *110 Livingston Street*. Indeed, it was probably the principals who were responsible for the fact that Stanley Lisser's notes to white parents to send their children to 201 never reached their intended recipients. To a large extent the principal was responsible for the difference between Miss Jersild's Harlem school and John Brown Junior High. But if, as we have seen, the merit system is blind to the difference between an orderly, controlled, civilized candidate and a disorderly, vulgarly authoritarian, panic-prone one, surely it has no instruments that can distinguish a candidate who is committed to "the elimination in his pupils of all that he feels is repulsive in their backgrounds and values" from one who "would be committed to utilizing these values as a resource for education."

This paragraph of Wilcox's was a gauntlet thrown to the "merit system," deliberate and crucial. Anyone on the side of the community-control advocates who might have believed for one moment that, despite this threat—to their careers, their security, and most important their self-image—the principals and the aspiring principals of New York City would support, or refrain from attacking, community control out of respect for the mere "good of the children" had to be an innocent. The same must be said for anyone on the opposing side of the board or the Council of Supervisory Associations who might have believed that the community-control advocates would withdraw this keystone of their program out of respect for a mere "merit system."

Whether the teachers would or would not acquiesce in a proposal that principals be chosen by their constituencies (instead of winning them as prizes in a board of education contest, as John Nailor, a black principal at a 201 school, once put it) I think could not have been so certainly predicted. The UFT had for years favored the election of supervisors by school staffs, and it looked for a little as if the union might go along with a plan for appointment of principals by a community-teacher governing board, similar to the one that 201 eventually created. But the teachers were balancing dangerously between supporting a revolution, limited in scope but daring, and supporting the status quo, which they themselves had so often before challenged.

Wilcox did not structure the issue of the principal in terms of a black male. But if this was not implicit in his formulation, it very quickly became a significant embodiment of it, and it was the point that provoked perhaps the greatest outrage from the defenders. Two silly arguments were put forth against the point.

One: "The merit system must be color-blind. Since when do we pick a man for a job or fire him on the basis of his color? Would you pick a surgeon to operate on your child because he was black if you knew a white surgeon was better? Those children are entitled to the best principal we can give them whether he is black, white, green, or polka dot."

Two: "Those people are not the least bit interested in the children or in education. All they are after is jobs. If you allow this thing to go on, every good job in the school system will be up for grabs."

Now the green and the polka dot argument is a tedious cliché evasion: everyone knows that what we are talking about in America, and have been talking about since 1619, is not green and polka dot but black and white. The merit system is not at all color-blind but has built-in devices for distinguishing the dark- from the light-complected. In general, in America, we do not of course choose an objectively inferior black man for a skilled job, but we do, often enough, base our choice of the white man on the assumption, possibly even in the face of evidence to the contrary, that the black man is inferior. Second, the black men were indeed fighting to get the jobs that the white men were fighting to retain. The collective gasp of outrage that issued from the throat of white liberal New York when the fight for the appointment of black principals began in earnest was another of the disingenuous and illogical responses which continued to mark the entire course of the battle.

The question "Would the children, and the black community generally, be benefitted by the promotion of black men teachers, qualified by the system's own criteria to be school supervisors?" was hardly ever asked. An educator is not a surgeon or an engineer or a computer programer. He is a human being who interacts with other human beings to produce change. What is beautiful and good and powerful is what looks and acts beautiful and good and powerful, and there is no doubt in my mind that the children would be infinitely more benefited by seeing black men in positions of authority, over whites as well as over other blacks, than by all the cant about black is good and black is beautiful.* Any one who grew up seeing Negroes only in roles subservient to whites and who is halfway honest about how this affected his concept of the relative dignity of the two races and of himself as a member of one of them has to understand this.

What would happen to the unemployed white principals who have put in a lifetime in the school system if black men were to be hired in large numbers to supervise predominantly black schools is another question, and it deserves consideration. Surely we would not want them standing on street corners or running off so their wives and children would be eligible for welfare. But to be answered seriously, the questions must be posed seriously. I should think there would be no good reason, except the prevailing view of the importance of principals and the unimportance of teaching children, why they oughtn't to be set to teaching children—and keep their principals' salaries.

This, in any case, was the wave massing behind the front wave that Lisser, and any other members of the white community who might have been watching from the shore, could see.

By August—irked to action, perhaps, by the Negotiating Committee's running all around the place enlisting the aid of the United States Commission on Civil Rights, the United States Commissioner of Education Harold Howe, and State Commissioner Allen, and by the threat of a parents' boycott in September—Superintendent of Schools Bernard Donovan and board of education President Lloyd Garrison themselves were finally meeting with the Negotiating Committee. They heard a new tune: either desegregation or "total community control." The representatives of the board said they had legal

* *The radical black view of the triangle white-man/black-man/black-woman in the American national neurosis is presented by the now enormously popular writer Eldridge Cleaver, especially in* Soul on Ice *(Delta, 1968). Cleaver is not interested, theoretically, in the significance of the triangle for the fourth party, the white woman. But we ought to be.*

responsibility for the schools and could not abdicate their responsibility; members of the Negotiating Committee said the board had already abdicated its responsibility by not educating their children. Elsewhere Lisser, still making swimming motions, was meeting with the few white parents he thought he might be able to persuade to send their children to 201, and once or twice with the local (black and Puerto Rican) parents to tell them what the school would be offering them. And the teachers, all black-and-white-together, including a Negro lady assistant principal, Beryl Banfield, were getting ready for first day of school.

Everyone says teachers and parents are the natural allies in wresting control of the schools from the distant bureaucrats. But if you ask people who were on the Negotiating Committee how come they didn't go to the teachers and Lisser to enlist support for their cause, they are likely to say, "They weren't our people, they were brought in by the board from the outside." And if you ask Lisser how come he made no attempt to deal in depth directly with the increasingly angry community, he says that while he knew there was a wider issue of desegregating the whole system, he felt that if the school was perceived to be running effectively and especially if it had an integrated staff, he would be let alone by the community while they "negotiated" the broader issues with the board (a ploy the New Leftists call co-opting).

The teachers and the parents didn't talk to each other partly because they were not accustomed to talking to each other. The distance between them was a distance created and sustained by a status system which makes teachers believe that black parents are not able to make a contribution to educational process and black parents suspect that teachers do not wish to make a contribution.

Lisser's comment that the board possibly intended him to be the buffer in a strategy of evasion and delay may well have been an accurate assessment. Undoubtedly the board would have been happy to go on indefinitely negotiating the broader issues while 201 functioned "effectively" (in the universe of Harlem schools), neither integrated in its student body nor controlled by the community. But the Negotiating Committee was making its stand here: in this place, at this time. A revolution has to begin somewhere not everywhere.

And it fell to the windowless, hollow-box building on 127th Street to be Harlem's Bastille.

When the guerrilla action of 1966 began, the two most intimately concerned parties (the community and the teachers) took strong independent stands vis à vis the board of education, and when it ended the board of education was stronger than it had been, and the two natural allies were on their way to engaging each other in one of the most vicious fratricidal slaughters of New York's history. It seems to me conceivable that the teachers, who are at the bottom of the professional status ladder and next to the bottom of the entire status ladder, might have made an alliance with those at the level below them—the parents—to become with them advocates of their common charge, the children. That they did not perhaps derived more from bad habit than from bad intention. Once, discussing some outrageous, complicated, but withal quite gratuitous miscarriage of justice perpetrated against some southern Negroes, I asked an experienced and decent southern white liberal if he thought the white establishment had sat up all night figuring to make it come out that way. "No," he said, "they just have to act the way they've always been used to acting and that's the way it comes out." That's what makes social change so tedious: habit is ever so much more insidious than conspiracy. As it appeared at that time, however, the teachers helped to shore up the crumbling bulwarks of the board of education against the second, unseen wave. Many will disagree, but I believe they did it unwittingly and inadvertently, just by acting "the way they'd always been used to acting."

Eventually the activities of a handful of teachers in the skirmish of September, 1966, rolled up a burden of strategic logic which propelled the entire United Federation of Teachers away from a "natural alliance" with parents and into a different alliance—with the supervisors and against the parents. Because the few 201 teachers in effect levered all the teachers' weight to that side at that time, it is important to observe in detail what happened.

Thursday, August 18, 1966. Community representatives demand that 201 not be opened until a satisfactory agreement has been worked out between it and the board of education; that is, they will boycott 201 when the school term begins.

Wednesday, September 7 (five days before scheduled school opening on September 12). The teachers at I.S. 201 organize a chapter of the United Federation of Teachers.

Thursday, September 8. Declaring that the school will not open on Monday, community representatives walk out of a meeting with board President Lloyd Garrison after he issues an ultimatum to them that unless they withdraw their demand for community control, nothing can go forward.

Friday, September 9. A representative from the UFT visits the new chapter and tells the teachers that they will have to decide for themselves whether or not they wish to support the impending parents' boycott, but that if they decide to do so, the union will protect them against reprisals from the board.

This little moment will not return.

Saturday, September 10. Parents of children scheduled to attend 201 receive a special delivery letter reminding them that school will open as scheduled on Monday.

The board is trying to bull it through.

Sunday, September 11, 2 a.m. A group of east Harlem representatives visit the board's assistant superintendent in charge of integration and urge him to use his influence with the board to delay school opening until some agreement has been achieved. They point out that opening school at this point may be dangerous.

In the summer of 1966, Chicago, the Hough section of Cleveland, and even quiet old Atlanta had experienced uprisings, most of them provoked by relatively minor incidents of injustice or harassment in black communities. The parents' suggestion that opening school might be dangerous may be viewed as an objective warning or as a tactical threat. For some of the 201 activists, the always hovering young black radicals in the streets may have seemed a potential danger to their movement; for others, a potential strength. For all, it was clear that the force was there; they could not wholly control it, but they had to take account of it.

Sixteen hours after the meeting, the board of education announces to the press that, to alleviate community tensions, children scheduled to attend I.S. 201

on Monday will report instead to the schools they had attended the previous school term. "The community and the Board of Education," the press release goes on in that lovely we're-all-trying-so-hard-together tone that the board likes to affect, "have been seeking a method by which the community can participate more fully in the operation of the school."

The community has apparently achieved at least a stand-off, the first in its years of negotiations with the board.

Monday, September 12. With picketers from the community on the sidewalk continuing the nonverbal communication, community representatives and Superintendent Donovan meet inside 201 to discuss ways in which a community educational council can help "make parents responsible for the education of their children." Dr. Donovan responds "with sympathy" to the community's demands and says that if necessary he will go to the legislature for enabling legislation to "make possible a creative role for a community council."

The negotiations take up: use of paraprofessionals in the school, after-school programs, curriculum (Negro and Puerto Rican history), and personnel. The community wants a black man principal for the school. There is some kicking around of that question.

Depending on the relative strength of the defending alliance and the rebel forces, board negotiators and spokesmen swung between the position that their legal mandate prevented this or that concession and the position that the board would request legislative action where it had no legal authority to make such concessions as it wished to make.

Saturday, September 17, after a week of discussion. A format for a community council (not too different from what eventually will become the Governing Board) is worked out. It is agreed that as the 201 children are not receiving much instruction in the elementary schools, they will be moved to an old unused building nearby, P.S. 103, for the few more days that it is expected it will take to arrive at a preliminary agreement. The community position is hardening into two immediate demands: that 201 not be opened until an agreement is reached between them and Donovan; that the immediate gain be at least the removal of Lisser and the appointment of a black or Puerto Rican male principal. It seems as if Donovan is getting ready to yield on the principal in order to get the school open: he instructs the parents to send their children to old P.S. 103 on Monday morning and orders 201 to be kept closed.

Monday, September 19. Now Lisser, with nothing in his training or experience as a New York City principal to prepare him to be a basketball, is dribbled around the floor and exchanged between teams in a dizzying display of game tactics, which only a slow motion replay can recapture.

8 a.m. The teachers send five of their members to inspect P.S. 103 and find it without sufficient books and equipment for teaching. Daring to violate Donovan's orders, they boldly march *into the officially closed 201* where they hold a meeting to decide how to proceed. A large delegation from the UFT office, including Union President Albert Shanker, is present and assures the teachers that the union will provide "full moral and material support" in their boycott of P.S. 103—a boycott, that is, *against the parents,* who need to keep I.S. 201 closed to win what they are demanding—even though, ten days before, the union had promised support for the teachers if they decided to boycott I.S. 201 *in support of the parents.*

"The announcement that the 201 teachers would refuse to go into P.S. 103 came as a bad shock," Dorothy Jones, one of the community leaders, wrote a few months later. "In an attempt to head off this teacher action, I was able to reach some of the Union leadership by telephone that day. Though some of the leadership was sympathetic, it developed that it was impossible to stop the action."[3]

UFT people with whom I spoke shortly after these events seemed to be proud of the independence and militancy of the 201 teachers at this juncture. One old UFT radical said of the teachers' maneuver that they "occupied 201 the way the workers had occupied the Ford plant in 1936," as if the repetition of its form could renew the grandeur and meaning of that now accepted older revolution. At last, a group of teachers were exercising professional judgment and decision making on behalf of their students, in defiance of administrative order! Was Donovan's order which the teachers defied (an order in support of the parents) serious? Or was it, like Miss White's admonition to the children not to laugh at poor Collins, whom she herself has been holding up to scorn, an order that screened a conflicting message? Whichever, the bosses capitulate to the teachers so fast that the union's material support amounts to all of fifty box lunches.

11:30 a.m. Donovan tells the Negotiating Committee: (1) he has decided to retain Lisser; (2) 201 will open on Tuesday.

The strength of character Donovan had demonstrated over months to the Negotiating Committee crumbled in a morning when the teachers took a stand.

12:15 p.m. The Negotiating Committee, feeling betrayed by the teachers' presence in 201 just at the point when they thought they had scored a point, sends representatives to the teachers' meeting "to attempt to interpret [for the teachers] what the parents' demands really were. There seemed to exist little understanding on the part of the teachers about what the parents had been fighting for so many months," the chronology reports. A teacher participant remembers the community representatives as being angry and hostile.

1 p.m. Donovan then informs community representatives that negotiations with them will go forward after all; that Mr. Lisser has requested reassignment; and that while Negro and Puerto Rican applicants for the principalship are being screened, one of the assistant principals, Beryl Banfield, will serve as acting principal. (It is said that Donovan informed her of her elevation by smacking her familiarly on some part of her and saying, "Well, Beryl, you're the new principal," in that style of condescending familiarity so many schoolmen adopt not only toward Negroes and not only toward women but toward all inferiors. But perhaps the story is apocryphal.)

In exchange for an agreement by the Negotiating Committee that they will allow the school to open the next day, Tuesday, Donovan promises that Lisser will be absent from the building. He agrees that 201 will move forward as a demonstration district with a community committee having some kind of function.

The various items in this agreement are announced to the press. The day is over.

Lisser may have been the sacrificial lamb, but after years of humiliating failure to achieve integration, substantially improved education, or power of any kind in the school system, representatives of the black community seem at last to have wrested one little symbol of success from the skirmish. One day at a time. One victory at a time.

Tuesday, September 20. Another long day. A day of tears, sermons, eloquence, principles reaffirmed, principals threatening to resign. A day of militance and independence. A day of defeat. The end of the skirmish, the beginning of the war.

The teachers ride out to Brooklyn to picket 110 Livingston Street to protest Lisser's removal. They enter the portals to confer with the "adversary" (Donovan). President Shanker has called an emergency executive board meeting of the United Federation of Teachers to support the I.S. 201 teachers. Thirty-five principals plan an afternoon meeting to protest the board action; there are rumors that they will resign en masse. The myrmidons are massing.

Lisser in tears meets with his teachers. Beryl Banfield follows with an eloquent sermon about how color should be and is irrelevant to competence.

The teachers vote that if Lisser goes, they go.

"All we knew,"one teacher still at 201 two years later said, "was that the board of education was using Lisser to make a deal. That they were trying to buy off the parents with Lisser." That seems a likely interpretation. But another interpretation is that the teachers did after all, even in the middle of the tears and histrionics, sense the significance for them of the board's gesture to the community. At the meeting between Donovan and the teachers, the teachers "reiterated that, *so long as community involvement did not conflict with basic teacher rights, the merit system and the UFT contract*, they had no objection" [italics supplied].[4] In other words they would buy it if it was not merely cheap but free.

4 p.m. The board of education announces that Stanley Lisser *is* to report to work as principal of 201, on Wednesday morning. Representatives of the parents arriving to speak with the teachers receive the glad tidings from Shanker's lips. "They were disappointed," the *United Teacher* reports.

7 p.m. The news of Lisser's reinstatement had been on the radio for several hours before Donovan finally telephones Mrs. Babette Edwards, one of the community negotiators, and tells it to her personally. Of such simple innocent snubs is the fabric of history woven: you just have to go on acting the same way you've always been used to acting.

Enter from the wings New York's analogue to the South's outside-agitator-nigger-loving-jew-from-the-north, black, Trinidad-born, Bronx High School of Science graduate Stokely Carmichael, fresh from the cotton fields of Alabama, and the highways of Mississippi. His entrance supports the stereotype of I.S. 201 that will terrify New Yorkers in their beds for some time to come.

Here are two versions of the script. The first is from the I.S. 201 chronology.

After Donovan's 7 o'clock phone call to the community, representatives met and framed a telegram:

> *WE OF THE HARLEM COMMUNITY ARE SHOCKED AT THE IRRESPONSIBILITY SHOWN BY THE BOARD OF EDUCATION TOWARD THE HARLEM COMMUNITY BY BREAKING A PUBLIC AGREEMENT BETWEEN THE BOARD AND PARENTS. ONCE AGAIN THE BOARD HAS SHOWN CONTEMPT FOR THE HARLEM COMMUNITY BY APPEASING THOSE FORCES WHO WISH TO DENY EQUAL EDUCATION TO OUR GHETTO CHILDREN. THE BOARD OF EDUCATION'S ACTION HAS PITTED WHITE AGAINST BLACK AND WE WILL HOLD THEM RESPONSIBLE FOR ANY ACTIONS THE COMMUNITY MAY TAKE. THE CONDITIONS FOR FURTHER NEGOTIATIONS WILL BE THE REMOVAL OF STANLEY LISSER AS PRINCIPAL OF I.S. 201. [Emphasis supplied.]*

The telegram was sent to Mayor Lindsay, Superintendent of Schools Donovan, and board President Garrison. Interested groups from Harlem—The Black Panthers, SNCC [the Student Nonviolent Coordinating Committee], The Organization for Afro-American Unity, and the Muslims—who had been watching the struggle with the board, now became actively involved in trying to force the Board of Education and the City back to the negotiating table.

The second is from the special I.S. 201 issue of *The United Teacher:*

[Late Tuesday afternoon, Roy Innis of Harlem CORE *and Livingston Wingate of* HARYOU-ACT *addressed the 201 teachers.]*

Both Mr. Wingate and Mr. Innis, who stated with pride his beliefs in Black Nationalism . . . said that because they considered that "Harlem was a colony" and because "the vehicle of integration has failed and is no longer workable" they would accept the schools "segregated-style," but only with a voice in running their own schools.

Mr. Innis added that by the teachers' action they showed they had every qualification but one: a lack of humanitarian understanding of the "revolutionary situation of the colony of Harlem because of their internalized false white values."

The next day, Wednesday, the parents and demonstrators attempted to "lie-in" in Mr. Lisser's path, got arrested in a near riot, the teachers entered the school as did over 60% of the children.

Stokley Carmichael of SNCC *was on the picket line and black power had officially come to east Harlem.*

We may recapitulate the maneuvers of the various groups at this time as some will be repeated and will again bemuse the average newspaper reader or TV viewer ("I can't figure out what's going on over there."), and also because many of the maneuvers did not have at all the effect that we would have expected from the avowed intentions of the maneuverers, so further contributing to the general bemusement.

The board carries on for many years the standard bureaucratic strategy of delay, postpone, disappear, and pass the buck. The community spokesmen (1) seek the attention of city, state, and national big shots, and (2) threaten street action. The board makes itself available for negotiations, meanwhile allowing to continue the previously initiated line of action (in this instance, by Lisser and the teachers). Negotiations proceed, with the board occasionally having to be again prodded by threats of street action into taking the negotiators' demands seriously.*

Recognizing that the threat of street action means that the negotiators must be dealt with, not as unusually troublesome clients, but as a party of enough potential power to command some respect, the board concedes to one of their major symbolic–and real–demands (for a black male principal). The concession involves the sacrifice perhaps not of real power but of one individual in the middling ranks of the hierarchy. But the remainder of the concerned individuals, down to the lowest ranks (the teachers), plus a number of individuals of the same class as the sacrificed individual, rally to the defense of the sacrificed individual, not in order that power rather than a mere symbol of it should be yielded, but so that nothing should be yielded. In the face of rebellion by its own underlings on its own behalf, the board retracts its concession, not even with courtesy ("I'm a teacher, and you're a child, I don't have to say please to you"). The balked negotiators accede to the entrance of the more radical forces (whether willingly or unwillingly no one will tell). And the defenders cry that just this violent radicalism is what they have been seeking to protect society against.

The status gulfs between the groups, the historical truism that power is never yielded but only extracted, and black suspiciousness of the goodwill of any whites explain most of the above maneuvers. I am left with two questions which I can only pose, not answer.

If, as I assume, there were some among the blacks who understood that the teachers were almost as powerless a group in the system as they and that some at least among the teachers would have seen the possibility that teachers and parents together could be a powerful force for improving the status of both (as well, perhaps, as the education of black children), why did they not hold their suspiciousness in abeyance and seek the support of the 201 teachers long before the very moment when the

* *A lucid and self-conscious description of how to develop this kind of bureaucratic strategy at a lower level in the hierarchy and also how to enlist and deploy bureaucratic underlings as defending allies appeared in a secret paper of the High School Principals Association three years later. See Part III, section 4.*

community's entire position was undermined by the teachers' refusal to enter P.S. 103 on that crucial Monday morning? Certainly by early in the summer when they knew that they were going to have to strong-arm the board into negotiating?

If, as I assume, the politically sophisticated, liberal leadership of the UFT was not interested in destroying the community but only in strengthening the teachers, why did they not play a positive guiding role rather than an apparently permissive one in respect to the young politically unsophisticated teachers? Why did they not attempt to educate them to the significance of the parents' boycott of 201, so as to add to the teachers' strength that of the parents instead of that of the supervisors and bureaucracy, and so as to bring teachers and community group into a mutually supportive instead of a mutually destructive relationship?

This seems to me to have been one of those moments in history when statesmanship on one side or both might have avoided not conflict itself but conflict so structured as inevitably to damage most the powerless and the vulnerable.

Getting Together in Harlem: September, 1966, to September, 1967

The board's strategy, enunciated by Lisser, of trying to hold the line on 201 while negotiating "the broader issues" downtown didn't work. On the contrary, membership in the conflict-community (previously limited to the geographical area around 127th Street and Madison Avenue) began to spread alarmingly. Old-time members—the 201 negotiators, the board of education, the 201 staff, the UFT, with the principals and black militants on 24-hour call—were joined by newly interested parties—the Ford Foundation, Mayor Lindsay, Ocean Hill-Brownsville (the community in Brooklyn), and some university professors and scholars.

On a stage in which these various parties were forever bowing and scraping to one another, grimacing, menacing, courting, snubbing, apologizing, snubbing again, somehow I.S. 201 became the fall guy. The audience, utterly confused about what-all was going on and endarkened rather than enlightened by media which in their own confusion and fear knew only to present the dramatic and the frightening, accepted as the upshot the idea that I.S. 201 was the center of chaos and anarchy and was probably bent on spreading chaos and anarchy to the rest of the city.

In a time of assaults on teachers, parent-teacher boycotts, citywide controversy over the "disruptive child," three day sit-ins at the board of education, arrests of educational activists (including one subsequently appointed to the board of education), a rage of hysterical public meetings throughout the city, charges of racism, of racism-in-reverse, and of anti-Semitism, and policemen in the schools, *plus* a three-week all-city teacher strike whose motto was "TEACHERS WANT WHAT CHILDREN NEED"–in a time, in short, when the extreme was the normal, it is hard to imagine anything that could have happened inside Intermediate School 201 to give it such a reputation for extremism. One must look to what was happening in the larger conflict-community of which I.S. 201 was one member to appreciate its unhappy distinction. This section focuses on the events in and immediately concerning I.S. 201 from September, 1966, to September, 1967, but the reader must bear in mind that behind the popping of small arms fire in east Harlem there was the continual booming of the big guns in the wider conflict-community, and that all the combatants were extremely sensitive to what was going on in all the other little skirmishes around the city and also were constantly adapting their tactics to meet not only their own immediate needs but also the needs of the grander overall strategy.

The major events of the year September, 1966, to September, 1967, provide a glimpse at the underlying grand strategies:

1. In April, 1967, the board of education "announced its desire to experiment with varying forms of decentralization and community involvement in several experimental districts of varying sizes."[5] I.S. 201, along with four elementary ("feeder") schools, was to become one of three demonstration districts. The Ford Foundation funded its

planning, and some professors and the United Federation of Teachers lent some initial support.

2. Mayor John Lindsay appointed a panel to draw up a plan for decentralizing the New York City school system, which panel was headed by McGeorge Bundy, President of the Ford Foundation, and the 201 storm began to be sucked into the decentralization tornado.

3. In September, 1967, the United Federation of Teachers conducted the longest and most successful strike in its history, rendering its membership euphoric and black New York intensely hostile.

Although the UFT participated in and the board of education tacitly sanctioned the creation of three demonstration districts (besides the 201 Complex the other districts were: Two Bridges, carved out of the multi-ethnic district 3 on Manhattan's Lower East Side; and Ocean Hill-Brownsville in Brooklyn, like the 201 Complex predominantly black and Puerto Rican), both did so with so much ambivalence that people in the three districts believe they were set up for the kill. ("Don't run you'll fall. Don't run you'll fall . . . OK, if you insist on running, go ahead run. Go-on, RUN [pushing] . . . . See-e-e. Didn't I tell you you'd fall? . . . [appealing to the bystanders] I tried to help him, but he fell. He wasn't *ready* to run. [kindly] Next time listen to me and you won't get hurt.")

The evasiveness, the hard stands and subsequent yielding, the appeals to the legal limitations followed by promises to request legislative changes that had characterized the board's stand during the first phase of the struggle continued. Now in this period the United Federation of Teachers at its own insistence became almost a full-fledged partner to the negotiations between the board and the community. Thus, while the union was making sure that the teachers' interests would be protected in any arrangements arrived at, it would later be able to say, "Us? Against community participation? Why we even helped develop the plans." (I myself believe that the union was not plotting for an eventual showdown with the community, merely hedging against the possibility of one.)

In September, 1966, after Lisser and his staff were briefly reunited with the children inside 201, the community group took another tack in seeking a voice in the running of the school. They solicited the help of Dr. Kenneth Clark, who met with the board, and with representatives of the UFT and of the Council of Supervisory Associations, to discuss with them a plan which he had worked out in consultation with members of the community. He came to those meetings, not in his capacity as a state Regent, but simply as an agent of the 201 negotiators. Still, his principals must have hoped that by virtue of his world prestige as a scholar and his position of dignity in the educational hierarchy, he would command more respect and courtesy from the board than they had.

He didn't. He told his principals after one meeting with the board that he felt he had been put on the stand and subjected to an inquisition. He had not gone there, he said, "in his official position [as a Regent] but ordinary intelligence and prudence would have required that they not get on a member of the Board of Regents if he were white." He threatened to leave. The board apologized. Then one member responded to his statement that it had long been known that the quality of education for Negro children was inferior by saying that this was not so. Clark told him that he wasn't going to sit there and argue facts but that if he, the board member, "knew the area which he should know in order to discharge his duties with responsibility, he would know that study after study has demonstrated this fact." The board apologized again. After the meeting, it issued to the press, over Clark's objections, a meaningless statement about having discussed "how to bring quality education to the schools." Later, Superintendent Donovan said he thought the meeting had been going well "until Dr. Clark collapsed."

Dr. Clark believed that the board's discourtesy to him was a racial matter. I believe it was a hierarchical one, that the board took him for what he at that meeting was, not a high-status Regent of the State of New York, but a spokesman for a very low-status group of Harlem parents. A Regent of the State of New York would have talked around about how to overcome the "cultural deprivation" factor. A spokesman for black parents says openly, "You're running inferior schools for black children, and if you don't know it, you're not fit to be holding the job you've got." Even among the most moderate, civilized, and educated of black men, once they become spokesmen for the black community to the white world rather than apologists for the latter to the former, there is a quality of candor that is found by the white world to be in bad taste. It is again a difference between defensive and offensive styles of combat.

Dr. Clark's plan was for a university to assume the responsibility for running a small complex of schools around 201 as a kind of model school district. The university model school is a familiar feature of many university campuses, where it customarily serves mainly the children of the faculty. A few times in educational history, notably in the model school of the University of Chicago under the direction of Dr. John Dewey, such schools have been hot houses for seminal educational innovation. Politically and historically, a university-run model school would, one would think, be far more conservative, more adaptable to going status arrangements, and therefore more acceptable to a board of education than would a community-controlled school.

Even this plan, however, produced negative reactions among various members of the emerging coalition of board, supervisors (Council of Supervisory Associations), and UFT.

The board said that any new plan must be "within the principle of the Board of Education's legal responsibility for operation and staffing of the public schools." The law, which is sometimes in history a shield for the powerless against arbitrary exploitation or oppression by the powerful may at other times, as we saw in the matter of due process, be a defense by the powerful against the just demands of the powerless. The board also opposed calling Commissioner Allen in on discussions because such discussions would likely be leaked to the press and result in "the Board's being presented as not having the resources to resolve the issue on its own and this would further erode the image of the Board as a 'self-reliant Board.'" It is interesting that the board was so aware of how much its power in the school world derived from its public image. This suggests that the attacks over the years on the board's poor performance as an administrative body were not without their effect on the board's position. One wonders whether, if the teachers had not played the role of shoring up the board's defenses, the power could not have been rather easily seized from its shaky old hands.

The president of the Council of Supervisory Associations said that the Clark-community proposal could not be implemented; that it would bring anarchy to the schools; and that his association would have to fight it—which determination would make of the first two predictions a self-fulfilling prophecy. Holders of power are likely to assume that the passing of power to others necessarily results in anarchy. Which it may do if the holders' grip is so tenacious that only a major upheaval can dislodge them.

Albert Shanker, president of the UFT, said that the proposal was illegal, that it would take away the board's power to make decisions, and that it would jeopardize the rights of teachers. Illegality was the conventional empty objection. The board's power to make decisions the union itself had been whittling away at for some time. And the extent to which the rights of teachers would be jeopardized would have depended on the extent to which the teachers union made itself an ally instead of an enemy of educational change and also on whether teachers do indeed have a "right" to perform in ways that diminish humanity and prevent growth.

Clark felt that the board was using the UFT and the CSA to run interference for it. (The metaphor might be appropriate not only to that occasion but to the Lisser controversy a month before—and to future events already in the making during the winter of 1966-67.)

This phase of the negotiations ended with the board's unilateral issuance of a proposal entitled "Proposals for Improving Education in Schools in Disadvantaged Areas." ("Disadvantaged" is felt among many black leaders to be another of those hideous hypocrisies by which the larger society conveys to itself and to the "disadvantaged" the idea that the burdens the dissatisfied labor under are somehow consequent upon their own inadequacies. "Cheated" would be more accurate if less elegant.) The so-called plan for I.S. 201 had been promulgated, verbally, to the 201 negotiators at a meeting a few days before, and when the negotiators protested (1) that they ought to see the plan in writing and (2) that they were being given a take-it-or-leave-it proposition, the members of the board one by one got up and left the meeting.

I once witnessed a comparable incident at a public

meeting of the board. A very emotional and to me very moving speaker was making an appeal to the board on behalf of the schoolchildren of New York's poor communities, accusing the board, among other things, of simply not listening to the people, when Superintendent Donovan, the then-president Alfred Giardino, board member Rose Shapiro, and one or two others proved the point. As the tearful lady was speaking, they neatly gathered up their papers and without once looking at her, at one another, or at the unbelieving audience, modestly and quietly left the meeting room in one's and two's. It was a tremendously cool performance. Chilling. I think that the harshest and most vituperative of the black power advocates, whose style is so offensive to us of the middle class, would not have been able to pull off such a devastating aggression. Even as you call a man "whitey," "Jew-boy," "pig," you are acknowledging his humanity by addressing him. When you remain calm and oblivious in the face of his tears or his anger, you are putting him in the realm of the inhuman or the nonexistent. This is the bureaucratic style of warfare, and that it may arise out of embarrassment, momentary impotence, or fury, makes it, like the black style, also human, but no less ugly.

The board's plan provided for what critics called a "glorified Parent-Teachers Association." The board said that its plan was "in substance" the same as Dr. Clark's plan (the way a spayed cat is "in substance" the same as a panther), and concluded brightly: "The fact that the 201 Board's functions must remain advisory should not impair its usefulness. The Board of Education will look to it for fresh ideas, for new and promising educational methods, and for frank evaluation of school performances; and no one will more eagerly hope for the success of its programs."[6]

The Negotiating Committee issued a scathing critique, agreeing only with the statement that " 'the fact that the 201 Board's functions must remain advisory should not impair its usefulness,' since the useful function that the Board intends for it is to serve as the latest buffer between itself and the black community." And the entire local board of district 4, in which I.S. 201 was located, resigned in protest.

During the remainder of the winter two professors of

Yeshiva University, Sol Gordon and Harry Gottesfeld, were working privately with the community negotiators and with representatives of the United Federation of Teachers to produce a plan entitled "Academic Excellence: Community and Teachers Assume Responsibility for the Education of the Ghetto Child," while publicly the Harlem parents' reputation as "trouble makers" was spreading. In September, the *United Teacher* had said that community control meant "black power fulfilling itself . . . the hiring and firing of teachers."[7] In October, Albert Shanker, UFT president, said on a radio news conference that the union opposed having an elected board of education because the elections would become "a battleground for extremism."[8] (By 1969, Mayor Lindsay's appointed board seeming a greater threat than the electorate, the UFT sponsored legislation which provided for an elected board, but, presumably so as to prevent "extremism," not on the basis of one-man-one-vote.) Many people in the black community believed that "extremism" was a euphemism for assertive black man ("uppity nigger"), and I should think that for many frightened whites in that surely frightening city, the word must have conjured up a black face with fierce eyes shooting out anger from beneath a bush of frizzly black hair.

In December, a group of parents and community people interrupted and then took over a public meeting of the board of education, functioning as a people's board of education. The New York *Times* was at first condescendingly amused, describing the costume of one of the lady disrupters in colorful detail (the *Times* never described board member Rose Shapiro's costume at meetings, apparently considering her a public functionary, not an escapee from the women's pages) and putting in quotation marks the words "members of the rump People's Board" and "election" of its "members" (in the old accounts of life on the plantation, "mock weddings" among the darkies are referred to with just such innocent delight). On television, however, the spectacle of, for example, the massive, deep-voiced Queen Mother Moore of Harlem booming, "Run them out, they're perpetuating idiot factories among us!" must have been frightening enough to people accustomed to the sweet reasonable voice of the regular board.

And *Dissent* magazine (January-February 1967) which described itself as "a bi-monthly of socialist opinion" published a guardedly pro-UFT, anti-board of education article entitled on its face, "I.S. 201: Disaster in the School" (by Jeremy Larner) and on the magazine's cover "Harlem: Turmoil in the Schools," as if the editor found it too hard to choose between two good anxiety-provoking words. *Dissent* hardly represents the mass media, but among its readers as well as on its roster of editors are some of those very leaders of the liberal-"socialist"-labor-union community whose support lent intellectual and political respectability to the community-busting tactics of the United Federation of Teachers a year and a half later. Reprints of the *Dissent* article were generously distributed, including to the teachers at I.S. 201, accompanied by the professional card of the president of the United Federation of Teachers.

Also in January a reporter from the New York *Times* visited 201 and reported it to be "turbulent" (another excellent word). He said children were running around, teachers were screaming, and "a wary principal [Lisser—was] facing a still hostile community. Many of its teachers feel encircled by tension and without support and its pupils are often defiant and undisciplined." Superintendent Donovan told the reporter, "Instruction of the children is going on satisfactorily. I haven't heard that the school doesn't have good, sound leadership . . ." That would depend on whom he was listening to: David Spencer and others of the parents group of I.S. 201 had written to the board complaining that discipline had broken down and teachers and children were asking to be transferred out of the school. The effect of all this news on white parents whose own children attended "good" schools, and who had no experience or knowledge of the common phenomenon of chaos schools, was to encourage a belief that somehow the community agitation had disrupted the normally placid and productive processes of education in Harlem.

But education was not going along placidly at all—not in 201 and not in many other schools scattered throughout the city's black and Puerto Rican neighborhoods.

In 201, Lisser and his teachers quickly settled in after their victory of September and assumed that, as the pickets were gone from the street, the main fuss was over. Their morale and esprit de corps was high, as was to be expected: they had fought for a principle (no pun), briefly but courageously, and had won. They were experienced, hardworking, concerned. As one teacher put it who had left a job in a "good" suburban school to answer the siren call to teach in a "showcase" school with an "innovative" program under a dedicated principal: "It was a great year. I became convinced that if given the chance the kids in the ghetto could learn the same things my well-to-do white suburbanite students learned."

It is precisely this kind of sentiment that enrages black people: that to confirm a child's humanity (ability to grow), he must be compared with an ostensibly superior, white model. The very dedicated and extremely hardworking teacher who made the statement might well have become sensitized himself to the kind of value judgment implied by his statement if he had had the opportunity to work for a period in a community-controlled school. Unfortunately, he twice lost this opportunity: the first time when the board put Lisser back into the school and the parents out; and the second time when the teacher left (he says by request of community representatives) after he had gone out on the three-week strike in September, 1967.

But the euphoria induced by the belief that 201 could become a first-class suburban school in the center of Harlem was short-lived. In early spring Lisser finally succumbed to the second wave and resigned from 201 and the school system. Beryl Banfield, Negro, popular with the teachers, but by this time without credit in the community, became acting principal. Morale inside the school began to deteriorate quickly and continued to deteriorate for the next year. A peculiar thing happens when teachers begin to distrust themselves, distrust their supervisors, distrust one another: the children, demonstrating a phenomenon physicists call resonance,* begin to go to pieces in whatever ways those particular children are most likely to go to pieces when they do.

* Resonance. *The phenomenon which results when, in the case of a forced vibration, the period of the force equals that of a natural vibration of the system to which the force is applied. It consists of a vibration of large amplitude in the system. If the force is due to a*

The children in Harlem, when they go to pieces, cut classes, play hooky, run in the halls, talk back, pull the fire alarm, start fires in wastebaskets, and fight among themselves.

Much of the children's fighting is mock fighting and I suspect it is frequently intended to "get" the teacher rather than one another. Adults, however, and especially adults with other cultural orientations, often can't distinguish between serious fighting and mock fighting. The children themselves will tell you if you can keep cool enough to pose the question. But if you let them "get" you, of course, then they've succeeded in what they intended and it doesn't matter, to you, whether the fight was real or not.

Now sometime in the spring of 1967, the pupil-system in 201 began to vibrate in response to two forces. One was its own teachers, themselves probably feeling exposed and anxious when Lisser left and the demand for a black male principal was renewed. The other was the increasing number of "incidents" in schools throughout the city combined with the UFT's response to these incidents: the notorious "disruptive child clause." This was a plank in the union's negotiating demands for its new contract which would have given enormous and quite arbitrary power to the classroom teacher to remove from her class and even have suspended from school children she couldn't manage. Throughout the city, parents and even teachers responded with a sense of outrage to the attaching of major responsibility for the difficulties and failures of the system on the system's most numerous but most vulnerable members. Probably never before in history were naughty children more rewarded with attention than during the months when the "disruptive child" was a topic of constant household and public discussion.

There is no record, but the incidence of mock fighting must have soared.

It was during these times, in this atmosphere of a frantic heightening of distrust at all levels, that the board designated I.S. 201 as the center of one of the city's

tuning fork in vibration, and if the system is a second fork of the same pitch, the latter will be set in vibration as a result of the waves emitted by the former, and consequently the sound heard will be louder. Webster's New International Dictionary, *Second Edition.*

proposed demonstration districts and that the United Federation of Teachers and the 201 negotiators began to "cooperate" in the development of a plan for the district that somebody may have believed would go down with the board of education. When one considers the fact that in September, 1966, no group produced a quality of statesmanship sufficient to overcome the mutual disregard and suspiciousness that prevailed then, it would have been miraculous if, after the teachers' balking of the community's almost achieved concession from Donovan, after the resentful community's implication in the breakup of Lisser and his staff's great plans and prospects, after the UFT had, as it were, officially put the blame for the schools' failure on naughty children, and while the children themselves were undoubtedly driving their teachers up the walls, it would have been miraculous if after all this, the UFT and the black community could work productively together.

Nevertheless, the two groups tried, or looked as if they were trying, or the UFT said later *it* had tried. UFT President Shanker paid several visits to east Harlem that spring, meeting with community representatives and with teachers of all the five schools proposed to be in the I.S. 201 Complex. He was trying to persuade the teachers to accept the proposal developed by the two Yeshiva University professors, the so-called Gordon-Gottesfeld proposal.

The air in Harlem was thick with distrust and hostility. A teacher present at one of the separate teachers meetings reports:

> I do not recall which one it was but either Gordon or Gottesfeld appeared at a joint meeting of interested teachers of all the schools concerned, the union leaders and uninvited[!] community representatives on April 14, 1967, at the Negro Labor Headquarters Hall on 125th Street. He was not made to feel very welcome. There were many doubters in the audience [presumably among the teachers] as well as Mrs. Helen Testamark [a community activist] who sneaked in through a back door.

It would seem to have been pretty tactless to hold a meeting in Harlem to discuss a community school project, to which community representatives were uninvited and to which one member of the community had to "sneak in through the back door," but so it was.

> Mrs. Testamark led the parent protests and boycott in September [1966]. I could never figure out why she was against it [the Gordon-Gottesfeld proposal]. It is also about this time that the anti-Semitism started to gather more momentum.[9]

A good deal of the suspiciousness and opposition to the Gordon-Gottesfeld plan must have derived from the way the situation was structured. The teachers and parents, each feeling so threatened by the other, might possibly have been able to work through their hostilities and distrust by working together on a common project. But for an outsider, who knows nothing of the travail the others have been experiencing, to offer a plan primarily of his devising has to produce the suspicion in each group that it is being used by the other. Further, during this time it was not members of the community of teachers themselves who were trying to work out a plan with the community of Harlem but their representatives from downtown, who then attempted to sell the plan back to their constituency. The structuring of the negotiations reflected the status of the UFT representatives as leaders and of the university professors as experts. Such a structuring may well produce paper plans, but it cannot produce human and group relationships which alone can effect social change. Only later, during the summer, when the I.S. 201 Planning Board began to make its own plans eliminating leaders and bringing in experts as low-status advisors rather than as high-status initiators, could some teachers and some community people even begin to find a basis of trust in common endeavor, demonstrating that the notion of community control must be worked out in the doing rather than on the drawing board.

But by the summer Shanker and the UFT were fully occupied in matters that seemed at that time more central to the UFT's existence and prosperity—their biennial contract negotiations with the board of education. If the 201 teachers' brave march into the 201 building on Monday, September 19, 1966, was not the point of no return in UFT-community relations, then the three-week strike of September, 1967, was.

One of the community people recalls that during the spring of 1967, Shanker had asked if the community would support the UFT against the board if it came to a strike and that they had answered "Yes, if you'll put our representatives on your policy and bargaining committee." "He laughed at us," she said. A UFT representative who had been present, responded to an inquiry regarding this incident:

> Al did go to Harlem in the winter of 1967. His purpose was not to ask for help specifically in the UFT negotiations but just to explain to community leaders the position and demands of the UFT, and to try to establish lines of communication. It was a very hostile meeting from beginning to end, with Roy Innis [of Harlem CORE] playing a leading role in union baiting. Al handled himself very well, I thought, and did not meet hostility with hostility and suggested—I *think* it was he who suggested—that perhaps another meeting might be held as a follow-up. The community leaders present were supposed to arrange for a follow-up meeting, but simply never did. I am sorry I can't remember the meeting in detail, nor can Al, but it does seem probable that some of them may have asked for representatives on our policy making and negotiating committees. I can say that I remember Al being very somber, serious, and rather soft-spoken throughout the meeting, and he certainly did not laugh at any of the things that were said in that atmosphere.[10]

Perhaps he merely smiled at what must have seemed to a trade unionist a bizarre proposal, but to the proposers would have seemed sensible enough. Whether one experiences a smile or giggle as "being laughed at," like whether one experiences an angry muttering as "being threatened," as we shall see shortly, is freqently a function of one's subjective state. That community leaders were hostile to the UFT there is no doubt. Whether Shanker did or did not meet hostility with hostility in a fundamental way must be determined by the subsequent history of the union's relations with the community.

During the summer of 1967, the taking of sides went on in the undeliberate, confused way that makes us feel at the time that all other choices are still open, and later that none were.

In May, Superintendent Donovan announced the suspension in many districts of the city's Open Enrollment Plan. The last of the first wave was slithering back into the sea in a froth of dirty foam.

Then, early in July, the board formally authorized the creation of three "demonstration experimental" school districts—201, Ocean Hill-Brownsville, and Two Bridges—in implementation of its April memorandum, "Decentralization Demonstration Projects."* Now, why were districts that were set up as a response by a stubborn stronger power to the nagging, persistent pressures of a weaker power, in other words that were the outcome of a power struggle, why were such districts called "an experiment"? In the first place, it's more dignified that way. An "experiment" has status in the world of reports and conferences in which educational administrators move, whereas "yielding to pressure" clearly tarnishes one's image and rusts the remaining residue of power. In the second place, calling the districts an experiment made it possible for the board to impose conditions that would make it very difficult for the experiments to succeed. For example, the Gordon-Gottesfeld proposal had promised that the schools in the 201 Complex be run as so-called More Effective Schools—a largely UFT-supported plan for providing selected schools with a good deal of extra personnel, space, and equipment (amounting to about $500 extra in cost per child per year). The board eliminated the MES conditions from the "experiment" on the grounds that if the community-run schools had greater resources than other similarly situated schools, then you wouldn't know which

* *In the earlier memorandum dated April 12, 1967, the board had proposed to set up two demonstration projects, one consisting of I.S. 201 and feeder schools, and the other of a junior high and feeder schools on the West Side in Manhattan. The Board dropped the second project—the junior high involved was called Joan of Arc—without consulting with the already mobilized community groups. As the Joan of Arc residential area was composed of blacks, Puerto Ricans, and middle-class whites, there were many white parents involved. The board demonstrated by its unceremonious dismissal of this project that its behavior to citizens and parents is status- but not necessarily race-oriented.*

condition had contributed to the success if they were successful; that is, the experiment would not be pure because there would be more than one variable. And, in the third place, as it later developed, if you call a project an experiment, you can decide later that the experiment didn't work, and end it. The community-control proponents could well have argued that if the parents and others in the community ran their own schools and there was no catastrophic decline in academic achievement, then democracy and parental responsibility ought to prevail. But as the board decided to call democracy an experiment, the community accepted what they could get.

The Ford Foundation announced planning grants totaling $135,000 for the three districts, of which $51,000, going to the Community Association of the East Harlem Triangle, Inc., was to be used for the 201 Complex.

Two days later the Mayor's Advisory Panel on Decentralization, headed by McGeorge Bundy, announced that it was drafting plans to spur closer cooperation between schools and communities. While the grassroots community-control people may have wanted to dissociate themselves from the higher (but, they felt, less significant) politics of administrative decentralization, others in the educational universe saw a clear and necessary relationship.

The UFT, which had played a prominent role, perhaps too prominent a role, in introducing the teachers into the planning for the new complex, withdrew available personnel from the summer's planning to work on its own now almost inevitable strike.

And in the complex throughout the summer a group of some thirty or forty people, including perhaps a half-dozen teachers recruited from its five schools (I.S. 201 plus four elementary feeder schools), tried to organize itself into the kind of school-community committee and to organize the community around the five schools into the kind of school-community complex that Preston Wilcox had proposed a year before. They worked hard, in the sense that they spent hours weekly in meetings, producing reams of minutes and a plethora of plans. They had less support from their sponsoring agencies than they had expected and more faith in them than was warranted. Because Donovan would be away on vacation for the summer, he appointed a special agent to act as liaison man with the Planning Board in his absence. But after a very short time the liaison man went away on his vacation for the rest of the summer. (It seemed odd to the planners that Donovan hadn't foreseen that.) Ford did not send representatives to help with the planning, and some of the planners felt they should have. (A funding agency customarily receives periodic formal and informal reports from a funded program but does not customarily participate directly in the activities.)

The board of education actually granted nothing when it authorized the planning for these projects, not even the funds for the planning itself, which came from Ford. The board merely "approved the concepts"[11] of parent-teacher-community planning for the specified districts, and stated the superintendent of schools and the board of education would review the actual details when they got worked out. Among the concepts so approved were: election of parents, community members, and school staff to a governing board; election of a unit administrator by the governing board; governing board participation in curriculum development; authority to hire consultants; and control of budgets alloted by the central board. In respect to staff, a Ford Foundation press release also says: "With the exception of staff presently in the school who may remain, staff will be recruited and selected by the new local board. Under safeguards to be negotiated with the teachers union, the governing board may remove professional personnel it considers unfit or unsatisfactory."[12]

The board's approval of the "concepts" was never to be transformed into an approval of details. There were important specific areas over which the Governing Board would never have control: it would never have control over budget, and it would never find any formal, official way of removing unsatisfactory personnel. But there was a more general problem. The board's failure ever to accept in actuality any of the results of the planning it had authorized (though not paid for), surfaced a year later in the Great Strike of 1968.

But during the summer the planners, coping with other difficulties, did not give too much attention to potential problems with the board. One participant reports, "It was the feeling of the parents and community people in contact with Ford Foundation that Ford would back anything they wanted to do and [that] the Board of Education would listen to the Ford Foundation. The board of education was considered no threat." Others were less confident—one said, "We were going to ask for everything we wanted and see what we could get." And another, "We never trusted them [the board]." But the community planners acted in the only way they could if they wanted to achieve; *as if* they would now finally get the authority to begin to create the kind of program that they had been demanding since the previous summer.

The style of operation of some of the members must have been extremely difficult for others of them. Besides the community leaders, who were verbal, facile, and sophisticated in intergroup and interpersonal relations, there were parents from each of these schools who were none of these. In addition, there were Spanish parents from one of the elementary schools, P.S. 39, who had straight-out language problems. Many of the parents complained that everybody talked so fast they didn't know what was going on half the time, and the people they complained to were likely to be, not their own black community leaders, but the teachers from their schools, usually white. Surface behavior was good, but wariness and confusion lurked beneath. From a personal communication by a teacher-participant to the author, this report:

> Several things were done behind the backs of teachers and others on the Planning Board. Letters were written without the knowledge and consent of the entire membership. Discussions were held with Ford Foundation and very skimpy reports were offered. Everybody seemed a little confused but nobody wanted to say that they doubted the intentions of other members. Nobody really had confidence in anybody else but this feeling had to be covered up. It was not uncommon to have some person come to several meetings, raise a lot of hell about some idea, even serve on a committee, and then disappear. During meetings, members of the Planning Board popped in and out at their convenience.

Observing blacks and whites at civil rights gatherings of various kinds in the South, I sometimes used to think that not cross-race sexual jealousies but merely cultural differences in respect to behavior at meetings and to time were what did in the movement. These differences also plague the relationships of school and community, teachers and children, and older and younger adults.*

Some time late in the summer Herman Ferguson, a black assistant principal from a Queens school and a candidate for a principalship in the Ocean Hill-Brownsville demonstration district, applied for the position of chief consultant to the 201 Planning Board. Later in the fall he was hired by the then elected Governing Board as assistant to the chief consultant, Berlin Kelly. Ferguson had been indicted for conspiracy to murder "moderate" civil rights leaders Roy Wilkins and Whitney Young, and he was subsequently suspended from his Queens post. His presence around the 201 Board exacerbated the internal tensions people were experiencing. While a man of considerable organizational expertise, he had a high-handed style of operation which irritated a lot of people. White members of the board felt that some of the community leaders—people who had been active in the 201 Negotiating Committee—went along with this style of operation, thus demonstrating a lack of trust in both the (predominantly white) teachers and the parents.

The teachers, and some parents, felt left out of the Board's decisions and felt manipulated by the Board. In terms of their present and previous experiences, none of the members were being unrealistic when they reacted to the others with suspicion. That somehow many of them continued to operate together, neither pushing the others out nor giving up in a huff, and to gradually overcome their distrust, is a kind of testimony to their commitment to the project and to themselves as serious adults profoundly concerned with children and with social change. The shifts in interpersonal relationships from a fixed hierarchical arrangement to a fluid give-and-take implicit in the idea of community control was beginning to occur in the process of creating the institutions for community control. It is likely that the individuals involved found themselves better able to cope with the interpersonal difficulties of this situation because no status considerations (at least none that were formally institutionalized) interfered with the

**For a good discussion of the cultural problem of time, I recommend Edward T. Hall,* The Silent Language, *the chapter "Time Talks: American Accents," offering the caution, however, that by "American," Hall means white American.*

expression of the difficulties. I should think also that there must have been a concrete idealism involved. For the first time in their lives as teachers and parents of schoolchildren, they believed they would themselves be able to influence the conditions under which the children who were their common responsibility would learn and under which some of them would work. It is not often nowadays in America that ordinary people (people not in positions of power) get the reins in their hands—even of a very small buggy, even if they are the only riders. That they continued to struggle for this goal in the face of the massive obstruction of most of the city's institutions hints at the power of autonomy and independence to serve as motivators of individual and group behavior.

Events in the Ocean Hill-Brownsville district and a citywide teachers strike interrupted.

Representatives of the three demonstration districts' planning boards had met together several times during the summer, recognizing that they had common problems and likely a common fate. In Ocean Hill-Brownsville, either the community people were more hostile to the teachers than were the 201 community people or the teachers were less able—or less willing—to tolerate the hostility. In any case, tension between the two groups, at least from later reports, ran higher. In an action that some of the teachers regarded as hasty and undemocratic, the Ocean Hill-Brownsville Planning Board had chosen Rhody McCoy to be Unit Administrator. One writer (Martin Mayer in *The Teachers Strike*) reports that to prevent McCoy's uncontested election, one of the white teachers nominated the white principal of one of the district's junior high schools. He suggests that this may have been a "frivolous" gesture. For a white teacher to have nominated a white principal to be director of a black community-control district is in the same category of "joke" as Miss Jersild's comments on her students' personal life: it couldn't seem funny to them. Following this contribution to democracy in the community, Albert Shanker came to a meeting in Brooklyn to protest McCoy's hasty election as undemocratic. People in the community were angry and it is reported that some of them threw chairs.

"By that time," says one former member of the UFT staff, "Shanker had overcome his earlier ambivalence to the experimental districts. He was no longer ambivalent."

The newly elected Ocean Hill-Brownsville Governing Board also moved quickly to do what the community control advocates had been saying all along they intended to do: fill principals' vacancies in the elementary schools where they existed. To accept these appointments, which came from outside the merit-system lists, Superintendent Donovan had to get a special dispensation from state Commissioner Allen. Allen authorized the creation of a special supervisory category "Demonstration Elementary School Principal."

Then in September, 1967, the UFT went out on strike against the board of education to achieve an improved biennial contract. (This three-week 1967 strike should not be confused with the ten-week 1968 Great Strike for "due process" and/or against community control.) Whether or not the 1967 strike was purely economic, it had certain clearly political consequences, in the sense of influencing the balance of power among the various groups of the school world. (Many of the details of the strike I leave for discussion in the section on the UFT to follow.)

The community—meaning not only the individuals involved in the 201 Complex, and those in Ocean Hill-Brownsville, but most of New York's black and Puerto Rican neighborhoods—experienced the strike of September, 1967, as a hostile act against itself and its children. Shanker claims that the mayor and the board aggravated these feelings. Likely, they did. Until the famous Thirty Years' War of autumn 1968, when the thing looked different, the establishment had always projected a teachers strike as some kind of hideous mass child murder, as if two days' or even three weeks' less of long division in a lifetime were going to create a generation of mental cripples. Now, topsy turvy, the community leaders, who knew very well that the more the children went to school, the less they seemed to learn, suddenly began to chant the same line.

Referring to the 1968 strike, Edgar Friedenberg, one of the few honest educationists I know, told a class at York University, in Canada:

> With the school strike, the urgency of settling became as

great as it did because nobody though to ask, "Look, what do these schools do anyway besides baby-sit?" And if we can't get along without that for a while (which may be true in a society so organized that both parents have to go to work to have a decent living), then you ought to look at that situation instead. However, instead of asking this question, the city went ahead and endorsed the teachers' assumption that education is something cumulative, that each day missed in school was a slice off the child's learning life. If you think back to the moments at which you learned relatively important things in your life, you'll find that the things that are, let us say of grade B importance . . . you learn in about a second. And the things that are of grade A importance, of course, you don't even know you know; you couldn't even say when you learned them. The notion of the cumulative effects of educational routine, however, is rooted deep: you should never miss a day.[13]

Of course Friedenberg is wrong, in the sense that everyone, including teachers, knows that the daily school compulsion is as irrelevant to education as the daily bowel-movement compulsion is to digestion. But we all play the you-should-never-miss-a-day game when it suits us. Parents keep children out of school because someone overslept or because Uncle Ike is about to arrive from Memphis, but they huff and puff if the children are sent home early so the teachers can do their paper work. Schools allow the children to sit around idle while a prodigious amount of foolish administrative detail is being transacted, or sometimes just to teach them to be idle without protesting, but call down the heavens if a child stays out one day because he feels like playing in the sunshine or reading a book or just moping in front of the TV.

In 1967 (and again in 1968) the community leaders played the you-should-never-miss-a-day game when the union went on strike, claiming that the strike was against the poor black and Puerto Rican children, "for whom every day of education counts." Really what counted, even in 1967, was the power of the union, which the community leaders felt to be a power that could be and would be used against their political demands.

At the 201 Complex all the resentment against teachers

and union that had been building up during the year (not to speak of a residuum of the resentment that most people build up against teachers in general during the dozen years, more or less, they are required to experience them in depth) was mobilized against the strike, and some leaders of black resentment (including H. Rap Brown, successor to Stokely Carmichael as chairman of SNCC) mobilized themselves. Again, as a year before, it was when the community felt most threatened and most impotent that its most "extremist" members and moods would take over. ("As usual," a very moderate community leader said on another occasion, "nobody listened until we got ugly.")

A few people, who at this late date sensed that there would be either a détente between 201 and the UFT or a slaughter, tried to persuade the union to except the three fledgling experimental districts from the strike. One 201 union teacher went to UFT headquarters with the tough line that as most teachers in the complex would not honor the strike call anyway, the union should prudently grant such a dispensation. He was thinking the UFT strategists might swallow it when, on his way back uptown, he heard the announcement—made allegedly without consideration of the full 201 Planning Board—that teachers who answered the strike call would be "screened" before being allowed to return to work. So history's foot slipped from another of those crumbling footholds over the murderous gorge, as it had twelve months before when Dorothy Jones telephoned the union leadership to try to head off the teachers' breaking the parents' boycott of 201, and the leadership were "sympathetic" but said it was too late. The "screening" threat scotched any possibility that the union would exempt the demonstration districts from the strike call.

The Executive Board of the UFT adopted a resolution that it would not allow screening. Some teachers in the complex struck and some did not. At one school, P.S. 133, where group morale was always high, the entire staff struck; they didn't take the screening threat seriously and they weren't screened. (Interestingly, in the 1968 strike, which was clearly a strike against the experimental districts, not one teacher in 133 went out.) At I.S. 201 about 50 percent of the staff struck.

Here I encounter contradiction as to facts. One of the

201 teachers who struck, a teacher member of the Planning Board, asserts that after the strike, eight of the teachers who had struck were asked to leave. He says that the pressure for this request, passed on to the eight by Beryl Banfield, the board-appointed acting principal who took over when Lisser left and would be leaving very shortly herself, came from "outsiders." The teacher writes (in a personal communication to me):

> All but one or two of us were Jewish. All were white. All were men. Most of us had important jobs in the school—department chairmen, program chairmen, union leaders, etc. [In other words, these were the teachers who must have seemed most threatening to the community leaders' intent that they themselves rather than the union or the board of education should control the centers of power in the schools.] We were told through another source [than Banfield] that if we did not leave, things would get tough for us and we would later want to leave. We all decided that if we want what the parents want then we should not stand in their way.

Now, another striking man teacher who allegedly was also told to go did not obey the summons and was not harmed. (He came eventually to be a strong supporter of community control and of the complex.) A community member of the Planning Board and later of the Governing Board has responded to inquiries about the situation that he knew nothing of the threats and knew for certain that the Planning Board was not involved.

There is no doubt, however, about the matter of "screening." The threat to screen striking teachers was publicly made by David Spencer, Chairman of the Planning Board, and in a short time "screening" came in union circles to seem the equivalent of the water cure. Insofar as screening meant being interviewed by a personnel committee prior to hiring, it was as a procedure no more humiliating than the various ceremonies a teacher candidate is called upon to perform by the board of examiners. But insofar as screening meant being reconsidered for one's job after having been out on strike, it was regarded with great horror by New York's trade union circles, which saw a return to the era of yellow-dog contracts, blacklists, and lockouts.

Besides the supposed threat to their job security, some striking teachers were personally frightened by the hostility of the community, reporting that they had been threatened. Questioned about the alleged threats, one of the community members of the Governing Board said, "Well, you know, teachers aren't very hard to scare. We feel that teachers like everyone else should grow up and face reality. I don't think anyone set out to alienate teachers or scare them."

Did they, or didn't they? True, teachers are easily scared—which may be one reason why it's fun to play at scaring them. Did Shanker laugh at the community people, or didn't he when they suggested he put some of them on the UFT policy and negotiating committees? True, some people are easily offended—which you may not think about if you haven't been walking around in their shoes.

The connotative and the denotative functions of language are involved. The mother who screams, "If you don't stop this minute, I'll beat your brains out," is merely connoting how angry she is. Tommy, knowing his mother and her style, understands this and, in most instances, stops at more or less this minute; in any case, he does not call the police for protection against an infanticide. The same threat made by an equally angry but strange adult probably sends Tommy scurrying. If the adult is of another race and/or Tommy is an especially timid child, Tommy may credit the denotation of the words enough to send his father back to avenge him.

Still there is no way of knowing how scared the community *intended* the striking teachers to be.

When it was all over (the details of the strike are discussed in section 3, on the union) and teachers and children were back in school, the Council of Supervisory Associations (representing all the supervisory personnel in the school system) instituted a suit against the board of education charging that the appointments of principals in Ocean Hill-Brownsville under the special designation of "demonstration school" principal and from outside the merit system violated civil service regulations and the civil rights of those on the regular principals list. The suit, if successful, would remove the keystone—appointment of principals—from the community school arch before the community schools ever even got started. The UFT entered the case on the side of the supervisors as amicus curiae. In respect to this decision, a union officer explained, "During the course of the strike, Al [Shanker] just announced at one meeting of the Ad Com [Advisory Committee, a kind of steering committee to the Executive Committee] that he was entering the case on the side of the CSA. The Ad Com passed it pro forma. I don't remember anybody saying anything about it one way or another." Later, when asked by a journalist (Martin Mayer) why he had done it, considering that the union had for years favored the election of principals by teaching staffs, which also would violate the "merit" system, Shanker is reported to have answered, "Pure pique."[14]

"Al handled himself very well . . . he was very somber, serious and rather soft-spoken," a colleague remembers of Shanker during the difficult meetings of the previous spring: "He did not meet hostility with hostility."

If you have courts, merit systems, lists, and examinations at your disposal, you can afford to handle yourself very well. If you have none of these, you may sometimes behave in ways that others find frightening.

"This is our community," an enraged mother in the 201 Complex once shouted, "and we don't own anything in it. Not even our own children. All I have is my mouth."

The Complex: People and Places

The size of the I.S. 201 Complex, one intermediate school and four feeder elementary schools, was on a human scale. In a district of this size a school could have a personality, a teacher or a mother could have a sense of a community with whose fate the fate of her particular school was involved, and a child could have a sense of the boundaries of the universe within which his existence mattered. And the district superintendent (the unit administrator) could know what was going on inside the schools. "I believe this little unit is a viable working unit," the I.S. 201 Unit Administrator once said. "A district [of 20 to 30 schools] is not. There's a power vacuum between the district superintendent and the principal."

You could walk from one to the other of the two schools of the 201 Complex that were farthest apart in about fifteen minutes. You could walk in ten easy minutes from any one of the schools to the building on 125th Street in which the Unit Administrator and Governing Board's offices were located. The Unit Administrator, the members of the Governing Board, and the teachers and principals of the district would be greeted by neighborhood adults and children in their comings and goings. What may or may not have been a self-conscious neighborhood before the I.S. 201 struggle began gained coherence during the course of the struggle.

The westernmost of the schools, P.S. 68, on 127th Street between Seventh and Lenox Avenues, bordered a great devastated urban slum clearance area (which in the summer and fall of 1969 was to become the site of another conflict between officialdom and members of the community). P.S. 68 was presided over by Principal John R. Nailor, who was once described by one of the school's best and most experienced teachers in this way: "If I were going to invent a principal I'd invent Nailor. He's a real person."

If you walk north three blocks on Lenox and then cut east on 130th Street, you pass through one of the nicest blocks in Harlem. Two-and-three story row houses fronted by tidy miniyards and occasional alienated urban trees. Cross wide, sunny Fifth Avenue and you face P.S. 133, a new block-long, red-brick building. P.S. 133 was (and is) one of the best schools in Harlem, no one quite knew (or knows) why.

The teachers trusted one another and did their own recruiting for staff openings; more parents from 133 voted in the Complex's Governing Board elections than from any of the other schools; the school undertook, on its own initiative, what was probably the complex's most successful innovative educational program. The school's accomplishments and the staff's esprit de corps, predating the creation of the complex, remained constant even when its principal changed. (These factors suggest that the tonus of a school may derive from the relationships among the staff, perhaps of merely a very few strong members.) During the time it belonged to the 201 Complex, the principal of 133 was Delora Hercules. A woman of considerable charm, she fit into her staff as prima inter pares, and was chosen by the entire complement of supervisors in the complex to be their representative on the Governing Board.

Down Fifth to 128th Street, east on 128th halfway to Madison. Looming over the narrow always twilit street was P.S. 24, old, grimy, dismal, with perhaps a mother standing outside by a post and waiting for her child to be brought to her.

P.S. 24 was scheduled to be torn down and merged with equally old P.S. 39 (the fourth of the complex's feeder schools) in a great new building. So, instead of two schools serving 483 and 593 children, there would be one big school, serving 1,076 children. (The more children the board of education assembles in one aggregate, the more each individual child becomes an ever-smaller fraction of an ever-greater aggregate and the less a whole entity unto himself.)

Neither the worst- nor the best-functioning of the feeder schools for I.S. 201, 24 was physically closest to 201, the center of the unit, and seemed to vibrate in response to all the discords and harmonies that sounded out from it. The P.S. 24 teachers agonized over every conflict between the Governing Board and the union, over every educational innovation, over every proposed personnel shift. They wanted to do the right thing. They didn't know what the right thing was or who now was the authority who could tell them. ("I don't want to hear anything more about the Governing Board, or the community, or the union. I just want to be left alone with my class to teach," one teacher at P.S. 24 said, not understanding that unless she could make herself into the kind of person who would examine conflicts and make decisions, she would never be able to teach a class very much.)

Across Madison Avenue was windowless I.S. 201, first beachhead of the revolution. In New York, where square feet per child are measured out as miserly as pounds of cornmeal in starving Mississippi, the school was fronted by a patch of fenced-in concrete wasteland, bearing neither utilitarian hopscotch squares and jungle gyms nor beautifying fountains and greens. Over the useless patio beetled the windowless second and third stories of the building, like a great eyeless forehead. Inside, the blank continuous walls (which neighborhood people used to say the board of education had devised so that the parents couldn't look in and see the kids weren't learning and the kids couldn't look out and see it was Harlem) contributed to that school alienation from the world that the educators of the 201 Complex strove to overcome. Walking around and around the hollow-square building, you had no outside, real-world point of reference to determine where in the building you were. If P.S. 24 was a dismal 1920s jailhouse kind of a building, I.S. 201 was a tortured construction of the 1960s were you could go hysterically round and round looking for the room where the meeting was supposed to take place.

In the morning until sometime after nine, again at lunchtime, and again at dismissal time, you would often encounter the school's principal, Ronald Evans (hired after Beryl Banfield, appointed action principal by the board of education, was given special leave by the board), out on the sidewalk. He worried about the drunks and addicts in the vicinity when the children came and went. If he wasn't there, he might have been in the wide first floor lobby reminding a chronic cutter to appear with his mother the next morning or discussing with a fifth grader where her coat could have disappeared to. And if he was in his office, his door was normally left open. (Many school principals like to say, "My door is always open," which is not a literal statement of fact but a metaphor meaning, "Moderately courageous students and teachers and very courageous parents may knock on my door if they can get past the secretary and I won't throw them out.") In the teachers' lunchroom at 201, they served soul food. (One of the minor planks in the community-control platform was that neighborhood women should be hired to prepare in the children's lunchrooms some of the kinds of foods that children in that neighborhood customarily eat.)

Exit to 127th Street, walk half a block east to Park Avenue, walk downtown one block under the railroad tracks, past the uncollected garbage and the open bars, half of whose customers are out in the street, and turn east on 126th Street. This is the route the children east of Park Avenue took to get to 201. P.S. 39, between Second and Third Avenue, on into Spanish Harlem, was the scene of another of the pitched battle of the community-control struggle, to take place during the 1968 Thanksgiving vacation.

The head of the 201 Complex was the appointed, paid, professional Unit Administrator Charles E. Wilson, the heart was the elected, unpaid, amateur Chairman of the Governing Board, David X. Spencer.

Wilson was tall, handsome, charming, ultimately cool. He could play at being tough, nasty, affectionate, heart-to-heart, intellectual, poetic, guy-in-the-street-down-to-earth – and always be in control of the game. "He's as true as a ten-cent tin whistle," said an associate who liked him very much, by which I believe he meant that you could never know which of his many notes he would emit next. But once in a confrontation with a high-stationed board of education messenger at a time when it felt as if the powers that be were giving the last turns to the hemp around the complex's neck, his voice cracked the thinnest crack for a syllable or two. From Wilson it was like a flood of raging tears.

Spencer was short, exophthalmic, bushy-haired, soul. He would threaten extravagantly when angry and had been known by his associates to weep openly at the mounting pressures and frustrations that they were all trying to cope with. His angry posture combined with his appearance seemed to arouse the deepest anxieties of TV and other public audiences. ("Watched you on TV. You look wild. Like a Cannibal," an anonymous correspondent once wrote to him. With an ethnicity that was a little less vulgar, a member of New York's liberal-intellectual bloc confided to a friend he thought Spencer "looks like he's crazy.") In person, Spencer was as direct and guileless as a grown man can be. In all the harshness and bitterness and mutual suspiciousness of a guerrilla warfare situation, everybody seemed to trust Dave Spencer. He exhibited in his attitudes and perceptions that cutting-through-the phoniness clarity which is characteristic of many poor black people and is distressing or delightful depending on whether one experiences the phoniness as a defense or an offense. He once said, "The whole poverty program is about self-help. And I guess the officials meant it at first. But now that our people are beginning to help themselves, the reaction is, 'Well now, look, we didn't mean for you to help yourselves *that* much.' " And he explained in the following way about parents' attitudes toward teachers: "Parents want to be involved in their kids' education, and they want to see a job done. They're not so hung up against teachers as you may think, but teachers are the only thing that's close enough for them to attack. We know that the Board of Education sets the rules and that we got to play by them. But we also know that we've asked the teachers to come out and try to help change some of the rules, and when they didn't do that, we *had* to attack the teachers."[15]

Bitterly antiestablishment as both Wilson and Spencer were, I did not sense in either that free-floating antiwhitism or anti-Semitism that became during the struggle the aggravating counterpoison to the kind of racism so familiar as to be invisible to most New York whites and Jews. Wilson said he thought that antiwhitism is nonproductive and puts too much strain on the gut – but he acknowledged that there were people in the complex who thought he oughtn't to be talking to whites, and I personally had some encounters that confirmed this. Spencer told a meeting of the Governing Board that when he found an anti-UFT picketer at P.S. 39 bearing an anti-Semitic sign, he tore it out of his hands: "out of respect for the children present here I won't tell you what I told him he could do with it. I want you all to know I'm not fighting the Jews. Did you hear me? *I am not fighting the Jews*!" One of the most esteemed members of the Governing Board was a white, middle-class Jewish lady schoolteacher, and another was a white Protestant minister.

The Governing Board consisted of ten parent representatives (of whom Spencer was one), two from each school; five teacher representatives elected by the teachers at each school (all but one was black); one representative of all the supervisors; and five community representatives, chosen by the parent members. The balance of power thus lay with the parents, or nonprofessionals, at almost 3 to 1, but in its deliberations the Board did not usually divide by professionals versus nonprofessionals.

The Unit Administrator was not a member of the Board; but he was chosen by and responsible to the Board and was expected to attend its regular weekly meetings, to report to its members on matters he or they thought they ought to know about, and to execute policy and directives voted on by them. On a few occasions the Board caught him up rather sharply when they thought he had overlooked or unnecessarily delayed doing things they wanted done. To appreciate the status shift here, one must recall that, while Wilson was a highly paid, educated professional, the Governing Board contained parents with far less schooling (not all of them even high school graduates) and teachers and one supervisor whose superior he was in the professional hierarchy. The Board made policy for the complex, operating as a whole and through a number of committees, the most active being the Education and Research Committee and the Personnel committee. To further widen the population of participants, parents and teachers who were not members of the Governing Board could be members of some committees, such as the Education Committee.

The Personnel Committee received resumés from and interviewed applicants for all positions, teaching as well as supervisory. Thus, Wilson, Evans, and Nailor—all appointed after the Governing Board became functional—underwent this selection process, as did many teachers. (The complex had to choose, in general, from among candidates certified by the board of examiners and had then to have its choices approved by the board of education's bureau of personnel.) What the committee and the Governing Board and Wilson looked for were strong, innovative, experienced educators with empathy for these particular children and some commitment to community control. Of the teachers they chose, many were young and inexperienced, qualities that are more likely to be overcome in time than timidity or hostility to the social environment, but that were enormously inconvenient in schools experiencing a constant drain of pre-Governing Board personnel while having each day to prove themselves to a doubting world.

The supervisors the Board chose (unit administrator and principals) all seemed to me to rank well above the average school supervisor, as I know him, in both strength and operating intelligence. In the case of both Evans and Wilson, the Governing Board was allowed to go outside strict "merit" system procedures for the appointments. Evans lacked one course in education required for state certification as a junior high school principal, and Wilson came from outside the public school universe entirely, which probably accounts for his somewhat flamboyant personal style and quite unschoolmanlike manner of operating – neither of which would have been likely to survive several decades in the school system. Nailor, who had been a strong supervisor and a kind of troubleshooter for the board of education for some time before the Governing Board and Wilson had the good luck to get him to come into the complex, did not have a principal's license; in other words, by board of education standards, he was not fully qualified and therefore not paid to do what everyone, including the board of education, thought he did so well.

The same was true of Mrs. Hercules. When a letter writer to the *New York Times* (May 23, 1968) questioned Evans' professional "qualifications," he neatly summed up the absurdities of the merit-system game by distinguishing between the "qualities that are crucial for one to assume administrative and instructional leadership in the complexities of today's educational scene" and the "so-called qualifications."

Perhaps more than anything else about community control, the idea that parents, some of them unlettered, and teachers should participate in the choosing of staff struck professionals, and many members of the public to whom they appealed, as outrageous. A board of education-appointed teacher on the staff of one of the complex's schools once said to me, "Look who they put on these committees. People off the streets. They aren't educators on the Governing Board. They are illiterate people." David Spencer wrote in response to just such a criticism, which could have been referring to him: "And when you say, 'How can lay people choose teachers?' I can only say that we got people who go to court for their *lives* to go on trial, and we pick from the run of the mill to sit on the jury and make a decent decision, and there ain't but three people in the courtroom that know law – the judge and the lawyers. But yet we still put enough stock in those plain people to come up with a decision by listening, thinking, using plain old common sense. We can do the same thing to pick teachers."[16]

Since all personnel had to meet at least minimum New York State requirements for the jobs they were appointed to and most of them city merit-system standards besides, what was involved in the hue and cry about parents' choosing their children's teachers was not the teachers' qualifications but the status shift involved in parents' judging teachers.

The notion that drifted about New York in those years that community control means that parents wander in and out of classrooms telling teachers what and how to teach and throwing them out if they don't like what they see was, for some who spread the idea, probably a disingenuous piece of propaganda designed to discredit community control, and for others the expression of a desperate fear of loss of status. The few times parents and community members were in and out of schools and classrooms were the times of climactic confrontation, and then, if they were to be considered outsiders, so were their fellow observers—union officials, bureaucrats, and policemen—most of them more irrelevant to classroom procedures than parents. The intent of community control was to create in the school world institutions of representative democracy, such as Americans are familiar with in both the political and the corporate worlds, so that a responsible constituency should be able to call professional management to account. That at no point did any communities in New York manage to develop such institutions must be ascribed primarily to the fact that almost all the established institutions from which the communities needed aid and cooperation offered instead suspiciousness, hostility, and massive resistance.

Beleaguered in Harlem: The School Year 1967-68

September, 1966, to September, 1967, had been a dismal year for what at about its midpoint became the 201 Complex, and it had ended worse than it had begun. In September, 1967, by the time the strike was over, the project was sick with internal complaints and punch-drunk with external battles. September, 1967, to September, 1968, was even a worse year for the complex, yet it ended with an interlude of out-of-this-world serenity. As with the year-in and year-out smooth functioning of P.S. 133, there is no way of prying loose the beautiful secret that would explain this gift that came to the complex. Perhaps some good spirit suffuses a group of people and brings to fruition their will to accomplish and their daily exertions.

I find in the developments of the school year 1967-68 overwhelming support for the thesis that the intent and/or the style of the board of education was throughout such as to mark for failure the demonstration districts they had allowed to be undertaken. I do not distinguish here between the appointed lay board and the bureaucrats who function either under or over them (depending on who ultimately does have the louder voice in that confused interplay of relationships). If there were any members of the board that brought the demonstration districts into existence who did intend or expect or even vaguely wanted them to succeed, there is no evidence whatsoever that they examined the network of events and relationships in which they were involved to see what role they might play to bring about the issue they publicly claimed they wanted when they said in 1966, prior to the establishment of the districts, "no one will more eagerly hope for the success of its [the community council's] program."[17]

The board's occasional gestures of good will (such as Superintendent Donovan's appointing a deputy to serve the projects while he went on vacation, which deputy then proceeded to go on vacation, or the board's half-hearted court fight on behalf of the specially appointed principals in Ocean Hill-Brownsville)[18] do not alter the case, although they might have slightly altered the image that the board projected to itself and to the public. The same was true of the United Federation of Teachers, although here I believe that there was for a brief period some genuine ambivalence, derived from differences of feelings and opinions among top union personnel, and tempory ambivalence on the part of Shanker himself (the union's only significant policymaker).

Image projection and introjection were probably a highly significant element in the entire struggle. Supposing a group of lower-middle-class and lower-class mainly black and Puerto Rican adults, without training, without status, without "superior education" themselves, aided merely by classroom teachers selected not by examination but only their own peers, were to succeed in creating education where an imposing system of prominent citizens and trained bureaucrats and supervisors and an elaborate arrangement of examiners and examinations had not. What would become then one of the nation's leading industries? And of one's image of oneself and one's professional group?

I tend not to believe (as do some critical analysts of the strategies of the board) that people actually stayed up nights inventing defenses for themselves, their group, their image. The defenses were already there, built up during individual life histories and during the histories of the institutions the individuals belonged to. One has only to believe in the defenses, the institutions, oneself. And believing, one knows that others (clearly less competent than oneself and one's peers) are not going to succeed where one has failed. And believing that others are not going to succeed, one acts in ways that impede their success.

The most immediate problem of 201 was shortage of personnel. If administrators can't choose personnel sympathetic to them, to their goals, to the particular children being served, they are going to have a hard time making their schools function as they want them to function. If they can't keep a full complement of any kind of personnel, they are not going to be able to make their schools function at all. Logic would have dictated that the experimental community-control districts be offered one of two arrangements in regard to personnel. Either they could have been treated like any other district, with personnel assigned by the board's bureau of personnel and no more than a very small percentage each year allowed to transfer out by request. (There are complex rules which normally control voluntary transfer out of a school. Permission to leave is granted to 5 percent of the tenured staff each year, and of these, senior staff members have priority. These rules are designed to protect "difficult" schools against excessive drainage of tenured personnel.) Or, recognizing the project's "specialness," teachers could have been brought in or kept in by consent of both themselves and the Governing Board and allowed to transfer out or be transferred out by decision of either, with some guarantees to both parties against arbitrary removal by the Governing Board or excessive departures by teachers. What the demonstration districts actually got, by an agreement between the United Federation of Teachers and the board of education (representatives of the complex were not involved), was the worst of both worlds: 25 percent of teachers would be granted transfer out in any year, but the Governing Board had no established authority to go either outside the so-called merit system to choose personnel or outside customary procedures to remove personnel. It was to a great extent this inequitous arrangement, which granted personnel special rights to leave the demonstation districts, but did not grant the districts special rights to dismiss personnel, that eventually produced, in Ocean Hill-Brownsville, the crisis that led to the Great Strike.

In practice, as always, there were "deals." During certain periods, more than the specially allowed 25 percent left the 201 district and others were in fact dismissed, with or without "screening," and with the agreement of the board of education's bureau of personnel. (Dismissed personnel, of course, got assignments in other schools.)

The situation in regard to teachers was bad enough – in September, 1967, there were twenty-five vacancies in I.S. 201 alone, about a quarter of the staff. The situation in regard to supervisors was even worse. Three of the five principals were on leave (P.S. 39, 68, and 133), and 201 didn't have a regular principal, even to be on leave, Lisser having resigned. Further, the board granted the school's two assistant principals (Beryl Banfield and Herman LaFontaine, an able though not highly experienced Puerto Rican administrator) special leaves as of the beginning of the second semester – without informing the Governing Board that it was going to do this.

I once asked the board of education's assistant superintendent in charge of the demonstration districts about the Banfield-LaFontaine transfers. He said that the assigning out of all of 201's administrative personnel at the same time was "unfortunate," it "wasn't helpful." (Whether it was or was not helpful would depend on what cause one meant to be helpful *to*.) He made it seem like one of those small slips that we also-imperfect-humans-of-the-board may occasionally make. I then asked how the board of education allowed such transfers without requiring that the 201 Board receive prior notice. He said the 201 Board did not have to be informed, as it was still only a planning board and therefore had no standing. But at this very time the board of education was in other respects acting as if the Planning Board *had* standing – for example, it was allowing teachers almost unlimited transfer-out rights on the grounds that 201 was a special situation.

In November, elections were held for the Governing Board, after the UFT had instructed its teachers not to participate and had urged a postponing of the elections. Nevertheless, over half of the teachers did vote, as did two-thirds of the supervisory staff and about a quarter of the parents. (These figures come from a report on the demonstration districts–the so-called Niemeyer Report–prepared at the request of the board of education. A member of the Governing Board quotes slightly higher percentages for teachers and supervisors.) Not a bad showing for a first election in a project nobody could on the basis of prior experiences have much faith in and among an electorate (the parents) who had never had much reason to have faith either in elections or in schools.

From the time the Governing Board was elected in November, 1967, until October, 1968, it received no formal statement from the board of education delegating or delimiting its authority. (On October 28, 1968, the board issued a bulletin delegating some of its powers to the city's 30 local school boards and to the three demonstration districts' governing boards. By this statement the three demonstration districts were demoted–or promoted–from their status as special experiments in community control to almost the same status as that of all the other local school boards. There remained, however, two important distinctions: the governing boards were elected, whereas the other local boards were still those appointed by the board of education; and the experimental districts were considerably smaller, thus more administratively manageable, than the other districts. This October statement also spelled out the powers of both governing boards and local school boards.) Nevertheless, as soon as the Governing Board was elected, the board of education cut the schools in the complex out of district 4 and treated them as if they were a separate district, in the sense that the board no longer made available to the schools the services (guidance coordinator, reading coordinator, etc.) normally provided for every school by its district office. The board did not, however, immediately provide the Governing Board with the funds either for these services or for any other operating expenses. The Niemeyer Report, sponsored by the board, relates:

Since the Project Board had no Project Administrator until March 27 [1968—when Wilson was hired for the position], it did not receive funds from the Board of Education for operating its central office. Thus, it had to rely on the Ford Foundation planning grant and two supplementary grants to pay consultants and the office staff. [Ford had never intended to finance operations, nor should have been expected to.] On one occasion, when the telephones were disconnected in the District office, the staff had to rely in part on the nearby office facilities of Bank Street College's Educational Resource Center to carry on its work.

Further, as soon as Charles Wilson was appointed unit administrator, the assistant superintendent of district 4, Martin Frey, immediately notified the principals of the five schools in the complex that they would henceforth be responsible to Wilson not to him. But Wilson had no staff, no facilities, and no experience with board of education routine. He protested that District Superintendent Frey's announcement was "both unfortunate and premature . . . you have pictured this completion of the transition period as if it had been accomplished rather than just beginning."

There was almost no administrative difficulty that Wilson's office did not encounter in its dealings with Livingston Street:

Item: As once before, when the building housing I.S. 201 was erected, now in the case of the new building planned to house the combined P.S. 24 and P.S. 68 (the building to be called P.S. 30 and 31), the board proceeded with planning the construction with almost no contact with the community. Although parents committees had been at work drawing up various requests, it was not until supplies and equipment had already been ordered that representatives of the Governing Board were granted a meeting with the board of education's architectural experts. The architect for the new building was the same one used for 201 (a structure that the community finds hateful).

Item: A teacher candidate whom the unit administrator's office sent to the board of examiners to take an emergency licensing examination was failed because he wrote a 200-word composition (with no errors) when a 250-word composition was called for. He retook the test and passed with a 250-word no-error composition. Then the board discovered that the candidate had a "record": he had been arrested on a civil rights charge in the South. Though his case had been dismissed, the candidate nonetheless had to procure a letter from his lawyer testifying that the case had indeed been dismissed—and then the letter got lost at the board. Eventually the candidate was licensed.

Item: From the 201 Complex newsletter, November 4, 1968 (during the period of the Great Strike):

> *Half of the faculty in I.S. 201 had not been paid since school opened two months ago. The first pay period in October, the payroll division claimed it did not receive the payroll sheet, even though we have a signed form that they did. This past pay period, they again claimed they did not receive the form, although this time it was sent by messenger and a signed statement obtained that is was received in correct form. At the same time the Board has been unwilling or unable to move on such basic essentials as the granting of additional positions or the correct disposition of payrolls, it has had the time and personnel to keep a close supervision of our schools in other areas. Every school in our Complex has been visited by several attendance officers who scrutinized our attendance records, apparently due to disbelief down at 110 Livingston Street that virtually all our children and teachers are in school. Health inspectors from the Board have made regular rounds to guard against violations. Parents organized brigades to keep those schools clean where the custodians were out [during the strike].*

Where were the health inspectors in 1966 and 1967 when the air-conditioning system at 201 wasn't functioning?

Item: Unit Director Charles Wilson received no salary checks from June, 1968, until some time in October when a secretary in his office was finally given the full-time assignment of pursuing Wilson's pay. Surprisingly, it took only two and a half days for her to locate his salary from June through August.

Item: From Ronald Briggs, Wilson's administrative

assistant, who always gave an impression of being on top of things:

When I call up there [headquarters], if I can possibly avoid it, I never say I'm calling from 201. I say 4A [as the complex had been cut out of district 4] or district 31 [the three demonstration districts were to be numbered 31, 32, and 33], or something like that. It's definitely worse if I say 201—you can feel them turning you off. Now, however, it's got so I can't say 4A because that gets them mixed up with 4, and I can't say 31, because Donovan has to decide which is 31, 32, and 33, and he's too busy to decide now. Sometimes, I just have to hang up the phone and get on the subway and go down there. They forget to send us some circulars and notices that go out to all the other districts, like about buses available for school trips, but we have friends in other district offices and they call us up and tell us about them. The staff here is determined to beat the system ["the system" being experienced not as a supporting institution but as an enemy that must be beat or circumvented if one is to survive]. We work 10 or 12 hours a day and take work home. We do it because we are recognized here as people. Our schools offer some hope for people, we're beginning to believe in success.

Briggs made this comment during a period of relative serenity. In the crisis that was to come over the district's P.S. 39, the serenity was to go.

Item: Candidates for office jobs whom the 201 office recruited experienced, in addition to the customary humiliations of petitioners for jobs before the board of examiners, special reminders of their, and the project's, unworthiness, implied in such remarks as: "Why do you want to work there with those people?" "What do you people up there think you're trying to do?"

I once overheard a sample of the kind of outraged incredulity that some of the old-time bureaucrats at the board were expressing in respect to the demonstration projects. It was the day after the assassination of Martin Luther King, Jr., and throughout the city the children's natural resonance was responding to nationwide shock. Fights, fires, and assaults occurred in several schools. In Ocean Hill-Brownsville, Unit Administrator Rhody McCoy, feeling that the staff was not able to cope, ordered the schools closed early. In a dim and dusty office at 110 Livingston Street, about as far from the schools and from the mourning over the killing of the dream as you could get, two officials were discussing this heinous act of sheer impudence: "Can you imagine Rhody McCoy just deciding to close the schools! Himself! I'd like to know who does he think he is." If you have built your life on the premise that rules and orders supersede reality (which Hannah Arendt in a different context referred to as the "banality of evil"), or constitute the only reality, then anyone who operates in another universe of reality is experienced as overwhelmingly threatening. For when the orders and the rules crumble, what will remain?

The 201 Complex was experienced as the highest order of threat, and treated with the scorn appropriate to such threats, not only at the bottom and medium levels of the bureaucracy but way on up to the top. Some time during the spring of the year, Wilson's office (lacking the facilities available at the usual district office) requested that a library consultant from the state board of education pay a visit to the complex's schools to evaluate its libraries. Wilson wanted help in figuring out what he needed, and he believed that the district would be entitled to federal educational funds if the libraries fell below a certain standard. The official came, visited the libraries, made notes, and left with a promise to send a report. Wilson's office never received the report, but there did come into their hands the following letter, which had been sent to the state official by a top confidential aide to Donovan prior to his visit:

I will leave it to your discretion whether or not to accept the invitation to visit I.S. 201. However, I can give you a little information on what to expect if you should accept it. You will be asked to evaluate the libraries and probably compare them with suburban schools or those in more affluent districts in New York [an act of social pretension ill-befitting black educators of poor black and Puerto Rican children] and to help seek or provide funds to upgrade these libraries. You may also be prepared to have any report you might issue to them used in an attack on the policies of the present Board of Education. This seems to be "par for the course" lately. However, I mentioned this to Dr. Donovan and he sees no reason why you should not go if you wish. However, he would appreciate it if you would let . . . his office know by letter that you are planning to go, when and if you do accept the invitation. Good luck.

The letter gives one a sense of the private club atmosphere in which the top bureaucrats operate, a private club to which newcomers can be admitted—when they have been recommended by old members and have passed through the prescribed initiation rites. But here from the center of Harlem came this ridiculous bunch of pretender upstarts trying to walk in through the front door, just like that! You don't have to use "nigger" to say "nigger."

February and March, 1968, were the nadir. Finally working with a unit administrator and a 201 principal of their own selection, the Governing Board was tying to wrest from the board of education some independent powers that would reduce the daily frustrations attendant on dealings with the Livingston Street personnel and that would give them instruments of operation somewhere commensurate with the responsibilities that they wanted to assume and that the public had been given to understand they already had. As Wilson put it in his first statement to the Governing Board. "The I.S. 201 Governing Board has never had the power to hire even one teacher or to buy a single piece of chalk."

Meanwhile, though the disparity between the Governing Board's powers and its responsibilities was not revealed to the public, three incidents had been keeping the complex in the headlines—all (so far as the general press was concerned) unpleasant. These incidents were generally treated as evidence of "extremism" at 201. The first involved a black teacher at P.S. 68 (the school of which John Nailor subsequently became principal), a man who was described by a not sympathetic colleague as a gifted teacher and a difficult person, John F. Hatchett. In December, Hatchett had published an article in *The African-American Teachers Forum,* "The Phenomenon of the Anti-Black Jews and the Black Anglo-Saxon: A Study in Educational Perfidy," which offended a lot of people.

The article was actually a response to an article published in the November 22 issue of *The United Teacher*, "I.S. 201 and the First Days of the Bundy Report." The title of the *United Teacher* article, one of a series of four on the Bundy Plan—which, issued in November, called for decentralization of the city's school system—and on the three demonstration districts, illustrates the UFT's strategy of hanging the worth of the one upon that of the other, that is, the strategy of hanging them together. The UFT article is throughout cool and reasoned in tone but based, with one exception, entirely on the testimony of teachers who were at that time negatively disposed to the project. The exception was Florence Thau, who, as a member of the Planning Board and then of the Governing Board, knew more about the project than any of the other teachers quoted but to whose testimony far less weight was given than to many others' and who is badly misquoted once: "As for rumors that what is really wanted by those in control of the I.S. 201 Complex is 'local control,' " the article maintained, "Mrs. Thau said that there was nothing to substantiate these charges, and that they were no more than rumors." Questioned about this statement, Mrs. Thau responded, aghast, "Miriam, how do you think I could say something like that? That's just what we do want."

In general the article gives a picture of secret conniving, grabs for power and jobs under cover of educational aims (the word "grabs," I might note, is used by people who have power and jobs to refer to people who can only get power and jobs precisely by "grabbing"), violence, threats, and general disorganization. The article quotes extensively two P.S. 68 teachers, a man with a Jewish name and a black lady, who were then antagonistic to the project (though they subsequently become its loyal defenders). It concludes:

The future of this complex of schools is not clear. No one seems to know exactly what plan the new Governing Board will be operating on, or exactly where the money for such operation is coming from. Teachers have not had an ideal role in many respects, and the teacher walk-out did create misunderstanding. Many parents and community people failed to realize that teachers were fighting for better schools. But beyond this, the activities of those others involved in the "experiment" must be evaluated, as must be the educational—and even political—theories on which their newfound roles are based.

If decentralization is to improve education, that knowledge which has been gleaned from the experience of the I.S. 201 demonstration complex must be examined. No opinion can be too conclusive—any experiment takes time—but three or four months must tell us something.

Like this passage, the whole article was a verbal putdown in the category of President Giardino's putdown of the local school board members or Miss Jersild's "fun" putdown of her students. The teacher walk-out created not "misunderstanding" but rage. Parents and community people didn't not *realize* that teachers were fighting for better schools; they didn't *believe* it. Putting "experiment" in quotation marks is, like putting the people's board of education "election" in quotation marks, a typographic ploy which suggests that the whole thing is a species of joke. "Newfound roles" is reminiscent of the way grownups talk about adolescents' "discovery" of sex. And the three or four months which should give us some evidence of the possibilities of community control ended three months *before* the Governing Board was even recognized, much less granted any powers. The article which seems to be withholding judgment barely veils an overwhelming contempt, hostility, and failure of honesty on the part of a writer who was considered to be one of the most sympathetic of the union spokesmen. (Less than a year later the UFT would be claiming solemnly that they were supporters of decentralization, and thousands of white citizens of good will would believe them.)

Nevertheless, the tone of the article was civilized. But the tone of Hatchett's response was not. It was strident and vulgar. Hatchett wrote that antiblack Jews and black Anglo-Saxon teachers were responsible for "years of miseducation coupled with horrendous abuse of the family, associates, and culture of the Black children who are forced to sit under their benighted tutelage."[19] He especially singled out his white male colleague with the Jewish name as being a "willing and obedient tool of the union hierarchy" and his black female colleague as being "blatantly stupid in her simplistic reasoning." (Both of these people, by the way, were exceptionally gifted and committed teachers with an unusual degree of rapport with and expectations of their students. I base this judgment on personal observation of them in their classrooms.) Anti-community-control teachers and others among whom Hatchett's article was passed around were horrified – and, in a perverse way, fulfilled. ("Aren't I talking quietly and reasonably to you? How do you dare scream such nasty things at me? It just goes to show what kind of a person you people are.") At P.S. 68, which was one of the schools that was suffering from having its regular principal on leave anyway, teacher morale plummeted.

The Hatchett Affair, which began with a noisy, ugly black response to a quiet, ugly white provocation, rose to a deafening climax in the memorial month of February along with the Malcolm X Assembly Affair and the Herman Ferguson Affair.

I believe that white Americans, or any people secure for some generations in their social and personal identities, cannot appreciate the extent to which identity and, during youth, the process of identifying constitute the rock on which we build our sense of self. We know so well who we are that we cannot know how we came to be so. As Erik H. Erikson, in *Childhood and Society*, wrote of the madness of Nazi Germany, "The world is apt . . . to underestimate the force with which the question of national unity [in this case, read "group identity"] may become a matter of the *preservation of identity,* and thus a matter of (human) life and death, far surpassing the question of political systems." And a dominant people cannot appreciate the extent to which the figure of The Liberator is a unifying and nourishing symbol for an oppressed people in the process of creating a new and dignifying identity for itself and its children. Malcolm X is on the way to becoming such a symbol – because of the way he lived, because of the way he died, and because of the quality of his being. (Father Abraham and the Kennedys are going to be replaced.)

So it was natural that some people at the 201 Complex (symbol of the new order in black schools) should plan to mount a memorial assembly for Malcolm X on the anniversary of his assassination, just as it was natural for other people at 201 to be nervous about such a memorial and for people in the educational establishment to be panic stricken and outraged. As it did for the assembly's promoters, the symbolism of mounting an assembly for Malcolm X rather than for Washington or Lincoln touched the opponents' deepest feelings of self and group. There "is the further fact," Erikson has written (in *Identity: Youth and Crisis*), "that the oppressor has a vested interest in the negative identity of the oppressed because that negative identity is a projection of his own unconscious negative identity – a projection which, up to a point, makes him feel superior but also, in a brittle way, whole."

On the Governing Board, many of the parents had grave reservations about the wisdom of holding the Malcolm X memorial.

It was some time around this period that the parent members of the Governing Board began to overcome their confusion and timidity and to express their opinions at meetings. They seem to have operated as a counterforce to the exclusionist tendencies of some of the more individually forceful community members in a more natural, democratic, and acceptable way than the teachers alone or certainly any nonsympathetic outside agency such as the UFT could. The parent members' anxiety was expressed in their insistence that Herman Ferguson (still their consultant) get permission from District Superintendent Martin Frey to hold the assembly. (This was roughly equivalent to asking permission of George III to hold the Boston Tea Party.)

Frey first refused to grant permission for the assembly to be held during the school day, saying, it would " 'disrupt' the educational activities of the school." (I think back on all those dreary Washington's Birthday assemblies, Memorial Day assemblies, Armistice Day assemblies, Boy Scout assemblies, and American Legion assemblies that "disrupted" the educational activities of my childhood, and I wonder if Malcolm X after a few years in the custody of educators is going to be that dreary a disruption.) In response to Frey's prohibition, a spokesman of the Afro-American Teachers Association, which was co-sponsoring the event, announced that the event would be put on "in the immediate neighborhood of the school and pupils would be asked to come out to attend." There was a change of plans and the program was allowed to be put on during school hours, but the children of 201 were not to be in attendance.

Sister Betty Shabazz, widow of Malcolm X, attended with her children. The press came, although they were not invited and their presence was inappropriate; they were detained in another room and the program was piped in to them. They said in their reports that they heard Herman Ferguson urge those present to obtain weapons and arm themselves for self-defense and heard other speakers and actors in a play by LeRoi Jones describe the United States as the "Fourth Reich," say "all white people will be killed," and urge Negro youths to refuse to serve in the armed forces and kill their "colored brothers in Vietnam." Teachers, including white teachers, who attended the event resented the press's failure to mention the "dignified" and moving parts of the program. (An unpublished letter to the *New York Times* from a group of teachers is reprinted below.) And Sara Slack, the black *Amsterdam News* reporter who attended, reported the poetry, the music, the appeals to (nonviolent) black pride, and summed up the program as follows: "The I.S. 201 Malcolm X Memorial Testimony, taken in sequence and context, was not an anti-white rally. If anything in addition to shaming Afro-Americans into 'waking up' it was a black pride festival dedicated to the slain man, whom they worship, El Hajj Malik El Shabazz, born May 19, 1925 and assassinated, February 21, 1965."[20]

The mayor, who did not get his information from the *Amsterdam News* reporter who was present or from the teachers who were present, was interviewed by a *New York Times* reporter at an Oregon ski resort, and his remarks were published under the head "MAYOR CONDEMNS ANTIWHITE PROGRAM AT I.S. 201." Among the mayor's remarks were: "It pays to avoid showdowns over questions that force the majority of the black community on to the side of a few militants."[21]

And Alfred Giardino, president of the board of education, said, fatuously, "Young and impressionable schoolchildren should not be subjected to racism of any kind"[22]—a remark which is the equivalent of scolding sexually experienced teenagers for playing footsies in the movies. "If *we* could remove every racist teacher who has referred to our children as 'niggers' and 'animals,' or to our schools and communities as 'zoos' and 'jungles,' half of the teachers in Harlem and East Harlem would be out," the 201 newsletter had commented a month earlier.[23]

That the assembly got such wild press notices can probably be ascribed not only to reporters' preference for the wild over the tame but also to their having been excluded from the hall. Accustomed as newspaper and TV reporters are to being granted privileged access to almost any event – sometimes to the disadvantage of the bona fide participants – the radical black power line of ignoring and excluding reporters altogether must offend not only their sense of what is important in society but also their amour propre. Somewhere Eldridge Cleaver refers to the press as "leaches." The intrusion of the press's ego demands can be just as offensive when they determine to "understand" the ghetto. "They come up here," Charles Wilson once said, "and they want the poor to scream for them. 'Show us how much it hurts. Show me your pains.' " (As with the guidance counselors at John Brown Junior High, turning one's inferiors from contemptible into suffering human beings is experienced as ennobling to oneself.) Whatever the motivation, there is no doubt that the press contributed to the massing public hostility to 201, community control, black people, extremism, and school decentralization, a hostility which would be expressed in hysterical crowd behavior the following autumn (1968) and in harsh political behavior the spring after that.[24]

After the Malcolm X memorial assembly, Herman Ferguson's bail was raised from $20,000 to $100,000 and his ouster as a consultant to the Governing Board became a condition for the Governing Board's recognition by the board of education. The scenario went like this. Ferguson, to cover the main facts again, had been suspended by the board of education from his job as an assistant principal in a Queens school because of the criminal indictment for conspiracy to murder civil rights leaders Roy Wilkins and Whitney Young. In the fall of 1967 he was hired as a paid consultant to the 201 Governing Board. His association with the Board had been sometimes helpful but often irritating, and with the possibility of hiring regular full-time staff, the Governing Board might have terminated his association in any case. At a meeting on March 1 between the board of education and the Governing Board where recognition of the Governing Board was being discussed, the board of education President, Alfred Giardino, announced that the central board would not allow the 201 Board to retain Ferguson even if the funds for his salary came from another source. He said, "The Board cannot have on its staff members who have been suspended by the Superintendent of Schools." This was the last item on the agenda. As the meeting moved to a close, a member of the board, Mrs. Rose Shapiro, "mentioned that members of the press were waiting down in the Board of Education Hall and that 'if we are to move together and are to explore together, we have to be very careful about what is said to the Press.' "[25] The Governing Board members stopped to talk among themselves briefly as they were leaving the meeting room, and when they arrived at the press briefing they discovered that the board's ultimatum regarding Ferguson had already been given out to the press. It came out in the *New York Times* the next day as "I.S. 201 PANEL TOLD TO OUST FERGUSON. Local Board Won't Be Given Recognition Until It Acts."

The maneuver was tactless at best, contemptuous at worst, and in any event certain to aggravate internal tensions on the Governing Board and make it as hard as possible for them to accept the ultimatum. (In its dealings with its own supervisory staff the board of education is almost pathologically delicate. An investigator questioning a district superintendent on a matter in which a decision he made was subsequently reversed said, "You were overruled?" The superintendent: "I don't like to use the word 'overruled.' Let us say there was a change in plans." The investigator: "That is a nice euphemism.") By some unexplained miracle, though the incident wracked the internal loyalties of its members, the Governing Board managed to get out of it without a major upheaval and with a decent show of delicacy of its own. The Board voted by a very narrow margin to terminate all consultants and provided that new staff would be hired by the new unit administrator with the approval of the Governing Board. It also passed a motion saying that Herman Ferguson had performed his job as administrative assistant "with a high level of competence." Perhaps it was the growing trust the board members had in one another as individuals working together on a very much beleaguered body that made it possible for them to retain their operating integrity in the face of such a sharp and potentially devisive provocation.

Also after the Malcolm X assembly, John Hatchett, who had responded so crudely to the provocative article in the *United Teacher,* and who had, over his supervisor's objections, taken his P.S. 68 class to the assembly, was dismissed from his post at P.S. 68 and had his substitute teaching license revoked. (The New York *Times* took the occasion to reprint two paragraphs from Hachett's offending article, but did not refer to the *United Teacher* article.)

Among members of the Governing Board and parents in the complex, many were distressed by the calls to violence at the assembly, although most had felt that most of the three-hour gathering was "dignified and solemn" in tone and they wanted to know why Ferguson intruded into the assembly the kind of ugly tone that they had said from the beginning they didn't want. Unfortunately, operating under the harsh kleig lights of a hostile board of education, a hostile UFT, and a hostile press made it more difficult for those in the community who disapproved to deal with that kind of ugliness. Their experiencing of the board of education, the United Federation of Teachers, the press (in other words, the white world) as hostile and bent on their destruction again and again made it extremely hard if not impossible for decent, humane people with a sense of decorum and taste to eliminate the reactions of violence and ugliness in their midst without seeming to betray their brothers and their cause.

In the midst of these events the Governing Board, elected in November, was formally installed—though there were no operating powers that had been delegated to it. The installation, a ceremony in the class of cornerstone laying which is usually given press coverage and was attended in this case by Borough President of Manhattan Percy Sutton, was duly reported by the *Amsterdam News,* but ignored by the *New York Times.* The new Governing Board and its new unit administrator acquired responsibility for: a supervisor's office with no funds for operation; a staff divided and short-handed; supervisory positions unfilled; reporters as hungry for evidences of "racism" as ten-year-old boys for pictures of breasts and thighs when all about them the real girls are walking around half-dressed and totally ignored; parents anxious and frightened; no formal authority to cope.

And the children vibrating like crazy, especially at I.S. 201 and P.S. 68.

At I.S. 201 (grades 5 through 8, ages about 10 through 15) the vibrations seemed to be in response to shortage of staff over a prolonged period, absence of trusted leadership ever (until Evans's appointment in March), inadequate and inappropriate teaching materials, and the general troubles of the world outside. Teacher morale and dedication were astonishingly good. The internal tensions among the staff—"be tough with them" teachers versus "understand them" teachers, black teachers versus white teachers, older teachers versus young teachers, black-culture teachers versus conventional-curriculum teachers, and UFT teachers versus anti-UFT teachers—were played down by loyalty to the project and the desperate wish that it should survive. In other words, the difficulties being experienced seemed to derive largely from events that were external to the teachers' relationships with the children and among themselves.

Of the three platoons deployed to wipe out 201—the press, the teachers union, and the bureaucracy—the teachers were more exposed to the press and their own union than to the bureaucracy. They kept writing letters to the newspapers trying to get their side of the story across. It was something like sending petitions of grievance to the general of the occupying army; the letters didn't get published. One of them, signed by a group of teachers, reads:

23 February 1968

To: The Editor of the New York Times

As a teacher at I.S. 201, I can only express disgust and honest rage at the news coverage the Times *has given 201. I and my colleagues are among those who feel the impact of your reporting most sharply. . . .*

The jungle-like conditions at I.S. 201 reported by the Times *on February 2 have existed for 30 to 40 years in ghetto schools all over New York, and, indeed, throughout the country. But it is only now, when black people are struggling to correct these conditions, that the press sees fit to explode the situation, with the unjustified effect of implying that the source of such chaos is in "community control," rather than in the existing school system. . . .*

The article in last Thursday's Times *[February 22] reported the expressions of violence by Negro speakers at a memorial for Malcolm X, but not a single line reported that James Baldwin ended his eloquent speech with the words, "What you must do is love your neighbor," followed by a long standing ovation. Given the fact that the building was fortified by scores of plainclothed and uniformed policemen, the very symbol of oppression and violence to black people, it is perhaps remarkable that no violence did occur. . . .*

The stories in the Times *and other news media concerning I.S. 201 have had ugly, unnecessary effects. The coverage has caused an over-reaction on the part of many community parents, it has distorted the concept of "community control" in the eyes of many (when, by the way, there is no community control at I.S. 201 as yet, the power being with the Board of Education), and it has thrown more obstacles in the way of the struggling Governing Board (witness the reaction of the Board of Education to Thursday's article about the Malcolm X program, that the Governing Board shall not "interfere" with I.S. 201 until further notice).*

We who are here because we believe in self-determination for Afro-Americans acutely feel the damage that the school has suffered because of your reporting. We hope that, if this unbalanced, irresponsible coverage cannot be righted, at least it will not continue.

There was still in the school a small UFT chapter, whose members were distraught at the way their school and their efforts were being defamed and discredited by their union. During the spring of that year, in public meetings, at the union's Delegate Assembly (the decision-making body of the union), in press conferences, and in political advertisements, the union had used 201 as a black symbol of all the terror held in store for New York City by the Bundy or alternative proposals for decentralization. In one *New York Times* ad (May 8, 1968) carrying boldly the scare words "APARTHEID," "CHAOS," "POLITICAL PATRONAGE," the following two sentences occur: "Our schools will be transformed from centers of learning into maelstroms of ideological and emotional conflict. This is already the scene at I.S. 201 and elsewhere." The 201 union teachers tried, and failed, to be heard at the Delegate Assembly. And they tried, and failed, to get a commitment from their president that he would consult with them before making statements about 201.

At a meeting (which I attended) between the union teachers at 201 and John O'Neill, the one UFT official who maintained contact with the black community during those years, a young white teacher said, "Those of us in the UFT are distressed at belonging to an organization that antagonizes the parents of our children. Our union isn't supporting us." And a black teacher said, "The UFT is there. But it is not interested in what we are saying." O'Neill, who predicted that sooner or later there would be a "clash between the revolution that's going on and trade unionism" (he was smack between the cymbals at that very moment), left with a rash promise that Shanker would stop making inflammatory statements about 201 without consulting the 201 UFT chapter. He did not deliver on the promise. (A few months later he was fired from the UFT and went over to the enemy.)

The earnest white teacher also told O'Neill, "In isolating the ghetto community, the UFT is setting up an obstacle to our success in the classroom." What the atmosphere in the classrooms and corridors at 201 was I can perhaps best convey by quoting directly from notes I made at the time about my experiences as a per diem substitute there. My observations are unreliable to the extent that, as everyone knows, a substitute is likely to encounter the highest level of disorder any school is capable of producing because the children know and she knows that her only function is the negative one of trying to keep order. This being the case, the children have nothing to lose in the way of good experience if they prevent her from fulfilling that function and everything to gain in the school game of one-upmanship. On the other hand, a substitute who knows schools can sense the general atmosphere of a particular school and can compare its social system with other schools. In my case, knowing, on the one hand, that I had no sanctions at my disposal to enforce any orders I might issue and, on the other, had not enough time to develop a relationship of mutual respect with the children, I limited my personal aims to making contact with individuals and small groups who reached out to me or accepted my reaching out to them and to preventing the rest from harming themselves or one another. This turned out to be not too difficult if I could keep myself from overreacting to provocations. In the end, I felt that I had had a few warm moments with a few children and that while I hadn't taught anybody much, I hadn't harmed anybody much either. My notes and retrospective comments on them follow:

Unventilated room with temperature in the 80s. Dreadful!

Teachers all seem very serious. Much more serious than at Garvey Junior High [an almost wholly black school in the Bronx where I had also done per diem subbing. There, teacher lunchroom conversation was likely to be the usual combination of inconsequential small talk and the kind of despairing hostility toward every aspect of their environment and their profession that Nordstrom and Friedenberg call ressentiment.] *Children, even when class is not in control, are not so wild as there—no fighting, throwing chairs, etc.—although a good deal of wandering in and out of the room.*

After lunch two big boys, perhaps high school truants, invaded the room. [The verb betrays the anxiety they aroused in me.] One grabbed my hands and waltzed me around a few times. Then both circled the room, kissed a few girls, and left. I was alarmed. The thought crossed my mind to send for help. [I still don't know why I didn't or whether I should have.] The children seemed merely amused and quieted down immediately on the boys' departure. This was the one controlled class of the day. [I always acted with each new class of the day as if I was in charge and expected to remain in charge. I would put an assignment on the board, distribute materials, and doing other such teacher-like things. Once in five or six times, a class would take me at my face value and we would have something like a regular lesson in an atmosphere of something like classroom order. I was never able to figure out what happened between us to bring about these occasional miracles.]

In the last class there was a very handsome, cool boy

whom the other children greeted as one who had been long-gone. Ronald. He said he'd been in the hospital and the doctor said he was crazy because he had tried to kill his brother. He reproached me for wanting to make him work on his first day back. I asked what did he come back for, and he said "to learn." I walked away. Later he put in my hand, saying nothing, a piece of chalk I was trying to get back from some boys. At the end of the hour I said I hoped if I ever came again he would want to learn something from me. He said "It's impossible. I don't know anything. I got no smarts." [The primary educational purpose of the 201 so-called experiment was to undo Ronald's conviction that he is stupid. And people were going to decide in three mad months, or even three years if the experiment was a success!]

Angela in homeroom explains to me the attendance procedures. She tells me I must take attendance again after lunch. But she won't be there. She never comes back after lunch. "Isn't that right, Thomasina, I never come after lunch?" Thomasina agrees. I say maybe today she will come. Why should she? I'll miss her. She does come after lunch, not saying anything to me but obviously putting herself in my way and waiting to see if her presence will be recognized. I say I'm glad she's back. But tomorrow I'll be gone and there will be a different substitute who won't know how to take attendance or how you line up before lunch, and who won't know to look for Angela after lunch. If Angela knows she will not be missed, why should she come? [One item that increases a substitute's difficulties in keeping order is that for the children authority is a matter of expertise in the school's rituals. Clearly if you don't know when and how "our teacher" takes attendance, you are not someone to be listened to. The shortage of regularly assigned teachers common to Harlem schools was aggravated at 201 by the central board's policy of allowing mass transfers out of the complex's schools. And the substitutes came and went.]

In the lunchroom I ask teachers about books and reading. The one department I've been in that seems to have plenty of books is home economics. In the closet are sets of three different brand-new books, beautifully illustrated with pictures of homes, kitchens, food. No black faces, no collards, or corn bread, or rice and beans. The teachers say the books are no good and there aren't enough of them. Most teachers produce their own material. The kids can't afford paperbacks and shouldn't be asked to pay for them if they could. One young man teacher tried, without too much success, to produce math materials out of cardboard. They can't get math materials. He takes his kids on street outings and to museums where they are always very interested in reading the signs, the leaflets, etc. [Children learn to read, and improve their reading, not from teachers but from books. The more there were no books to be read day after day, and week after week, as their middle-class age mates were doing in schools and libraries a few miles away, the more the children wouldn't be able to "pass" the standardized reading tests and the more it would be possible to say the "experiment" in community control was not succeeding. But when the "experimenters" demanded control over their budget so they could purchase books that the children would want and be able to read, they were told that this would violate the purity of the experiment.]

During the afternoon I have a class which consists entirely of four boys (word must have gotten around that there was a sub in that room and no one would know you were cutting). We start to talk about some work when a girl comes in and slowly walks behind Leroy who is sitting with his back to the wall. Leroy says, "Go way, I don't trust you." I, "Who don't you trust?" "Nobody. I don't trust nobody. But Leroy. Yeah, sometimes I trust Jay [the boy next to him]." Some bouncing of this back and forth, with Leroy saying alternately that he trusts nobody but Leroy and that he trusts Leroy and Jay. I, "Anybody trust you?" "Yeah. Lady give me five dollars go to the store for her. She live on 32nd Street [that is, 132nd Street – the children customarily drop the "hundred" as superfluous; real 32nd Street would be "downtown."] And I live all the way on 24th Street. But she know me cause she call me Leroy." [This was clearly a brag, although it may also have been true, and it inspired the others try to top it.] Jay, "Lady gave me $25 (!) to go downtown to pick up some flowers for her!" Received with appropriate amazement but no outright disbelief. We now settle down to my worksheet. The boys work with considerable interest and don't stop *when the bell rings. I have to tell them it's time to go. [In Charles Wilson's talk to the first open meeting of the Governing Board after his appointment, he said, "What we have to do is build a system of trust." Clearly this is what the children were dreaming about.]*

The school is gathering up all its forces to become like a "real school": hall patrols, cut slips, attendance books in order, offenders sent to dean. Over the loudspeaker Evans warns that kids are not allowed out of class without permission: "You are responsible for the children in your class at all times. Remember that if a child is out of the class without your permission, you are responsible for what happens to him." In the lunchroom teachers are congratulating one another on the new get-tough policy – they are happy that Evans is getting tough with the kids and also with them and determined to show him that they will perform. Evans is a constant presence in the halls. The teachers discuss joining other groups who will be picketing the UFT spring conference to confront newsmen but decide against it on the grounds that they want to stay out of the public eye and build up their school. They completely don't trust newsmen. One lady teacher: "Whatever you say to them, it somehow gets twisted around and comes out different."

[At Garvey, the children's disorder was greater: mass fights in the lunchroom; fire alarm being pulled several times a week; large items being thrown from windows; central light switches being pulled with great waves of children swarming and screaming in the ensuing darkness; and teachers and monitors constantly hitting, a whack with the bare hand or with a yardstick being considered an appropriate accompaniment at almost any time to almost any order. There, the principal was to be seen only if you happened to pass a particular point in the outer office with a view toward her desk when her inner office door was opened for a secretary to enter or exit. Unlike its treatment of 201, the press reported on this school only in the event of major interruptions of the humdrum daily routine: a parent-led student strike for improvement of lunches, or the dismissal of a teacher chosen to be a scapegoat for the entire misery. Some months after I had been a substitute at Garvey I formally interviewed the principal and she claimed

that there was no corporal punishment in her school and that any child could have access to her at any time. An avowed advocate of community control, this principal was very hostile to her staff, blaming them entirely for whatever difficulties the school experienced. They in turn had no trust in her. In contrast the 201 supervisors never denied the difficulties they were experiencing, and they were trying to cope with them.]

M. L. King murdered last night—looting in Harlem. Parade of police cars four cops in each, almost all of them white, driving down 127th Street at 8:30. Evans in shirtsleeves outside calling children in from sidewalk. Two of "my" children on arrival independently report in detail dreams of cops, chasing, guns, robbers. One dream ends with the dreamer chasing and catching a robber and turning him over to the cops and getting a medal, this detail told with as much pride as if he actually had won a medal.

In one class, since the children are paying no attention to me, I decide to pay attention to them. This is home economics; only girls. I find four girls sitting in animated conversation talking about the assassination. They say they're having a play and they give me permission to be the audience. They seat me rather ceremoniously and begin again from the beginning, which consists of two of them meeting the two others in the street and embracing with cries of "Long time no see." They all agree to go to one "lady's" house to visit. A bowl of artificial flowers serves as pretend refreshment, although they probably all have M & M's, potato chips, etc. in their pocketbooks. The beginning conversation is a bit stilted, as they are being mothers. But very soon they are speaking out of themselves. One by one, other girls join and listen. One of the newcomers keeps trying to say something and when I point this out to the four, one says, "She can't talk, she isn't in the play." "Couldn't she be in the play?" "No, she was running around." "If she sat still and showed she wanted to be quiet, could she get in the play?" Eventually, all are allowed to speak, although the play continues to be dominated by one or two big talkers. I, too, am allowed to speak if I raise may hand and say, "Can I be in the play for one question?" The play quickly degenerates, or rises, into a discussion, but once in awhile the hostess remembers it is a play and passes around the artificial flowers. It is all about the assassination, peace, violence: "Those people that broke the windows, they're not really sad Martin Luther King was killed, they just want to steal things. Martin Luther King was a man of peace. I believe in peace. And he wanted to help people everywhere. All over the world. He even went to Africa to help make the Africans equal. When I grow up that's what I'm going to do is help people to have peace and be equal. Nonviolent." The children change my name first to Washerman, then to Washnwear. How did they discover my fiber content so quickly? [We are in, naturally, a home economics class.]

[Later.] A child is telling another child whose parent owns a store she should write "SOUL BROTHER" in the store window. Another girl, who had been very hostile to me the last time I was in the school, comes up to me, "Aren't you afraid to be in Harlem?" (Why I, who am grown up, and not she? Isn't she afraid to be in Harlem?) "I'll tell you what you should do. You should put black on your face and then put a sign here [pointing to my chest] that says 'SOUL BROTHER.'" What made her, since last time when I thought we were enemies, decide I am to be saved?

By after lunch, the halls are wild with kids who wander in and out of rooms and duck in and out of stairwells when you try to catch them. Teachers seem pretty cool. Resigned. The final two or three periods the whole school is sent to the auditorium. Four kids I encounter on the stairs beg to come to my room with me. Looking for sanctuary? At first they sit around and talk about their own simple affairs . . . like allowances. "My father give me five cents every Friday [with heavy scorn in respect to the amount]. I mean my stepfather. My real father he died. He hung himself." Very calmly, eliciting no particular response from the other three. I, "How come?" "I guess he felt bad 'cause he cut up my mother face." Running her finger down the side of her face to show where, while the other kids, finally reacting, say, "Don't do that, you'll leave a mark on you face."

This girl came from Puerto Rico when she was eight. Her mother speaks no English. She is one of the famed culturally deprived, language-handicapped, emotionally scarred. She has good control of the language, is bright, very eager, reads fluently. Maybe what we need is fewer explanations and more trust.

The day ends, not gloriously, but without catastrophe. I feel less hostile to the apparatus of control being set up here. There is too much intrusion of the world's violence to wait for the children to begin to control themselves only as their interest in learning is engaged. I suspect Paul Goodman is not right, that it would be best if the school could somehow quickly be made into an oasis of relative calm and order even if that means an imposed discipline. But who wants this except for the parents and the teachers there? What's in it for anybody else? For the press, or the UFT, *or the board of education?*

[Now as I reread my notes, I have new doubts about this at-the-time judgment. Maybe the children can achieve the calm and order which they need to grow up out of themselves, out of their plays and their bragging about who trusts them, without cut slips, deans of discipline, hall patrols, etc. There is something to be said on both sides. But clearly it must be said by those adults who are side by side with, care about, and are responsible for these particular children. The crucial dilemma of how to raise a generation to responsible adulthood in a world of mass irresponsibility is going to be resolved not by men and women behind desks on which are many scholarly reports and two telephones but by men and women who stand with and touch and are touched by the children themselves.]

At P.S. 68, where, among other things, the children were younger, their disturbance derived more from the disturbances that their teachers were experiencing with one another than from the disturbances of the world beyond. Internalization by the staff of the pro- and anti-community-control struggle, plus the absence of a regular principal, had made the school one of the most chaotic of the chaos schools. Hatchett taught in P.S. 68. A teacher there explained the conditions like this. Her beginning remarks refer to the period before Wilson became unit administrator of the complex.

In the summer and fall of '67 some of the teachers felt that dictatorial methods were being used on the Planning Board. The chapter chairman [the chairman of the UFT chapter in the school] and the UFT got together to try to prevent this group from taking power. When we couldn't, we decided to withhold cooperation. We went politicking in the neighborhood, which was not the right thing to do. There was the strike in '67. Whatever the real reasons for the strike, we *thought* we were striking for smaller classes, and better conditions for the children. Then came Hatchett's article. The school was torn apart, a lot along racial lines, but not all the black teachers went along with Hatchett. Morale was terrible. Some teachers left. Others went to the board of ed to say they didn't feel safe in the school. The assistant principal left, and only one newly appointed assistant principal was an experienced supervisor. The kids were coming apart. Fires, fights, gangs of kids running wild, furniture turned upside down. Teachers wouldn't get to their rooms at 9 o'clock and the kids would be alone in there. Hatchett was picketing outside after he was fired. His class was divided up among other classes. Once I went down and found four little girls from his class crying by the principal's office. The teacher whose class they'd been sent to refused to let them in, said she had no room for them. The principal's office had a gate and these big metal file cabinets blockading her from her door. [Nailor, soon to become principal of the school, had them removed.] I went to the board of ed, with UFT backing, to say the school was unsafe and we needed four or five additional teachers and a dean of discipline. They'd just given that to a school in the Bronx that had got into the same kind of trouble. Wilson went with the same request and they said, "Sure, ok, you get them." I got the feeling they wanted this thing—they had structured this for failure. At that time I didn't believe it of the union, but I believe it now . . . .

Then Wilson came in like 500 volts of electricity. He gave us the leadership we hadn't had all year. He did something that was absolutely brilliant. . . .

The Complex: Plans and Programs for Change

When Charles Wilson, Ronald Evans, and the 201 Governing Board headed by David Spencer assumed responsibility for the education of the children in district 4A in the winter of

1967-68, the immediate crises they faced—inappropriate and inadequate supplies, responsibilities far outweighing powers, shortage of personnel, teachers at war with one another, and children distraught with anxieties—were merely a bubble on the sea of disaster which is education in Harlem (many would say in New York and in America).

The board of education had given 201 three years to demonstrate that a misery of order or chaos could be turned into a process of education if the parents of the pupils were accorded status and could exercise power. What they got was a total of about six or seven months, separated by a summer vacation, and very little power. I am counting the months of the spring of 1968, from the time Charles Wilson was chosen to be unit administrator by the Governing Board, and Ronald Evans to be principal of I.S. 201, plus the autumn of 1968, until, with the termination of the Great Strike which crushed Ocean Hill-Brownsville, the defenders of the school system turned the heat on 201, so that the following spring they could accomplish in Albany the destruction of all three demonstration districts and probably the possibility for community control in New York in this period.

In those very few months, during which most of their energies were given to trying to cope with board of education hostility expressed as bureaucratic pathology, the 201 Complex also tried to effect some of the kinds of educational and social change that Preston Wilcox had proposed when he wrote, "We must find a better balance between scholarship and citizenship."

Programs to involve and support the community were planned and some undertaken.

At I.S. 201 itself, which was becoming a kind of symbol of the educational, cultural, and political aspirations of the community, the auditorium was booked for concerts, poetry readings, and meetings.

In one school there was a proposal to train a group of parent aides who would work regularly with the teachers and be available as per diem substitutes in the teachers' absence (a far better arrangement than the customary one of bringing in a stranger).

In the fall of 1968, the complex office published a 250-page manual, *The I.S. 201 Complex Community Information Manual.* It tells where to go if you experience employment discrimination; three ways in which high school dropouts can get a high school diploma; what emergency equipment and services you are entitled to if you are a welfare client; what city office to call if you have a complaint about removal of dead animals, a street cave-in on your block, or a water or gas emergency; how and where to apply for college scholarships and admission; and how to start your own business. It has a chapter on cultural heritage, one on narcotic addiction, and one on special agencies for the Spanish-speaking. Beyond its useful information, the book carries to the children's parents the message that the people in the children's school know about Harlem and about their lives. The publication of the *Manual* was the kind of gesture that could reach across the cold gap that separates the homes of Harlem from the alien schools of Harlem.

There was a program to provide medical examinations for all the children in the project. The complexities and coldness of most New York City free clinics mean that few medically indigent families are recipients of any preventive medicine at all and that many ailments are long neglected. Thus in an examination program in one school, of 470 children examined, 270 were referred for further treatment; of these, 79 had vision problems, 62 required dental work, 59 had a positive TB tine test, 29 positive sickle cell preps, 21 anemia, and 20 urinary problems! The same school defenders who recognize so well that sick, undernourished, near-sighted children cannot be energetic learners tended to oppose the community-controllers' medical and social service projects as going beyond the schools' proper domain.

One way of perpetuating an oppressive system is just by fragmenting responsibility. What the people at 201 were trying to do was to use the school as a lever to effect social change in many significant areas.

There were plans for after-school study programs, a "live-arts" program, community seminars, a home-management program. One reading consultant conducted an evening program to help parents help their children learn to read.

Although there were several brave and quite successful educational innovations, and although one heard among staff a good deal more serious talk about teaching, curriculum, and children than one does in most schools, in general, it must be said, the schools were run conventionally enough.

Some educators, including Wilson himself, thought far too conventionally. In the great gloomy indoor yards which are one of the less charming architectural features of New York City schools, there was still morning and afternoon shape-up by classes; the teachers still ticked "ssh, ssh, ssh" and "dontrunyoullfall" as the lines proceeded to their classrooms; in the four elementary schools, the children were ordered into homogeneous classes with infinitesimal distinctions astonishingly perceived by their teachers and themselves among as many as ten different groups; teachers still clocked in and out and brought notes from their doctor when they were sick; and the principal, if he was doing the job teachers, parents, children, and Governing Board expected him to do, was still in command. When one or another of the principals didn't do his job, everyone was likely to feel pretty unhappy and to want to find a way to replace him, a maneuver not encouraged by 110 Livingston Street or facilitated by the always staring angry public eye.

Perhaps the most intensive of the straight educational programs was the Schools for the Future program devised by Caleb Gattegno and instituted at P.S. 133, Mrs. Hercules' school.[26] For two weeks before school opened the teachers to be involved were trained by a math specialist and a reading specialist, who then remained to work with the teachers in the school for the entire following school year. They were both people whose high level of teaching energy charged up all the teachers who worked with them, and the children.

The reading method combined a kind of phonics system, a reading vocabulary of very active and emotionally charged words, and original writing by the children. So that instead of dragging through years of "See Dick run. Dick can run," in a very few months first-grade children were writing sentences like "Dad's impossible," "My brother is a pest," and "My mother is a nag." In other words, six year olds were using writing to communicate with the teacher and with one another, instead of merely submitting to it because their elders told them they had to. I watched Dorothea Hinman, the reading specialist, spend about twenty minutes with one third-grade class as they figured out "fatal," a word whose sounds they were just learning to decipher and whose meaning they didn't know. After the children had learned to read (pronounce) the word, she led them to its meaning, offering the phrase "fatal shooting," and then saying that Dr. Martin Luther King had been the victim of a fatal shooting. Then *they* told *her* what "fatal" means. It was twenty minutes of concentrated hard work, with teacher and children all putting forth intense efforts; but, having the prior experience and therefore the expectation of success, they were able to work together patiently to solve their puzzle. To have patience you have to have faith. The twenty minutes were spent not so much in teaching the word "fatal" as in renewing the experience that words are there to be deciphered and that if one will have confidence in one's skill, one will succeed in deciphering them. For there to be effective learning, there has to be self- and mutual trust at the level of each teacher and each child, and each child and each word. Unlike Miss White's class, where class and teacher were engaged all morning in trying to find out what the other was trying to convey—and about half the time not succeeding—here class and teacher were engaged in a common problem, which from their past experience they knew they were going to solve. The teacher was too busy helping the children solve the problem to bother about where they were putting their hands and feet, and the children were too busy solving the problem to be thinking up ways of bothering the teacher.

The principal and the small group of teachers of the lower grades who participated in this program during the 1968-69 school year were so impressed with the extraordinary progress their classes were making in both reading and math that the following year the program was undertaken for the whole school.

Because of the need for new training, for change in old-established classroom ways, and for a high degree of intellectual energy (as distinguished from disciplining, that is, status-reinforcing energy), it is most unlikely that a program of this kind could be imposed on teachers by a principal, a reading supervisor, or the board of education curriculum department, even supposing that any of these would be interested in introducing a radical new program.

In this case, a teacher on the very well-functioning staff of 133, hearing about the program, had asked its creator to come to the school and explain it to a group of teachers and parents. It was a small group of volunteer teachers who undertook to work with the method during the first year. The way in which the program was introduced and instituted suggests the kind of initiating, professional role that teachers might be able to play in a school system in which education rather than status preservation is the primary concern.

From the time he came to the 201 Complex, Wilson tried constantly to direct his staff's attention to the children, to the parents, to the community, and to the ways in which they all interact. When, on Wilson's introduction to community and staff, an earnest young teacher asked what he thought should be done about curriculum, Wilson responded, "Schools are about people; they aren't about curriculum. People have different ways to learn. Maybe we have to find out how people learn. When they don't learn, it means we've muffed the ball." Sometimes, laying on the canvas another of the myriad metaphors that colored (and sometimes obscured) his messages, he would say, "All these years when the children didn't learn, the educators blamed them. When a company's business starts falling off, you don't blame the customers. You try to find out why your product isn't selling and you change your ways to make it sell." He saw the old school system as being unable to do this. "Those guys," he'd say, "can't even conceive the problem."

Wilson himself conceived the problem in terms of restructuring people's relationships; rethinking all educational procedures; and developing viable administrative arrangements.

In administration he tried to be responsible without being the sole center of decision making. He wanted supervisors and his office staff to make decisions on their own, but did not pass on or delay questions that came to him to be answered. This was at variance with the customary bureaucratic procedure of passing the problems around and around the table not only until they get cold but until they get smelly and somebody drops them under the cloth. Wilson also tried to restructure the administrative arrangements between the unit administrator's office and the schools in such a way as to encourage responsibility and change. Feeling that even in the relatively small complex of five schools, he had too many people reporting to him for him to be an effective executive, he used one of the personnel openings in his office for an educational director. "We have educational administrators," he said of the old system, "but no educational leaders. Principals have too many teachers under them, supervisors too many schools, and so on."

Wilson's major concern was with people and the way they relate to one another. He felt that one aim of the "experiment" in community control was to help parents mobilize so that they would and could demand more of their children's schools, and so that they would force from the teachers the respect for them as human beings to which they and their children were entitled. Claiming that educators had never recognized parents as adults, he often announced that the parents of the complex were his boss and that if he pushed the teachers to perform it was because he was being pushed by the parents.

His sympathy for the parents and concern for the children, did not, however, make him an enemy of the teachers. He believed that teachers don't want to fail and that his task was to help them find ways to succeed. Similarly, Miss Hinman conceived her task to be to help the children find ways to succeed at reading. Wilson would have recognized the analogy: he sometimes spoke of education as a way of extending the opportunity for everyone to learn and develop—"find himself and what he's about." He sought opportunities for staff to meet and communicate informally and so overcome some of the cold artificiality that characterizes bureaucratic communication. Friday mornings from 8:30 to 10, staff members who had a free hour were invited to breakfast together on ham and eggs, grits, and biscuits, around a big table at a store-front community-action center dining room accessible to all five schools. And he visited the schools a lot, walking the halls and popping in and out of classrooms. On leaving a classroom, he would comment on the interaction among the children and between the children and the teacher, the teacher's rigidity or freedom, the physical arrangements that inhibited or encouraged flexibility in teaching and learning. For teachers for whom supervisory visits had always meant being rated and being judged, his visits may have been very difficult and frightening. For others, who sensed what he and the project were about, they apparently were not. In the hall of a school he was visiting, a teacher, trying to break up a fight between two boys, got drawn into the fight. Leaving the school, Wilson said, "Why do teachers have to feel personally affronted because a kid gets into a fight?" A half-hour after he had returned to his office, he received a phone call. "That's OK, I'm not there as a punitive observer. I'm there to learn why people act the way I see them act . . . If you helped him save face, then you're a big guy . . . You can't break up a fight if you start fighting. Well, teachers learn, too."

I should think that it has not often occurred in the history of the New York City school system that a classroom teacher called up a superintendent to inform him that he'd apologized to a child and the superintendent congratulated him for it.

Wilson's style was open, impulsive, dramatic, sometimes ostentatiously "tell it like it is" – quite unlike the typical schoolman's measured dignity which is so often a defense against communication rather than a means to it. He was familiar with personnel practices of big business, with a number of relevant academic disciplines, and with uses of psychology and sensitivity training in restructuring relationships. He was willing to re-examine every accepted school tenet and routine for its relevance to the needs of educating the children of Harlem. He ascribed his own sensitivity to the nuances of interpersonal relationships to his experience in working with the deaf, and his comments on classroom situations suggested to me that he had the kind of inner ear the deaf must have for the messages people send with smiles, posture, bodily movements, and physical positioning in relation to others.

These qualities, important if one is to be able to receive and interpret feedback (from one's pupils if one is a teacher, for example, or from one's teachers if one is a supervisor), are generally not cultivated by and not relevant to the status-superior, whose chief preoccupation is control. Both Miss White and Miss Jersild were unaware of how their pupils were reacting to the signals they were sending, except when the children were bad, and then they could say that that was the fault of the children's bad home environments. Likewise, Mr. Giardino was undoubtedly not aware of either the tone or the effect of the tone of his remarks to the school board members. (Even Giardino's top aide, who followed the events of the meeting most attentively, did not hear Giardino's put-down words or tone and after the meeting expressed apparently genuine surprise when confronted with the irritated reaction of some members of the audience.)

The fact is that a status system has a one-way communication line: talk goes from above to below. And there is no way for a status system to train sensitivity to the needs of those below and to the way in which one frustrates or meets those needs. Also there is no way for the merit system to select and promote individuals whose gifts lie in this area. The ordinary parents, community members, and staff people who comprised the Governing Board at 201, however, did manage to choose from among several applicants an individual whose gifts and training were applicable to the situation of their schools and their children. But although Wilson clearly *had* the requirements, he was judged by the board of examiners not to have *fulfilled* the requirements to be unit administrator of the complex. He was therefore hired as a per diem consultant, with no contract, no tenure, no pension, none of that bastion of security defenses without which most educators would feel even more insecure than they do.

Wilson's severest tests in his attempt to "build a system of trust," which was the aim he had stated to his Governing Board when he took over his job, occurred in I.S. 201, where the staff was agonizing over the relationship of black liberation to junior high school education, and in P.S. 68, where staff and children were tearing each other up in the aftermath of the Hatchett affair.

On assuming his post as unit administrator he gave his first big attention to P.S. 68. He went in and dressed down the entire staff for their atrocious behavior and then he took them away—along with some parents, some Governing Board members, and others—for a sensitivity weekend in Westchester County. Edward Gottlieb, one of the few principals in the New York City school system, as I have noted, whose focus of interest was the children and education, once wanted to use some special community-relations funds he had to hire a bus to take a group of parents and children to his country house for an all day Saturday outing. The funds, amounting to $40, had been allotted for after-school coffee and cake for parents ("Can you imagine," Gottlieb says, "$40 for coffee and cake!"), but the board of education official in charge of approving Gottlieb's expenditures said that obviously school funds could not be used on Saturday, not a school day. On another occasion Gottlieb's district superintendent refused permission for him to take two teachers from his school to an out-of-city school to observe a reading method which he thought the teachers might want to try out. A combination of bureaucratic refusal of imagination and infinitely petty stinginess would have made a sensitivity weekend in Westchester County seem to 110 Livingston Street the equivalent of a go at the tables at Las Vegas.

But for all those who participated in the sensitivity weekend, it seemed to have been something like an experiencing of grace. Afterwards they talked about it as one does of a miracle cure, with self-love and pride in their achievement. "You should have seen how terrible it was here last year!" Or, "We were simply awful before that!" Or, "Did anybody tell you what was going on here last winter?"

Then Wilson and the Personnel Committee set out to find the "strong, black male principal" that everyone felt P.S. 68 needed, and to persuade him to come into the complex and to persuade the board of education's bureau of personnel to assign him to P.S. 68. It was not an easy task. (To a young woman teacher from 68 who told Wilson how he had given them all a "breath of hope" and who begged him to find them a strong male principal, Wilson responded, "I'm trying, I'm trying. We educators make it a point not to take strong males in. Therefore it's hard to come by one.") When the schools of the 201 Complex opened in September, 1968, most other schools in the city being closed by the Great Strike, the staff of P.S. 68 were on top of it. They felt that with John Nailor as principal to guide and support them, they were going to be able to work well with one another and with the children.

Meanwhile the board of education's Bureau of Zoning and the board of education's Office of Personnel coincidentally each made a slip so that the rabbit almost disappeared into the hat forever. Zoning described a boundary line that, if sustained, would have removed 68 from the complex; but the Governing Board went in and got it back. And Personnel, having arranged Nailor's assignment to the school, nevertheless sent back the principal who had been away on leave for the whole previous year while the school was dissolving in bile. Wilson telephoned Personnel and said, "Either she's out in twenty-four hours or I call in the 'community' and they tear up the whole project. Then I resign and leave you to put it back together." The board, having its hands full at that moment with the "community" in Ocean Hill-Brownsville, arranged matters satisfactorily. Wilson preferred to be gentlemanly, but the complex had put a lot of money and time into 68 and they weren't about to let it slip away.

A sensitivity weekend is a quick-acting leaven, but too expensive to apply to all the schools' staffs. For the most part, staff and children's hopes would have to be raised gradually over time by the attitudes of their supervisors, by new programs, by the introduction of hopeful young people among them and the removal of the hopelessly hopeless, and by the staff's own sense of participating in an experience in democracy and learning instead of merely serving as instruments in a fatal operation.

I.S. 201 itself, symbol of the revolution, was beset by all the theoretical and interpersonal problems that had agitated the civil rights movement, the black power movement, and the struggle for power in the schools. No planned sensitivity sessions could have resolved the problems that vexed the staff there, but only working together on behalf of the children they all cared for, writing, talking, and sometimes bitterly wrangling about the issues that were agitating not only them but all of America. At I.S. 201 the resolution of the problems would have had to be sought in the carrying on of the struggle.

On the staff of the school were a group of strong black-power advocates, most of them young men, some of them indiscriminately hostile to whites; a group of youngish white men and women, tending to be sympathetic to black power but confused or angry when it was turned against them by their colleagues; a few older, more politically conservative black teachers; and a number of teachers who fit into none of these groups. Among the groups, as well as among individuals within them, there were considerable differences with respect to discipline, curriculum emphasis, and norms of staff relationships. Some blacks used positions of authority to assert control over those by whom they felt they had always been controlled (that is, they played the old status games); and some other blacks resented authoritarianism exercised for its own sake. Children raised hell with young teachers who were beguiled by libertarianism or incapable of establishing control, and older teachers exuded disapproval, sometimes ascribing the turmoil to the ineffectual teacher's color. Thus, a strong, middle-aged Negro lady teacher scolded a young white teacher because his class was in disorder: "If these were white Bronx High School of Science children, you wouldn't be letting them run all around the place like that." And a strong, experienced white teacher whose own classes were highly structured and disciplined disapproved of a philosophy that emphasized black pride but let the children run wild.

Wisely, Wilson refrained from interfering in the factional and philosophical struggles that were going on at 201, feeling that the participants themselves would have to find their way out. (Some of the black-power advocates disapproved of him because they felt his interpersonal-relations approach had insufficient black content.) All concerned recognized that finding their way out would take time. "We're finding our way," one teacher said. "We're going to have to have ten bad years before we get anywhere. Still I'd rather work here than any other part of the system. In the system, there's no hope for the kids. I'll go along with anything that tries to change."

Trying to stay afloat in the sea of public hostility, to avoid being swamped by the storms over Hatchett, over Ferguson, over Ocean Hill-Brownsville, left the I.S. 201 staff little enough peace and energy to resolve the grave racial, educational, and sometimes generational conflicts from which they suffered and which anyway were not peculiar to them but merely replicated in miniature at 201 the problems of the nation. Still they made stupendous efforts. They stayed when they might have left, like those who participated in the exodus accompanying Principal Lisser's departure early in 1967. Many of them did quite effective jobs of teaching. Some of the young men had come to teaching in order to get draft deferments. (For this, they and their counterparts at Ocean Hill-Brownsville were sometimes referred to by UFT President Shanker as "those draft dodgers"; likewise Socrates might be referred to as "that traitor.") They found teaching at 201 demanding and fulfilling in a way they had never expected. They learned about children, about themselves, about political struggles, and about black and white in America.

For some time, the staff at I.S. 201 published a little rexographed four- or six-page paper called *Focus*, in which they wrote of their belief in what they were doing, the problems of teaching, and the problems of society. In one issue, Barbara Gill, a young black teacher who was the I.S. 201 teacher representative on the Governing Board, published a series of papers written by herself and her students on the subject of "boredom," a common school phenomenon which certainly deserves serious investigation by teachers, students, and psychologists. A perceptive seventh-grade girl explained that students are bored when they don't understand what's going on and when their teacher is bored.

In times of crisis, *Focus* served as a medium for reducing tension and for personal reflection. A few weeks before the Malcolm X memorial assembly, LeRoi Jones had presented the same play he staged on that occasion to a student-writers workshop for I.S. 201 students and teachers, and some of the children in the audience had screamed antiwhite slogans. A white teacher wrote later in the next issue of *Focus*:

> *For perhaps the first time in their lives, it was possible for students to express some of these emotions openly in school. If the force of their reaction makes me uncomfortable I must wonder what sort of pressures produced that reaction.*
>
> *Later, many members of the audience apologized to those who had not joined in the shouting. For the first time in their lives, these students were in a position, relative to the Whites to whom they apologized, where the apology was meaningful.*

And a black teacher wrote:

[The] whole question of racism in America is very seldom really discussed. Most discussions start with a group of rules tacitly agreed upon by both Black and White, and the painful search for truth is already lost. . . . We at 201 have the opportunity to start this search anew. The relationship of teacher and student must be elevated to a new plateau. . . .

We might share with [our students] the fact that we too have fears, weaknesses; there is much that we do not understand . . . .

. . . Mr. Jones didn't create these questions. His plays only serve to bring to the surface something that has always been there. Maybe together here at 201, we can begin the painful search for some of the answers.

In effect what these two teachers were saying was that to overcome the school unreality, unrelatedness, phoniness that turns off most black and many white teenagers and makes them unable and unwilling to learn whatever it is the syllabuses say they are supposed to learn—in other words, makes them feel "bored"—the school must become involved in the agonizing issues that control the children's and their own lives and futures. The people at I.S. 201 and in the complex as a whole tried to do this, themselves tolerating the harshness and tensions that necessarily ensued. The effect was intolerable for an educational establishment that buys the myth that "racism"—or, as it came to be called, "racism in reverse"—is a rare characteristic found only among the lunatic fringe, say, such as LeRoi Jones.

In the end, though, 201 was not allotted its bad ten years in which to work out answers to questions and ways for effecting social change. Between the month of LeRoi Jones, John Hatchett, Herman Ferguson, and the Malcolm X memorial assembly and the ending of the 201 "experiment" hardly more than a year later, the defenders of the established ways fought skirmishes across the Brooklyn Bridge in the slums of Ocean Hill-Brownsville and up the Hudson River in the halls of the New York State Legislature. And the most forceful of the defenders was the United Federation of Teachers, the organization to which many of the 201 teachers had once owed loyalty.

3. THE UFT: DEFENDERS OF THE FAITH

The Leader and the Style

The passage from challenger of the establishment to junior partner, which in an earlier day took the American labor movement as a whole about sixty years to accomplish, was accomplished by the United Federation of Teachers in this, the jet age, in less than ten years. During the course of the trip, the union, like the great family of trade unionism to which it belonged, gained respectability and power and achieved a share in the decisions of management and a larger share of the proceeds of the business. While employing the militant language and tactics of the early labor movement, and adopting a liberal stance on racial, political, and educational issues, the union's actual direction and clearly apparent destination in regard especially to the emerging community-control movement nevertheless won over a substantial body of conservative teachers; threw it into the arms of right-wing politicians and conservative middle-management groups; and alienated, probably irrevocably, the most recent challengers of the system, the urban blacks, plus the white groups both among its membership and beyond it who were most seriously concerned about improving the schools and effecting social change. It consolidated its own power and prestige not only in the school system but in the political life of the city and state, and also the prestige and popularity of its president both within the union and in the wider political arena.

While the direction which the union took in the years 1964 to 1969 can be ascribed partly to the collapse of New York as a viable human settlement and the political atmosphere of the jet age—law and order, the self-delusive efforts of major portions of the population to blink away the existence and significance of hippies and black nationalists, Mayor Daley, and various repressions associated with waging a ferocious but unpopular colonialist war—a good part of the credit for the speed and successful completion of the voyage must go to its president, Albert Shanker. A tough fighter although generally restrained and eminently rational, sometimes without a firm policy but always sensitive to the many possibilities of the moment, democratic in public style but running a tightly controlled one-man operation inside the union's leadership cadre, a convincing manipulator of liberal lingo but never letting lingo interfere with sound strategy, modest in demeanor but an indefatigable TV performer, Albert Shanker became for middle-aged, middle-class New Yorkers what Frank Sinatra had been for them a quarter of a century before. After the Great Strike, a man teacher wrote to the *United Teacher* proposing that the teachers give a testimonial dinner for their president, and a lady teacher, clearly one of the old conservative antiunionists wrote:

As a teacher who was violently opposed to the unionization of teachers, I wish to say, I was wrong. Thank God the union exists.

A special, personal thanks to Mr. Shanker for his selfless dedication and his admirable conduct, dignity, and patience, in the face of such opposition. He represents the profession professionally.

Thank you.[1]

The UFT was an open, honestly run democratic union, in which the shifting, inchoate, sometimes contradictory sentiments of the membership were gradually forged into tough policy by one man. Among the inner leadership (executive board and top office staff), Shanker was both admired and feared for his strong personality, intellectual and verbal virtuosity, and self-assurance. Charles Cogen, the union's previous president, had had about him some schoolteacherish mildness and indecisiveness which won him affection but far less command than Shanker achieved. Shanker admired polemical skills and was himself a gifted polemicist, both in style and in analytic ability. He would be harsh and contemptuous—angry—with disagreeing colleagues, and many found it hard or impossible to tolerate this, so they didn't disagree. In addition, the fact that the union was still young and insecure and had some of the old trade-union sense of the need to present a united front to the outside world made it impossible for leaders to disagree openly, especially in times of crisis. Shanker sometimes exploited this vulnerability by making public statements which committed the union to a way of action without first consulting his fellow officers. His decision, for example, to enter the supervisors' case against the special appointment of the Ocean Hill-Brownsville principals (made, he said later to Martin Mayer, out of "pique") was actually a decision of tremendous policy import—aligning the union with the supervisors and against the community—an import that was perfectly clear in Harlem and Ocean Hill-Brownsville. But he announced it to the union's Advisory Committee so casually it was almost a throw-away line which no one there would think to debate. "Al makes policy through the media," a colleague once said. "He makes a statement that commits us to a policy, and then all you can do is try to chip away at it, chip away at it a little at a time."

Actually his strong style and firmly enunciated principled positions for a long time masked the considerable uncertainties that made the union course very wavering—in respect to More Effective Schools, the disruptive child, election of supervisors, and the union's relationship to community movements. To some extent the period of wavering may be said to have represented the teachers' indecision about whether to consolidate their strength through an alliance with those below them on the status ladder or through an alliance with those above them. In the end, the wavering produced a historical record which could be pointed to as evidence that the union had always supported whatever principle or program they might wish to say they had always supported.

In the larger population of the union's membership or its Delegate Assembly, Shanker showed himself to be a strong though generally fair chairman, a commanding figure, and a gifted manipulator. He could quickly rouse the delegates to such a pitch of commitment on a highly charged issue that when a speaker in the opposition took the floor, they would immediately start to holler and boo (the Delegate Assembly often sounded like a bunch of irascible kids on a ballfield playing without a referee), whereupon Shanker would say, "It is very hard to get up here and talk before all these people. It is especially hard to express an unpopular point of view. You should give your fellow delegates every consideration." And the rhubarb would subside instantly, the hecklers ashamed of themselves and respecting their leader for the reproof. ("It isn't nice to laugh at Collins, children.") In his appeals to a meeting to adopt this or that line, Shanker would combine a soft with a hard approach – reasonableness, principle, shame, ridicule, appeals to anxiety and fear. "That's all this great, big, powerful teachers union can do–appoint a committee," he might say if further consideration of a touchy issue was proposed. Or, "It'll be one teacher at a time, one school at a time, until no teacher is safe in any school in any borough and public education is destroyed," when presenting the threat of community "screening." Against his cleverness and certainty at any given time (even if later he would take another position), the ambivalence of teachers who were searching for ways to protect their rights as teachers without alienating the black community seemed somehow ineffectual and naïvely idealistic. Young, New Leftist, white teachers who spoke against him in the Delegate Assembly were sometimes hooted and booed. Blacks were listened to with sympathy and respect but gained no converts. Eventually they left the union.

In the city at large Shanker came to be among certain groups a kind of folk hero who in his principled upholding of group, class, and race interests resolved the nagging contradictions people were experiencing between their picture of themselves as liberal, decent, nonracist citizens and the role their status and racial anxieties were leading them to play in the city's racial-political dramas. During and after the Great Strike, many old liberals and labor union leaders understood how Shanker was defending their stake in society; newspaper dealers and taxi drivers gratuitously expressed their admiration and appreciation when they encountered him in the streets; and people began to imagine him as mayor of New York.

In the meantime those very qualities that commended him to his followers—the powerful combination of principled ethics and self-interest—made him anathema to his enemies: the black community, angry students, white school reformers, some old liberals, and teachers who opposed the union policy. Forgetting how powerful a social-political engine it takes to keep a Shanker airborne, opponents burned him in effigy, picketed his home, invented hate slogans around his name, and constantly inflamed themselves and one another by repeating his latest statements delivered on TV or to the press. I suspect that the variance between Shanker's tone and apparent intent, and between what the union said and what it did, were more responsible for the rancor that Shanker's enemies bore him than was the simple fact that he was determined to beat them in a struggle for power. For while the union would claim that it was trying—and perhaps with a kind of schizophrenic sincerity really was trying—to "build bridges to the community," it would at the same time be engaged in so roiling up the waters beneath, that Roebling himself would have fled in despair. (A case in point was the union-supported teacher bust, in effect, of the community's boycott at 201 in September, 1966, which then was followed by a period of the union working on the Gordon-Gottesfeld proposal along with the community and at the same time putting forth the odious disruptive child proposal.)

I think the union conceived itself always as a friend of the black community. A close associate of Shanker described in a letter to me a meeting she had attended with some of the Harlem activists after the 1967 strike, "so we could again begin to cooperate with the community." She complains, "They were extremely hostile in their greeting, and throughout our conversation, quite unfairly and needlessly so, since the last thing I conceived of myself as was an enemy of theirs." She assumed, of course, that her conception governed the case. A young black man I know once commented on this common phenomenon: "A white man can choose his own friends. But not a black man. Any white man that says he's your friend, you got no way of getting rid of him. Well, god-damn, I want to be able to decide myself who's my friend."

The union's enemies were enraged alike by both the union's constant affirmation and even acts of concern for the black and Puerto Rican communities and civil rights and its subversion of black and Puerto Rican aspirations. Thus throughout the whole struggle for power between the union and the community, the union was conducting courses and developing classroom materials in Afro-American history; at the very time the union was out to crush the 201 Complex and legislative decentralization with a single blow, Shanker and a large group of fellow-unionists marched with Martin Luther King in the Memphis garbage strike; and one of the strongest points in the union opposition to decentralization was that it would create a system of apartheid and destroy all hopes for school integration—hopes that the union was trying to keep alive long after they had been killed by the white community, including some school people, and buried with bitter farewells by the intended beneficiaries of integration.

Among the theoretical or principled matters on which the union (or Shanker) took diametrically opposing positions at different times were whether teaching ability is a universal regardless of the kind of child or community; the validity of the merit system for promotion; and the most desirable means of choosing the members of the board of education. In addition, during the period of the Great Strike, the union was dishonest about its early policy regarding decentralization and about the response of black teachers to the strike. Examples follow:

In 1964-65, when the integration pressure was becoming really uncomfortable, the board of education proposed to improve things for ghetto schoolchildren, not by stepping up desegregation, but by the forced transfer of experienced teachers from academically high-achieving all-white schools to academically low-achieving predominantly nonwhite schools. The union strongly opposed these forced transfers (which would indeed have upset the horizontal promotion that most long-term teachers count on), Shanker saying in a radio interview that he opposed the "concept of transferring a teacher who has been in a middle-class Bayside school for the past fifteen years as being prepared to cope with the many problems faced in a slum school." "Such a policy," he claimed, "fails to take account of realities . . ." But three years later, he opposed local qualifying interviews for teachers, saying, "If he's not qualified to teach in your district, he's not qualified to teach in mine." In addition, after opposing both "forced transfers" and salary bonuses as ways of getting more teachers into "bad" schools, he opposed decentralization because it would take away the central board's power to assign teachers where they are needed most.[2] From as far back as the 1920s, the UFT and its predecessors had consistently advocated teacher participation in the selection of supervisors, eventually demanding election of supervisors by teachers.[3] Clearly such a plank was an attack on the conventional merit system and a recognition that unmeasurable qualities which are recognized better by people than by examinations qualify a supervisor. Then the UFT not only joined in the CSA suit's defense of a very rigid interpretation of the merit system in 1967, but the next year when the board proposed to give the full title and rank to "acting" supervisors as a way of qualifying more blacks and Puerto Ricans in those positions, the UFT opposed the plan as an attack on the merit system.

For many years, the UFT opposed an elected board of education on the grounds that it would involve the schools in power politics (!); but it favored an elected board in 1968-69 after its own tremendously political strike of 1968 had generated UFT support from among great portions of the city's electorate.

It opposed decentralization with tremendous vigor throughout the academic year 1967-68, but during the Great Strike claimed it was not opposed to decentralization but merely upholding the need for due process. And when in September, 1968, it had by its policy driven from its ranks almost all its black members ("I can't go into my community now and say I'm a UFT member," one deeply torn black member said), it planted in the *New York Times* (September 20, 1968) an advertisement signed by friendly liberals which claimed that the danger lurking in the Ocean Hill-Brownsville dismissal of nineteen teachers "is understood by black and white teachers alike—which explains their strong solidarity in the most effective strike in teacher union history."

To understand why maneuvering and dishonesty, which after all have characterized power struggles throughout history,* should have so enraged the union's opponents, both black and white, I think one must look not to their naïveté (for I don't believe they were naïve) but perhaps to some feeling they may have had of having been personally betrayed. The type of man who though politically opposed to Nixon, let us say, would still not be personally outraged by him, or even by a Humphrey or a Kennedy, because he would have expected nothing of them in the first place, nor ever credited their expressions of good intentions–this man did, after all, believe in liberals, in Jews, in trade unionism, in educators, and in the political morality, fairness, and honesty of his neighbors and fellow New Yorkers. And when that very belief was used as a tool in a power struggle, which was fraudulently denied to be a power struggle, then the believer felt that it was he who was being used, and he responded with rage. I speak now of those white teachers and others who bitterly opposed the union policy, but I think the same might apply even to some blacks, however much most of them later protested that they had never had faith in white liberals, etc.

The firm belief in school integration on which the union based its opposition to community control and decentralization had been less firm only a few years before when the black community was making its last big push for integration. In February, 1964, after a spring, summer, and autumn of board of education evasiveness in respect to integration, the Reverend Milton Galamison, pastor of a middle-class Negro church in Brooklyn and a man who probably had some political ambitions, called for a citywide boycott against the schools to support demands for integration. At the last minute the diffused and somewhat disorganized boycott forces were coordinated by Bayard Rustin, coordinator of the 1963 March on Washington.

* *With the exception of such rare refreshingly honest though brutal events as the debate between the Melians and the Athenians in the sixteenth year of the Peloponnesian War and the Athenian's subsequent act of genocide. See Thucydides,* The Peloponnesian War, *Chapter 17.*

Considering that it professed to be a strong supporter of school desegregation, the union took a curiously ambivalent position on the boycott. In many schools the local chapters simply let it go by. In the predominantly nonwhite high school where I was teaching, the union chapter chairman, who considered herself a militant "progressive," evaded requests for a chapter meeting to discuss what position we should take in respect to the boycott. Though not a chapter officer I insisted on calling a meeting and arranged for the principal Edward Gottlieb, a boycott supporter, to speak, and the chapter voted to support the boycott. I was convinced that only the insistent intervention of one person brought about this support—that is, that the union would not otherwise have given it.

Of course this also happened in other schools, and many individual teachers as well as some whole chapters did support the boycott. But the UFT as a whole sidestepped. The UFT Delegate Assembly met to consider an unhappily indecisive resolution offered by the Advisory Committee. It was:

MOTION

A. *The Delegates reaffirm the UFT-Executive Board position that the organization will support teachers against reprisals if they respect picket lines of civil rights groups at their school because of their individual consciences.*
B. *The Delegates reaffirm the UFT's stand that the Board of Education come forth with an effective city-wide plan and timetable.*
C. *The Delegates reaffirm support for the UFT's Effective Schools Program as essential to achieve quality education.*
D. *The UFT urges immediate negotiations between the civil rights groups and the Board of Education in order to achieve quality integrated education.*

The resolution recommended nothing in respect to support of the boycott. It said it would protect *teachers.* It supported its own MES program. And it recommended that the board of education "negotiate" with the civil rights groups, knowing both how long the civil rights groups had tried to do just this and, from its own decades of experience, how fruitless was negotiation from a position of weakness. At one of the irritable, noisy sessions of the Delegate Assembly, a number of speakers (including an especially lucid and persuasive black teacher who later assumed an administrative post in the 201 Complex), urged unqualified endorsement of the boycott itself. And a handbill was passed out signed by one Reuben R. Gordon, a teacher, which concluded: "The issue for the leaders of the UFT and for the Delegates stands out stark and clear. Will you or will you not recommend that the teachers of New York City honor the picket lines set up by the City-Wide Committee for Integrated Schools? On that issue and on that alone you must now stand up and be counted."

The count supported the weak resolution proposed by the Advisory Committee, and the UFT started to slide down the road toward the Great Strike of 1968. In a conversation with John and Vivian O'Neill (the UFT vice-president and his wife, both long-time militant members who broke with the UFT at the time of the Great Strike), I once raised the question of what would have happened if the union had been consistently strong and committed on integration at the time when that was a live issue. "They would have had a lot of trouble with the membership," they agreed, "but they would have been in great shape now if they had weathered the storm."

Two and a half years later, in September, 1966, after a period of mounting teacher and public concern over pupil assaults on teachers, came the crucial confrontation between the community and the UFT outside the "windowless showcase," I.S. 201, and later that school year the resignation of Principal Lisser. That was the year of the disruptive child.

The Disruptive Child Issue

Albert Shanker explained the genesis of the disruptive child issue from the union's point of view in an interview with me:

> The disruptive child issue is a major issue for teachers. There's hardly a teacher who hasn't had the feeling or experience in a particular class that there is one kid or two

who take 95 percent of the time and attention and prevent them from functioning as a class and prevent other children from learning. But of course it's a somewhat subjective issue in the sense that you probably have about 5 percent of all the teachers who don't have any trouble with any child and you may have another 5 percent where most of the kids are considered disruptive. But by and large, there are children who, with 95 percent of the teachers year after year, day after day, time after time, exhibit certain types of behavior—call it disruptive. We have always had pressure from the membership. "Do something about the disruptive child." And a lot of the pressure was put in the form of "Why don't we have a contract provision that lets us kick kids out of classrooms?" The expulsion idea. We always resisted that. [Once at an annual conference] we had with us the president of the Detroit teachers union. They had negotiated a contract the year before last which didn't have very much money in it, but it did have a provision whereby teachers could expel children from the classroom for a one-day period requiring the parents to come in the next day and have sort of a conference to adjudicate the particular dispute. When our teachers heard that up there, they just went wild over it. So we printed it in the paper. But then we got a lot of flak the other way. A lot of our teachers said, "This really is a bad procedure and we don't want the right to throw kids out of the classroom—very antisocial." We had an executive board committee who worked on it and they came in with a plan that was very much modified from the Detroit plan.[4]

On March 11, 1967, at the same Saturday meeting of the Delegate Assembly at which the delegates, against the wishes of their president, voted to dissociate the UFT from the prowar, pro-Humphrey policy of the national AFL-CIO (thus demonstrating that on an issue to which they were strongly committed the delegates could use their union's democratic machinery to assert an independent position), the Executive Board proposed "A Program to Remove Disruptive Children from Regular Classrooms." The resolution would have passed primary responsibility for suspending a child from the principal to the teacher. Grounds for suspension included "endangering health and safety," "intimidation of teacher and/or students," "defiance of authority," theft, vandalism, gambling, obscenity, profanity, and inciting to violence. While the child could be immediately removed from the classroom, before he was suspended from school there would have to be a "planning conference" with the principal, which would include some or all of the following: counselor, social worker, psychologist, attendance teacher (truant officer), UFT representative, anybody else the teacher or supervisor wished to call in. *After the planning conference the parent would be called in and informed of the conference's decision.* (This from an organization that would shortly build a righteous mass movement around the ringing cry "due process"!)

A howl went up from the black community, from civil libertarians, even from some teachers, and the union eventually softened its disruptive child demands so as to exclude defiance of authority, theft, vandalism, gambling, obscenity, and profanity as reasons for suspension. In actual practice, the formal grounds are relatively insignificant. As we shall see in the case of Brad Dalton below, and as we know in respect to teachers who are marked for purging, a case can always be made against an individual whom it has been decided to axe. The union, discomfited by the mounting fury of the black community, kept toning down its disruptive child clause, never, however, giving up the principle that the teacher should bear a major share of the right to decide whether a child should be suspended. They were never able to understand why the same black parents who complained that the teachers let their children run wild, that there was no discipline in their schools, and that the children weren't learning anything were so opposed to a simple device for getting rid of offenders in order to produce in the classroom the peace and quiet necessary to learning.

President Shanker believed that the board of education "inflamed" the black community against the union, as a kind of union-busting device (the trade-union equivalent of the conservative outside-agitator theory as an explanation of black discontent). Shanker explained, "Every time the superintendent was on television, he said 'We're not going to allow teachers to throw kids out just because they don't like them.' "

It is true that the superintendent used the issue to help create opposition to the union, but the black community did not need the superintendent to make them understand: (1) that what amounted to chaos schools and chaos classes are created by the interaction of many social forces, not by a handful of disturbed children; (2) that teachers, and especially white teachers, are likely to be far more distressed by the culturally different and generally more open expressions of hostility provoked by school repressions in black children than by those provoked in white children; and (3) that the individual child up for suspension likely would get neither a fair hearing to determine how far he was responsible for the offenses complained of nor, if he were truly disturbed, the kind of services that might help him to overcome his disturbances.

A grave fault in the theory that if only the occasional disruptive (deviant) child (one in a class, perhaps, or two or three) were removed (suspended), all would be well, is dealt with by the sociological theory of deviant behavior. There is a good deal of literature on the subject, some of it taking off from the writings of Émile Durkheim. A most important contribution, in the form of a sociological-historical study, is the brilliant work of Kai Erikson, *Wayward Puritans,* which argues that deviance is not a property inherent in the behavior but is conferred on it by those who judge it; that "deviant forms of conduct often seem to derive nourishment from the very agencies devised to inhibit them"; that the deviant is significant and relevant to the normal life of the community; that the style which the deviant adopts is directly related to the community's most cherished values; and that the volume of deviant behavior in a community tends to remain constant over time.

The relevance of these propositions to classroom deviance is apparent. Aside from the relatively rare children who are so alienated from reality that the fashion and intensity of their disruption bear little relation to classroom norms, most classroom deviance seems to be a pushing out of just those behavioral boundaries to which the school and that particular teacher attach most importance. In every class there are likely to be one or a few children who will misbehave in precisely those ways that are most maddening to the teacher, and suspending them will do as much good as cutting off the hydra's head. Erikson writes: "Men who fear witches soon find themselves surrounded by them; men who become jealous of private property soon encounter eager thieves. And if it is not always easy to know whether fear creates the deviance or deviance the fear, the affinity of the two has been a continuing course [*sic*] of wonder in human affairs."

A strict and perceptive teacher at I.S. 201 once explained to me how he kept order, even in the worst chaos times. "I have to decide where to draw the line," he said. "If I draw the line at getting out of your seat, a couple of kids will get out of their seats, but they wouldn't dare get into a fight. That would be too great an offense. If I draw the line at talking, they might talk a little, but they wouldn't dare get out of their seats. If I insist they look at me the whole time, then they won't even talk. To keep control I have to not make issues over nonessentials, but when I make an issue, I have to follow through on it." Understanding the school game, this teacher could coolly decide how he would play it. But for most classroom teachers, deviant behavior is a nerve-racking, anxiety-provoking phenomenon which a few children produce out of some mysterious evil which they bear within themselves, and the teachers see the elimination of the afflicted child as a miracle cure for the social disease.

Since many teachers are more anxious and more repressive in respect to poor nonwhite children, expect them to misbehave, and take the smallest infractions as symptomatic of rampant intentions to commit the worse, and since also the feelings of hopelessness in respect to fruitful learning do lead poor black and Puerto Rican children to misbehavior in greater numbers than white middle-class children, the black and Puerto Rican parents were justified in fearing that it was their children who were the targets of the union's disruptive child clause. And the eloquently angry mother of the black birds for whom the sky was the limit was somehow right when she said, "If they're disruptive, *you* made them disruptive."

The fact is that nonwhite children are suspended from school with far greater frequency than are white children, and, I suspect, often for offenses for which white children would be let off with a simple reprimand. (During the school year 1968-69, however, as we shall see, student rebels, and the children of opposition parents were suspended in great numbers regardless of race.) A study of school suspensions during the 1967-68 school year in district 5 of Manhattan, which includes black, Puerto Rican, and middle-class white children, found that 1 of each 90 black children had been suspended at some time that year, 1 of each 180 Puerto Rican children, and 1 of each 1,250 white children.[5] Suspension proceedings were often casual, records in the district office kept with lamentable casualness (largely because of lack of personnel), temporarily suspended children sometimes forgotten for months, and seriously disturbed suspended children left unschooled and untreated.

How suspension is experienced by the child and his family—the one of every 90 black children or one of every 180 Puerto Rican children—is suggested by the experience of Brad Dalton, a thirteen year old in the seventh grade. I'm going to tell the story as Brad and his mother told it, without questioning the factual accuracy of their account, since what is important here is not whether Brad did or did not hit a teacher or commit the other offenses complained of, but how he and his mother felt about the school during and after the suspension proceedings, and by implication how they would feel about an organization that advocated increasing suspensions as a way of improving the schools.

Brad's whole class was running down the stairs to the lunchroom, and Brad was caught by his teacher and told to go to the end of the lunch line because he had been running. (It is not uncommon for a teacher to single out one of a group of offenders as an example to the others.) Brad answered angrily, "I ain't goin' in the end of the line, man," and the teacher told him he would throw him back there if he didn't go. Brad said, "You not throwin' nobody." The teacher grabbed him, and Brad resisted. (Later the teacher charged Brad with unprovoked assault in response to the order to go to the end of the line.) Eventually the dean got involved, and Brad was sent home that afternoon with a message for his mother that he was not to come back to school the next day and that she should await formal notice of a suspension hearing.

There had been previous difficulties between Brad and that teacher. Brad described the teacher as "a troublemaker"—that is, he made trouble for Brad. The expected letter appeared under Mrs. Dalton's door the next morning, announcing that her son had been suspended and that she would eventually receive a notification from the district superintendent's office to attend a suspension hearing. (This meant that longer than a five-day "principal's suspension" was intended.) Mrs. Dalton said of these procedures:

I thought it was mighty strange. I felt if my son had any problems in the school whatsoever, it was the school's place to get in touch with me or his father, to bring us into school and tell us exactly what happened. I had never been through anything like this before. I've been through many experiences, I'm the mother of seven children and I have never had any child suspended from school. I have been in many times talking to the teachers about the behavior of my children, if there is a behavior problem. And then if I do, I give them my cooperation, I try everything that I possibly can do, to gap this error, to discipline my children in a way that they probably won't go for this thing again. I always tell my children, "Right or wrong, if a teacher tells you to do something, you do it. If you have any questions later, you bring this question to me. If I feel there is something wrong, I'll go into the school and I'll check into it. But you are not to try to handle your own problems personally. You are there to learn." I do chastise my kids and I don't condone any of them for disbehavior or being disrespectful to a grownup. But children will do things when you're not lookin' at them. So I'm not here to say he wasn't disrespectful to a teacher, I'm only here to say that if he has a problem in school, that I feel as his parent, I should be aware of it, the school should get in touch with me to let me know what happened. And I felt kind of left out as a parent. I felt I was being looked over as a parent. This I resent. I resent it very much. I resent it to the fact that I said I should go in to the school immediately and discuss it with them. But they said in the letter, "Stand by for further notice. We will get in touch with you." In other words they was tellin' me *not* to come. "We will call you and wait for us to get in touch with you."

Mrs. Dalton was "completely kept in the dark" for ten days, the principal refusing to see either her or a member of her local school board whom she had asked for help. All this time, of course, she had to keep Brad out of school. When she came to the hearing, the district board member who had been acting as her advisor was not allowed to come with her and she had to confront alone a whole room of people, most of them stand-ins for various school people who she had been told were supposed to be present. Further, the teacher who had instituted the suspension action was not himself present. Mrs. Dalton did not know what offenses Brad was going to be charged with, and she got a bad shock when they were presented:

At the hearing, eight pages was presented and from the way this paper was presented you would think this was a completely corrupted child, a child that wasn't even fit to live in society. He'd have to be put away, you know. I mean this is the way they had him to be. When I as his parent know he is not particular that way. Like I told them at the hearing, not only does Brad go to school, Brad also participates in other places, he participates in the settlement, he participates in church. Any organization on the south side that's good for children—the Dalton family is in there. And this is the first I have heard of what Brad actually did in the school was at this hearing. So how in the world can I really prepare myself to answer all of these charges when this is my first hearing from any school authority what my child did?

She insisted on another hearing so she could confront and respond to Brad's accuser, and then she asked him why he hadn't told her Brad was doing all those bad things. He said he has tried to help Brad many times by talking with him, but that he hadn't wanted to bother her. She was pretty mad about that, and disbelieving. She said she knew children were sometimes disrespectful to grownups and then if you really wanted to help them, you'd best call in their parents. Her phone number was listed in school. She didn't believe he really was trying to help Brad. She also explained to the interviewer that she found out from some other teachers that although this teacher had been represented by the dean as an old-timer at the school, he'd actually only come a few weeks before, in the middle of the term.

Teachers in the school that sees him, you know, they went over to meet this boy, he was nice and polite. Of course they're not going to come up against the dean of the school and the principal of the school, you know, but I have been approached many times by them and they can't understand why Brad's in trouble, I mean they wasn't aware of it, they don't know what happened, it was kind of like a secret.

Mrs. Dalton was groping her way towards a new perception of how the school system works.

This is the funny thing that I was trying to tell you about, I find when it comes to the school and the child . . . I always thought that the school was there to protect the child, in so many ways, but when I got to this hearing, I find out as a parent it's a different way: that everybody is there to protect the school, and the authority in the school, and the people in the school, even down to the district superintendent, and his job.

Brad Dalton's suspension adventure has an incredible storybook ending. The district superintendent—a man of unusual compassion and concern—said that in cases of assaults on teachers the child is never returned to the same school and that this is the policy he would follow; however, instead of continuing the suspension or sending Brad to a "600" school, he suggested a transfer to a nearby, predominantly middle-class white school. Mrs. Dalton, now very suspicious, said she was first going to check the school out.

And it really is a nice school, and they have a lot to offer children. As a matter of fact, they offer the three languages in the seventh grade, which they don't ordinary do in other schools [i.e., in nonwhite schools]. Sometimes they don't get that until the ninth grade and some children never get to it. The principal invited me to stay as an observer for the day. She invited my son to stay because she said, "Over here our schools are run a lot different from your schools." Where he came from, they go as a group, whatever they do, they do as a group, you know as a class, but in this particular school they don't go as a class, they go as an individual. You have to trust a child. You will have to believe a child will be able to get their next assignment without the teacher on his tail all the time. They wanted to let me and Brad observe a day to find out if Brad was able to participate in this type of a program coming from a different one. So, it seems he came out with flying colors. I stayed until twelve o'clock that day and one particular teacher . . . a social study class . . . even I, at my age as a parent, got something out of that class. This teacher was something else. She was very anxious to hear the children's opinion, you know. I wish there was more like her.

She called the district superintendent's office to say yes, she wanted Brad to go to that school. But now the guidance coordinator to whom the case had been turned over tried "some of her wheelin' and dealin' "; the coordinator said she thought that wouldn't be too good a school for Brad and proposed instead another predominantly nonwhite junior high school. Mrs. Dalton had to argue with her, reminding her again and again that this was the school the district superintendent had recommended, and finally she had her way.

At the school from which he had been suspended, Brad had been in a middling seventh grade—around 7-9 or 7-10. As a matter of fact, Mrs. Dalton had maneuvered around some about that, feeling that if the work were too hard for him, he would get into trouble because he'd be discouraged, and if it were too easy, he would get into trouble because he'd be bored. A few weeks after he started in the new school, she telephoned there just to make sure he was doing okay.

I called the school just yesterday and they told me he was just wonderful. They can't imagine this child being in trouble, "because he's beautiful here. I mean we have no problems, he do everything accordingly." I just hope it continues. And they find that on ability and his reading level they was able to put him in 7-2 there. And he is doing wonderful there. They're happy with him and he's happy with them.

At the time she was interviewed, Mrs. Dalton was trying to figure out how to get her three other junior high school children transferred too.

The marvelously lucky outcome of the Dalton family's experience with suspension (which I suspect that the unusual district superintendent had deliberately manipulated) did not however in any way blur Mrs. Dalton's perception of the unfairness of the proceeding and the self- and system-serving callousness of most of those who participated in it. Few suspended students are as lucky as Brad. Many are forgotten for months. Many are sent to "600" schools, which are generally mere holding operations and attendance at which leaves a mark on a child's record—and often soul and development—only one step away from commitment to a training school. Many are eventually transferred to another "bad" school, where the child's sense of the injury he has received at the hands of the system is added to whatever drove him to deviance in the first place so that he will surely "get himself suspended" soon again. The really deeply disturbed may be recommended to more or less adequate psychological or educational agencies, and the parents may or may not follow up on the recommendations. Of the 195 suspension cases in the (1967-68) study of district 5, 174 were referred for service, and there was "strong evidence" that contact was actually made in 103 cases. In any case, in respect to a number of these agencies, including the notorious "youth houses," we may properly quote Erikson's caution, "Indeed, the agencies built by society for preventing deviance are often so poorly equipped for the task that we might well ask why this is regarded as their 'real' function in the first place."

If the district 5 ratios of 1 in 90 black children and 1 in 180 Puerto Rican children suspended in a given academic year are anything like representative for the city's black and Puerto Rican population as a whole, then it would be a rare black or Puerto Rican family that would not over a period of, let us say, five years have first- or second-hand knowledge of a suspension case, and likely one much more distressing than Brad's. No wonder the whole of nonwhite New York was revolted by the disruptive child demand! And by the organization that by sweetening it up a bit sought to force the demand past the disgusted parents' clenched teeth—the organization that after using the disruptive child demand as the long spring initial buildup for its 1967 biennial new-contract demands, went on strike in September with the slogan "TEACHERS WANT WHAT CHILDREN NEED."

War Games: The 1967 Strike, Bundy, and George Fucillo

For the Board of Education of the City of New York and the United Federation of Teachers to reach their biennial agreement on salary, class size, working periods, sick leave, and so on requires an elaborate ceremony lasting many months and involving the mayor, the press, the media, "the public," various supervisory organizations and various citizens organizations, plus, if it comes to a strike, the courts, mediators, other labor unions, draft boards, and any other groups or prominent individuals who have a stake or an interest in the power plays being enacted.

The ceremony customarily begins quietly in the spring with occasional public announcements that negotiations are in progress for a new contract. The two parties are of course far apart on salary and other issues. The union accuses the board's negotiators (usually the superintendent of schools) of foot-dragging (the board being, as we have seen, a congenital cripple when it comes to negotiating with "inferiors"), and the board accuses the union of trying to usurp its educational decision-making powers. In addition, the board says the union's salary demands are totally unrealistic; it just doesn't have that kind of money. This claim may be reinforced by the board of estimate's annual budget which actually reduces the amount of money the board had asked for to keep going merely on the old scale. The union persists, knowing that when the authorities have stretched their resistance to the snapping point, the mayor will dip into some hidden pocket and bring up the funds necessary for a good compromise agreement. Through June, public pronouncements become increasingly frequent and increasingly acrimonious, and uninvolved groups and the New York *Times* are saying that they hope both sides will exercise good sense and moderation out of consideration for the children. But by the time the school year ends in June, with no agreement in sight, the union spokesmen say they don't see how a strike can be avoided in September, although the board of education, with its big investment in cheeriness stocks, is sure they will reach an agreement before September.

During the summer, mock negotiations proceed, as both sides feel obligated to convince "the public" that they are working frantically toward a settlement. Of course, with children and teachers gone from the schools, "the public" not turned on to school problems, and the two sides thus having no tools to use in the prying out of power advantages, they do not expect to reach an agreement. But to ensure that the game will be played out fairly quickly once school is due to open, the mayor may intervene himself sometime along in August, or appoint a mediator. The weekend before school is due to open, there being no settlement, the union calls a mass membership meeting to take a strike vote.

The union is determined to get enough more for the teachers so that each teacher will recognize some little improvement in her daily routine or her monthly salary check and so that the membership as a whole will emerge with a sense of solidarity and victory. The mayor, knowing he's going to have to put his hand into that hidden pocket, nevertheless has to make it look tough enough so he can fend off all the other unions in the city when they come around for their piece. And the board of education, confronted with the union's demands for participation in making educational decisions, has to try to protect its own house-of-cards system of prerogatives, which is its sole claim to function in the running of the schools. To determine if there is to be a strike, and if so, how long it is to last, the delicate interplay of these contending forces must again draw in "the public."

The union must convince the public not only that the teachers' salary demands are legitimate, but that both the salary demands and the working condition demands are directed toward improving the schools. The union may even sometimes have a difficult job persuading its own members of the necessity for a strike, as some of them regard a strike, and especially a strike for money as unprofessional, and others regard a strike for anything but money as idiotic. Thus the leadership's decision to call for a strike and then to recommend a settlement at any particular point must take membership attitudes as well as public attitudes into account. The mayor and the board have to convince the public that while they are doing the best they can, the union, by holding up a settlement, is doing terrible damage to the children. Normally the conservative newspapers more or less support the mayor and the board, while the liberal prolabor New York *Post* supports the union.

The negotiations and strike of 1967 followed the customary pattern, *except* that the events of the preceding academic year, in the fall of 1966 in the affair of Principal Lisser and during the spring of 1967 in the pushing of the disruptive child clause, turned some of the public and some of its own members against the union and prepared others to support it even before the appropriate time for the lining up of public opinion. Already in the spring of 1967, black and Puerto Rican community groups and the African-American Teachers Association were lining up in opposition to a possible teachers strike. Otherwise things proceeded more or less according to the usual program during the spring, with salary and some working conditions the major bargaining items. The disruptive child clause was not dropped from the union's demands, but the union did not make a public issue of it. The board, as Shanker said, used the demand as a way of reinforcing the black community's opposition to the union.

It was some time during the summer when another of the union's demands surfaced as a significant item in the negotiations. This was the demand for continuation and extension of the More Effective Schools Program. "MES was the issue of the strike," one high-ranking union official told me. "MES was a blind," John O'Neill said. Whichever, MES served powerfully in that critical period of mobilizing public support for the strike and convincing strikers of the justice of their cause.

More Effective Schools, proposed by the union and instituted by the board in ten elementary schools in 1964 and eleven more in 1965, was a program for upgrading the schooling of poor nonwhite children by providing more space, equipment, and personnel. Classes were smaller and the children had more space to move around. The total register of the school was lower. The ratio of teachers to children was higher, and there were more paraprofessional personnel than in a regular or a Special Service School. Classes were heterogeneous instead of ability-grouped. There were also more guidance, counseling, and psychological services. The total cost per child of these improvements was $218 in 1964-1965, about $300 in 1967-68, and probably about $500 at the time of writing. The aim of the MES Program was to approximate in "ghetto" elementary schools the objective teaching conditions found in academically high achieving middle-class suburban schools, with the addition of guidance-type personnel who would supposedly help to reduce the special "adverse effects of poverty."

The MES Program provided the conventional measure of more money, which the UFT believed to be the key to improving the education of poor nonwhite urban children. Its effectiveness was measured by the conventional measure of reading tests. Studies of the effectiveness of the program by this criterion–plus one evaluation that purported to measure objectively such subjectively experienced classroom phenomena as "quality of instruction," "creativity and imagination" (of teacher), and "general attitude of children toward the teaching staff"–produced ambiguous results.[6] The children seemed to show some slight improvement in reading over control schools, but were still behind national and New York City norms. Teachers, parents, and perhaps children in ME schools probably had higher morale than those in non-ME "bad" schools, certainly those in chaos schools. In some cases, however, this improvement was accompanied by a worsening of matters at a neighboring ordinary school. As a small total register, small classes, and lots of space were among the essentials of the program, the board would sometimes have to shift a couple of hundred children out of a school being converted to MES status, thereby aggravating space and related problems in the school to which they were shifted. The popularity of the program among some parents and staff was therefore bought partly at the expense of children and staff elsewhere. Thus, while some black and Puerto Rican parents were wholeheartedly in favor of MES, others were indifferent, and the activist groups tended to oppose MES as a program for *any* school.

In effect what MES was doing was again trying to overcome some of the effects of the internal contradictions of the system–the conflict between serving the status system and serving the children–without seriously challenging the system's ways. MES, limited as it was to elementary schools, did not address itself at all to the problem of why poor children are increasingly turned off by school as they approach adolescence. And although many community people were employed as paraprofessionals, and parents were generally happy about the nice atmosphere, there was no real status or power shift as between parents and school personnel. It was, as a matter of fact, in one of the best ME schools in the city that I observed two very young lady teachers of a prekindergarten class assign their middle-aged paraprofessional classroom aide to such chores as cleaning up after the children's lunch, helping the children on with their rubbers, and so on, while they read to the children or conversed with them to "help improve their verbal skills" and performed other functions which, unlike showing a four year old how to put on his rubbers or set the table, they labeled "teaching." They said the paraprofessional can do everything but "teach." Surely the lesson would not be lost on the parents, perhaps even not on the children, that there is a hierarchy of tasks to which the hierarchy of persons is fitted. The union's summary statement of the qualities of an MES emphasizes this point: "Teacher aide time . . . frees the teachers from nonteaching duties so that they may devote their energies and time fully to their professional responsibilities." This concept, appealing to teachers, emphasizes the status differences that lie between "professionals" and "paraprofessionals" and ignores the creative, productive ways of bridging the gap which some Headstart programs and experimental schools throughout the country had been developing.

MES, although a UFT-proposed remedy, only gradually came to be an item to which there was strong union commitment. In January, 1967, when the topic was still cool enough to be objectively appraised, a writer in *The United Teacher* defended it thus: "We must frankly recognize that it is not realistic, considering the financial, physical, or professional resources which are available or can be made available to the schools, to plan in terms of immediate, total improvement of the New York City school system; therefore the most critical areas of the city should be singled out for total improvement first."[7] This honest explanation also helps to explain why, although the MES parents may have been pleased, responsible spokesmen for the whole black and Puerto Rican community would not be interested in a program which would benefit slightly and perhaps only temporarily twenty or thirty thousand, less than 6 per cent, of the 350,000 black and Puerto Rican elementary school children in the city.

But by September, 1967, MES was represented by the union as a major program for improvement of the school system.

Just before school opening day in September, 1967, both the teachers and the board of education had turned down a series of proposals by the mayor's mediators which offered the teachers substantially the pay raise they eventually received after striking for almost three weeks but next to nothing in respect to getting rid of disruptive children, reducing class size, and ensuring the continuance of the MES Program. The theme of the strike that ensued, "TEACHERS WANT WHAT CHILDREN NEED," enabled the teachers to say during the strike and when it was over that they had been fighting for *educational*, not monetary, gains. This had a clear public relations advantage.

The black activists and some black teachers opposed the strike bitterly and persuaded parents to come in to man struck schools, providing a little preview of the lineup and maneuvers of the Great Strike the next year.* The union responded by warning parents to keep their children out of schools manned by "undesirables" or people with tuberculosis (a reference to the regular chest x-ray requirement for all school personnel). These warnings further aggravated the black community's hostilities. The city got out an injunction against Albert Shanker under the state Taylor Law which prohibited strikes by public employees, and some supervisors sent to draft boards the names of young teachers who had occupational deferments. Black and some young white teachers, including some of those who in an earlier period would have been among the most militant unionists, were extremely ambivalent. But an element of conservative, generally older teachers, who had been pretty stalwart opponents of teacher unionism and

**Except that in 1967 the principals and the board encouraged parents to act as strikebreakers, while in 1968 they discouraged them to the point of sometimes having them arrested for attempting to enter the schools.*

had never struck before, joined the strikers, and joined the union. One can only speculate, but I think that Shanker's personality, the frightening opposition of the black militants (dramatized by the 201 "screening" threat), and the educational issues for which the union was fighting, accounted for the adherence of this conservative group. The strike lasted almost three weeks and the strikers' morale in general mounted steadily throughout. The threat to jail Shanker was a booster rather than a deterrent.

On money demands, the teachers got more or less what the mediators had recommended (and the board of education had turned down) before it began. On educational issues, it got a small reduction in maximum class size, an increase in the number of "preparation" (nonteaching) periods for most classroom teachers, considerable concessions on the disruptive child, and some concession on MES. In respect to the disruptive child, the significant factor was that board of education procedures on suspension became an item in the union contract, thus recognizing the union's rightful interest in the matter. Ten million dollars was won for special educational programs, including MES, to be recommended by a special work group which would consist of two union representatives, two board representatives, and two parent or community representatives *to be chosen by the first four* (a colonialist mode of selection generally in line with board and teacher treatment of their low-status clients).

With the 1967 strike and contract, the struggling United Federation of Teachers achieved junior partnership status in the New York City school system. The strike itself had been an exhilarating experience for many teachers. "It was a *wonderful* strike!" a teacher friend told me on my first visit to the city after it had ended. The altruistic aims of the strike, the new enemies encountered and overcome, the exciting sense of risk in staying out so long, all must have contributed to the feeling. If the strike itself gave the teachers and their fellow citizens a consciousness of the UFT's power in the affairs of New York, the settlement inscribed some of the ways in which that power might be used. Likewise, Albert Shanker's power as the three-year president of the union was consolidated. His emerging personal popularity within the union and throughout the city was fed by his well-publicized fifteen-day jail term in

December, celebrated by teacher and other trade unionist picketing of the jailhouse. "It is a sad day in these United States," he told his Delegate Assembly while the sheriffs stood by waiting to take him away, "when anyone has to go to jail because he has been fighting for smaller classes, for More Effective Schools, for more regular teachers, for more money for education and for teachers."

Whatever the reasons for which the teachers went on strike and stayed on strike in September, 1967–and they must have been different for different individuals–the outcome was a vast strengthening of the power of the union. The teachers had flexed their muscles, and the board of education had hollered uncle. The whole city saw it happen and were impressed or appalled depending on how they expected the union would use the muscle they had bared.[8]

Then in November came the Bundy study on decentralization, *Reconnection for Learning*. The board of education was walloping the demonstration projects with bureaucratic truncheons while the UFT was snapping around at their heels and the press was delightedly reporting the rout as an attack. And now the mayor and the Ford Foundation, who had been moderately helpful behind-the-scenes supporters of community control, came in with a grand plan for decentralization, which they said was more or less the same thing as community control.

In the spring of 1967 the New York State Legislature, thinking perhaps to put an end to the recurring crises and scandals and the insatiable monetary demands of the New York City school system, had directed the mayor of New York to "prepare a comprehensive study and report and formulate a plan for the creation and redevelopment of educational policy and administrative units within the city school district of the City of New York with adequate authority to foster greater community initiative and participation in the development of education policy for the public schools . . . and to achieve greater flexibility in the administration of such schools."[9] In May, Mayor Lindsay appointed a panel of distinguished citizens headed by McGeorge Bundy, chairman of the Ford Foundation, which at just that time was interesting itself in the struggling-to-be-born community-control projects.

The plan, issued in November, carefully printed and

adorned with meticulous index, footnotes, charts, tables, and appendixes, is another of those evidences we Americans keep producing of our silly belief that power relations can be altered in favor of the powerless by public-relations scholars seated in fine offices overlooking lush hot-house gardens. The Bundy Plan attacked some internal contradictions of the system—for example, the complex and restrictive procedures for accrediting teachers in a time of teacher shortages; the tight administrative control over a school system exercised by an autocratic agency which has neither administrative know-how nor an interest in education; the mistreatment and apathy of those adults who are most important to the children but least important to the system. But it deliberately fails to confront the issue of power and status in the system. Thus:

> *We are further convinced that increasing the role of one party (and we are emphatic that real participation implies a real share of authority and responsibility) does not imply robbing other parties.*
>
> *. . . If one assumes, as the Panel does, that the interest of an overwhelming majority of all New York City parents is the quality of education in the schools, not the exercise of power for power's sake, then pressures for ethnic preference are likely to subside after the initial period of reorganization.*

Watching McGeorge Bundy before a meeting of the UFT Delegate Assembly, I personally sensed him to be innocent rather than disingenuous. I thought that he did not understand that unlike material wealth which, when subdivided and shared, can generate more wealth all around, the kind of authority and responsibility which confer status no longer confer status when they are shared. So the acquiring of authority and responsibility by those of lower status does indeed rob other parties of the very kind of authority, status-authority, that is most valued in the school system. And power was precisely what the powerless parents did want. What else is the education race about?

That, in the end, if it did not confer power, decentralization would be simply another game run against the poor, the plan itself somehow recognized:

> *At the same time it is important to emphasize that the best possible reorganization of the New York City schools can*

be no more than an enabling act. It will not do the job by itself. Reorganization will not give New York the additional funds it needs to improve schools in all parts of the city. It will not wipe out the generations of deprivation with which hundreds of thousands of children enter the schools. It will not meet the great deficits in health and welfare services that beset many families. It will certainly not wipe out the poverty and physical squalor to which too many children return when they leave school every afternoon. It will not wipe out the shortage of qualified, imaginative, and sensitive teachers and supervisors. It will not automatically provide insights into the uncharted terrain of the basic mechanisms of learning and teaching.

By comparison with Preston Wilcox's rationale for community control, this passage indicates how little the Ford Foundation scholars understood the relationship of school to society, the possibilities of using the school as an instrument of social change, the extent to which teachers may be rendered "qualified" and "sensitive" by the relations of power in which they operate (for example, teachers are very sensitive to the needs of their superiors), and how much very good charting of the mechanisms of learning and teaching has been done, only to be neglected by school systems far more interested in status preservation than in learning.

While the Bundy Plan was either innocent or hypocritical in respect to power relationships at the level of the school, the teacher, and the parent, it recognized the possibilities of power struggles at the district and city levels, and created ingenious devices as a protection against direct democracy.

The community school boards, for example, would consist of: six members selected by a panel elected by parents in the districts, and five more "selected by the Mayor from lists of qualified persons presented by the central education agency after consultation with parents and community organizations." By comparison, the Electoral College, devised by the Founding Fathers to diffuse (or defuse) democracy in the new nation, was a model of simplicity. Indeed, the plan's justification for the arrangement sounds for all the world like a twentieth-century Alexander Hamilton:

The proposed selection procedure is not simple. It is designed to balance the desire for the greatest possible parental participation with the need for successive safeguards against block [sic] voting, partisan politics, and other noneducational influences in school affairs. . . . Arguments against direct election of members include the danger of domination by political clubs; the expense to candidates of campaigning; the distastefulness of election campaigning to men and women who would otherwise be willing to serve . . . ; the possible domination of school affairs by majorities of residents who were not parents or by sectarian interests that might not hold the interests of public education uppermost. *

So do the aristocrats yield to pressures from below by setting up a simulacrum of popular control whose complexity is a defense against serious assaults on going power arrangements, these being labeled "the permanent interests of the community."

The Bundy proposal was a bundle of elaborate administrative rearrangements designed to rescue a bankrupt operation before the depositors started a run on the bank. I should think that Shanker and the UFT and all the other defenders of the system against the Bundy Plan were right in sensing that even a slight tampering might have so exposed the system's fundamental weaknesses as to make it even more vulnerable to attack by those who were truly aggrieved. In addition to real faults in the proposal, of which the proliferation of expensive bureaucratic machinery was a serious one, each of the many groups that attacked it had its own stake in preserving the status quo. The board of education (bureaucracy and lay board) would have been quite shorn of power and status. The supervisors would have been made responsible to district boards, a perilous change from their going arrangement. The teachers

* *Change "sectarian interests" to "factionalism" and you have the Federalist Paper Number 10 on how republican government helps to overcome the effects of that "dangerous vice." "By a faction," Madison wrote, "I understand a number of citizens, whether amounting to a majority or minority of the whole, who are united and actuated by some common impulse of passion, or of interest, adverse to the rights of other citizens, or to the permanent and aggregate interests of the community."*

union would have lost the power base of a body of members all appointed by and responsible to the same authority and at the very moment in its history when it had succeeded in forcing its way into a seat near the head of the table.

The major action of the school year 1967-1968 was a steady pamphleteering-debating campaign for and against the Bundy proposals. No one could deny that the system was in a pretty bad way, so even those groups that were defending it put forth their own "decentralization" proposals. But there was, of course, no serious intention on the part of any of the defenders to hammer out among themselves a redistribution of the power arrangements in the kind of hard bargaining of the interested groups that alone could have produced an acceptable, workable compromise. (If the Constitution of the United States of America had been devised by an assemblage of disinterested scholars, even with all the shrewd compromises it does contain, the states' representatives for sure would not have bought it.) In the pamphleteering war, one of the least impressive of the counterproposals was that put forth by the UFT. Shanker must have recognized that the counterproposals were a public-relations gimmick designed to make the public believe that their authors were seriously interested in reform, whereas what was necessary was first of all to defeat Bundy or anything like it. The UFT therefore concentrated its energies on sending speakers around the city to debate the various civic-minded parents, organizational representatives, and community-control people who were supporting the Bundy proposals.

As the New York City school system is a creature of the state government, the battles were being directed toward influencing both the public and the state legislature, which in the spring would be considering some kind of reform legislation. Backing up the pamphleteering-debating war against Bundy was the vendetta against the demonstration districts being conducted over this period by the board of education, the UFT, and the press. Meanwhile inside the city's nine hundred-odd schools, life was proceeding more or less as usual, with perhaps a few more chaos schools than before as pupils everywhere set up sympathetic vibrations to the grownup's tremors—and perhaps more chaos on the surface too.

One small incident and the reactions exemplify the terms of the citywide controversy. The pattern is as follows: an incident occurs in which community adults or children respond to the frustrations of their situation—more often than not hostilely, inappropriately, or toward the wrong people. (Bad language, sit-ins, pupil rampages were the most common responses. Physical assaults by adults were extremely rare.) Community leaders react with a qualified disclaimer of bad language, violence, whatever, but point out that this is what happens when the community has no legitimate means to redress grievances or control the institutions that are supposed to serve them. The defenders of the system suggest that the outrage has occurred because too much has already been yielded and warn of catastrophe unless there is a pulling back. And proposals are made or tentative steps taken which will come to maturity at the next stage of the conflict. In this case, the incident occurred in a poor Negro and Puerto Rican section of Brooklyn adjacent to Ocean Hill-Brownsville, named Bedford-Stuyvesant, where a group of extremely militant parents were reinforced by a couple of fist-swinging young toughs. A letter to the editor in the January 16 issue of the *Amsterdam News* commented on the circumstances that led to the fracas. "The day is Monday, the date is January 8, 1968, the temperature is 8 degrees. Despite the subfreezing temperature a group of Negro and Puerto Rican children are huddled at the door but not permitted to re-enter the building of J.H.S. 117, Brooklyn, after eating lunch outside the building, due to the unreasonable and inhumane directive of the school administration."

Three days after the episode outside the school, on January 11, the New York *Times* reported on the front page: "Four men with Afro-style haircuts and wearing Black Muslim crescent symbols on gold chains knocked down the principal and two officials of Brooklyn Junior High School 117 yesterday in a fight over whether pupils had been locked out in last week's freezing weather."

In the ensuing controversy over the brutal attack, the militant district parents association issued a statement which said, "These men of the community used the only means open to them to protect our youth. Therefore we must condemn the school system which denies our community the control necessary to educate and protect its children."[10] And the Council of Supervisory Associations demanded the ouster of Superintendent of Schools Bernard Donovan on the grounds of his softness to community control. The New York *Post* reported the CSA statement and the associated comments of its chairman, Joseph L. Brennan:

> *The Council of Supervisory Assns . . . said that the Board of Education and Donovan are "creating situations" that block "meaningful education" and threaten the safety of pupils, teachers and supervisors. [The Association statement said:]*
>
> *"Friday's beating of one of the most respected junior high school principals in the city is one of the latest in a long series of harassments and intimidation of staff and yielding to small pressure groups by the Board of Education and the Superintendents."*
>
> *The Post asked Brennan for an example of "yielding to small pressure groups."*
>
> *He replied: "The creation of the Ocean Hill-Brownsville district is one. Obviously it's not working."*[11]

Donovan asked the board of education for authority to put security police in schools where necessary. Community people, knowing that it would be their schools that would get the security police, protested, one militant being quoted in the *New York Times* as saying the secutity force plan "means trouble."[12] A year later his prediction was more than fulfilled.

A similar contretemps was occurring in the very same weeks and the very same district that the assault took place on the J.H.S. 117 supervisors, providing a dry-run for the issue, the policy, and the strategies of the Ocean Hill-Brownsville dismissal of the nineteen members of the district's school personnel and of the Great Strike of 1968.

District 13 of Brooklyn experienced the often distressing interventions not only of the militant parents group but also of the Brooklyn chapter of CORE, headed by the intemperate Sonny Carson. Apparently Carson would move in as reinforcement when there were disputes in the district between school authorities and parents.

In Macon Junior High School, a district 13 school in which hostilities the previous spring had led to the transfer of a Jewish principal and the appointment of an Irish one acceptable to the community, hostilities among students, black teachers, white teachers, principal, and community had mounted to manic pitch during the fall of 1967. The school was a little exemplar of the Hobbesian universe of all against all, children fighting among themselves, and grownups, even the custodial personnel, hitting indiscriminately. The distraught parents were accusing teachers of not keeping order; the teachers were accusing the principal of being too permissive and one another of being lax; and the principal was accusing the teachers of goofing off. When a mother got up at a parents meeting on Monday night and claimed that her son had been hit and had two teeth knocked out by teacher George Fucillo, a cause was found. Fucillo, a mild-mannered and generally likeable man, was called in to the principal the next morning to explain. He said he had taken the boy's arm to get him on line and the boy had bolted from the room. At 3 o'clock he received a letter from the principal giving him a "U" rating and notice that he was fired. The union's chief cool-it man and perhaps the last man who could still talk with community activists, John O'Neill, was called in to negotiate.

Acting in the manner that they had learned over the decades, the principal and the district superintendent proposed a deal: in the interests of the school system, George would have to go, but they would drop the "U" rating, pay him for days lost so far, and transfer him to a "good" school if he would agree to go quietly. (In effect, this was the same kind of deal, not usually available to students, that had been offered Brad Dalton and that he had had no choice but to accept.) Over the years many teachers had accepted such deals, sometimes on union urging. A teacher who might refuse the deal would have to accept the "U" rating and then appeal it before a system-appointed person or panel. In fact, John O'Neill himself had for years been urging the union to take a strong stand against both deals and the biased panels, to no effect. But now, at this moment, when the instigator of the action against the probably innocent teacher was not, as before, a hostile or personally prejudiced or judging supervisor, but a hostile community, the union decided the time had come to make a stand.

The Executive Board brought the case to the Delegate Assembly along with a two-part resolution:

In view of the fact that the educational system at all levels—school, district, and central headquarters—is no longer capable of administering fair review and appeal procedures because it gives in to local pressures: (1) That when a teacher is charged with action which may result in an involuntary transfer, a "U" rating or dismissal, that the matter be referred to impartial third party arbitration with a presumption of innocence until such time that the Board establishes its case. (2) That upon failure of the board to follow this procedure, the UFT will shut down all schools in the given district, with all other teachers in the city providing the financial support in the district until impartial review is obtained.

Only one delegate questioned the first part of the resolution, somehow strangely missing the point, which everyone else understood. He hollered out angrily in the middle of O'Neill's account, "Why was George picked to be the hero? Why aren't others given the same treatment? Why? Tell me why!" Poor fellow, he must have been one in whom was rankling a deal he hadn't wanted to accept and had been advised to. O'Neill answered, "Because most teachers take their transfer."

The second part of the resolution met some opposition. "We will further antagonize the black community." "A shut-down would discriminate against kids in ghetto schools, which is where such incidents are more likely to occur." "Why strike? Why not just make it a grievance case?" "Why strike against the community when our enemy is the board of education?" "Let's appoint a committee to work out some other sanction than a strike." But with powerful rhetoric, Shanker, who had never responded to O'Neill's earlier demands to make an issue of deals and kangaroo courts, mowed down the opposition. He said that if the union merely appointed a committee to consider sanctions other than a district strike, as a substitute motion proposed, "you are announcing to every pressure group in

New York City that they can get rid of any teacher they want to get rid of and all they have to worry about is a committee that is going to sit and talk about it. That's all this big, big, powerful union of teachers that believes in doing something is capable of doing after teacher after teacher after teacher is pushed out, to appoint a committee to see what can happen." He said, "There are a few crucial times in the last few years when if we hadn't taken the right action, this union would be dead! There will be a dozen schools next week and another dozen a week later and another dozen the week after that." He said the newspapers would play up the racial overtones but "this is not a racial issue. It is a question whether a school system can be run in a context of terror."[13] (When teachers hear that kind of rhetoric, they are likely to forget that many schools *are* run in a context of terror: of principals against teachers, and teachers against children.)

Both parts of the motion were overwhelmingly carried. There was then a motion from the floor, planted by the Executive Board, to add a third part to the effect that there be set up in each district a compaint board of outstanding citizens who would be available to hear parental complaints against school personnel. This motion too overwhelmingly carried. After which the entire resolution sank from view into the roiling waters of the hastening storms.

The clearly political, rather than juridical, substance of the Fucillo case was revealed by the union's response to the Hatchett case in the same month. Hatchett, it will be recalled, had taken his P.S. 68 class to the Malcolm X memorial without the permission of his supervisor and for this was dismissed and had his substitute teachers license revoked. He received the customary administrative hearing. He had telephoned the UFT to ask for their representation at the hearings, but his request, first received by a junior staff member, was eventually lost in the union's embarrassment at being asked for help from a leading enemy militant. Those watching from the communities saw an interesting contrast in the two cases: one teacher, white, accused by a parent of having struck a child was first given a "U" rating and then offered a transfer with clean record, and became a symbol in the union's emerging fight for due process; another teacher, black, accused by his supervisor of having taken a class to a community function, was kicked out of the system while the union tried not to notice it was happening.

"If George got reinstated tomorrow," Shanker had told the Delegate Assembly, "everybody would say it's because the UFT is so strong that we got him back in. If he doesn't get reinstated, then as far as all the teachers are concerned, it's because there were community forces that kept him out."

The strategy of a districtwide strike in defense of teachers penalized by their supervisors under pressure from the community was tried on at home in the Fucillo case, but never worn in public. Fucillo neither accepted the transfer deal nor did the board appoint an impartial outsider to give him a fair hearing. Actually he hung around the UFT office for a good part of the spring semester, as Hatchett hung around the 201 office. For reasons which I do not know, the union did not call a strike against district 13. Perhaps it would have been too risky a venture to strike against the established authorities of district 13, Brooklyn, without having first done the obvious thing of exhausting administrative procedures, that is, bring a grievance case. Perhaps the bread was not yet ready to come out of the oven.

Ocean Hill-Brownsville and the Nineteen*

It was a rising, self-consciously powerful teachers union and a declining, confused board of education that confronted the Ocean Hill-Brownsville Governing Board when it announced dramatically early in May that it intended to

* *Sources for this and the next section include the usual interviews, conversations, and attendance at street confrontations and meetings. I had no direct contact with the Ocean Hill-Brownsville Governing Board or its unit administrator's office, but only some with persons on the fringes of these groups, and also with UFT people involved. Most useful periodicals were the New York* Times, *the* Amsterdam News, *the* Village Voice, *the New York* Post, *The* New York Review of Books, *and the* United Teacher. *Useful documents included: "Administrative Hearing into Complaints of Rhody A. McCoy, Unit Administrator of Ocean Hill-Brownsville, Requesting Transfer of Teachers, Report and Recommendations of Francis E. Rivers, Esq.,"*

fight for meaningful existence. The board of education having lowered the barricades just enough to endow Charles Wilson and his Ocean Hill-Brownsville counterpart, Rhody McCoy, with the title of unit administrator, then was powerless to prevent the headlong swarming over of the community followers demanding to take over the fortress. And meanwhile it was rapidly losing credit among the white citizenry. For the citywide decentralization debate had focused embarrassing public attention on the board's lamentable inadequacies as administrator of the city's schools. Between the push in Albany and the push in Ocean Hill-Brownsville, the board of education, defenders of the elaborate, suffocating power and status system, might have gone down, had not the teachers, to save their own place of lowly privilege, come to their defense.

Two months after the Fucillo Affair, the Governing Board of the Ocean Hill-Brownsville demonstration district in Brooklyn ordered its unit administrator to dismiss thirteen teachers and six administrators, and the union was ready. That each plane of the conflict's ascent had had to be separately traversed without knowledge of what would be encountered on the next is no denial of the fact that by meeting, or creating, each crisis in the way it did, the union

Board of Education, August 26, 1968; the City of New York, Commission on Human Rights, Education in Crisis: A Report on Decentralization, Teacher Training, and Curriculum in the New York City Public Schools, *December 1968; New York City Commission on Human Rights,* Report on Three Demonstration Districts, *February-March 1968;* Final Report of the Advisory Committee on Decentralization *("Niemeyer Report"), July 1968. Some of the documentary material and much of the best analytical and polemical material on both sides have been gathered together in a book edited by Maurice R. Berube and Marilyn Gittell,* Confrontation at Ocean Hill-Brownsville, *Praeger, 1969. In addition, the following were useful or may be of interest to the reader: Martin Mayer,* The Teachers Strike *(New York: Harper & Row, 1968), Edward P. Gottlieb, "Ghetto Schools Need Black Power,"* WIN Magazine, *November 1, November 15, and December 1968; Agee Ward, "Ocean Hill: Education, Community, Power, and the Media,"* The Center Forum, *November 13, 1968. Tom Brooks, "Tragedy at Ocean Hill,"* Dissent, *January-February 1969; "The Mason-Dixon Line Moves to New York,"* I.F. Stone's Weekly, *November 4, 1968; Carol A Wielk,* The Ocean Hill-Brownsville School Project: A Profile, *Queens College Institute for Community Studies, February 1969; and Steve Zeluck, "The UFT Strike: A Blow Against Teacher Unionism"* New Politics, *Winter 1968.*

prepared, or determined, the way for the next confrontation. It had tested and augmented its power in the strike of the previous September. It had sensitized the public and its own members to the "extremist" dangers lurking in decentralization and community control. And it had sketched out a strategy and rationale with which to meet the crisis.

Beginning with the planning phase during the summer of 1967, the history of the demonstration district of Ocean Hill-Brownsville runs roughly parallel to that of the 201 Complex. It encountered the same frustrations in respect to the board of education, the same maddening ambivalence from the UFT, the same panicked exodus of teaching and supervisory personnel, the same heightening of tensions among the children in the schools, the same slightly jeering condescension on the part of the press and the media, and the same tendency for the most militant individuals and the most hostile feelings to surface in crisis situations. Like 201, the Ocean Hill-Brownsville district was trying to find a fingerhold until perhaps it would be rescued by legislative action on decentralization. And, just as 201 was to watch its sister district's perilous clinging to the rocks in the forthcoming months, knowing that in the end either both or neither would make it, Ocean Hill-Brownsville had been watching 201's engagement in the Ferguson Affair, the Hatchett Case, and the Malcolm X Memorial Scandal.

In the flood of polemical and analytical literature provoked by the dismissal of the teachers and the ensuing confrontation, there were hints at a conspiracy underlying the dismissal. The exciting idea of conspiracy has been gaining in popularity generally in America, doing damage I fear not only to social justice but also to social intelligence. From the point of view of the conspirators, a conspiracy is merely a private, organized plan, and subsequent developments suggest that the various elements in Ocean Hill-Brownsville were not together enough to make a conspiracy even if they had wanted to. In any case, Occam's Razor enjoins me to provide as explanation for the dismissals merely the more or less publicly known facts.

First, with the drainage of personnel and especially experienced supervisory personnel and the hostilities being experienced throughout the Ocean Hill project, as in the 201 Complex, several of the schools in the project had been reduced to chaos schools, children running wild and staff morale terrible. After the 1967 disruptive child/MES strike, which the Governing Board and the schools' black teachers had refused to support, there was considerable bad blood between the white striking teachers and the black "scab" teachers. And with the opening of the school year 1967-68, seventeen of the schools' twenty-one assistant principals had offered their resignations, and the board of education was requiring the district to accept new assistant principals as they came off the top of the competitive lists of the merit system. (Some of those so appointed were among the nineteen whom the district sought to dismiss later in the year.) At one school some teachers either left or, in that atmosphere of hostility and suspiciousness, were believed to have left, their classes, and then gone home for the day, in the middle of a fire alarm which found all the pupils and teachers outside the school when 3 o'clock came.

Early in April parents organized a two-day pupil boycott of the schools demanding of the board of education that their Governing Board be given real power over the schools. Community activists who were undoubtedly involved in organizing the boycott were among the groups that the Governing Board had to reckon with in its struggle to survive.

Second, the Governing Board was completely stalled in its attempt to establish with the board of education the extent and limits of its powers. Helpless to cope with its multitude of troubles without a clear delegation of authority, it had, along with the governing boards of the two other demonstration districts, submitted to the board a set of "Draft Guidelines" for demonstration districts spelling out what the districts thought ought to be their powers. Relevant to the matter in hand are the following four proposed clauses from the section on personnel:

b. All power of appointment of other instructional and supervisory personnel [other than the unit administrator] presently exercised by the Board of Education and the superintendent of schools is vested in the governing board acting upon the advice of the unit administrator.

d. The governing board, upon the advice of the unit

administrator, may remove or deny tenure or suspend any teacher or supervisor who fails to meet standards of performance established by the governing board. Removal, suspension, or denial of tenure of a teacher or supervisor under the jurisdiction of the governing board may be effected only upon a recommendation of suspension, removal, or denial of tenure by the governing board.

g. In the process of collective bargaining with representatives of teachers and supervisors, representatives of the governing board shall participate in all matters pertaining to the governing board; in addition, the governing board may enter into supplemental agreements with representatives of teachers and supervisors.

h. The governing board shall function as the "district level" in the processing of grievance proceedings under the existing collective-bargaining agreement between the United Federation of Teachers and the Board of Education.[14]

The provisions say in effect that in community-controlled schools, the community, as represented through its governing board, should be responsible for the personnel in the schools. Paragraph *d* suggests that standards of performance and procedures for evaluating them would be developed by the governing board. Paragraphs *g* and *h* recognize the inevitability of the United Federation of Teachers and suggest that the responsible authorities for the schools in question should have power to deal with it. (While the governing boards may very well have had hostile feelings toward the teachers union, so had the board of education for many decades, and nevertheless the two parties eventually could bargain. The governing boards would surely have done the same, whether they liked it or not.) There is nothing to indicate that the board of education had the slightest intention of accepting or even seriously negotiating the "Draft Guidelines."

Third, the UFT was believed to be an enemy of community control, and the UFT leaders in the schools (chapter chairmen especially) to be fifth columnists. The disruptive child strike, the UFT-CSA suit against the specially appointed principals, and Shanker's constant public philosophizing about "vigilantism" and "extremist takeovers," all contributed to a natural distrust of the union. In the face of that distrust, the individual union leaders in the schools would have had a hard time at best convincing the Governing Board and McCoy of their loyalty to the project. (But it should be noted that at 201 some union teachers did succeed in doing just this; in the process, however, they gave up their loyalty to the union.)

The individual union leaders half-heartedly did try. They worked on committees to try to get the schools back on their feet. They urged fleeing teachers not to flee. And, oddly, when the suit against the specially appointed principals went against the appointments in the trial court, a suit to which their union was a party, these lower echelon leaders wrote a letter to the board of education urging them to appeal it. (It would have seemed more appropriate and more effective to have written a letter to their own union in the first place urging them not to be a party to the hostile suit.)

But with the other half of their heart, they did just the opposite. They made public clamors that the election of parent representatives to the Governing Board was not democratically conducted, aptly playing the very role—the imperialist bringers of democracy to the barbarians—in which some of the harsher community militants sought to cast them. (If the charge of improper election procedures was true, and there may be evidence that it was, the ruckus made about it by an outside—and white—organization could only inhibit the aggrieved parties within the community from making their own fight for justice, and there is also some evidence that it did just this.) Union leaders had opposed the electing of community members of the Governing Board solely by the vote of parent members. And they charged that the special principals were hastily and undemocratically chosen. Finally they withdrew from the Planning Board entirely and organized an effective teacher boycott against election of other teachers to the Governing Board. A number of the strong union people, especially a man named Fred Naumann, chapter chairman at I.S. 271, kept turning up at some of the innumerable Bundy debate meetings at which McCoy was a pro-decentralization speaker to heckle and oppose him from the audience. He would publicly assert that the Governing Board elections were undemocratic and that the chaos conditions at J.H.S. 271 were the consequence of community control. At one such meeting, on Manhattan's West Side, a member of the audience pointed out to Naumann that conditions at the local junior high school, with no community control, were just as bad, to which Naumann is said to have responded, "You don't even know what anarchy is till you've seen 271." It is alleged that McCoy called some of the hecklers into his office at one point and said, "I don't want you people following me around any more."

When the Governing Board sent dismissal letters to thirteen teachers and six supervisors, they could have thought they were dealing with all three problems—a school situation that was getting out of control, unclear demarcation of its powers, and a hostile union—plus one more.

Some of the Sunday quarterbacks speculated that the Governing Board intended by the confrontation to spur on the laggard legislature to pass one or a combination compromise of the decentralization proposals offered by Bundy, the mayor, and the state Regents. Others lamented that their headstrong behavior undercut the serious and patient proponents of decentralization at precisely the inopportune moment. The Governing Board may or may not have expected that the legislature would throw it a rope in its perilous ascent. Some of the activists didn't believe it would. But the UFT knew that if the legislature dislodged the weak and discredited the board of education, its own place in the power system would be threatened, and it was attending seriously to the legislative scene.

The Governing Board's letter advised the recipients that the Governing Board had voted to terminate their services in the district, that they should report to 110 Livingston Street for reassignment, and that if they wished to question the Governing Board's action they might meet with it on a specified date. Among the recipients were some good, some bad, and some indifferent teachers; some teachers with regular licenses and some with substitute licenses; and a number of UFT chapter chairmen. Clearly the Governing Board was trying to get rid of personnel who, while the project and community control were fighting for their existence, were felt to be actual or potential traitors. It was also expressing the simplistic notion held by so many school people that what you have to do to overcome a chaos situation is clear out a few ineffective people. And while it was doing these two things, it was serving notice on the board of education that it was going to exercise control over its personnel *openly, without deals.*

This was indeed a bold gesture, announcing, in effect, that the Governing Board not only had the powers of a district superintendent but was going to exercise them without the prescribed pussyfooting around. The Governing Board may have thrown down the gauntlet in this way because it considered the appropriate supervisors were too disorganized, too harried, or too unreliable themselves to get up a case against those the board decided to axe; or because the politically determined decision to dismiss the Nineteen was so hastily taken that there was no time to get up a case; or because some or all of the teachers were so impeccable that it would have been too difficult to get up a case (unlikely); or because they knew or supposed that Superintendent Donovan would not make the same complementary moves when playing the game with them that he normally made when playing the game with board of education-appointed district superintendents asking for the same thing; or because they wanted to announce that they intended to get out from under the old hypocritical rules and arrangements. Likely different people among those involved in making the decision had different reasons. The one overriding consideration was clearly to strengthen both the Governing Board's control over the schools for which it was responsible and its bargaining position in relation to the central board and the union. The Governing Board may be faulted for having made a strategic miscalculation, but they can hardly be faulted for striving to survive.

The union's response to this move in the power struggle was equally political. It could have acted like a straight, nonpolitical trade union and advised the dismissed teachers to appear before the Governing Board and follow the regular grievance procedures from that point on. This would have put the responsibility for enforcing the board of education's rules on the board itself. But that weak vessel's small residue of power was fast seeping out. Whatever board of education rules were to be enforced would have to be enforced by the union. And this would require a massive show of strength from the membership.

Indeed, even the power of the United Federation of Teachers plus the support of most of the press was not sufficient to enforce orders that had no legitimacy among those against whom they were being enforced, and the orders eventually had to be backed up by the naked force of the police. The districtwide strike which was proposed but never used against district 13 on behalf of George Fucillo was now invoked against Ocean Hill-Brownsville on behalf of the Nineteen.

All through May and June the battle surged back and forth as Superintendent Donovan ordered the teachers back into their schools, parents and community activists blocked their way, police escorted them through the blockades, principals refused to assign them to classrooms, personnel loyal to the project scorned and/or threatened them, and the teachers pulled out again in protest against the humiliations and distress. Three hundred and fifty teachers in the district went on a sympathy strike to enforce the union's demand that the dismissed teachers be accepted back in the schools and back in the classrooms. (Suddenly out-of-teaching assignments, heretofore considered special plums provided for the principal's favorites, were no longer an acceptable substitute for classroom assignments.) Parents and other community people went in to try to cover the uncovered classes. Donovan closed down three of the "community's" schools as punishment for their treatment of the union teachers, and the community responded by closing down all eight. Donovan told McCoy he had "gone far enough," and Shanker asserted maybe we needed a new superintendent "who would keep his word." At one point McCoy "suspended" seven of the thirteen teachers he had already "transferred," and even the seasoned Ocean Hill-Brownsville buffs got lost on that one. The *Amsterdam News* called it "musical chairs." A mediation attempt by a labor mediator collapsed. (Sending him in the first place was like sending in a tennis linesman to mediate between Israel and Syria.) And through it all the police swarmed. They escorted teachers into schools and escorted community members out, evidencing the fact that power and legitimacy had collapsed in Ocean Hill-Brownsville and only force would prevail, and lending support to the enraged, such as Ralph Poynter, who wrote in a leaflet, "If these police from other communities succeed in putting this community out of its schools, it will be absolute proof that in Black and Puerto Rican Communities the schools do not belong to the public, but to a police-state."

The alliance of teacher and policeman, once a somewhat fanciful sociological theory explaining society's two-pronged instrument for control of its most oppressed peoples, was becoming a practical day-to-day operation in the streets and schools of Ocean Hill-Brownsville that spring. (In one of my visits to the UFT headquarters at this time I observed hanging around the offices a number of square, neatly attired, not-Jewish types whom I had never seen there before and sensed not to be teachers. I thought they might be reporters. A union official explained that they were plainclothesman. "You know," he said, tactfully taking me out of earshot, "they've got a really good class of guys that they're training nowadays." Roughly paralleling Thoreau when Emerson came to him in jail, I felt the only honorable place that day was in the street below beside the picket line manned by not such a good class of guys.)

During the summer, Ocean Hill Brownsville agreed to submit its demand for transfer of the Nineteen to impartial adjudication, *the first time in the history of the New York City school system that a teacher had ever been able to carry a grievance against a supervisor directly to an impartial (outside) judge.*

The judge, Francis E. Rivers, cleared the Nineteen of any cause for punitive action, and pointed out in his decision that due process includes the "right of the respondent to be informed of the nature and cause of the charge against him; to be confronted with the witnesses against him and *be able to cross-examine them*; the right to call witnesses in his defense and to be represented by counsel; *to be presumed innocent of the charges until his accuser has proved them by a fair preponderance of the credible evidence*; and to be accorded equal and non-discriminatory treatment."[15] I have italicized the items that are those not granted at standard board of education hearings. Judge Rivers did not even note, because it goes without saying, that due process implies that the issues in dispute be judged either by a panel of the disputant's peers (a jury) or by an individual without interest in the dispute (a judge). Except for those rare cases where tenured teachers had pursued grievances into the courts, a judgment in respect to a teacher's competence had never before been made either by peers or by an impartial outsider.

I believe that the Ocean Hill-Brownsville Governing Board goofed tactically in several respects when it agreed to a quasi-judicial hearing. Not only was it illogical to hold a hearing in respect to a procedure which had always before been executed as a deal, and not only was the hearing more rigorous in respect to defense of the teachers rights than customary procedures for more serious actions (for example, "U" rating, withdrawal of license), but the only rules by which adjudication could proceed were precisely those board of education rules which were inapplicable to Ocean Hill-Brownsville's needs—or any school's needs for that matter.

The consequence was, on Ocean Hill-Brownsville's side, a hodge-podge of charges some of which are ridiculous according to common sense and others ridiculous according to the rules. One teacher, for example, was charged among other things, with "failing to decorate the classroom properly and excessive use of the blackboard." The judge must have wondered how foolish that Rhody McCoy could get: the school is in a shambles and you want to get rid of a teacher because he doesn't tack up crepe paper on the bulletin boards. Another teacher (one of the union leaders) was charged with hostility to the district, evidence for which was offered in some remarks he was alleged to have made to another teacher at a Christmas party. The judge said that what the teacher was alleged to have said at the party, "even if it were credible," was protected both by the First Amendment freedom of speech prerogative and also by the privileges adhering in a Union official under the Fair Labor Practice Provisions. (The judge also found "incredible" the testimony of an unlicensed educational assistant that another teacher had used profane language to pupils, incredible because of the nature of the testimony or because of the status of the witness he did not say.) The Rivers decision demonstrates that if scholars and experts cannot resolve power struggles, neither can judges.

Of course, a serious educational system would need some kind of "due process." But criteria for judging a teacher's performance that would be both meaningful and manageable, judges who would be both critical and fair, and the procedures that would protect the teachers, the children, and the school institution could only be determined by the concerned groups over time in a situation of mutual trust and common concern. Each area of society had to develop a "due process" that fits its peculiar purposes and processes. That to the union "due process" meant little more than "maximum protection possible for the security of teachers," it demonstrated once again when in 1969 it opposed the board's proposed new suspension proceedings, which allowed students to bring counsel when confronting their accusers in a suspension hearing. Union spokesmen said they opposed the "creation of an adversary situation whereby a teacher may be put in a position of having to answer accusations and charges. The UFT believes that such a situation would be contrary to law and to the fundamental due process rights of the teacher." (*The United Teacher,* November 2, 1969.) It is as if the educator's security is threatened by "due process" for students. And so it is if the educator's security is to rest merely upon his superior status.

Meanwhile, old and newly organized citizens groups and most of the liberal New York City legislators were pressing for passage of a decentralization plan formulated by the New York State Board of Regents, which eliminated some of the unwieldy features of the Bundy Plan. The mayor and the governor were backing it. Shanker flooded the corridors of the state capitol with leaflets and literature, with frightening remarks about "extremism" and "vigilantism," and with 500 supporting teachers at a total cost to the union alleged to be about $500,000. Threatening the political future of legislators who opposed the will of the teachers, Shanker won the support of traditionally conservative upstate Republicans and of enough downstate Democrats to have his way. The sponsor of the stalling, confusing "decentralization" compromise bill that finally passed with Shanker's consent was the Staten Island representative to the state senate, John Marchi, a conservative, antilabor, anti-civil-liberties Republican who would celebrate his legislative contributions in the spring of

1968 by becoming a law-and-order mayoralty candidate of New York City in 1969.

As the reformist forces were strong enough to prevent a complete defeat of decentralization and as the still gathering powers of the teachers union, in alliance with lesser conservative forces, were not going to allow definitive legislative reform of the ailing administration, the compromise bill put the whole matter off for another year. Recognizing that the members of the lay board of education stood with the bureaucracy in opposition to decentralization, the Marchi Act authorized the mayor to appoint four members to an expanded board. This board would be empowered to delegate any of its functions to the thirty local and three demonstration school boards and mandated to prepare a plan for a "community school district" for New York City, which plan should be forwarded to the legislature for its consideration by March, 1969. The board of education might allow the local school boards, which had hitherto been appointed by it, to be elected, and the local boards should have the power to hire district superintendents under contract. The Marchi Act and the enabling provisions which the new board of education passed the following autumn did little either to rationalize administrative procedures or to shift power and status. But it ensured at least that the struggle for both could and would continue for another year. In respect to the demonstration districts, the act empowered the board to delegate to the governing boards of the demonstration districts any or all of its own powers, subject of course to applicable contracts and other legislation (for example, the contract with the United Federation of Teachers and the legislation governing board of examiners procedures). The law provided the possibility of a lay board sympathetic to both the mayor and decentralization and less unsympathetic to community control. And it gave the union a chance to try out the strategies and alliances that it would use on the next plane.

A howl went up from the reformers and rebels. Kenneth Clark, after having threatened to resign from the board of regents if its plan did not pass, urged the governor to veto the bill, calling it "a cynical, political playing of games with deprived people" and charging that Shanker's behavior had "promoted anti-Semitism in the Negro Community."[16]

The *New York Times* in an editorial calling the bill a "watered-down version that bordered on a mandate for inaction," warned, "Foot-dragging on decentralization involves a flirtation with disaster . . . The UFT and the Board, in seeking to protect their powers, have exposed themselves to all the hazards that spring from efforts to maintain a discredited bureaucracy amidst popular dissatisfaction and distrust."[17]

Community activists from all around the city stomped back and forth before the entrance to the UFT's recently purchased office building, chanting "Down with Shanker," while up above the new-type police and the new-type unionists watched them from the windows. And among the teachers who had had the experience of throwing their weight around in the halls of the law-makers, there was renewed respect for Shanker as a strong leader who knew what he was about.

But the universe of Shanker fans and Shanker haters was only beginning to expand. The issue of the Nineteen still vexed, a nasty nettle that would have to be dealt with.

The Great Strike: Issues and Outcomes

The ten-week Great Strike of autumn 1968 was a putdown by several of the city's major institutions of the black community's challenge to the school status and power system. Structured by the United Federation of Teachers as a strike against the board of education, the occasion of the putdown was chosen and the forces behind it were dominated by the United Federation of Teachers. A number of the individuals and groups that contributed did so perhaps reluctantly (the mayor, the mayor-appointed board of education), others more eagerly (the custodians, the police, the supervisors). The central issue—power—was obscured for many by the sometimes esoteric discussions of the apparent issue—due process—and by the failure of most observers and participants both to perceive what schools do and how people in them normally treat one another. But the way the conflict was structured, the way the parties to it played their roles, and the way it was ended all indicate clearly that it was a power play to put down a nascent black movement. As we are able to observe events, relationships, and outcomes, we have no need to argue about what the union teachers "intended," or whether or not Albert Shanker was "sincere" in his appeal to due process (although in respect to the latter, my personal opinion is strong enough to be apparent, I believe, in the following exposition).

Although the decentralization pot had been put to the back of the stove to keep warm for a year, the matter of the Ocean Hill-Brownsville Nineteen plus three hundred and fifty was not going to simply evaporate in the meantime. Nor could the mess be settled during the summer in the absence of all those who have to be around while the trouble is cooking to make it come out right.

But when school was about to open in September, 1968, the union was insisting that Ocean Hill-Brownsville take back not only those of the dismissed teachers who still wished to go back, but also those who had struck the district in their defense during the spring and had been replaced by the Governing Board for this offense. Having held out throughout the spring agony and having now staffed their schools with young and sympathetic teachers, the Governing Board was stubbornly refusing. Perhaps pressures and factional struggles within the community plus rancor against Shanker for his great victory in Albany also stiffened their backs.

For the union, while the Marchi Act was a holdoff, dangers remained. One was the power the supposedly antiunion mayor now had to appoint a board of education that might undercut the union's power, perhaps by actually strengthening that of the demonstration districts. A legal memorandum concerning the effect of the Marchi Act on the demonstration districts explains that under the new act the board of education would have the power to delegate some of its powers to the governing boards, whereas previously the governing boards had been limited to advisory functions.[18] The demonstration districts were a power base for community-control advocates. The new legislation made it legally possible for them to be strengthened. They had demonstrated their enmity to the UFT and the possibility of using it to weaken the UFT, as in the dismissal specifically by Ocean Hill-Brownsville of the UFT chapter chairmen. Even the old board of education had shown itself powerless (or unwilling) to prevent this. The mayor's board of education would undoubtedly be even more so. A final legislative determination would be made in six or seven months, and intervening developments would clearly affect that determination. It was a natural decision for the union to have recourse to its habitual playing out of educational conflicts on the citywide screen of public opinion by mounting a strike.

Natural, but not easy.

The membership sensed that a strike at this time would be a strike against decentralization, against community control, against the black community; and still shivering from its exposure to black hostility the previous September, it hesitated at the edge for a few moments before plunging in again.

My notes on chapter chairmen's meeting which I attended a few days before the formal strike vote evidence some of their hesitations, and also Shanker's superb ability to sense the group's undertones and improvise an orchestration to meet his standards of performance.

The union membership within each school was known as a chapter, and while the assemblage of all the chapter chairmen had no official standing in the union's organization, they were sometimes called together for the purpose of testing out major policy decisions before a meeting of the official, larger body, the Delegate Assembly.

Talking among themselves before the meeting opens, people are confused, upset, conflicted. I meet Dan G., from my old school, a young but pretty conservative guy. "Decentralization is going to come," he tells me, "I live in Rockland County. The people run their own schools, there. We've got to find a way we can adjust to them [community-control people] and they can adjust to us."

Shanker opens the meeting calmly, explaining the events and the issues of the Ocean Hill-Brownsville Nineteen. He is cool, informative, no rhetoric. His occasional glancing references to job rights and union protection produce restrained little burst of murmuring or applause.

He claims local people are saying, "We've got too many expensive teachers at upper steps—let's get rid of them and hire lower-paid ones, so we can have more teachers, more equipment." A gathering groundswell of murmuring greets this and continues till he asks for quiet. "Membership is way down at 201," he reports. He says "We have to make sure decentralization is not used as a union-busting device: we are asking for an agency shop as a protection [applause], and super protection for chapter chairmen [more applause]."

Then he takes a quick turn. "We have not talked about, we are not considering, we are not recommending striking against decentralization. Decentralization is the law. We opposed it, but it was passed. You do not strike against the law. That's what you have a government for." (But a strike is a violation of the Taylor Law.) Now he takes up in a serious way what is bothering everybody: the effect of a strike on public relations. He says, "I believe we will have more public support for this one than we've ever had before." Burst of outraged "No's" followed by some "Yesses." [He himself probably couldn't have then imagined how right he was.] "But if we don't strike, we might as well vote to close up the union." Voice behind me, "That's his stock-in-trade." He expresses sympathy for the black community but reminds his people, "You don't give rights to people by taking them away from other people who just got their own rights." [This has the same specious logic as Bundy's moralizations about power.] He returns to the law-and-order issue, saying, "We won under the Rivers decision, and we have to insist that others abide by a decision that we would abide by if we had lost." Referring again to the dismissed Ocean Hill-Brownsville people, he says "What will happen to the system, what is the use of a contract if we let this happen to these people?"

So, appealing to his audience now as citizens, now as educators, now as union members, he ends, and opens the floor to discussion. Still the tone is of a troubled group conscientiously searching for a way.

There is a good deal of dissent, restrained and questioning. Prostrike sentiment has more of a feeling of rancor, and therefore determination, than antistrike sentiment, which is more ambivalent, testing. "You have to deal with the fact that a strike now would be viewed as a race war between a white union and the black community," one undecided speaker says, revealing the underlying dilemma. Shanker answers questions, sometimes hedging and prevaricating. The statement "We may have no strike on Monday" draws applause. A lady asks, "If we strike, who will we be striking against?" A prostrike speaker says he fears a very long strike because "no one has any interest in opening the schools. The only group that is interested in getting the schools open is the parents." Nobody laughs but me. A New Leftish young man, terribly sincere, makes an appeal to "empathize with the dynamics of social revolution" (audience expressions of disgust); a tentative reference to Vietnam by way of analogy (hoots of "Sit down"). He says, "The union has parlayed the specialized OHB incident into a generalized attack on decentralization." Mounting hostility as he proceeds. Hopelessly begging for understanding, he returns to his seat. But a black teacher receives courteous attention in his appeal: "We must find the best way of resolving our differences with the black community; what has happened in Ocean Hill-Brownsville will not necessarily happen elsewhere. Suppose we strike and win, how can we enforce such a victory? You cannot have due process in a hostile community."

More and more, people stop saying "If there is a strike," and drop the conditional. Suddenly, Shanker announces that, while the members may go on discussing if they wish, he has to leave for another meeting. He makes a warm, kind summation speech, saying that he thinks decentralization is going to succeed. And then, "We will always extend a helping hand provided we are treated fairly." Rising in one movement to their feet, moved and flushed, they cheer. And the meeting is over.

I remain in my seat, stunned. I mean, that rabbit came out of the hat and she stole a carrot and produced a litter while I was still figuring out what the act was about.

A week later amid warnings from dissident teachers that a strike would destroy the union (how wrong they were!), the schools were closed by a citywide teachers strike.

That power, rather than due process, was the issue of the strike was apparent to some at its beginnings, to all by its end. In the playing out of the power struggle on the huge screen of public opinion, everyone became an actor, including those who thought they were only watching on their little TV screens each evening. What roles were played by the public, that is, the many publics, of New York City is recounted more fully in Part III, section 2 below. How the top actors were conducting among themselves ferocious mock battles which they believed were for real is told in exhaustive and also somewhat exhausting detail in Martin Mayer's *The Teachers Strike*.

The negotiations were carried on primarily by the mayor, the mayor's appointed prodecentralization board of education, Superintendent of Schools Donovan, and the UFT negotiators, and secondarily by a number of mediators including New York State Commissioner of Education James Allen (now U.S. Commissioner of Education), labor mediator Theodore Kheel, and State Regent Kenneth Clark. Rhody McCoy and the Governing Board said that the whole issue of the transfer was an administrative matter that concerned it and Donovan, and that the UFT had no business in the quarrel at all. And Shanker said that since McCoy was Donovan's subordinate, Donovan had complete authority to resolve the issue and that therefore neither McCoy nor the Governing Board Chairman, the Reverend C. Herbert Oliver, had any business in the quarrel. On this issue Shanker more or less prevailed. While McCoy and Oliver had some quasi-friends in court (the Reverend Milton Galamison, the 1964 boycott leader, now a member of the prodecentralization board, Kenneth Clark, and even, the union said, John Doar, chairman of the board), they had no standing there themselves. In the circumstances, however sympathetic the mayor and John Doar may have been to what are commonly called "the legitimate aspirations of the black community," Ocean Hill-Brownsville could not exercise a power in the protracted negotiations anything like commensurate with its interests in the matter. Again and again, decisions agreed to by the chief negotiators were imposed on the Governing Board, or as the Governing Board would say, "forced down our throats"—and promptly vomited up again, as when the teachers were marched into the schools by armed police, the principals refused to assign them to classrooms, and the "loyal" teachers and community members annoyed and frightened them into leaving.

How, in negotiations so structured, could a negotiated settlement be reached? It couldn't. There would have been only one possibility: offer the three demonstration districts power, authority, a recognition of their right to be, in exchange for a negotiated settlement on hiring and firing procedures which would honor the UFT contract and deal fairly with the dismissed Nineteen. What Ocean Hill-Brownsville, like the other two districts, needed was a measure of dignity and a recognition of its authority—and this is precisely what every single proposed solution denied it. Four little instances illustrate the point.

John O'Neill reports that when he and three associates first went hot-footing it out to Ocean Hill-Brownsville to try to cool it with McCoy, McCoy said:

"Maybe we could transfer the teachers to my office (McCoy's) while we tried to work out a solution of the issue." I indicated that this was certainly within the realm of possibility (this is exactly and precisely the way in which we, the union, have handled this type of problem in other situations and I speak as one with probably more experience than any other union representative in handling school level disputes—legal and extra legal), but my three associates demurred and called President Shanker at the office in New York and he supported them in their opposition.[19]

Second: Shortly after the events recounted by O'Neill, I heard from some community-control people that at a meeting in Brooklyn of Ocean Hill-Brownsville people, union people, and some people from the Urban Coalition (a group of businessman sympathetic to black problems), the Ocean Hill-Brownsville people had offered simply: "Give us community control and we'll give your people a fair hearing." The offer was not taken seriously. John O'Neill, who had been present at the three-way meeting, confirmed what I had heard. Another union man who was present when I asked O'Neill about it was shocked that such an offer could even be made. He said, "What kind of a bargain is that? First, let them give them a hearing."

Third: Edward Gottleib, the only school person I knew who didn't seem to be angry at anybody during these angry times, advanced a four-point proposal during the strike as follows: (1) recognize the legitimacy of community control by the Governing Board; (2) adopt the districts' "Draft Guidelines" of March, 1968; allow the UFT to challenge the dismissal of the Nineteen *de novo*, with all rights of appeal, arbitration, and ultimately strike if necessary; (4) meantime assign the then ten remaining of the Nineteen (nine had accepted transfer) to Ocean Hill-Brownsville under the direct supervision of an outside educational organization, such as the Center for Urban Education. The article claims that Donovan, district negotiators, and UFT loyalist teachers from the district had agreed substantially to these proposals but that Shanker rebelled at a decision taken without his presence.[20]

Fourth: An article by the president of the New Rochelle, New York, chapter of the American Federation of Teachers, Steve Zeluck, reports an attempt at a genuine resolution of the genuine conflict as follows:

Those who still had doubts about the UFT's goals in the strike should have been convinced by an event just prior to the third resumption of the strike on October 11. Several labor leaders brought Shanker a proposed basis for settlement which had the tentative approval of the Board of Education and the local governing board. The main points were: 1. Recognition of agency shop for the UFT; 2. Restoration of the disputed 83 teachers [the details here are not relevant] to their teaching *positions in the district; 3. Written guarantees of due process; 4. The UFT to publicly recognize and support community control and decentralization; 5. the UFT to join the governing board in demanding funds from the Board of Education to assure the effectiveness of the experimental districts as well as for general education purposes; and 6. The details of the previous points to be negotiated between the UFT and the local governing boards. The UFT rejected this proposal.**[21]

So instead of being accorded some dignity and power, Ocean Hill-Brownsville lost ground steadily throughout the

* *Zeluck's article provides a realistic analysis of the political forces involved in teacher unionism in general and the UFT posture of the years 1967 and 1968 in particular. His authorities for the material quoted, he reported in a letter to me, were a top procommunity New York labor leader and John O'Neill. Further, he says, the matter was not denied when brought up at a New York State teachers convention. Zeluck himself experienced considerable pressure as a result of his article, the state AFT convention censuring him, at the urging of the UFT, for "anti-union activity."*

strike and reacted with increasing fury, until it was exhausted and beaten, but still hollering. The mayor scolded the union, accusing them of seeking to usurp the board of education's authority over the school system and of bringing the city to its knees. And John Doar ordered district superintendents to open the schools where parents and antistrike teachers wished to teach. But if the board of education's rules and Superintendent Donovan's orders had no legitimacy in the black community and could only be enforced by police, Doar's orders, not to speak of the Taylor Act (which made strikes by public employees illegal), had no legitimacy in the school-bureaucracy community, and nobody was about to call in the cops against them. (John O'Neill asked Galamison at one point why the board didn't fire a few of the district superintendents, as they were disregarding board orders. Galamison looked shocked, "Oh, come now," he said, "we couldn't go that far!") Perhaps only the mayor perceived how legitimate power in the city was ebbing away, when he was quoted in the *New York Times* as saying, in his eighth-grade-civics-teacher tone, "The issue now is whether we can continue to survive as a city if each dissatisfied group breaks the links which bind it to a common purpose of preserving order. The issue now is whether we can halt the drift toward paralysis and polarization that grips us now, and get back to that measure of cooperation we have begun to achieve up to now."[22]

While the structuring of the conflict seemed to preclude its ever ending, short of military occupation of Ocean Hill-Brownsville and imprisonment of its leaders, the struggle was not a stagnant one but had its own inner dynamics.

In the drift towards paralysis, the union's demands kept toughening. Its first minimum demand was for return of the dismissed teachers to classroom assignments and a guarantee of impartial review of local districts' actions against teachers. As the Governing Board, McCoy, and the Governing Board's principals kept "violating" agreements to which *they* had never agreed, the first two would be suspended, and on one occasion the mayor ordered the closing of the district's key school (I.S. 271). So, among the union's escalating demands were removal of these offending persons, barring Governing Board members from entering their schools, and even declaring the "experiment in community control a failure" (so do the mixed metaphors of science and politics turn language into gibberish). But escalation has its limits.

In the drift toward polarization, the union came through stronger and stronger on the screen of public opinion up to a point, and then as dissident teachers, dissident liberals, dissident trade unionists, and moderate black and Puerto Rican leaders more and more coalesced with the black rebels, the union's image began to fade some. It was at the moment when the union was beginning to have to yield that a court decision was handed down which could be used to resolve an especially troublesome item.

When, in the case of the specially appointed demonstration district principals, the decision handed down was favorable to the UFT-CSA, the board of education appealed the decision, meanwhile keeping the principals in their positions. On November 14, the Appellate Division denied the appeal, that is, declared the principals illegally appointed. Although the board would appeal that decision, too, to the Court of Appeals, it agreed to use the Appellate Division's ruling as grounds for suspending the three principals involved, all located in Ocean Hill-Brownsville.* As it had been the principals who were directly involved in refusing the dismissed teachers classroom assignments, this was a victory for the union.

Generally the strike agreement was a victory for the union and specifically for Shanker. (The *New York Times* story of a Madison Square Garden meeting of the teachers to vote on the settlement pictured two lady teachers each bearing a huge sign. One read "GOD BLESS YOU, AL," and the other, "BLACK AND WHITE UNITE, U.F.T." Neither lady was black, nor were many others in the hall. The second slogan, pathetically anachronistic, was an echo

* *Eventually the Court of Appeals upheld the board of education's right to create the special category, demonstration school principals, and the three principals were returned to their posts. However, the decision ordered the board to submit the new category to the same kind of "merit system" procedures as govern other positions. See Lewis M. Steel,* Community Control and the Courts *(Queens College Institute for Community Studies, March, 1969).*

of the old trade union slogan of the thirties, "Black and White Unite and Fight.") The agreement provided for the appointment of a three-man "watch-dog committee" to ferret out and bring to a hearing cases of harassment of teachers throughout the school system. The union was understandably anxious about the reception the returning teachers would receive by parents and other teachers who had opposed the strike. The chairman of this committee was Harold H. Israelson, a labor lawyer who had represented among other groups the now defunct Secondary School Teachers Association and also Local 740 of the Custodial Workers Union, a group that had supported the strike. The committee functioned subsequently in defense of anti-Governing Board UFT teachers in the 201 Complex, but maintained a hands-off policy in respect to the wave of reprisals during the ensuing school year by supervisors who had struck against teachers who had not.

The union was assured that there would be no reprisals against striking teachers. Time was added to the school day for a limited period, and holidays were withdrawn to make up for lost instructional time and to allow teachers and supervisors to make up for lost pay. This clause was a hook on which hung a whole new series of troubles.

The subject of involuntary transfer and due process was dealt with as follows: "Pending the negotiation of a mutually satisfactory clause, any dispute involving the involuntary transfer of an employee shall be subject to the grievance procedure including arbitration. Pending such decision, the status quo of the employee shall be maintained." The inclusion of the clause suggested that "involuntary transfer" itself had not previously been subject to grievance procedure. There was no provision for a revision in the grievance or appeal of "U"-rating procedures so as to provide fair hearings (due process) for all teachers on all occasions. But this would come soon after.

Commissioner Allen appointed a state trustee to run the Ocean Hill-Brownsville schools. The Governing Board remained suspended. McCoy and the remaining principals were put on their good behavior. The union teachers were to be given classroom assignments. Three antiunion teachers who had been accused of harassing union teachers were to be taken out of the schools and sent to the district office pending disposition of their case (a violation of the clause specifying that teachers be kept in their posts while hearings were in progress; but these were pro-Governing Board, antiunion teachers). Unauthorized persons were to be kept out of the schools. This last clause, aimed at the members of the Governing Board and other community activists, was used throughout the system during the ensuing school year to protect the schools and the principals against procommunity citizens, including members of various district boards.

The settlement did not either provide due process for teachers throughout the system or squelch Ocean Hill-Brownsville objections to the return of the dismissed teachers—the two ostensible aims of the long strike. First one state trustee and then another despairingly tried to deal with the latter issue for months while members of the Governing Board, sometimes reinforced by community activists from other parts of the city, did gain access to the schools. From the time the strike was settled, the calm that had prevailed inside the Ocean Hill-Brownsville schools while the union teachers were outside was shattered. But the strike did project a bright image of the UFT, and Shanker in particular, as defenders of law and order, an image which continued to shine over the city for a long time, warming many civic issues, including a mayoralty election. And the settlement gave the UFT power in the school system, and local UFT leaders power inside the schools, which no teachers union had ever had in any school system in the country.

Two demands that Shanker had enunciated from time to time remained unfulfilled. One was for an agency shop, that is, automatic dues-paying membership for every teacher. (An agency shop would have not only liquidated the anti-UFT factions among the teachers but would have helped resolve financial difficulties that the union was experiencing as a consequence of having lost its check-off after the 1967 strike and having spent $500,000 lobbying to get the Marchi Bill passed.) The other was for abolition entirely of the demonstration districts. But that was to come. It required another street skirmish, this time a small one, and another excursion to Albany.

The street skirmish occurred outside P.S. 39 in the 201 Complex.

4. BATTLE'S ENDING

Mopping Up: Return to 201

The Germans' anti-Semitism made them feel that "something must be done about the Jews," which in turn led them to covertly delegate to the S.S. the task of doing that something. It then became important to the Germans to fuzz over the gory details, to conceal from themselves, as well as from others, exactly what was being done. . . . This shameful work that nevertheless must be done, is, then (morally) "dirty work." . . .

As the urban ghettos have grown, so has the cohort of functionaries who receive the covert assignment to "keep the colored out of our way." . . . If the teachers . . . and cops were ever to spell out in detail what their duties are . . . they would threaten the delicate balance preserved by silence about their dirty work. . . .

—*Lee Rainwater,* Transaction, *November 1967.*

In east Harlem the five schools of the 201 Complex opened quietly every single schoolday during the strike. The children came regularly—after a sound-truck had informed the neighborhood that the schools were open. (In Harlem, striking teachers prudently did not try to prevent children and nonstriking teachers from entering their schools.) A few custodians stayed away and refused to yield their keys, but the teachers and parents managed to break in and to keep the buildings clean and in good running order. At P.S. 133 the new reading and math program was filling the school with excitement. At 201, the teachers were busy planning their black-studies curriculum, putting out their teachers newspaper, trying out the new paperback books, undertaking new ways of coping with the old discipline problems. At 68, once the question of who was to be principal was resolved, John Nailor got down to getting to know his staff and introducing an intensified reading program. At the unit administrator's office, Wilson was busy working out new ways of delivering district services to the schools more efficiently.

Only ten teachers in the whole complex went on strike, nine of them from P.S. 39. At each school the staff met as a group to decide on its course. Some teachers say they went in because they were threatened, or *felt* threatened, and this notion was spread around by UFT people. Some responded to David Spencer's desperate plea to "please don't strike . . . don't let us lose our schools to the militants . . . help us keep our project alive." "He was like crying," one young undecided teacher said. "You saw how much it meant. I didn't know what to do. Now I'm glad I went in."

Many teachers in the complex who did not go out in the 1968 strike had gone out in the 1967 strike, although with some ambivalence. They had seen the 1967 strike as a genuine union strike against management which, unfortunately, happened to be damaging or was felt to be damaging to the black and Puerto Rican community. But they saw the 1968 strike as directed specifically against the black and Puerto Rican community and against their project in particular. Seventeen teachers at P.S. 133, where the entire staff had answered the strike call in 1967, distributed a letter explaining why they refused to strike in 1968. They said, "If there is any doubt in anyone's mind why it was so different here than elsewhere in the city, let us make clear why now. We have a stake in the children we teach and their future just as the community does, and our responsibility is to them—not to any union or bureaucracy which seeks to maintain a status quo which has never given our children a chance and does not intend to. . . . Our teachers, our parents, our community, and above all our children are 'together.' " Many old and formerly loyal UFT members, as well as many younger, idealistic New Leftish teachers, who had been drawn to the complex by their social concerns, felt the strike to be a betrayal not only of the community which had won their loyalty but of the ethic which underlies trade unionism—defense of the underdog. (In assessing the political and educational potential of community control, an element which must be considered is the social orientation of the people the movement drew to it and of those who massed against it. The people in, around, and at the head of a movement are the movement and help to determine what it will be.)

Thus, alone in the city, the 201 Complex (with the exception of the ten striking teachers) went quietly and harmoniously about its daily business, happily unseen by the public. The Complex had had its bellyful of publicity for two solid years and, feeling that so far as it and the newpapers were concerned, "no news is good news," tended to shun reporters in a most un-American way.

But their satisfaction with their own progress and good morale was countered by a sense of doom if Ocean Hill-Brownsville should be destroyed, and the two feelings put the people in the 201 Complex in a bind: To go quietly about their own business as if Ocean Hill-Brownsville were not being mortally attacked and prove by their own accomplishments how community control could work—only to be chosen the next victim? Or to use all their resources to defend their brother community from the enemy—and so invite the enemy to turn his guns on them at the very moment when they first began to experience anonymity and accomplishments? A parent member of the Governing Board wrote an appeal to all the parents in the complex saying, "We should not take it for granted that Shanker will leave us alone—they might attack us like Ocean Hill-Brownsville. As parents, we should prepare ourselves in case something like what happened in Brownsville happens to us, that they may decide to close our schools." She asked that parents send in suggestions about what they should do if the threat became a reality.

The people involved in the complex temporized. And they were able to temporize, because in the absence of publicity and outside hostility, the various elements among them could express and work out their differences. (This is exactly what was prevented in Ocean Hill-Brownsville by the massive outside attacks.) The Governing Board minutes of September 13 (1968) report that members of the Board had attended negotiations between the Ocean Hill-Brownsville Governing Board and representatives of the board of education. "We were there most of the day, and the Governing Board [of O H-B] didn't agree to anything. . . . As it now stands, open war has been waged against the Governing Board and everyone is talking. . . . A suggestion was made that we send a telegram to the Board of Education demanding that they turn over all powers to the [O H-B] Governing Board. Our Board decided that this issue needed more discussion and inside facts . . . We know that anything that happens to Brownsville happens to us."

Seen from only a short year away, their comments have a sad innocence about them, especially the idea of sending a telegram to the board of education. Later at the same meeting the Governing Board took up teacher grievances: "We will develop the mechanics to handle grievances that our teachers have. We must tell our teachers that we will handle their grievances and that we are not involved in the strike."

Individuals associated with the 201 Complex participated in critical street and school encounters in Ocean Hill-Brownsville. But when a rather badly attended open meeting of the Governing Board decided one evening to call a rally of parents and children in support of Ocean Hill-Brownsville, opposition the next day by parents and teachers who had not attended the evening meeting led to calling off the demonstration. The minutes read: "most of the parents are afraid for their children to participate in a rally. The consensus of the Governing Board was that we had not done enough planning and we had too little time. In the future when we make decisions, we will make plans together in order to avoid this kind of confusion."

They backed away again. Likely, only the kind of tough-minded leadership that the union had and that their enemies inaccurately charged them with having would have made it possible for 201 to act in concert with all the other community-control forces in the city to save Ocean Hill-Brownsville, themselves, and the possibility of community control in New York.

The weeks went by with no untoward incidents and only two difficulties, to both of which the parents responded voluntarily and in considerable numbers. Custodians in two schools walked out and threatened to fire their assistants if they went in. Parents and teachers together kept the schools in good shape. There was some attempt to have the parents put on the payroll so they could be paid for the work—jobs being not all that easy to come by in Harlem—but the complications of sending the people downtown for fingerprinting and other "procedures" seemed too great. The parents' response to the schools' call for help was felt by all to be both an evidence and a builder of community support. (One of the great unsolved problems of the complex had been the enlisting of continuous, active parent support—attendance at meetings, participation on committees, and so on. The Governing Board and other interested teachers and parents had all along recognized the need for more widespread and more active parent participation, without having the energies or the personnel to spare to enlist it. But in the two crises the complex encountered in the year 1968-69, it got the kind of participation it had wanted to stimulate all along.)

The second difficulty was that of the nine striking teachers at P.S. 39. Nine missing teachers leaves a big hole in an instructional staff of 35. Teacher aides were used to help, and efforts were made to find either volunteers or sympathetic teachers who had been locked out of other schools. Members of the Governing Board seemed especially galled that striking teachers were being paid. At one Governing Board meeting after another, throughout the period of the strike-lockout, one member or another would ask if it was true that the people on strike were collecting their paychecks, as if, for all their cynical understanding of what was going on, they still couldn't quite believe that the politics of collusion would go that far. At one point, in the kind of pointless desperation that is emotionally comprehensible but often politically unwise, the Governing Board sent letters to all the striking teachers telling them their children needed them and they should return. The letter said that if they did not return, the Board would be forced to seek replacements for them (leaving ambiguous whether it meant permanent or temporary replacements). The Board did not get replacements. The striking teachers did not return. And the rest of the staff at P.S. 39 limped along without them.

The working teachers must have felt resentful that they had to work that much harder because the striking teachers were at home, and especially so when the striking teachers turned up on payday to collect their checks while there was all that mixup and delay with the working teachers' checks. Nevertheless, when the strike ended on November 19, the striking teachers returned to their school and went back to work.

Teachers who had been working all along said they were welcomed back. The UFT made some vague charges that they were "harassed" on their return. I should guess that there were dirty looks and nasty cracks, which, politicized, become "harassment." Not only were the working teachers resentful of the striking teachers, but they believed the striking teachers were opposed to their project. One middle-aged, Jewish lady teacher who had worked in the school for many years, said, "There was always a good spirit here. We had our get-togethers. Those teachers, they didn't *want* the Governing Board. The Governing Board notices you're supposed to send home with the children, they'd always just tear them up." While this may or may not have been true, the teacher's telling it demonstrates a sense on the part of teachers loyal to the Governing Board that the striking teachers were not loyal to the Governing Board.

The school operated without incident for just one week following the end of the strike when the clause in the settlement that no schoolman in his right mind should have allowed to be put there delivered the missile that the 201 people had tried by playing it cool all during the strike to avert but that, in their honest moments, they had known was on its way to them. But whether a man is or is not in his right mind depends on what reality principle governs his decisions.

In the case of the disturbing clause of the strike

settlement, if the reality principle was the wish to "make up" the days of education the children had lost during the strike (in accordance with the you-should-never-miss-a-day doctrine), then the clause in question was mad. If it was merely to recompense the teachers for having been the shock troops for the defense of the system, then the clause in question was quite sensible. ("The whole trouble with the system," said the middle-aged lady teacher at P.S. 39, "is all that double-talk. They never say what they mean.")

The striking teachers had received their first three semi-monthly paychecks in September and October. Thereafter the checks were stopped and except for some nonstriking teachers, there was no pay for the duration of the strike. To help compensate the teachers for the pay they lost during the strike, the strike settlement by a calculation whose arithmetic rationale is too difficult to be worth untangling here, but whose political rationale was simple if not primitive, added forty-five minutes to each school day for a period of months and several conventional holiday days to the school year. For working overtime and on the holidays, teachers would receive time-and-a-half pay. The entire arrangement, agreed to by the mayor, the negotiators from the board of education, and the negotiators from the UFT, was proclaimed to be a way in which "lost instructional time" could be recovered. (The teasing problem of recovering lost time which has intrigued man since he first discovered his mortality was thus solved by American know-how in November of 1968).

In respect to lengthening the school day, every teacher knows that most children have "had it" by 3 o'clock in the afternoon. Younger children have often had it by lunch time; in many schools the rest of the day is merely marking time. (This is one reason why after-school remedial programs are likely to be a fizzle.) At the high school level, with so many of the city's high schools on overlapping double and triple sessions, running from around 7 a.m. to after 5 p.m. anyway, adding the provided time to each student's schedule would keep the school open some two hours longer. And the students wouldn't come or wouldn't stay anyway. The earlier you open school in the morning, the more latecomers you have, and also the more truants, because many students don't bother to come at all if they can't make it on time. And the later you keep it open, the more late-afternoon cutters you have. All that means extra little pieces of paper to be filled in and moved around to record the latenesses, the cutting, the absences. As for the canceled holidays, they were an even more unrealistic way of "making up lost instructional time." The day or two before and the day or two after any holiday are hard days in a school–a lot of absences and greater than usual difficulty in keeping the students in control. In some schools, this is so even on normal Fridays and Mondays. To open the school the Friday after Thanksgiving and the days between Christmas and New Years would be to combine in one session the before-holiday hysteria with the after-holiday blues. But everybody understood what the clause was really about, and in the black and Puerto Rican communities, angry as they already were at the UFT, the board of education and the supervisors, they were furious that so hypocritical a pretext was being used to reward the striking teachers for the damage they had helped to inflict on Ocean Hill-Brownsville and community control. The issue of opening or not opening schools on the holidays became another of the symbols of the struggle.

At its first meeting after the board of education had announced the new holiday arrangement, the Governing Board passed unanimously a resolution to honor the customary school holidays, "because our schools have been open and our children have been attending, the Board feels that our schools should be closed on holidays." Elsewhere in the city there were rumblings of discontent. Many teachers did not wish to work, despite the time-and-a-half bonus. High school students staged demonstrations. (This important phenomenon I will turn to in the next part of the book.) And the board of education took cognizance of its previous foolishness by ordering that students should not be penalized for absence on holidays and that no tests should be given on those days, saying, in effect, "the schools will be open, but we don't really expect you to come."

The 201 unit administrator foresaw that the Governing Board's decision about the holidays might create difficulties, writing in his monthly report:

Governing Board members should be most aware of the fact that the month of November will be an increasingly important time. A major challenge is approaching concerning the school holidays we at 201 plan to observe. The Governing Board should be aware that its determination to follow the traditional school calendar will be subject to considerable criticism, not only from external forces who are bent on discrediting every action taken, but internally from some who feel that the bureaucracy sould not be challenged. The Unit Administrator is not counseling a change in the decision, he is merely pointing out to Board Members areas where there will be conflict—and the Board should be prepared for conflict, disagreement, and, hopefully, for effective resolution of the differences between yourselves and some members of our community.

Some people had always thought that the unit administrator tended to be an alarmist, and this time, they were half-right: the community was undivided in its support for the school holidays and for its Governing Board. Even the Puerto Rican parents of P.S. 39, hitherto among the most conservative and cautious of all the parent bodies, did not want or intend to send their children to school the day after the turkey and fixings and felt it a matter of principle that the school not be opened.

But the Governing Board office was going to be open, and the unit administrator informed the nine teachers who had struck P.S. 39 that if they wished to earn their time-and-a-half for the holiday, they should report there for the day; the unit administrator was merely expecting trouble, not looking for it. All the schools in the complex remained closed on Friday, November 29, the day after Thanksgiving, except P.S. 39, where mysteriously the custodian opened the school. The nine union teachers, who had informed their classes that school would be open, appeared, plus thirteen children and a few parents who had got or attended to the teachers' message rather than the Governing Board's. If closing the schools was a symbol for the community, clearly opening them was a symbol for the union teachers—or a planned provocation.

They were met at the door by several members of the Governing Board, who barred their entrance. They then went, not to the Governing Board office, as they had been instructed by their superior, but to 110 Livingston Street, in accordance with instructions from their union headquarters.*

After three months of playing it cool, the 201 people lost their patience—all of them, including the most conservative parent body in the complex, and without any assist from "militants" or "outside agitators." When the teachers refused to report to Wilson's office for an administrative conference, they were informed that they were under suspension for insubordination and should report to the unit administrator's office until their case was disposed of. Then when Donovan countermanded Wilson's orders, the parents were hopping mad and said that no matter what happened in those hearings, they weren't going to have those teachers back in their school. UFT spokesmen charged that "the district had been 'looking for a ruse' to get rid of the nine instructors without due process"[1]; the district believed that the UFT was "looking for a ruse" to get rid of 201.

The strategy of apparently and perhaps really independent moves and countermoves by the board of education and the United Federation of Teachers which in 1966 had defeated the first move for community control and put Principal Lisser back in I.S. 201 and then in 1967-68 had discredited community control before it ever began was carried back from Ocean Hill-Brownsville to Harlem in autumn 1969, reinforced by the police.

The Governing Board's charges of insubordination against the nine teachers were countered by charges of harassment against Charles Wilson and David Spencer. The Governing Board's choice of a lawyer to hear the charges against the teachers was vetoed by the board of education on the grounds that the (left-wing) lawyers association to which the lawyer belonged was not "a bar association." Board member Rose Shapiro, arch-foe of decentralization, said: "It would seem elementary that lawyers' groups which exist primarily for political purposes and take partisan positions on political and social issues would be

* *The fact that the teachers intended to report to school must have been relayed to Livingston Street by the union, which then claimed that the deputy superintendent had informed the union that if the teachers could not get into their school they should go on out to Livingston Street.*

automatically excluded from being involved in personnel proceedings which basically stem from such issues . . ."[2] The charges against Wilson and Spencer, however, were brought to the watch-dog committee headed by the veteran labor-union attorney Harold Israelson. Partisanship, like most questions in the struggle, was determined by power.

But, as in Ocean Hill-Brownsville, power alone would no longer serve. A police line was thrown around the school. And for months, the teachers (reduced by resignations to seven) were escorted daily to school, each by two policemen, and protected by them through the day, each threesome in an otherwise empty classroom, while in the under-policed streets of Harlem, daily and nightly, residents were mugged and teachers had their pocketbooks snatched. Parents were adamant in not wanting their children in those teachers' classes. (To a well-wisher who suggested that prudence would have dictated that the Governing Board yield to superior force, a member of the Governing Board responded that to do so in this case would have made a mockery of community control and parental responsibility.) The children were crowded in with other classes. Numerous observers from the board of education, the union, the Israelson committee, and the press also came around. On several occasions police surrounded the building and interfered with evening meetings of adults going on there. Efforts of the Governing Board to negotiate through John Doar, the presumably pro-community-control (according to the union and on the basis of his appointment) president of the board of education, were fruitless. The effect on Mayor Lindsay and Doar of the skewed Ocean Hill-Brownsville negotiations plus the massive white anger of New York city was to push them relentlessly into more and more anticommunity positions. (Doar and his board were retired soon after by legislative mandate. But Lindsay remained, and was re-elected mayor in part on his promise of good behavior to the white voters.)

David Spencer, summing up, told a press conference:

It is with deep sadness that I face you today. For I must report that all the channels to a just and peaceful resolution of the present conflict at P.S. 39 seem to be closed.

We are not surprised at the present confrontation with the U.F.T. Albert Shanker has been attempting to create such a situation for the past year and a half. We feared that once his vendetta against Ocean Hill-Brownsville cooled he would again turn his attention to us. Anticipating this, we have been attempting to meet with the Board of Education for several weeks to present our problems, clarify responsibilities, and anticipate possible crises. . . . However, there has been . . . no indication of any real desire on the part of the Central Board to assist our demonstration project in any meaningful way.

We can only conclude that the Board has embarked on a policy of wiping out any significant attempt by Black and Puerto Rican people to exercise authority over their children's education. Today, Donovan's and Lindsay's Gestapo in blue have pushed us up against the wall. We are not about to back down. We are fighting for our most precious possessions, our children. We hope the general public will bear that in mind.

Finally I would like to thank everybody for the wonderful support we have had from our community . . . Blacks and Puerto Ricans in Harlem and East Harlem are united to fight for their children's education and future. They have been joined by the staff of P.S. 39, most of whom are white, many of whom are U.F.T. members. Our enemy is not nine teachers; it is a racist union that is exploiting nine teachers to whip up fear and insecurity among its constituency and racial polarization in the rest of the city. This strategy may defeat decentralization. But it will surely destroy Public Education in the process.[3]

The reference to "Public Education" was pure rhetoric; what Spencer had been battling for all along was to destroy a "Public Education" that was destroying children. And, caught up perhaps in his feelings about the immediate enemy, he gave undue credit to the UFT. Surely they were not the instigators either of the destruction of the children or of the destruction of community control. They merely had the job, along with the policemen, of coming into Harlem to do society's dirtywork.

Surrender Terms

The actions of the school years 1968-69 had a successful issue in the spring with, first, the passage of another "decentralization" act and, second, the signing of a new collective bargaining contract. The legislation included the building of bridges between the lay board of education and the city's political parties, the casting into legislative bronze of some of the UFT and CSA key demands, and the molding of a crude simulacrum of a democratic apparatus. The contract included a happy raise for the teachers (in which the supervisors would automatically participate*), a strengthening of union power and influence, and a reduction toward the zero level of the likelihood of any further serious trouble from community-control quarters.

Not only the substance but the processes by which these treaties were negotiated were significant of the new era. Unlike the situation of the year before when the old board of education bitterly opposed any decentralization, now the state Regents and the mayor's prodecentralization board of education more or less agreed on a decentralization program. And the mayor and the governor had both favored decentralization all along. On the surface, therefore, the decentralization forces were stronger and more unified than they had been the year before. But only on the surface. The almost complete destruction and the forces' own repudiation of their left flank in Ocean Hill-Brownsville and east Harlem meant that the bargaining would now begin from a point much closer to the status quo. In addition, with mayorality elections coming up in the city and the white electorate turning sour on minority rights, justice, reform, and on any candidate closely identified with those goodies, the mayor and the governor had very little to say throughout the hard legislative bargaining for a new act to succeed the temporary Marchi Act.

* *A New York State law, referred to as the "index," provides that supervisors should automatically receive a salary increase of equal percentage whenever the teachers get an increase. The union had long objected to being made a porter for the supervisors in this way, especially as the supervisors, until 1968, always crossed their picket lines; and defeat of the index was a permanent plank in the union's legislative program. One of the chief supporters of the index had always been the very same John Marchi who became such a friend to the union beginning in 1968.*

So it was that the bill, which Shanker and the conservative legislators managed to pull out of the legislature and which the governor signed with as little comment as he would sign a bill ordering a plaque to be put up to honor some innocuous patriot, barely reduced even the worst of the administrative abuses and inefficiencies much less got down to the fundamentals of power and status inside the schoolhouses. Far from even rationalizing administration, by erecting a dummy system of district control so as to project an image of democracy, the act probably will prove to have increased rather than diminished the bureaucratic tangle. And by writing into law the defenses that the union and the CSA felt they needed against their collective nightmares, it certainly strengthened some heretofore merely conventional status and power arrangements.[4]

The new act substituted politicizing at the upper levels of the system for democratizing at the lower ones. An interim board of education, to supervise the passage to the new permanent arrangements, would be composed of one member from each borough to be chosen by the borough presidents, figures always close to the party machines. This board was to take office immediately, thus neatly disposing of the mayor's prodecentralization board. The permanent board would be elected, one member from each borough—that is, one as well by the 221,991 inhabitants of Staten Island as by the 2,627,319 inhabitants of Brooklyn. Like the Electoral College and the Bundy proposals, this arrangement would diffuse the power of the (black and Puerto Rican) common folk.

District boards, chosen by a complex proportional representation system, would administer the 30 to 33 school districts. Minimum size requirements for districts would eliminate the three demonstration districts. The district boards were empowered to choose their own district superintendents, but otherwise the distribution of specific educational and administrative powers between the central board and the district boards was confusing, even to the lawyers examining the legislation. In addition, whatever their powers might prove to be, the district boards, for a number of reasons, would be unlikely, unwilling, or unable to use them in any innovative or status-changing ways. One of the most significant restraints was that the central board had the specific power to suspend or remove members of the district boards. Thus, the district boards were not in the end responsible to the people who chose them—the parents and voters of their district—but to the people who might remove them, the central board, or ultimately, the same old bureaucratic hierarchy.

In respect to the matters that had been agitating the teachers and the supervisors, the bill's provisions rewarded their rapprochement many times over. The rattly Model T "merit system" was given a new fan belt and a set of plugs and declared good for another 200,000 miles. One positive element was that districts which were identified by average reading-test scores, the fever thermometer registering, inversely, degree of nonwhiteness—as normally experiencing chronic teacher shortages were empowered to go outside the board of examiners regular procedures in hiring new teachers in certain specified ways and during specified months of the school year. Further, all supervisors eligibility lists were made qualifying rather than competitive. This meant that the few black and fewer Puerto Rican candidates who could survive the promotion procedures now need not come in among the first in order to be appointed, but could be chosen from anywhere on the list. In exchange for this concession, the supervisors got a clause providing that *all* persons on the current competitive list for elementary school principal had to be appointed by April, 1970, thus protecting the investment of those who had made it before any newcomers should appear. (Since the number of openings for elementary school principal in that period would not equal the number of eligible candidates, the designees would have to be granted the salary and other prerequisites of the position without its duties.)

Otherwise in respect to personnel, the old methods of hiring and promoting were retained; all personnel were employees of the central board, not the district boards; and special protections were provided for personnel against the district boards. District boards could transfer teachers within the district only for specified reasons, not transfer them out of the district at all, and discipline them only subject to certain procedures never before provided in the system. Even with the protection of these procedures, disciplined personnel would have the right to appeal to the central board, which would not be bound by the so-called due-process procedures. The act (which one commentator described as an elaborate, legislated collective bargaining agreement) thus inscribed in the law books a new definition of the ancient, many times reinterpreted principle of due process. Due process was to be a procedure protecting the teacher, not against a remote, powerful, status-superior bureaucracy but against an immediate, powerless status-inferior local board. The teacher might have to go on being humble toward her superiors, but they in turn would protect her against her inferiors (a kind of feudal allegiance-protection arrangement).

The replacement of the prodecentralization board with a new politically appointed board occurred in the middle of negotiations for a new collective bargaining agreement, the contract signed as the outcome of the 1967 strike being now about to expire. The negotiations quickly concluded by the new board were a model of how contract negotiations may proceed when labor and management have each other's confidence. There was hardly any union barking about a strike at all. After a spring in which the board of estimate was offering the city a budget that would have killed all the city services without even providing enough for a decent burial, and less than two weeks after the board and the union were announced to be "far apart on salaries," an agreement was signed providing salary increases and other benefits estimated to be worth $500 million. Otherwise the contract closed up a few little pinholes left in the legislation. The union would have an agency shop as soon as any other union in the city got an agency shop (a most-favored-nation clause). The union would have veto power over names on the panel designated to serve as trial examiners in the "due-process" procedures of district boards against teachers (it having been established at the previous stage that impartiality is a product of power). The union's check-off was restored. Adequate supplies would be made available in teachers washrooms. The union was empowered to bring "special complaints" that a district superintendent was not protecting employees against "persons or groups . . . engaging in a course of harassing conduct, or in acts of intimidation." In other words, if in return for loyalty from their liegemen, the district superintendents did not provide protection against the barbarians, the liegemen would be able to appeal to the duke.

On educational issues, as an article by John O'Neill points out, the union dropped entirely or reduced substantially demands in respect to class size, remedial services, teachers for the non-English speaking, a teacher internship program, more textbooks, more guidance personnel, and more paraprofessional workers. And in respect to nonteaching periods (needed to cool off, calm down, use the now adequate supplies in the washroom, and prepare lessons), the contract provided a monetary compensation for lost preparation periods. O'Neill comments that this arrangement "turns teachers into 'piece workers,' frozen, probably permanently, into the current teaching loads. When teachers decide to give up preparation time for pay, the aura of 'professionalism' has been stripped away."[5]

Something went for education, notwithstanding. Of the $500 million which the contract awarded the teachers, $10 million were allocated for such educational improvements as a nationwide teacher-recruiting drive, scholarships to children from "disadvantaged areas," another ten More Effective Schools, and establishment of early childhood centers in about fifty schools. These programs would cost the teachers, who would be getting an annual increase of between $2,000 and $3,000, about $160 per teacher over two years. And the first-page story in the *United Teacher* summarizing the new contract happily reported:

UNION SETS ASIDE $10 MILLION
FOR EDUCATIONAL IMPROVEMENTS

It's not every day in the week that a union passes up $10 million in benefits for its members in order to help children in disadvantaged areas. But that's exactly what the United Federation of Teachers did in its bargaining sessions with the Board of Education, completed on June 24.

The UFT *reached agreement with the Board that this sum should be utilized for educational improvements that "we and the Board felt would be good for the children," Dan Sanders, coordinator of negotiations for the union, said.*[6]

One of the greatest powers that came to the union in

those troubled times was the power to believe in itself and its own beneficence. Its displays of liberal lingo stunned everyone, including itself. So the union rushed toward the floodtide of its power and prestige. Meanwhile, there was some disturbing evidence that one price of its increased public power would be a reduction of freedom and democracy inside its own organization. The dismissal of John O'Neill, harsh treatment of members who had opposed the strike, and a reduction in size of the Delegate Assembly in such wise as to virtually eliminate minority representation suggested that, as in the nation at large, dissidence was going to be inhibited as identical with disloyalty.

And meanwhile, too, outside the union, there was a gathering resistance among many hitherto passive members of the system. And you couldn't take in these new rebels with any of that old jive.

Part III.
The Struggle against Power and Status

This is your system, and we don't like this crap and all the things that you-all do. We believe that as long as we have to stay in this system, we are always going to be at the bottom.

—A black high school student

It seems as if the whole thing is just one big preparation for nothing.

—A white high school student

1. THE SCHOOLS AS DESPOTISM

Sometime during the school year 1968-69, the charge of energy directed at the unyielding, status-enforcing, race- and class-biased school system had passed from the mainly adult community-control movement to the mainly student take-over-the-schools movement. What appeared in the media and in the mouths of principals and politicians as an epidemic of fires in wastebaskets, fights in cafeterias, and sassiness to teachers among overcrowded, racially hostile, or semicriminal youthful types was in reality a quasi-political movement to break out of the constraints of body, mind, and spirit that constitute the framework of the normal urban high school. The kids, in a phrase, were seeking to liberate themselves. But everybody had learned a lot from Ocean Hill-Brownsville and the Great Strike. While New York's revolt of the high school youth was typical of mounting student revolt throughout the nation, it was also, as a consequence of the previous year's politicizing of both the attackers and the defenders of the system, more advanced and more organized than that in many other cities.

The student demands in New York dug at the roots of the school fix in a way that the community-control demands did not. Condensed, the student demands were as follows: to end the educational irrelevance of the curriculum; to end the invidious status differences among various groups of students; to end the educationally irrelevant status differences between students and teachers; to end the dovetailing of student status differences into societal status differences; and to end the security measures employed by schools to enforce the irrelevance of the curriculum and the system of status differences. Black student groups also demanded the deliberate upgrading of the status of black and Puerto Rican students, teachers, community, and culture, and the construction of high schools in black communities.

Now, what the students were striking out against was not just a local matter or even conditions peculiar to urban high schools. In certain ways, it was an attack on what "school" has traditionally been in Western civilization. A neat description of this traditional role and of the dangers inherent in it is to be found in an analysis originally published in 1932, Willard Waller's, *The Sociology of Teaching*. Waller writes:

> *The generalization that the schools have a despotic political structure seems to hold true for nearly all types of schools, and for all about equally, without very much difference in fact to correspond to radical differences in theory. . . . It is not enough to point out that the school is a despotism. It is a despotism in a state of perilous equilibrium. It is a despotism threatened from within and exposed to regulation and interference from without. It is a despotism capable of being overturned in a moment, exposed to the instant loss of its stability and its prestige. It is a despotism demanded by the community of parents, but especially limited by them as to the techniques which it may use for the maintenance of a stable social order. It is a despotism resting upon children, at once the most tractable and the most unstable members of the community.*

Waller's book (reprinted in 1967) gives an excellent account of the kinds of maneuvers that the school despotism employs to maintain its "perilous equilibrium" in the face of the mutual enmity of the various groups that make up the school community. His exposition can be very revealing to adults, including, it is likely, many adults who regularly practice those maneuvers. But among students, only a few self-deceiving achievers are not fully familiar with the entire school repertory of defensive and offensive maneuvers.[1]

The school as despot has usually managed to maintain its equilibrium because its immediate subjects (the students) or their advocates (their parents) believed the despotism to be a benevolent one—that is, believed it to be intended for and in the long run tending toward the students' own good. The teacher was accorded obedience (or, as Loretta put it, respect) because even the most obstreperous students knew in their hearts that she had something to teach that would do them good to learn. Hence the prevailing folk wisdom among teachers that if you have a good lesson, well-prepared, you won't have trouble with discipline—or its latter-day variant (a significant falling off from the standards of the recent past), you won't have trouble with discipline if you keep them busy copying something off the board, which will make them believe that they are learning something. Further, the teacher as a matter of course believed that she *could* teach what she had to teach and that her students *could* learn it—a belief, as we saw in the case of Willie Gallagher, that teachers no longer regard as manifest truth. In essence, the school's authority lay in the subject matter it intended to convey.

Until fairly recently, whenever the subject matter ceased to commend itself as relevant to a teenager's needs either as a human being or as a future producer, he simply left school and went to work. Now, with society changing a hundred times more rapidly than the high school curriculum, the student is being kept in subjection to an increasingly irrelevant schooling for increasing number of years, and the school despotism no longer has the natural authority of curriculum on which to rest. The student no longer believes in his heart that identifying a predicate nominative, being able to recall in what circumstances Jarvis Lorry and Miss Mannette first encountered Madame Defarge, reciting the social, economic, and political causes of the Spanish-American War, or translating daily two pages from a nineteenth-century bit of French nonliterature is going to do him good.* With the erosion of its natural authority, the school must fall back on other measures to sustain its equilibrium and its despotism.

The measures that the high school has come increasingly to use in the last several decades have been the power of the compulsory education law or, alternatively, what we might characterize as the "law of competitive accreditation." Students in New York are required by law to attend school until they are seventeen and, if they persistently fail to do so, may be fetched from home or the streets and dispatched to institutions of even higher security and lower intent to educate.[2] To this formal law, the social ruling of competitive accreditation adds its complementary weight. The ordinary career routes and economic institutions have few openings for young people unless they have been accredited as high school graduates and not many more unless they have been well enough accredited at that level to be admitted into the next level, from which they can eventually be accredited as college graduates.

But these relatively abstract matters cannot substitute for an authority that is self-evident. Thus, in the face of mounting disrespect for the school and its subject matter on the part of the students (not to mention the doubts of the teachers), the high schools in particular are dependent on elaborate security, grading, and status systems which then further erode whatever shreds of legitimacy the curriculum and the school personnel may have retained. There has thus spread through the New York City high schools a nasty ambience of snobbery, cynicism, shame,

* *Many New York City high school students whom I interviewed reported intellectual pleasure with the discussions they had in some of their history classes. In the end, however, their success as students was measured not by the seriousness with which they discussed or read history, but by their observance of the school ceremonies and their willingness to repeat meaningless or even obnoxious historical clichés on tests and examinations. See the experience of Benny below. Also, many serious academic students do tend to value science courses, because science facts have a kind of universal currency which they can respect. See Carl Nordstrom and others,* Society's Children *(Random House, 1967). The authors point out, however, that the more imaginative of those who early chose science tend to abandon it when they discover that a career in science offers most people little possibility for original, creative endeavor.*

and distrust, descending in moments and times of crisis to brutality and vengeance, such as to taint the dignity and decency of all willing participants—students, teachers, and administrators. The effect is that only those who are misfits or rebels, who implicitly or explicitly deny the system's legitimacy, can play the role of teacher or student with self-respect and respect for the other.

The various groups in the school population are variously damaged by the irrelevance and shabby falsity of a good deal of the course material and by the status and power (and most recently force) arrangements which bolster the school despotism. The teachers, by being forced or forcing themselves to serve up a hash of moralistic and patriotic platitudes in the classroom; by acting as policemen and guards in halls, toilets, and lunchrooms; by spending a good part of their time keeping records of their students' general complaisance—called grades, which serve in general as accrediting data—lose respect for themselves, for their students, for their subject matter. One student said:

> I don't like to put too much blame on people as individuals. I blame the system. [The teachers] don't know what to do . . . they can't reach us . . . and there's a war between us. They call us zombies. We're not related to each other. I think all these teachers have to go along. I think it grows on them. It's the way things are done. They just do it without thinking . . . without even knowing what they're really doing.

Frequently, teachers who have not reached the point of questioning the system as system will still refuse to enforce some of its more humiliating rules, such as informing on cutters, challenging student loiterers in the halls and toilets, and so on. In the last years, however, more and more teachers who have begun by questioning the rules have ended by questioning the system. And especially in the time following the Great Strike, the most meaningful student-teacher relationships came to be those founded on a, not necessarily explicit, common rejection of the system's premises as well as of its rules.

The top Academic students (those destined to be accredited to the next step), by accepting with a minimum of questioning the travesty of learning that goes by the name of subject matter in exchange for a good ranking within the student status system are corrupted intellectually and socially—and kept in ignorance of the world of their fellow students (as the stories of Temma, Kenny, and Rachel below show).

And the bottom group of Academic students, General students, Commercial students—those in attendance because of the compulsory education rather than the competitive-accreditation law—in addition to the waste of their intellectual energies, are held in low esteem by their teachers, by the higher-ranking students, often by themselves. "You've got to remember what kind of student body we get here," a school psychologist in a predominantly black and Spanish-speaking high school once said to me. "Remember the cream is skimmed off by the specialized high schools . . . . A great many teachers are really disillusioned because they can't teach."

Loss of Legitimacy: The Irrelevant Curriculum

A school curriculum may be relevant in one or both of two general ways. It may train individuals to play productive or at least remunerative roles in the larger society. The subject matter of a medical school, a TV repair training course, a police academy, a lesson in running a switchboard, or a school for interior decorators is relevant in this sense. So is teaching a child in a gathering-and-hunting society how to spot game or a gypsy child how to tell fortunes. Alternatively, or concurrently, a school curriculum may be relevant as education. It may help students to understand themselves, their society, their world, and the natural universe; and it may teach them how to ask the questions that will help them go on increasing their understanding. A psychoanalysis, a novel, a scientific experiment, a newspaper, a conversation, or serious academic study may be relevant in this way.

Most of the customary high school curriculum is not designed to be relevant in either of these ways, and if it is sometimes relevant in one of them, that is a matter of chance. It is designed mainly to be a means to a further experience (trade school, professional school, college, life, apprenticeship) which, it is hoped, will be relevant in one or both of the above ways.

As compulsory education laws function, they do not provide any significant training or serious education for teenagers; they keep them off the streets and out of a labor market that has no use for them. In the age group 22 to 24 there is very little difference between the unemployment rate of high school graduates and the rate of school dropouts, of both sexes and all races: 5.0 percent and 6.8 percent. For nonwhite males (the group in New York which is most urged to "stay in school and get a good job"), unemployment among those 22 to 24 who were dropouts is 6.9 percent, among high school graduates, 8.2.[3] As there are more armed service rejects among dropouts than among graduates, the unemployment rate of graduates would presumably be considerably higher if so many were not taken off the streets by the army. It may also be presumed that as holders of an Academic diploma are less likely to be unemployed than holders of a General diploma, the unemployment rate among the latter would be barely above that for dropouts.*

The statistics must be viewed with some skepticism. Determined by registration at state employment services, they leave uncounted the unemployed who do not register there at all. (They also, of course, do not reveal the numbers of employed who are in dead-end, unskilled jobs.) But however faulty, the figures do disclose the results of a high school curriculum that, even where it is designed to be vocational, is out of date, inefficient, and unrelated to actual job possibilities.

In general the vocational courses in New York City high schools train students in skills for which there is an ever diminishing demand or train them so badly that the graduates customarily go on to private vocational schools in order to be able to qualify for the job openings that do exist. Moreover, the curriculum, which is designed essentially to accredit people to college, does not, as we have seen, do this for most of New York's black and Puerto

* *The high school's function of keeping young black men off the streets was sharply highlighted in October, 1969 in Washington D.C. when a high school principal's request to dismiss school early because of an uncontrollable disciplinary situation was refused by the assistant superintendent who explained that "keeping unruly students in school was preferable to having them roaming the streets."* Washington Post, *October 25, 1969.*

Rican students. They are not prepared for college, not expected to go to college, and not acceptable to most colleges. "Why do we have to go out into the street, to Harlem self-help teams, to poverty programs, to get ready for college?" a rebel student at George Washington High School asked. "Why can't we get it here?"[4]

There remains the other relevant task that the high school curriculum could perform—to help students understand themselves, their world, the physical universe. The students' eager responsiveness to the occasional classroom discussion that really engages them suggests how ready they are to explore ideas and the world. But the school is prevented from meeting this need by the emptiness and dishonesty of most of the curriculum.

Why should people with a live musical idiom of their own—be it rock, soul, or Latin-based—fulfill the school's music requirements by sitting an hour a week trying to close their ears against Beethoven? Why should boys and girls who despite eight years of the weekly spelling rituals never learned to spell, sit day after day pounding at broken typewriters? Why should students whose own adult sex lives may have begun two or three or more years before be instructed in the meaning of adolescence by men and women whose only wish is to retreat from the sexually charged atmosphere of a gathering of teenagers?

But the problems with curriculum go deeper. The most dramatic incidence of irrelevance and dishonesty is in courses in social studies and in English. In the latter, language instead of being developed as a tool for thinking, expressing, and appreciating is seen as a body of precepts as rigid and unreal as the rules governing school behavior. And literature, instead of an expression of the most creative uses of language and ways of exploring men and the world, is composed of plots and characters to be remembered, vocabulary words to be learned, and little moralisms and lessons tucked away between the rhymes and inside the themes.

Most high school math and science courses are more or less relevant to the needs of college-bound students in the sense that they meet the college demands for attainment in these areas. Whether or not they are the best courses for general background or for those who will not specialize in science or science-based technological areas is another matter.

(I myself think that one basic science course plus a survey of the history of science might be more generally useful.) Foreign-language courses, again, are usually directed toward meeting college entrance requirements rather than toward meeting students' real-life needs. In New York, few native English speakers can converse in Spanish with their Spanish-speaking neighbors, even after having studied Spanish for two or three years, and many teachers who are New York born and raised cannot communicate with their Spanish-speaking students.

In the social studies, especially in the required high school courses in world history and American history, the realities of the human and the American experience are strangled in a net of half-truths, unrelated details, and idiot clichés. The course in world history typically purveys the concept that all civilization has been carried along the Greco-Roman, Judeo-Christian traditions, with barely a mention of the contributions to the west of Byzantium and Islam or of the relatively independent civilizations of ancient Ghana and Mali, of the Orient, or of the empires of the New World. These courses thus render the nonwhite peoples of the world invisible in historical time, as the Negro in America is invisible in physical space, and perpetuate a stereotype of the Third World as populated by peoples whose emergence from nonhistory and barbarism was achieved only by the intervention of Europeans and Americans. While student pressures in New York, as elsewhere, have resulted in the introduction of Afro-American history courses (usually given as electives), these can remedy the distortions of the basic, required history courses to only a limited degree, and only for those students who elect them.

Of anthropology and archaeology, which might help the inheritors of our distraught world to accept with a little more equanimity the many ways there are to be human and to conduct a human society, I have seen only the smallest trace in the New York high school curriculum—in the form of hundreds of copies of a pamphlet by Ruth Benedict and Gene Weltfish, *The Races of Mankind*, published in 1943 by the Public Affairs Committee and intended then to serve a nation at war by combatting Nazi racist ideas. I found the pamphlets high on a dusty shelf in my English department's bookroom; once the war was won, the booklets were left there to gather dust. I distributed them to my students and conducted some discussions on race. I found the students fantastically ignorant of the simplest facts about the subject—for example, they did not know the terminological distinctions between "race," "religion," and "nationality," and, although they all had had some exposure to a course in biology, most of them believed that race differences were carried in the blood stream. "He's Negro, because he has Negro blood." "You are Negro if you have one-thirty-sixth Negro blood." "Jews have Jewish blood." At the same time, they were eager to clear up their confusions and to air their opinions.

American history, as written up in the textbooks and taught by most teachers, is an exercise in not seeing black; not seeing power struggles except as a kind of magnified family quarrel caused by misunderstandings and soon smoothed over; and not seeing the United States as a great power engaged in power struggles. The radical black students call these books racist texts, and whatever the intentions of the writers and publishers, I know no effective refutation for that point of view. Many of the texts are so written that they can be sold on a national market and so must withstand the shrewd scrutiny of southern boards of education. But even many of those liberal texts that mention the contributions to American history of individual Negroes, or groups of Negroes (for example, the black cowboys) fail to confront honestly the class and race conflicts that lie at the very heart of the American story. The history of the Civil War and of the Reconstruction is still conveyed with the southern viewpoint of Ulrich Phillips, as if C. Vann Woodward, John Hope Franklin, and the whole school of revisionists had never existed. The slaves and the freedmen are conveyed as mere objects of history rather than as men who also played their role in the struggles of the nation. "Black Codes angered the North" (not the black men?), "Abolitionism angered the South" (who in the South?), and the "tragedy of Reconstruction" (because the plantations were ruined and the slaveowners embittered, not because the freedmen were returned to virtual slavery) are expressions repeated again and again from one book to the next, giving the impression, which indeed is the fact, that what is being written is not history but myth.[5] (A similar analysis might be made of the schoolbook treatment of American Indians, as at first a kind of nuisance, like mosquitoes or a harsh climate, and then, when they were overcome—like mosquitoes or a harsh climate, by superior technology—as a kind of burden that we have done our utmost to bear with patience and ingenuity. But never treated as a people, also born to the human condition.)

Many history teachers at the high school level (whose own training would have included a good deal of history reading as undergraduate and graduate students) try in their classes to refute and overcome the nonsense contained in the texts they use. Their efforts are likely to be balked, however, by the years of indoctrination that their students have already experienced at the hands of elementary school teachers whose knowledge of history is derived from a combination of what they remember from *their* high school courses and what the especially foolish elementary school social studies books say. In one fifth-grade social studies text, for example, *In All Our States*, by Paul Hanna and others, a unit on "The Changing South" proceeds calmly without the intrusion of a single black face. Cotton is being hand-picked by whites (a changing South, indeed!). And the text reads: "In this part of your book you will learn about two important crops grown on Southern farms. You will learn about some of the problems caused by the way people used the land. And you will see how Southerners today are working on these problems and are finding new and better ways to use the resources of their region." The history teachers themselves have little or no say about what texts they will use in their classes, texts being chosen by department chairmen and principals from lists approved by the board of education. (But when dissident parents and students called for the destruction of "racist" books and for control by the community or the students over the choice of textbooks, the teachers union took the position that while the community might have some say in what subjects should be taught, it would be an infringement of "academic freedom" for them to interfere with how the teachers taught or what books they used.)

The erasure of black from the American experience and of the non-Western world as creators, as well as recipients, of civilization defiles what is called the study of history and damages white students quite as much as black. As the cultural historian Harold Cruse wrote in answer to Cleaver's opposition to "cultural nationalism":

The black search for "identity" . . . only underscores the fact that all *Americans are involved in an identity crisis. Since whites and blacks do not identify with each other, it only means that neither blacks nor whites are really identifying with the realities of the American experience which bound them together so fatefully in what is supposed to be the "cultural matrix" of a nation. Thus the implied threat of the division of the nation into "two nations black and white" is another way of saying that the American experiment in nationhood has been a historical failure of the first magnitude.*[6]

It is in a nation's schools, and especially in the inculcating of the nation's history, that the sense of nationhood begins to be conveyed.

If the subject matter served to Academic students is a kind of mockery of scholarship, the subject matter dished out to the General students is a mockery of a mockery. Must the Academic and Honors students learn hard vocabulary words, like "lethargy," "sagacity," and "dilemma," in order to score well on their College Boards? Then the General students must also learn vocabulary words, only easier ones, like "leisure," "numb," and "scorched." These items are taken from midterm examinations in a "bad" Manhattan high school. ("Relevant" and "irrelevant," two words that up until a few years ago were among those imprisoned by teachers on their vocabulary lists, have now been liberated by the students for free employment in their own speech.) Must the Academics read *The Prince and the Pauper, The Mill on the Floss*, or *The Tale of Two Cities*? Then the Generals will read the same, but "abridged and adapted."* Must the Academic students commit to memory the factual material contained in a ten-page chapter on the Renaissance? Then

* *I have these titles from a booklist provided me by a teacher who explained, "There are newer books [in the stockroom], but they've never been put on the list, so they're never used. Most—or much—department money is spent on replacing* Jane Eyre, Tale of Two Cities, *etc. The higher-track teachers get first crack at the books, so that the lowest tracks wind up with the garbage or no books at all."*

the General students must commit to memory a half-page of such exciting nonsense as "Europe began to awaken from the deep sleep of the Middle Ages"; or "The people of the Far East have had little practice in the art of ruling themselves." These statements are taken from two texts currently used in the New York City schools—*World History Study Lessons* (Follett Publishing Company) and *Our World and Its Peoples* (Allyn & Bacon Inc.). The former, a workbook-textbook in world history for slow readers covers the Crusades in 380 words, ancient Egypt in 440 words, the fall of Rome in 470 words, and the civilizations of ancient India and China in 540 words.

The response of most students at most levels to the course material is one of measureless boredom. "It's so *boring*! She's so *boring*!" breathes the cosmic sigh through hour after hour of student interviews. The teachers, too, are bored, by a task and a subject matter which if acknowledged to be irrelevant would make *them* irrelevant. Those for whom the discipline—science, literature, history—commanded respect in their college days are likely to be disgusted with the empty shells of learning that they are expected to try to convey to their non-college-bound students and often they come to displace this feeling of disgust onto their students. Out of student and teacher boredom with their common task, with themselves, and with each other arise certain rituals designed to sustain the system and the relative status of the parties to it. The rituals have mainly to do with grades and privileges.

Grades and Privileges as Instruments of Control

Second only to the student complaint "It's so *boring*" is the complaint "The teacher always has to be right." Most teachers are loath to explain reasons for a command or an assignment to students, either because much of what they demand of their students is in the category of ritual, for which, of course, there is no reason that might appeal to logic, or because explaining diminishes authority.

After the strike of 1968, some students at Gandhi High, a mixed Manhattan high school, began to challenge their teachers in class. "What's the purpose of this assignment?" "Never mind the purpose. You do it because I'm the teacher and I told you to." In one class, students objecting to a book that was assigned were asked by the teacher if they'd prefer to read something else. A student suggestion of John Updike's *The Centaur* was rejected out of hand: "Because I said so. If I'm the teacher and I say 'No!'—therefore 'No!' " After class the teacher told the student that *The Centaur* would have been too difficult for many of the students. "Which I really would have accepted if he had said it in class," the student commented. "But just this business of 'No. I'm the teacher.' It's this, constantly."

"It seems clear that the reason for a command should never be explained," Waller writes. "Although it may be desirable on other grounds to explain it, it should be recognized that the explanations, by introducing an element of doubt concerning the command, or by the suggestion that it might not be obeyed . . . detracts from the force of the command." The initial mistake of the teacher who rejected *The Centaur* was to ask for student suggestions for a title. Or perhaps the initial mistake lay with the decision of the teachers union to call for a strike, as that very same girl student suggested when in response to a scold question, "Where were you during class yesterday?" she asked, "Where were you during the strike last month?"

The students, for their part, use the innocent question as a way of one-upping the teacher. Through the ages, students have developed as rich a repertory of ways of one-upping the teachers as teachers have of ways of one-upping students. Probably richer. Because while the student must always rely on his own cunning, the teacher, tripped-up once too often or at a bad time, can always give up that game and fall back on sheer power.

The conventional power of the teacher is the power to grade. Conscientious teachers take grading very seriously. They keep minute records of attendance, promptness, homework handed in on time, reciting in class, and performance on tests. Some teachers add to these items extra points or extra zeros for being helpful, doing extra assignments, chewing gum, talking back, leaving your seat without permission, and so on. Conscientious teachers weight various kinds of grades differently, with, for example, a 90 on a big test being worth twice a 90 on a little test, a zero for nonattendance graver than a zero for chewing gum. Two or three times a semester, teachers tally all their records and give each student a grade—in accordance with which he passes or fails; passes well or badly; moves up to an Honor class or down to a General one; and eventually is accredited to college or drops out (or is asked to leave). Conscientious teachers consider themselves, and are generally considered by students, to be fair. The student knows what he's going to get a zero for, so he knows where he's at. If a student respectfully questions a conscientious teacher about his grade, she will redo her bookkeeping in his presence, and if she finds she has made an error, change the grade. It is considered bad practice—tending to give one a reputation as a soft mark—to change a student's grade once it has gone onto his permanent record, but the teacher who wants to be fair will sometimes do it anyway.

The teacher who is not conscientious, who doesn't care if she is considered fair or not, who hates calculating weighted averages, or who in general is just lazy hands out grades more or less by instinct. That is, she honestly and openly uses the power to grade as a way of making students behave correctly and answer correctly.

Neither the conscientious nor the lazy teacher's grades are necessarily closely related to the student's intellectual attainments—or even to his merely academic attainments, except among obviously college-bound students, where grades are likely to be more closely related to academic performance, with items like forgetting to bring one's book to class or even handing in one's homework late less likely to earn a penalty and final grades being more dependent on test and class performance. But even among the college-bound classes, some teachers weigh observance of the rituals quite high.

All students, whether college-bound or not, report that not only conformist behavior but also conformist thinking is required for good grades. Among high school students interviewed for this book, almost all felt that agreeing with the teacher was necessary if one was to get a good grade. Their sense of outrage in regard to this seemed to be limited to those occasions when a student was marked down for more or less innocently disagreeing with a teacher, that is, without consciously intending to provoke. Ishmael, for example, reports that he was reproved for making the classroom into a forum for subversive ideas and given a low grade for a talk in speech class on "socialism." Disappointed in the grade, he openly charged the teacher with grading him on his opinions. His shocked classmates reproved him: "You were right, but you shouldn't have said that." More often, however, the "debates" between teacher and student are a dialogue about status and independence. For many if not most teachers, as we have seen, grades are a way of telling a student if he is "right" or "wrong." And in the ambience of status and anger that prevails, the distinctions between correct behavior, correct facts, and correct opinions tend to be blurred. On their part, students' questioning of their teacher' opinions is likely to betray not cool intellectuality but a nastiness aroused by their unhappy low-status position. Where they persist in being provocative, as a few do, it would be an unusual teacher who would not be moved to respond with the weapon she has, grades. How often students are actually graded low for merely disagreeing with the teacher is less important than that most students believe this to be the practice, and therefore regard questioning not as a way of learning but as a way of "getting" the teacher. Students who don't want to "get" the teacher play it safe and keep doubtful questions to themselves.

Among the college-bound the competition for grades is as fierce as the competition for entrance to "the college of one's choice." Ché Lopez, one of the students from Gandhi High, tells about the middle-class white students in his school: "I mean, the things that they do, they are *so conditioned for that mark*! If they didn't get a 93 in their subjects, they would pass out cold. If they got an 85, they never saw anything as low before! I don't begrudge them the marks. I do feel sorry for them in the sense that they are being driven to get it, they don't even know why." But among the non-college-bound, and especially among the Generals, passing is generally considered good enough, and a General student can pass if he attends regularly, behaves well, does his homework some of the time, and shows that he is "trying." It is considered cruel to flunk a General student who "tries." (Loretta Tubman said that her history teacher was "too nice" to flunk her, so he gave her a 65, but she thought it would have done her some good if he had flunked her once.) For the non-college-bound, which means most black and Puerto Rican (and working-class white) students, comparative grades above passing are of minor importance.

But when the teacher is deprived of competitive grading, he has lost an important teaching prop. In the absence of meaningful subject matter only the grading process is left as educational dialogue. And, when grading, too, crumbles, the teachers become further demoralized, and many hours of classroom time are empty of even a pretense at instruction. A common student complaint is of teachers who talk at length to the class about their personal lives, or even read the newspaper. The students, also demoralized, cut class, play hooky, and hang around the cafeteria or bathrooms insofar as possible. A few come into school high on wine or pot. Others bring the instruments of repose with them, to be dispensed half-secretly among their fellows. There are occasional sexual encounters, shakedowns, and heroin shooting in stairwells and bathrooms. At every predominantly black and Puerto Rican New York City high school, compulsory education gathers in thousands of young men and women who, reduced to despair or at least to lethargy by the insolent tedium of their daily experiences there, serve as potential customers for marijuana peddlers and dope pushers. And many students and their parents blame society for nothing so much as the way in which "their" schools and their children are degraded by this relationship with the underworld and with illegal and sometimes frightening practices. "They call this school pushers' heaven," a student said in disgust. "Nobody wants their school to be called pushers' heaven, not even the pushers."

In addition to grades, a conventional instrument for control of students is that of privileges and honors. Here, too, as with grades, the instrument is relatively effective among the college-bound students and relatively ineffective among the non-college-bound. For the former, a one-period-a-day job (unpaid) in the attendance office puts one in personal touch with the school's most important personnel, gives one various authority advantages over one's fellow students (or if one is a good guy puts one in a position to do them an occasional record-changing favor), and perhaps gets one out of an oppressive study hall. A job in the program office gives one the opportunity to make out one's own program (that is, pick the most popular teachers, a lunch hour at the same time as one's friends, etc.). A job assisting a teacher in her bookkeeping during one's lunch hour provides at once an escape from the unsavory, steamy lunchroom and the private company of a teacher who may pass on faculty gossip, give advice about academic problems, or even be a kind of friend. (The teacher is meanwhile getting the student gossip, so that these arrangements serve as something like the meeting of enemy nationals in neutral territory.) Serving on the G.O. (student government) Council or being elected one of its officers serves all the preceding functions on a grander scale. For these chores and privileges, students earn "service credits," commendation slips, and other academic emoluments which may be exchanged for election to honorary societies, recommendations for still other, higher privileges, and eventually letters of recommendation to college. Performing chores of these kinds is considered to be "serving the school" and thus being a "good school citizen."

The students who serve in this way are usually the school's least alienated ones, least alienated from the teachers and from the school game, that is; they are often quite alienated from their fellow students, including, in the case of G.O. representatives and officers, the students who are supposed to be their constituency. Nonelite students in the high school in which I taught were so uninterested in the student government apparatus that the administration made membership therein (which involved a small fee) compulsory, and in most nonelite classes it was difficult to get two students to serve as the student government representatives. While some students are simply uninterested in the school exchange of services for privileges, others (both elite and nonelite) regard it as hypocritical and demeaning. College-bound students, however, sometimes cynically put in a certain number of semester hours in school services "because it'll look good on my transcript."

Social prestige distinctions between college-bound and non-college-bound students generally reflect the distinctions of the larger society.

At Turner High, a predominantly black and Puerto Rican high school, until quite recently different groupings of students were assigned to different lunchrooms, all

Honors students and seniors to a small fairly clean third-floor lunchroom and all others to a huge unpainted basement lunchroom which its patrons called "the dungeon." As almost all the white students were Honors students, and as the dropout rate among the non-Honors ran to 70 or 80 percent, the upstairs lunchroom had a clientele of about 50 or 60 percent white in a 10 or 15 percent white student body, and "the dungeon" had a clientele of 95 or 98 percent black and Puerto Rican. There was a general belief among the basement clientele that a different menu was served in the upstairs lunchroom and that soft music was piped in.*

Benny Wilkinson: "I just got sick and tired of all that old mess."

Benny Wilkinson is an example of a black young man who experienced the high school atmosphere of irrelevance and repression, as a negation of his educational aims.

Benny's mother, Mrs. Wilkinson, was a strong, ambitious, assertive woman who told each of her children, "I didn't send for you. I didn't call you. But now that you are here, you gonna conform to all the rules we make here." The rules, carefully lettered and tacked up around the three-bedroom, municipal housing project apartment, included instructions on hanging up clothing, respecting other family members' privacy, washing out the bathtub, and doing one's homework. There were bookshelves in almost every room bearing a couple of sets of encyclopedias, three or four dictionaries, a few novels, books on child care. There was a globe and, on the wall, a large map of the world. Benny's room was bursting with technical books and magazines, history books, prints of old sailing ships, maps, a much-used old chemistry set, and uncounted model airplanes. As with Miles Randolph's

* *The official reason for running two lunchrooms was that the special privilege involved would motivate students to want to get to be Honors students or seniors so they could eat in the better lunchroom. Actually, as the school had so few white students, it was hoped that the provision of a clean and civilized eating place would serve as an inducement to white families to continue to send their children there.*

family, the Wilkinson's may have been poor, and, in addition, lacked, as they say, a resident male—but the family certainly did not conform to the conditions of the "deprived child" cliché.

Benny got his first library card when he was in second grade, and he was a habitual user of the library throughout his school years. He was passionately curious about history and science, mainly technology. "I used to read a lot about trains and cars and stuff like that. I was beginning to wonder about some things, you know, wonder why they were like that. I began reading about stuff like that, you know to satisfy my own curiosity. You know, wondering what made boats run this way. Why do we have to be this way? Why not another way? The physical make-up of things. What went on inside us." Somewhere along in his high school years, he began to patronize the research room of the great New York City 42nd Street Library in pursuit of facts about American history and technological development.

Grade school was boring to Benny—"you were sitting in one place all day and looking at one face all day and hearing the same voice all day"—but the world was a fascinating bundle of riddles to be solved.

Benny attended a predominantly white junior high school under the board of education's Open Enrollment plan. That was much less boring than elementary school had been. There were good discussions in the history classes and he was introduced to biology.

He looked forward to high school, which he thought would carry him even deeper into the worlds he loved to explore. Entering Simón Bolívar High School as an Academic student, he found instead a world that disheartened and demoralized him.

> A lot of teachers really didn't know what they were teaching. You know I found that to be true in history and the sciences. Those are the two subjects I always used to know and that is why I really used to catch them.
>
> You could say they wasn't interested enough in their job to try to help out anybody. You know, like go to them and ask them a question about this and that and the other, and they would say, "Ah, well, right now, I have to do this, and I can't answer right now." But they didn't ever come

around to answering it at all. The school itself has a real bad reputation. So that a lot of the teachers there, they just normally think "Okay, these kids are not going to care anyway. So I don't have to do this." So after a while you just lose interest.

It is just a small minority [of students who made the school bad]. They mess it up for the rest. You can see those guys a mile away, especially the way they used to come in. They used to practically crawl up the stairs. A lot of times the ladies [aides] at the door would look at them and not do anything. Usually in the winter time they would go there drunk. They don't go to their classes. They hang around. [Or they] just sat around in the back and wheezed and whoozed. I know of one guy, he was caught in the bathroom [drinking] and all he got was a two-weeks suspension. And after his two-weeks suspension was over . . . whamm [back to the same offense]!

[The administration] figured that the only way to improve it was to tighten down on us. [Make it] like a penitentiary—that was their long-range plan to so-call "improve the school."

I just got sick and tired of all that old mess, and I was getting kind of disinterested in the classes so I began to cut a couple of classes.

His grades reflected his demoralization and bad attendance, he flunked a course or two, and finally he was "busted" to a General course. This meant that, despite his considerable background in history and science and his demonstrated high reading ability, he was programed for General instead of Academic history and English, some shops, and record keeping, a kind of kindergarten-level bookkeeping which the General students get as a math course.

The last year before he and the school agreed on the one thing they could agree on, to part, he and a small group of students with the support of one white lady teacher organized a small group to try to "clean up the school." They distributed a pamphlet in which, Benny said, they announced that they "were cleaning up Simón Bolívar High School. We were making the school . . . trying to make it a respectable school where people could come to learn. We were trying to have the school for the purpose for which it was built. A hall of education, instead of a flop house or a juvenile penitentiary, as it was." The group was perhaps impolitic in focusing its attention on the boys' dean who they felt was responsible for allowing the school to run into the ground.

Benny's attendance record made him vulnerable. He and his mother were called in for a suspension hearing.

When I got to this, it really tore me up. By that time my attitude was nilch. That is the year I supposedly was going to graduate [with a General diploma]. And I was hot and bothered about the whole deal. [At the hearing before the dean] it was just like out there in Times Square. The whole world could hear. Everybody was around. Down in his office, talking, waiting. [You] trying to hide your head, and everybody in school knowing what is going on—that makes it kind of bad.* [The dean] said, "You are always cutting." So I said, "How many times have I cut?" And he didn't give a number. I said, "Well, half these people around here right now have cut more in one year than I have cut in three years." And he said, "Well, that is beside the thing. The thing is you were caught." So I didn't say anything else.

There was a couple of teachers came down and they was willing to sign a petition, you know, to have me passed. But he wouldn't take that. [The charges] were just cutting—not being in class—that was it. They had no record of bad actions or anything like that. I never gave anybody a hard time. I wanted to stick around. But at that time I was going back and forth to the recruiting office and down to Whitehall [recruitment headquarters] for my examination. I wanted to fight that guy. I wanted to see why—where does he get the authority to throw me out when all them other guys have been going like that for years? Why did he jump down *my* throat? [My mother] wanted to know why, too, and she felt that the reason he had given wasn't good enough. She wanted to hear another

* *By contrast, the UFT contract requires and the board of education recently reaffirmed a teacher's right to privacy in a grievance hearing. (See* The United Teacher, *August 31, 1969.) Also, it goes without saying that teachers may be accompanied by counsel or other representative of their choice. On the other hand, teachers and administrators have generally been unconcerned about or opposed to the granting of privacy and procedural protections to students.*

reason. I wanted to hear another reason, too. I wanted to satisfy myself that there was nothing I could do about it. I wasn't thrown out. I had a six-month suspension.* I was supposed to come back the next September. But that September I was in the Air Force, up in Illinois.

At the time I was interviewing Benny, he had a highly skilled technician's job in the Air Force and was taking courses on his own time to be a pilot. He was teaching himself the math he needed. "Most of the things, I have now," he explained, "pertains to my work and that makes it a whole lot easier. Now I have nobody pressing me about you have to do this or you have to do that. I know I have only four years [to accomplish] about five different things to make it better for me. So therefore this has to be done and I better do it." Like Miles Randolph, Benny was not only highly competent, he was also highly motivated, except that Benny's school was not able to harness his will to achieve.

Though Benny thought he had been treated unfairly in high school, he considered himself to be responsible for his school failure. Three years later, an Air Force man for two years, back and forth a couple of times to Vietnam, tears rose to the surface of his voice when he remembered his last days in school—rather different from the cap-and-gown ceremony that he may have imagined for himself, that his mother had surely planned when she delivered her lecture to him about the rules of life as she saw them.

I asked him if he felt the suspension was his fault.

Yes, it was. I could have ignored all that stuff and just gone along anyway. People have done it before me and some was doing it while I was there. I don't see why I had to be so different. But it just happened that way . . . I would say it was my fault. Whose else was it? But I feel that it is not too late for me to come out of it. That I will *have* to come out of it or else I will be like those guys up on 135th Street. You know, I just can't see myself as that. Can't picture myself as that. That is how they started.

* *The school here did not observe board of education rules, which would have required, for a six-months suspension, a hearing before the district superintendent, with the dean appearing as witness rather than as judge.*

Benny's story illustrates how a hollow and insulting curriculum upheld by an array of repressive security regulations produce that very student disgust with school which the regulations are apparently seeking to mitigate. And as the professionals continue to administer the cure which increasingly aggravates the disease, they solemnly explain how this disease is caused by environmental conditions beyond their control.

Loss of Legitimacy: The Security System

With the curriculum having little legitimacy as authority among non-college-bound students, and grades and privileges little strength as power, the New York high school, like high schools in many other cities is bereft of sanctions for maintaining control over its unwilling subjects. More and more, it has come to rely on an elaborate security system which in crisis situations can itself be maintained only by naked force. I calculate that in most predominantly black and Puerto Rican schools more energies are devoted to keeping school and class attendance and punishing nonattenders than to any other single activity. New teachers are warned that keeping attendance records neat and up to date takes precedence over all other activities. Mere paperwork, however, is unequal to the task. Most schools leave unlocked from the streetside only one door, so that students entering late can be screened and reported. Some years ago the fire department prohibited the until then common practice of locking doors also from the inside, so now guards (teachers, student trustees, paraprofessional aides) are commonly stationed at other doors, too, to apprehend students who try to cut out early. Most students give up without a fuss if they are caught trying to leave, but occasionally there will be a show of physical force between a student determined to leave and a, usually male, teacher determined that he will not. A student who uses force against a teacher, even if it is a resisting not an attacking force, is considered disruptive and is usually summarily suspended, transferred, or expelled.

The more the security rules are felt by students to be

unjustified, oppressive, or even only a nuisance, the more they will find ways to cheat and evade. And the more they cheat and evade, the harsher the rules must be made to catch the cheaters and the evaders, with the explanation, "If we could trust them, we wouldn't have to have all these rules. But they are always trying to get away with something. Without the rules, this place would be just anarchy." With distrust eating into the very marrow of the school organism, only more rules and evasions are possible.

To prevent the student from trying to get out by pretending that he is ill, most high schools have a rule that a claim of illness must be accompanied by a measureable fever for the student to be allowed to leave. (Shrewd first-aid room attendants prevent students from holding the thermometer under the hot water tap.) Students experiencing menstrual cramps, vomiting, fainting, headache are sometimes sent back from first-aid rooms with a note to the classroom teacher, "Please allow this student to put his head down on the desk as he doesn't feel well." School rules forbid the dispensing of aspirin, and frequently there are not enough cots in the first-aid rooms for the number of (real or imaginary) patients.

Many high schools, especially overcrowded ones, try to schedule as many students as possible without lunch, in order to cut down on use of the cafeteria, a place especially vulnerable to wildness, fights, running around, and so on. Thus a student may go through four or five hours of running from class to class with no break at all, a schedule that most adults would find impossible, and that the union contract does not allow for teachers. Guards, usually under the direction of a strong, experienced male teacher, patrol the cafeteria to enforce order and prevent smoking, and there, to the din of hundreds of teenagers in a huge hall without soundproofing, is customarily added the continual blare of a guard's commands emanating from a bullhorn. To prevent students from cutting out, and also from having a smoke after lunch, or (considering the food usually served in the cafeterias) from having an edible lunch, most high schools forbid students to take their lunch at home or in nearby luncheonettes.

To prevent smoking (tobacco or pot), many schools have padlocked all student washrooms except the two near the cafeteria, and they are usually locked during the first and last periods of the day. When open, lacking any soap or paper supplies whatsoever, toilet seats scarred with cigarette burns, floors often soiled and puddley, and booth doors missing or without catches, students are watched from the outside through an always open door by a guard who is sometimes of the opposite sex from the users. ("Quit peeking through the door!" I once heard an irate girl student holler out to a boy student guard barely beyond the open door. He answered, seriously, "I'm not peeking, I'm watching.") All this proceeds within a few feet of the cafeteria. In order to prevent needy students from using the teachers' toilets, usually one men's and one women's to a floor, these must be locked too and each teacher given a key. I once asked an administrator and a school psychologist in a school where the device of locking the toilets had recently been instituted how the students had responded. The administrator said, "They fussed a little at first, but they got used to it pretty quickly." And the psychologist said, "Most of them don't seem to care. But it does bother some of the more sensitive ones." (By "sensitive," he may or may not have meant "white.")

Because most high schools buildings are three to five stories high and elevators are reserved for teacher use, students normally do not have time to get to the one open toilet in the short interval of changing classes and still arrive in class before the bell. They must therefore go to class and ask the teacher's permission to go to the toilet. If the teacher grants permission (which teachers sometimes do not do because, as we saw before, students often use going to the toilet as an excuse for getting out of the classroom, meeting their friends, grabbing a smoke, and so on), she writes the student a pass, including thereon the date and time and the student's destination.

In corridors, pass or program card must be produced on demand in order that the student may be identified and his right to be at that spot at that time checked. In the corridor, too, a student may be challenged by any teacher or guard in respect to other school rules—which forbid, for example, wearing a hat, carrying outer garments, or wearing dark glasses. Because a student and a teacher who meet in the corridor may well be strangers to each other and therefore without even that modicum of humanity that exists between enemies who know each other's names, corridors, like cafeterias and toilets, are the areas of most open hostility between the two groups. Commands and challenges are often uttered harshly and without any courtesy word (some teachers say, "a teacher does not have to say 'please' to a student"), and teachers will walk down corridors growling "get that hat off your head" to every hat wearer who does not snatch off the offending garment at a teacher's approach.

Of course, many teachers, particularly lady teachers, are customarily polite to all students, and, until the high school rebellion began, after the Great Strike, most students seemed to accept all the rules as just, so long as they were justly and courteously enforced. Most teachers, probably the majority, regard the rules as necessary but the experience of enforcing them as humiliating and unprofessional. Paraprofessional aides are frequently deployed to guard duty at toilets, doors, cafeteria, and so on, thus enabling the teachers to pretend that they have nothing to do with the whole nasty business. A few teachers, however, will use the rules and the corridor encounters as a way of riding, humiliating, and sometimes seriously discomfitting students. Miss Weber, a teacher at Norman Thomas High School tells the following:

I had a nice boy student, Roosevelt Jones, whom I had assigned to me from a study hall to help me with my clerical work during my free period every day. I never bothered him if he came in a couple of minutes after the bell, because he was really doing me a favor helping me with my chores. One day he dashed in all red and panting, and upset. And right after him stomped in Mr. Elkins. He had a reputation for being very tough. Elkins was in a real fury. He said the boy had been fresh to him in the halls. He said he was taking him down to the dean. They were both so angry I was afraid of what might happen, so I said I myself would bring Roosevelt to the dean in a few minutes after he quieted down. Elkins said, "You mean you refuse to relinquish him?" As he put it like that, I had to say yes. He stormed out. Roosevelt, seventeen years old and a very cool type, burst into tears. He said no teacher had ever stood up for him to another teacher. He said Elkins had met him and a girl on the stairs and made some crack insulting to the girl. Roosevelt rose to the insult, and Elkins turned on him.

Both students took off, Roosevelt to my room. In a little while I took him to the dean's office as I had said I would and found that Elkins had reported *me* to the boys' dean. I didn't want there to be bad blood between me and Elkins, so when I saw him again, I explained why I hadn't wanted to let him and the boy go off alone together in the then empty corridor and stairways. He said, "You didn't have to worry. I could have taken care of him on the stairs."

For every offense for which a student is sent to the dean, a record is kept in the dean's office. An occasional lateness or absence is relatively easily excused, especially if the student can think up a good reason. Chronic cutting and lateness are likely to be more harshly dealt with, and can be used as grounds for summary action if some other offense is reported. In a serious dispute with a teacher, impudence or any kind of physical force by the student is prima facie evidence against him regardless of the provocation. After one case of hitting or a few cases of impudence, a student who is under age seventeen may be suspended, or transferred to another school. Neighboring "bad" high schools for years engaged in the practice of regularly exchanging a dozen or so bad boys, under the theory that at least during the first few months, friendless in a new school, the worst bad boy will more or less behave.

Suspension for a limited period is another possible penalty. Board of education rules regarding suspensions provide for notification of the parent and a hearing, called a "guidance conference," attended by various school personnel, the student, and the parent, but, until recently, specifically excluding counsel for the student. In 1967, Judge Constance Baker Motley ruled that a student had a right to counsel at such hearings, declaring in her decision: "The due process clause of the 14th Amendment is applicable to a district superintendent guidance conference. The 'no-attorney' provision deprives plaintiffs of their rights to a hearing in a state-initiated proceeding which puts in jeopardy the minor's liberty and right to attend public school." School personnel, many of whom eighteen months later would participate in a two-and-a-half-month strike on behalf of due process for teachers, were outraged by Judge Motley's ruling, one principal being quoted as saying,

"They [lawyers] will interfere, telling the child or parent when and what to say and obstruct the whole purpose of the hearing," which observation accurately reflected the intent of the ruling. The board of education appealed the decision, and it was overruled by the Court of Appeals.[7] In May of 1969 the governor signed into law a bill allowing students right to counsel at hearings for suspensions of over five days and also the right to cross-examine at any suspension hearing witnesses against them—presumably teachers. Despite intense public interest in school matters at just that time, the press paid almost no attention to this piece of important legislation. And when, six months later, the board of education revised its suspension rules to meet the mandates of state legislation, the High School Principals Association warned that the new rules would "create chaos in the schools," and a spokesman for the United Federation of Teachers suggested that that organization was not happy about the rules but was "willing to give them a fair trial."[8]

The next penalty after suspension is expulsion. The New York State compulsory education law requires the state to provide an education for persons between the ages of six and twenty-one and requires students to attend school until age seventeen (unless they graduate from high school before that). Misreading the law, school administrators have for years simply expelled students at the age of seventeen if they failed egregiously to meet school expectations. Younger students who come into conflict with the authorities are frequently dealt with thus: "How old are you?" "Sixteen." "When's your birthday?" "March 18." "Uh, huh. Well, you better watch out." Students and disciplinarians alike understand very well the signals in this conversation. That the threat and the action are illegal is, to co-opt a students' word, irrelevant, for clearly the school has a more practicable power over students than do the courts over school personnel. The possibility of expulsion at age seventeen is one way to keep in line non-college-bound students actively striving after that piece of paper which society's spokesmen keep telling them is worth everything despite their secret suspicion that it is worth nothing.

For those whom the school acknowledges to be college-bound—white middle-class and a tiny elite of nonwhite—the school's system of controls and threats is likely to be less rigorously enforced. For one thing, school personnel often feel that the rules are not made for the "good" students, but for "those others," or, like the school psychologist, that "sensitive" students should not be pressed too hard by the rules. While harsh and rigid bureaucratic types do come down hard (and white parents often feel unfairly) on all students, college-bound students, or white, middle-class students are rarely subjected to the sterner penalties, like suspension or transfer or expulsion—that is until the high school revolt began, when, as we shall see, rebellious white students also began to be suspended by the dozens and the scores.

In case a student's physical appearance is not a clear guide to how he is to be treated—and it usually is—his program card indicates whether he is a General, an Academic, or an Honors. Ishmael tells the following:

> One time when I was sent down to the dean for something or other and he asked what class I was in and I said 10-4. And he said, "Oh, that's the Honors class." And I said, "No, it's not." And he said, "Well, kind of like it. It's almost Honors." And at that point I felt that the conversation between us turned. Like I was one of them. Like, "Oh, you're one of us. OK, so it couldn't have been that bad." Like obviously, you know, it was just a momentary rebellion.

In an all-black school, of course, or in a passion-laden corridor encounter between a teacher and an anonymous black or Puerto Rican student, even a top Honors student may be in a vulnerable position. The following, from my notes on a teaching day at a chaos junior high school, illustrates this point, and, more significantly, illustrates the response by a very decent teacher to the adult manhandling of students:

> Sol, a teacher, told at lunch about a boy, one of his best students, so good, never any trouble, bright, always did his homework, etc., who had his hat snatched in the lunchroom by another student. The boy ran after the hat snatcher and was grabbed by an aide who threw him down on the floor and put his foot on his back. I gasp at this, "You can't do that!" Weary looks of cynicism from the

teachers around me. "It happens all the time." When the aide lets the kid up, Sol goes on, the kid takes after him with a chair. The kid is then suspended for two weeks. Sol went to the suspension hearing to testify for the kid, what a good boy he is, but it didn't get him off. He said he gave the boy some fatherly advice: "No matter what happens, never go after a teacher."

Then he said to us, "Just shows how things have to happen to the wrong kid."

To understand the inhumanity of these ordinary security measures, one should observe several factors. The first is that when human beings operate in a system of rules rather than a system of people, it is easy for them to ignore one another's humanity. Thus many teachers or aides who customarily are unthinkingly ruthless in enforcing the rules would of course be more flexible in the case of students with whom they have personal relationships. School size and arrangements, however, severely limit the possibility for personal relationships between teachers and students. Second, many teachers carry about with them chronic feelings of resentment, aggressiveness, against the students (as we saw in Part I), and feelings of aggression tend to choke off empathy.[9] Third, the race and social class factor undoubtedly reduces for many teachers the sense of their students' humanity. "You don't understand what these kids are like." "Toughness, that's all they understand." "Well, they're used to it, they don't mind the way we would." "They'll try to get away with anything, these kids." These are variants of commonly offered explanations. That the rules are normally less rigidly enforced against the elite (middle-class or would-be middle-class) students is an evidence of this point. However, black teachers and aides take on the rationale of the system. Once when I was interviewing a Harlem mother employed as an aide as she sat guard duty before a girls toilet room, a student who had no pass tried to get past her into the toilet, squunching and grimacing, "Oooo, oooo, I gotta." After the aide had turned her back, I asked if she didn't find it difficult to do that. "Yes," she said, "but those are the rules. What can you do?" She continued, "Terrible things would go on in there if we didn't keep the rules. That girl was just putting on an act anyway." Finally, like a good lawyer, throwing all the arguments into the summation for the jury, "It's all because we're too crowded, and we don't have enough personnel. If there was more money for the schools, it wouldn't be like this."

Ché and Temma: Hostile Comrades

The distance between the classes and the races is expressed in the following remarks by two children of our time, eyeing each other, across an institutional gulf, with suspicion, with rage, and with yearning, each sensing that he has something important to say to the other, not yet finding the right words or the voice that will carry across the gulf. The first student is Ché Lopez (his first name self-taken), a politically revolutionary black Puerto Rican Honors student. In a mood of passionate fury, Chê said of his fellow Honors students:

The student today doesn't know his ass from his hand. So-called intelligent, so-called smart people . . . Honors . . . I have never in my *life* . . . and this is not out of bitterness or anything [because] I'm going to college—I don't think I'll have any trouble getting in—but I have never met such an ignorant lot of . . . demented . . . *poops*! [He explodes the word, giving at the same time a hard hand smack.] They're *nothing*! They can't feel! They know nothing about life. And they don't know where they're going. And they're just latching onto things that people told them they should work to. They have no mind of their own. Their minds are . . . *idiots*! They're programed. They're oriented to white society. They want to become honkies. They have no real ambition. They don't know what they want to be.

As far as I'm concerned I've never met people that are more like people than the so-called lower, underprivileged . . . Because, you see, they're privileged in their own way. They got the hard knocks. And they're wise. And they know that they've lived . . . .

These other guys, these other people, I don't think they ever will.

Temma Fields is a highly intellectual white student in a specialized and therefore nonsegregated high school.

Temma told about a history class in early April of 1968 as a comment on the remark of a friend and fellow student who had said, "The school is integrated, but, like, the minds don't . . ."

Last year, right about the time that Martin Luther King was killed, there were several classes where we talked about it, and all this bitter resentment began on the part of the four or five Negro kids in the class.

It was incredible how much bitterness was there, and everybody in the class was sort of awestruck. And the white kids were just sitting there very innocent and wide-eyed, trying to understand what was going on, and feeling sort of helpless and lost. It also frightened me: the fury was an understood thing among *them*, and I was out of it.

They were telling us stories—just small anecdotes. And we were listening to these stories of the kind that you read about—usually taking place in the South, and many years ago. And they were telling us that they were happening right all around us *at this time.* And they knew it, and they'd known it all their lives, and they took it for granted that they were happening. And we didn't know anything about it at all!

And all of a sudden I realized how much of their lives was completely unknown to me. Stuff that I just couldn't imagine—couldn't conceive of. I'd always known that it is difficult to be a Negro in America and it is difficult to be poor in America and that there are all kinds of horrible people who are prejudiced and all kinds of bad things like that. But I never knew anything like that at firsthand. I never believed it. I never thought that my parents' friends were prejudiced or that if I happened to meet a Negro person there would be any reason why we shouldn't become friends. We would just have to like each other. But it didn't occur to me that everything is really, really different. And that's one of the things that no one's admitting. None of the white liberal-type people are willing to admit it—that there really is a difference.

I was really glad that they told me . . . that finally everything was honest. Because I never . . . that was the only honest moment I've ever lived about black and white—was that moment.

They said, "Well, here it is. This is all that's going on.

Now you understand why we hate you?" And we said, "But *we're* not that way." And they said, "It doesn't matter." And then we understood. Sort of.

What did you understand?

That they hate us just by association. That they didn't want to bother to figure out who was responsible for what particular thing.

And some of us [white kids] would raise our hands and say, "Well, what can we do? We want to do something? Why don't you want us to take part in any betterment thing? You say you want to be the prime movers of the whole thing, but can't we help you because we agree with you—that blacks should have more power in this society?" And they said, "Well, no, because we hate you and we don't want anything to do with you." And we said, "That's not fair, because we didn't do anything to you." And they said, "It doesn't matter if *you* [personally] did something. You did something because you're white." And I left the room really, really distressed because for the first time in my life something which I was convinced was the right thing and the good thing was being rejected by the people for whom it was intended.

We are *not* all guilty. *I* am not guilty. *I'm not guilty for existing in this society.* I'm guilty for not putting myself out more individually, let's say. But I am not guilty in the same way that many people are guilty. And I don't see why I should suffer for what *they've* done. I also think that I can be of value to this group of people. I think I can give them something. I don't know exactly what it is. But I don't see why they should reject it right off, before they can find out whether it's worth something or not.

The word "guilt" is too theological and too deeply personal to describe the kind of responsibility that Temma does bear. As one of the most successful in a system where success for one group is bought with failure for another, Temma, however guiltless in her feelings and beliefs, did indeed, from the viewpoint of her black fellow students, earn their resentment. Psychologically speaking, it is not surprising that those who had been picked from birth to be the losers in the educational race were not about to accept "help" from those picked to be, and (so far as the ordained losers could tell) eager to be, the victors.

But while some of those destined to be losers, like Ché for example (who would probably escape his destiny), knew that even the victors were victims—"programed," "poops,"—they did not know to what extent some of the victors recognized their own entrapment. Temma's "honest moment about black and white," in which the blacks told the whites what they were feeling, was in a sense not reciprocated. The whites did not tell the blacks what *they* were feeling about the system in which they played the winning parts. But one day Temma, her brother Kenny, and a white girl friend, Rachel Harris, did tell one another how they felt victimized by their complicity with success. It was the day after the ending of the Great Strike of 1968.

You know, there are some kids who have effectively dropped out of school by the age of fourteen. Could you conceive of yourself doing that?

Kenny: Yeah. I was thinking . . . during the strike particularly. The fact is that [then] there *wasn't* any school. Everybody knows that there always is school—always will be school. But the fact that there wasn't really made me think.

What did you do during the strike?

Kenny: Well, most of the time I suppose I wasted. I had my job, of course. That took a couple of hours a day . . . . The rest of the time I spent reading, bicycling, and walking around the city. When school was about to start, I was shocked by thinking that I really could live without there being school. And in fact, you know, now I had something to compare against, I think I would really be living much more if I weren't going to school—living in my old romantic sense of it: thinking, feeling. [Yesterday] I came home from school, and I sat down and started doing homework, just writing things off, and even seeming very intelligent. And—I was kind of looking back on it—it seems to me kind of like a different sort of state from living. I mean just separated somehow.

Temma: The things that we [Rachel and I] take most seriously, both of us, are music and also principles, and being able to get outside. We'd play music together [during the strike]. We sat around and talked and talked and talked. We went out on bicycle rides. We went to concerts.

Rachel: It was just a whole different . . . It is part of the

American pattern of life. Like I was discussing this with my mother. I said, "All right, look at it the way it stands. School's horrible for me. I can't stand it. I'm horribly bored. There is no joie de vivre in this city at all. No one enjoys what they're doing. No one even enjoys the food that they're eating. They eat a lot, but they don't enjoy it. They don't have artistic tastes for anything." And I just said to my mother, "Well, we've got to make it great this year! We just gotta have joie de vivre not matter what!"

Temma: I can't make it great till after this weekend. I have to catch up on all the work I have to do.

Rachel: Oh, I have so much work to do, but I'm doing it [making it great] anyway.

Could you ever conceive of when you fall behind, you just say, "Well, fuck it"? I mean and just flunk that course?

All together: I couldn't do that. I couldn't flunk anything. I couldn't do it, not consciously.

Rachel: I think it is more complicated to flunk a course than it is to pass it. Temma, don't you often get this feeling? Like you're in the class? If you go out of the class, let's say, go to the bathroom—you can't get out of the school, our school has guards. So you're sitting in the bathroom flunking the course, right? [Everybody laughs.] And you end up in the god-damned office with filling out a cut card. You're getting a reputation. Your mother's getting called up. You're having all these things happening to you at once. It's so ridiculous. I would rather just . . .

[The only way Rachel could conceive of flunking a course was by absenting herself from the classroom.]

Temma: It's more complicated than just running to avoid the bureaucracy. It's not such a big problem for me to do enough work so I can do well in a class. But I have never been able to do the amount of work that would give me, say, an 80 average. Instead I force myself to get a 94 average. *That* I don't understand. I mean, I really don't approve of it. I think a lot of it has to do with the need for my teachers' approval . . . and my parents' approval.

Do you expect *your teacher's approval?*

Temma: Yes, I take it more or less for granted. Only I have the feeling the first few days [in a new class] that I have to let the teacher know that I'm one of those people of whom she should approve.

What if you just didn't come to school?

Temma: We both have the feeling one ought to be doing something with one's life.

Rachel: Like my parents wouldn't be home, my friends wouldn't be home. I could walk around the streets. I've done that. I goofed off a whole summer. I wasted . . . You just got to have a life. Some kind of life.

Temma: School is an anti-life.

Well, there are a lot of kids who don't follow the pattern [prescribed by the school]. They just stop doing it.

Temma: I'm already a conditioned part of the society. Before I even went to this school I think I was. The point is you're expected by your parents to fit into the society to the extent where we will go to college.

Are you also expected by the school to do that?

Temma: That's right, yes. The whole purpose of education it sounds like to me is, in elementary school to get into a good junior high school, and in junior high school to get into a good high school, and then from high school . . . the whole big ultimate thing is for college. And why you are going to go to college nobody really knows, except the implication is it's probably to get a good job, but everybody is ashamed to say that, so they vaguely pretend it's because you want to become an educated person. But very few people believe that. Or get to that stage. School prepares you to go into a society and to expect to dislike most of the things that you are going to be doing in your life. The things that are your everyday life—from nine to five, or whatever it happens to be. You can expect to have to travel every day to the same place, and to do the same thing, in a completely scheduled routine, and you come home really tired. And to accept it just sort of passively and do what you are supposed to do and then possibly you may have a couple of hours maybe on the weekend when you can supposedly do what you really like to do if there is such a thing although by the time you have gotten to the stage where the people one sees on the subways are at, you probably don't even know what you like any more. You probably don't like anything as a matter of fact.

It seems as if the whole thing is just one big preparation for nothing.

2. RESISTANCE—AND NEW DIALOGUES

One Monday in March, 1969, a day that the black students of a given high school had designated as "Black Monday," a group of students from that school, standing on a street where they were overpowered now and again by the relentless trains above them or by the restless policemen who urged them from one corner to the next, rapped tirelessly with an interviewer for several hours. "They were more than happy to talk to me," the interviewer said. "Nobody's asked them anything about anything in years."

* *Sources, both printed and interpersonal, for this and the next two sections were gathered with the assistance of a young collaborator who acted as a participant-observer in some phases of the student and community resistance described. He interviewed student and adult activists and attended meetings, both formal and informal, in several parts of the city, taping some of the proceedings and providing notes on others. He had the assistance on a few occasions of a black friend, and on others of a young woman friend. I myself interviewed a few students, usually after he had made the initial contact. I also talked with numbers of teachers, parents, and community activists, as well as with representatives of the New York Civil Liberties Union, the National Emergency Civil Liberties*

The group was a shifting one, but a small core of white working-class youth (of Irish, Italian, and German background) were present throughout. During the first couple of hours, they expressed their resentments and hostilities with gradually increasing bitterness, as well as increasing saltiness.

About the black students: "They want everything from us. They want the shirt off our backs. They want our jobs. They want our everything." "These people [black students] have worked their way up to have, like, control. Why? Because everybody is afraid. When they have a problem, all they do is pick up the phone and call in the Panthers, and it is solved. The school is afraid that if they do anything against a black student, then all the black students will get together and have a protest, will riot."

About the principal: "Any papers we give him, like the petition to go outside in the lunch hour, he just ripped it up and threw it in the wastebasket. He didn't even know what it was for. He shut the door in our faces." "He's white. And a filthy bastard too. I wouldn't be surprised if he smokes acid. He gets around the hippie kids in the school. I wouldn't be surprised if he's a homosexual. Did you see that time he picked his nose?"

About the toilet rules and the cafeteria: "They lock the bathrooms. You have to do it in your pants or on the floor. Somebody shit on the stairway and pissed on the stairway. They couldn't hold it in and they weren't allowed to go out. I got thrown out last year because I walked out of the room just to take a piss, and I told the teacher that I would piss for the class if she wouldn't let me out. Like this school

Committee, and the Mayor's Task Force on Student Unrest. The New York Times, *the* New York Post, *the* Village Voice, *and the* Amsterdam News *provided some information. I examined many student "underground" newspapers, of which the most prominent were the* Weakly Reader *(Washington Irving and Stuyvesant High Schools), the* Neo-Dwarf *(Seward Park High School), the* New York Herald Tribune *(Stuyvesant High School), and the* New York High School Free Press *(citywide). Single copies of mimeographed "student demands" issued at various schools throughout the city were also examined. My interpretations of the events described combine the insights of many individuals interviewed, my collaborator's, and my own, based on my experiences as a teacher in a predominantly black and Puerto Rican "bad" high school.*

is a prison!" "That lunch is shit, man. I wouldn't feed that to a fucking dog. I wouldn't feed it to a nigger. Have you ever eaten horseshit before?"

About the teachers, the dean, and the UFT chapter chairman: "This school isn't run by the principal any more. It's run by Kafker [the UFT chapter chairman]. He's in charge of everything. He has no right to. He wasn't elected to. But you can't get rid of the UFT." "You go to the dean's office for something and he will curse you out, he will say 'If you get the–if you fuck this school, I'll kick your ass!' or 'I'll kick you out,' and stuff like that. I didn't sign into one of my classes this year, he said, 'If you don't sign into that fucking class, I'll work you over.' " "She's a liberal and she can't stand me. She hates me because I am white. She hates me because I am conservative. And that goddamn fucking thing, she hates me for everything."

And about the police: "They had the cops. And they went after the kids and were busting heads. And they had these leatherneck guys from the motorcycle squad, and their boots you know, and their big giant sticks. Today, this morning, I would say every five inches there was a cop, separated with barricades. Tomorrow there will probably be barbed wire and machine guns out there. Now that's some living, boy! Standing around watching school kids! You gotta feel sorry for them. There's no need for it. Like they say, they are a bunch of pigs. There's no need for it .. no need for it."

After a couple of hours a few black students drifted into the group. They were more cool than the white boys, and more focused in both their resentment and their racism. One of them said: "This is your system, and we don't like this crap and all the things that you-all do. We believe that as long as we have to stay in this system, we are always going to be at the bottom." In answer to the interviewer's question, "Why are black students and white students fighting each other?" one commented, "*Who's* fighting each other? Just answer one question: Why don't white people like Negroes?" And in answer to the remark that the white students were getting their heads beat too, one said, "Yeah, but you can get on their side if you want to. I can't do that. Under this situation I *got* to fight. And when they start shooting you-all, you will say 'Fuck this, I'm getting on the other side.' You know damn well, you ain't going to be out there with me and try to stop a tank when you can get *in* one. And we are going to be in this thing by ourselves, so we have to fight by ourselves."

In the presence of the black boys, the white boys were silent. But when the black boys left, the discussion moved onto another plane. The word "nigger" was dropped, and the boys reverted to "colored," which they had used at the very beginning (as in, Adam Clayton Powell "is a white man trying to pass as one of them colored people"). And they began to direct their conversation away from their rankling feelings, and toward their situation and the situation of their black fellow students.

"Let's take the colored person. The way they are now. They're getting pushed around. And what are they supposed to do? If they're not supposed to go out and tear up things, how are they going to do this peacefully? They have no leg to stand on. Nobody has a leg to stand on."

"People who have made it don't give a shit about people who haven't made it. They aren't looking out for the other guy, the other people's interests. They're looking out for their own. I'm sure that a lot of people don't realize that they are fucking somebody else to make themselves better. [But] I don't think you have to destroy the country. Just change. Not destroy."

"Well, if you have to change something, and the person who is in charge doesn't want to change, what do you do then?"

Just as the entrance of the few black boys changed the terms of these white boys' dialogue about the schools, so the entrance of the militant black students citywide changed the terms of all the students' dialogue with their schools and changed the status relations between black students and white students. The emergence of the militant black students led white student radicals to confront the damages and indignities that they must endure and inflict as the price of retaining their status over black (poor, Puerto Rican) students—and to recognize the indignities which they share with all their fellow students.

The entrance of the articulate black students into the educational conversation also helped change the terms of the black adults' dialogue with the school system's defenders, and this in two important respects.

What the integration movement lacked and the

community-control movement lacked was an aroused mass constituency. By and large black and Puerto Rican parents either have believed that the schools were after all doing their best and that their children were indeed too naughty or too stupid or too lazy to succeed. *Or* they were misled by their children's good conduct marks into thinking that their children *were* learning. *Or* they didn't know that middle-class white children and poor black and Puerto Rican children are exposed to quite different learning experiences in New York City schools. *Or* they were too hard working, too preoccupied, too distraught, too ill, too confused, too tired to be able to act on such knowledge about the actual situation as they did have. Whatever the reason, the movement to improve education for black and Puerto Rican children in New York City was carried primarily by a tiny handful of devoted men and women seeking to arouse a largely quiescent mass of parents to the plight of their own children. (This led critics of the movement to suggest scornfully that the whole thing was the work of a few obsessed, merely self-interested outside agitators—as if, though themselves the products and admirers of the trade union movement, they had forgotten how that movement was created out of a mass of frightened, insecure immigrant wage slaves by a few devoted leaders.)

Although more and more parents were educated by the events of the years 1967 onward, black and Puerto Rican parents tended to appear publicly in relatively large numbers only at moments of extreme and specific crisis, such as the occupation of J.H.S. 271 in Ocean Hill-Brownsville in the fall of 1968 or of P.S. 39 in the 201 Complex some months later.

But the teenage children of the black and Puerto Rican parents had the energy, the time, and the immediate concrete sense of grievance to be able to overcome in a day the education-reform movement's previous lack of a mass base. The students were happy to empty out a school, fill up a park, or bust up a subway station at an hour's notice. They were also more likely than their job- and home-bound parents to move about the city in defense of fellow students in other boroughs or other schools. (Contrariwise, the long-term problems for effectuating meaningful change posed by a student constituency are that it annually loses great numbers of experienced personnel and that students tend to spend their abundant energies in often ineffectual and sometimes dangerous destructive actions. Some of the cadres of young adults and former students, along with an occasional rebel teacher, sought to provide the kind of support to the student movement that would overcome these disadvantages.)

The other and more important way in which the entrance of the students began to change the terms of the black and Puerto Rican community's dialogue with the school system was that the students were less interested than the adults in perpetuating the schools as a status-reinforcing institution. To a large extent the adult reformers wanted no more than a fair chance for some black and Puerto Rican and poor children to get onto the status ladder—more I.G.C. classes for black children; more Harlem children to be admitted to the elite Bronx High School of Science; more intensive coaching for black children so that more of them could get into good classes, good schools, good colleges; and more openings for blacks and Puerto Ricans as teachers and as supervisors. Many of the students, on the other hand, aimed to axe down the status ladder entirely and to use education for personal—and political—fulfillment. ("We believe that as long as we have to stay in this system," said the black boy under the elevated, "we're always going to be at the bottom.") In this dual aim, the students with the Afros and dashikis were joined by those with the long hair and beads. Perhaps if the system's defenders had foreseen that after the adults, who merely wanted everyone to get a fairer shake, would come the students, who would threaten to bring the whole structure down, they would have negotiated early on, instead of battling. But the defenders did battle, and in such a wise as to aid in creating at least for a time the very mass constituency that the community-control leaders lacked and needed.

The entrance of the black and white students together also changed the terms in which the system responded to the educational reform movement. To adult reformers, the system responded with subterfuge, evasion, delay, and prevarication (as demonstrated in the dialogue about 201). And while all the system's defenders chimed in as and when necessary, the UFT was its leading spokesman, bringing to bear the strongest argument in defense of the system in the

Great Strike. To the students, the response, first of all, was more direct and more brutal: it was banishment from the school community and cracked heads. And while some leaders of the UFT played a role in fingering the student activists to be dealt with, a good deal of the action was carried by the administrators, the politicians, and the police. One advantage of a complex bureaucratic establishment is that no one individual or group has to do all the dirty work all the time.

An unintended by-product of the system's cynical and brutal response to the student activists was the quick radicalization of people who before were either moderate reformers or wholly nonpolitical. Each clonk on the head from a billy club, each clearly political suspension of a student or firing of a teacher, served as a hot liquid which created a steaming radical out of a dry cynic or a cool idealist. The conditions surrounding and following the Great Strike produced among moderate reformers and liberals a backlash radicalism whose extent we still do not know.

It is a radicalism that is status destroying in more than one way, tending to bring together parents and children, teachers and students, home and community, and black and white, where the school had for so long kept them apart.

Early Beginnings of the Student Movement

The student movement of 1969, affecting almost every high school in New York City and many junior high schools, had its roots in the school social system. It began with tiny reform groups in individual schools here and there at the time of the 1964 school boycott, such as the group to which Benny Wilkinson belonged at Simón Bolívar High School. Sometimes led by white teachers and usually meeting outside of school, these groups generally had the aim to improve lunchroom conditions, get toilet paper and soap into the washrooms, get the pushers out of the school, agitate before the board of estimate for more funds for building maintenance and construction, and so on. The students, as well as their supporting teachers, tended to feel both very brave and very frightened about organizing to change conditions, but in general the school administrators, while disapproving and sometimes administratively harsh (as in the case of Benny), were relatively cool in their response. The groups remained tiny and ineffectual.

During the years 1966 to 1968 a few black and white high school students began to be aroused variously by the struggles around I.S. 201 in Harlem; by the college student movement, which hit New York City with the Columbia revolt of 1968; by the appearance on the New York scene of civil rights activists out of the battlefields of the South; and in general by the peace movement and the New Left. Some leaders of the community-control movement, sensing that the oppressed and aggrieved black and Puerto Rican high school students constituted a potential mass base for an attack on the school establishment, began to work with groups of high school students in terms of specific high school problems and also of the larger problems of the entire black and Puerto Rican school population.

On April 26, 1968, high school students throughout the city participated in a nationwide high school and college student strike to protest the war in Vietnam. In some schools relatively few students went out, in others almost the whole student body. In many, sympathetic teachers joined the students' picket lines. Some administrators were only mildly jittery—one scheduled midterm examinations for that day, hoping thus to entice the strikers in. Others were panicky and brutal, indulging in behavior that foreshadowed the nasty outbreaks that characterized the Great Strike six months later. A student leader from Nat Turner High describes the day:

We had a total strike . . . we got all the other schools around . . . we had 2,000 kids on the street. People started throwing things from the window. There were a number of eggs that were thrown.

Who started that?

You're missing the point. One guy that was hit was from the City Human Rights Commission. He will insist until this day that he saw the assistant principal there [throwing things from the window] —or at least an adult, if you push him up against the wall. About fifty people saw adults [throwing things], and the only adults in that school that day were teachers. [This was the point.] After that, April

26, these teachers were calling each other "Communist"—and the deans too, because the eggs came from the dean's office. There's a rift that's unbelievable [in the teaching staff]. The teachers are split in half now. Everybody who participated in the antiwar demonstration, and anybody who was with us when we did our thing for Rap Brown was labeled a Communist. They stick letters in mailboxes—"you communist," "you anarchist."

The "thing for Rap Brown" was, in effect, an open rebellion which occurred slightly over a month later, early in June, in the wake of the school administration's refusal to allow Rap Brown into the school to address the students, who thereupon decided to arrange to have Brown speak to them out in the street. A group of students called a meeting in the cafeteria and prepared to carry their demands to the principal. Police were called, and a dean shouted, in reference to a student speaker addressing his fellow students from a cafeteria table, "Get that nigger down from there. Get that nigger down from there." The students tried to seize the school's PA system. The principal locked his office. The police were turned loose. The student speaker (a former SNCC worker from Mississippi and Atlanta), trying to flee from the building, was finally caught in a classroom and clubbed. He was carried out of the building in handcuffs when the situation outside had quieted down and had his split head attended to only three hours later.

A few students had their baptism of fire that day. Some others, mainly white, had had it a few weeks before in Washington Square Park where on May 18 a contingent of students, hippies, and various other young radicals had massed to march to Central Park to join the very respectable adult citywide peace demonstration being held there. The students were assaulted by the city's known toughies, the Tactical Police Force, who also arrested a few reporters and the head of the New York Civil Liberties Union.

There were other similar incidents. In August students made their way to Chicago again to confront and be confronted by club-swinging police. Throughout the summer, student activists, both black and white, met on and off, planning ways and aims of organizing high school students. Intermittently they were joined and encouraged or held in check by various adults–Panthers, community-control activists, and teachers. Students I have spoken to say that some of their meetings during June were infiltrated by police seeking to enlist informers. By the academic year 1969-70, it was officially acknowledged that youthful-looking plainclothesmen were being assigned to pass as students in several high schools.[1]

Out of their summer meetings, they began to distill a program of demands. It was a program based upon a radical, New Leftist, black-powerish view of America, of conventional education in America, and of the daily personal indignities the students experience in submitting to that education. What they did not develop then was a strategy for increasing their active following or effectuating their program.

The United Federation of Teachers did that for them.

When the Backlash Hit New York

New York City is not a typical American city. In the first place it is a union town, in which nobody had better bad mouth trade unions or trade unionism. Then, it is a town still carrying within it the children and the children of the children of those who for decades had come pouring through Ellis Island–the Greeks, the Chinese, the Italians, the Irish, the Polish, the Ukrainians, the Germans. Many of these still live in definable neighborhoods, patronizing their local native groceries, butchers, bakeries, and restaurants. But downtown they share offices and go out to lunch and do business with one another, and often they even invite one another to their sons' bar mitzvahs and their daughters' weddings. New York is also a sophisticated, civil libertarian town: it knows what the score is; it opposes authoritarian high-handedness; it doesn't indulge in embarrassingly exaggerated patriotic and moralistic clichés; and it generally scorns obviously nasty racial and group epithets.

Given these distinctions, it might have been predicted that when the backlash hit the fan in New York, it was going to smell different from other towns' backlash. But despite its distinctions, New York City is still an *American* city and, given the appropriate conditions, as subject to backlash as any other American city. The conditions were appropriate in the fall of 1968—appropriate for backlash, and appropriate for the peculiar way in which New York City could express backlash.

With increasing public squalor and increasing numbers of black and Puerto Rican residents, it seemed to many white New Yorkers logical to blame the latter for the former. Unbelievably delayed postal service, hideous overcrowdedness of public transportation, and streets where even the pedestrians were bumper-to-bumper, so the general feeling went, probably were related to the "influx" of Negroes and Puerto Ricans. Muggings in broad daylight, garbage in gutters, and the declining number of "good" schools surely were.

One day during the Great Strike, I visited a neighborhood stationery store run by a middle-aged Jewish couple I had long appreciated for their inexhaustible good humor, friendliness, and wit. Now they were pale with anger. Mr. Simons did most of the talking:

I'll tell you what the problem is: it's the influx of colored and Puerto Rican. We been robbed in here twice in the last three months. My wife sits here on this stool the whole time so she can watch the door who's coming in. Believe me, I'm not prejudiced! I know I shouldn't condemn a whole race because of what a few individuals do. But what can I do? I'm nervous and scared whenever one comes in here. Did you read the article in the *Times* Sunday? [He was referring to Christopher Jencks' "Private Schools for Black Children," in the *New York Times Magazine*, November 3, 1968, an article which, for some, helped to provide an educational rationale for the kind of backlash sentiment my friends were expressing.] It explains the reason the colored don't learn is because of slum conditions.

So why do they want to pick on the teachers? [In their distress, they recalled events of a few years before.] You know we had to take our daughter out of Emma Goldman Junior High on account of conditions were so bad there. The colored hit her and took her money away twice. We put her in a private school on Lucas Street. [A possibility not open to nonwhite parents whose children also were sometimes assaulted.]

Declining public services, including police protection, and the spread into many schools of the "chaos" conditions which the children and teachers of Harlem had lived with for decades were producing in many white parents the kind of general anxiety that Mr. Simons expressed. It was only natural to put the blame somewhere, and only American to put it on the highly visible increasing black and Puerto Rican population from whom the threat seemed to emanate.

If the ecology of the city was ripe for backlash in that autumn of 1968, so were the politics. Mayor John Lindsay (called by one sympathetic non-New York journalist the "world's most persecuted WASP") was long regarded by many blacks as well as by many whites as a friend of the dark and the poor. He was a "cool-it" mayor who in moments of crisis sought to restrain some of the overreacting to black anger which, as in Detroit for example, aggravates the anger and prolongs the crisis. But many middle-class people, suffering, as did other less well-to-do citizens, from the physical and sociological dysfunctioning of the city, felt that Lindsay was indifferent to their distresses. Early in 1969, the New York *Times* reported on a group of middle-class and lower-middle-class whites of German-Jewish extraction who lectured him one night at a meeting. "We of the Chamber of Commerce of Washington Heights have our own ideas about riots," the speaker of the evening was quoted. "We do not believe in wheeling and dealing [with rioters]. We must have law and order at any price." The story went on to report that the speaker "also urged more policemen, a new high school, a replacement for a local public school, and a parking garage for the community. He opposed the proposed increase in the sales tax."[2]

Further darkening his image with the white, liberal, union-oriented citizens, was his selection of McGeorge Bundy to help him in the formulation of a school decentralization policy. Bundy was one of the architect's of America's Vietnam policy, and the fact that he was chairman of the Ford Foundation did not help either. ("We all know old union-busting Henry Ford" said a representative at a UFT Delegate Assembly).

Into this nicely bubbling cauldron was dropped the catalyst of community control versus teacher status and security. The reaction almost broke the vessel. When the United Federation of Teachers went out on strike in September, 1968, the masses of the white population—shopkeepers, policemen, bus drivers, office workers, professionals; parents and nonparents; well-to-do and struggling—all gathered themselves to defend their teachers' and their own threatened status. From the point of view of the struggle and the fears, it was historical accident that the bulk of the teachers happened to be Jewish, for in the struggle Jew and Gentile, Protestant and Catholic, Italian and Polish, were identities forgotten, at least temporarily, in favor of a common *Americanness,* which was defended under the common white banner of due process.

If the antagonisms that once divided ethnic groups were lost in their common embattled whiteness, so, too, were the issues that had divided teacher and principal, teaching staff and custodial staff, school personnel and headquarters personnel. First, supervisors, speaking through their organization, the Council of Supervisory Associations, and then custodians, speaking through theirs, Local 891 of the International Union of Operating Engineers, joined the teachers in reinforcing the strike by making it a lock-out. Doors locked and keys spirited away by cooperative custodians, absent principals and hard-to-locate district superintendents, and vociferous teacher pickets reinforced by parents and shielded by police, all protected the empty schoolhouses from their few would-be scholars.

That the issue was racial in the sense that a racially biased system was being defended against a political force seeking to overcome that bias, almost everyone understood—if not with the head, then with the gut. Only a few confused intellectuals (who took the mask of due process for the reality) claimed and perhaps believed otherwise. But that it was also racial in the sense that both the defenders and the attackers openly expressed their racial hostilities distressed and surprised a lot of New Yorkers, who had been long accustomed to avoidance of publicly expressed racism. Probably not since the draft riots of 1863 (when whites attacked blacks in what also had begun as a "mere" labor dispute) had New York City seen such *outspoken* white racism, and probably never before outside the privacy of in-groups at neighborhood bars such crude anti-whitism and anti-Semitism. The difference in style between the public and private face appalled the civilized. The Mayor, surprised like other decent citizens at the stink that rose when the lid blew off the sewer, appointed a committee to investigate "racial and religious prejudice, focusing primarily on the school dispute." The committee pointed out in its report that:

The prejudice emanating from blacks generally takes a form somewhat different from that which has emerged among whites. The countless incidents, leaflets, epithets and the like in this school controversy reveal a bigotry from black extremists that is open, undisguised, nearly physical in its intensity—and far more obvious and identifiable than that emanating from whites.

On the other hand, anti-black bigotry tended to be expressed in more sophisticated and subtle fashion, often communicated privately and seldom reported, but nonetheless equally evil, corrosive, damaging and deplorable.[3]

The most important difference between the racism of the defenders and that of the attackers was not observed at all by the mayor's committee: that is, that the one was primarily functional whereas the other was primarily verbal. Negroes who sense themselves to be victims of a whole school system which operates in a racially biased way simply laugh a loser's laugh when they are accused of being racist. While much of the Negro community, like much of the white community, disapproved of the bad manners of the name callers, it did not regard even the nastiest epithets as having anything like the force for evil of an entire apparatus of repression and discrimination.

Nevertheless people on both sides did indulge in name calling. The newspapers printed ugly pictures of picketers jeering at students, parents, and teachers who were crossing their picket lines (pictures such as had not been seen since the first black children fought to attend white schools in Little Rock, and Mississippi, and Alabama). Individuals reported that "scab," and "nigger-lover" were among the most commonly used epithets. Some antiunion blacks retaliated with anti-Semitic epithets (which they denied to be anti-Semitic). Union President Shanker gently scolded his followers for their bad manners ("It isn't nice to laugh at Collins, children."), but then the union reprinted and distributed widely thousands of copies of a black anti-Semitic leaflet that might otherwise have got lost in the deluge of abuse.

What the name calling on both sides revealed, besides frustration and sometimes despair at the crowdedness, the meanness, the indignity of life in that city at that time, was a jockeying for power among racial groups experiencing different degrees of crowdedness, meanness, and indignity. The blacks wanted a little more of what the whites had, and the whites, looking around and seeing that there was only so much, didn't want to yield any. At a private meeting (which I attended) arranged by some civic-minded New Yorkers during the strike, this exchange took place between the president of a national conservative Negro organization and a moderate from the UFT:

UFT representatives: Well, we favor decentralization.

Negro leader: What power would the union give up to make decentralization work? What are you willing to let the community control that you now control?

UFT representative: The powers we have are not great.

Some analysts have absurdly maintained that the issue was not racial but only political, and others, equally absurdly, that it was neither racial nor political but only educational. It was absurd to say the conflict was not political, because education, or anyway schooling, in America is a road to power, or to powerlessness, and therefore a political issue from kindergarten up. And it was absurd to say the conflict was not racial, because racial groups that felt an identity in themselves and recognized an identity in the others were struggling either to overcome or to defend established status relationships—or, in the case of the radicals, to deny status relationships altogether. In America politics is almost never not racial.

Thus what was billed as a strike by the United Federation of Teachers against the board of education of the city of New York was a massing of most of the white interest groups in the city against a racial-political-educational rebellion. To the first group of rebels—the community-control advocates—there accrued groups of other teachers, parents, and students who for interested or disinterested reasons supported their cause.

Initially, Mayor Lindsay and several of his appointees to the board of education were among the rebellion's lukewarm supporters, but their support, both ineffectual and half-hearted, probably merely prolonged the struggle without at all mitigating the ultimate defeat of the rebels; a more conventional mayor and board would likely have found a way of bringing the rebels to heel–thus ending the "strike"–more quickly than did John Lindsay. It was Lindsay's failure to deal firmly with the rebels that earned him such great unpopularity with large segments of the city's white electorate (an unpopularity that he strove, more or less successfully throughout the following spring, summer, and autumn to overcome).

With very few exceptions, the black community closed ranks in the struggle against the UFT and the school establishment. Even very conservative or very union-loyal Negro teachers, in addition to very conservative Negro leaders, joined the community-control advocates in opposing the strike. A few black teachers may have honored the picket line, but I know of none who helped man it. Where the schools were open, black parents sent their children in far greater numbers than did white parents. Puerto Rican parents were more divided than black parents, some siding with the black community in a struggle that they felt was also theirs, and others identifying with the more "respectable" forces.

Throughout the city, black, Puerto Rican, white, and integrated groups who had for years composed the vanguard of educational agitators, first for integration and then for community control, supported the antagonists of the system. In general, they provided the organizers and the cadres of neighborhood groups who expressed their opposition to the school system paradoxically by opening up the schools when the striking teachers closed them.

By their side were the teacher "misfits," now turned rebels. The odd teacher who did not distinguish in degree of humanity between a black and a white student or in degree of professional worthiness in teaching a 7-2 and teaching a 7-14 class; the teacher who would take the part of the assaulted student against an assaulting colleague; the teacher who joined the students in condemning the school's jailhouse rules instead of merely wishing someone else would enforce them—these were the individuals who sensed, or knew, that the teachers strike was an action in defense of an abhorred system. Some of them were old-time union members, expressing their belief in human dignity now by crossing instead of manning the picket line.* Most were young men and women only a few years out of college whose idealism had been aroused in adolescence not by the trade movement but by the civil rights and the peace movements. Some of the teachers formed dissident groups within the union or dropped out when they felt powerless to influence union policy. Others had never joined.

And then there were the students. Some of them had demonstrated for peace and been chased or conked by the police; some had petitioned the principals for the right to go out for lunch or the board of estimate for a new school building and been thanked or ignored; some of them had organized and demanded reforms and been harassed or suspended; and all of them had profound grievances regarding their treatment as human beings and as students. The few who had met during the summer of 1968 had begun to formulate a philosophy and a program. Then the strike-lockout that closed their schools provided them with both a strategy and a new phalanx of allies.

Defenders Out, Rebels In

During the last phase of the buildup of the community-control movement in the winter and spring of 1968, a few tiny militant mainly black groups, downgrading "decentralization" as a legislative gimmick, had operated under the slogan "we will take our schools." They meant,

* *For this, they were scorned as "scabs." The word "scab" denotes one who crosses the picket line or goes to work when there is a strike on. But it connotes the evil of betraying one's fellows for personal gain or out of cowardice. Among the many teachers who did not honor the union's strike call in 1968, there were probably very few who were "scabs" in its connotative sense. In most cases, teachers who went into school during the strike did so for principled not personal reasons.*

literally, that members of the community together with sympathetic teachers would occupy the school buildings and conduct the schools for the benefit of their children. On actual educational philosophy there was considerable disagreement among members of these groups. Unlike the students who had a program but were vague about tactics, these activists had a strategy but were vague about program. The tactic "take the schools" earned for members of this group from the teachers union the epithets "vigilantes," "extremists," and even "black fascists," epithets that came to be applied by extension to all community-control advocates, many of whom came to understand them to mean simply "nigger." Even among the more conservative community-control advocates, some of these community-control activists were seen as pretty way-out. Of one of the most vociferous, a black teacher named Ralph Poynter, a community-control newsletter said: "The ways in which Mr. Poynter chooses to express his zeal for community control may have made him unpopular among those who share his goals."[4] And even to many of those who supported both his goals and his methods, the tactic "take our schools" seemed romantic political adventurism.

And then in September, October, and November, 1968, with the school buildings and children abandoned by those hired to preside over them, communities of kindred souls throughout the city did take their schools. Respectable teachers and parents, people who had never before in their lives committed a crime worse than such as cheating on their income tax, broke windows and picked locks whenever they could not procure the services of a locksmith. High school students who had spent all their best energies figuring out ways of breaking out of school when the teachers were in, turned their energies to finding ways of breaking in now that the teachers were out. Men and women for whom a weekend at the seashore would have required days of planning and packing hurriedly decided to sleep in where they had broken in so that the wary custodians should not replace the locks and bar them from the building again the next morning. They took turns sleeping in night after night, while neighboring parents brought them meals, and then the occupiers conducted school when the children came the next morning. Bookish men found out how to turn on the water and the electricity which the custodians had turned off, and tired fathers swept stairways and emptied trash baskets.

During the three previous conventional strikes called by the UFT, principals and custodians had opened the schools as a matter of course, and in 1967 most principals had welcomed the parents who came in to take the places of striking teachers. By and large, administrators under the rank of principal had crossed the picket line, as had many nonunion teachers. And after these earlier strikes, the hostilities naturally aroused by strike breakers' crossing the picket line were not expected to and more or less did not endure long beyond the settlement. In the case of the Great Strike, however, after some initial shilly-shallying and confusion on the part of a few administrators and a few teachers, the lines were firmly drawn. Except in Harlem and other wholly black and Puerto Rican communities, most principals closed their schools, and many joined the picket lines. In general, up until they themselves voted to go out on strike, the custodians locked themselves into their buildings and everyone else out–including sometimes the mailman. After they went out, they simply disappeared with their keys. Official announcements from the board of education that schools were open where teachers were prepared to teach had no effect on this situation. And even after John Doar, the mayor's newly appointed president of the board of education, authorized teachers and community persons to secure the services of locksmiths to gain entry into their schools, the police, who had been protecting the empty buildings and striking teachers against the system's enemies, continued to make arrests of persons doing precisely what the president of the board of education had told them they might do. Court cases against persons who entered buildings for the purpose of conducting school continued to be pressed months after the strike had ended. As we have seen, the closing of administrative and instructional ranks against the rebels also applied to matters of salary. Many nonstriking teachers who managed to get into open schools to teach during the strike were for many months denied salaries for those services, while nonworking teachers who reported to their district superintendents that they had been locked out of their own schools against their will did receive salaries for that time. Clearly, whatever the official line or even the highest officials' sympathies, the sense of law and order and rightness of almost the entire white community was with the striking teachers as defenders of what amounted to white society's schools.

Now, what happened inside the elementary schools and junior high schools that were opened by rebelling parents and teachers varied from school to school, but in general more or less conventional procedures were followed, lightened somewhat by the smallness of many classes and the sense of freedom imparted by the unusualness of the situation. Of the special classes and schools conducted in churches, halls, and homes by devoted striking teachers for children who were respecting the strike, the same may be said. They tended to be more open, lighter, in short, more fun than regular school. (Which suggests something about the dead weight that school as an institution lays upon relations between teachers and children.)

But inside the high schools, the situation was somewhat different. There, not the parents but the students themselves had broken down the doors, and the possibilities began to be explored that students might become active participants in their own education. Some time after the strike, in the spring of 1969, a student who signed himself "Harpo" wrote in the *New York High School Free Press*, "Remember we've got the power to make our education worthwhile without disciplinary power hanging over our heads if we get together."[5] And "together" is here more than a preposition, more than an adverb, more than Madison Avenue's "together*ness*." It is a philosophy, a way of being, a state of political awareness, a call to action.*

The ten-week Great Strike, agonizingly too long for the striking teachers and the rest of the school establishment, was tantalizingly too short for the school rebels. Because what they were trying to do was no less than overthrow the entire school way of being—the irrelevance of the

* *My etymological "authorities" provide the following definition:* "Together. *Being together is trying to find out who you are.* Together *implies a certain wholeness or unity within a person, and a consistency of words and action.* Examples: *Eldridge Cleaver is together; Roy Wilkins is untogether. John Coltrane is together; Johnny Mathis is untogether. "Black" is together; "Negro" is untogether. An Afro is together; a do-rag is untogether. Knowing what a do-rag is is together; not knowing is untogether."*

curriculum, the status arrangements, the coercion, and to find new ways of relating and learning. "If we are to build a new society," Harpo wrote in the same article, "it must be as we destroy this one. If we separate the two, we'll just build new bureaucracies and new rulers after we destroy the present ones."

Finding ways of getting school going during the strike—which meant meeting and planning, picking locks or breaking windows, braving the jeering picket lines, enduring some police beatings and, more commonly, arrests, and encouraging more and more other students to join them—was in itself an experience that brought rebelling students and teachers together—and began to get them "together." The process continued as they organized daily programs, ran classes, and formulated rules. Finding their way toward a new definition of school (I hesitate even to use the word, naked as these groups were of most of the encumbering shrouds commonly used to turn a group of human beings into what we usually mean when we say "school") was indeed more a process than a product. In most of the "liberated" schools, the standard disciplinary rules were abandoned, as were distinctions among students as to Honors, Academic, and General. In many, students and teachers met together in general assembly daily or several times weekly to discuss organizational and procedural problems, and teachers gave up their customary practice of meeting *in camera.* Likewise among the teachers a tone of common endeavour obtained quite unlike the customary top-down, faction-ridden, competitive chore-shirking atmosphere. Most groups ran four or five classes a day and had their general meeting either in the middle of the day or in the afternoon. In some, students decided each morning which classes they would attend. Classes in math or in the natural sciences tended to be straightforward and conventional. Classes called "English" and "social studies" sought new areas to explore; they read Dylan Thomas, Paul Goodman, A. S. Neil. One group studied music as affecting social change and started out by discussing The Doors (a rock group). In one school, a small group of students experimented with T groups—a form of encounter group. In many schools, the student newspapers that would become one of the most immediate and refreshing products of the subsequent student rebellion began to be published.

For many students, being free to act like themselves inside a school building was an enchanting experience, which they savored by wandering around, smoking, playing cards, or guitars. Since they could have stayed out not only without penalty but with less effort than it took to come in, by coming and "fooling around" they must have been testing the teachers and enjoying the simple experience of indulging openly in ordinary pleasures which all their school lives had been illicit and confined to secret staircases and smelly washrooms. Others, despite their brave antiestablishmentarianism of coming to school against the "real" teachers' wishes, were made uncomfortable by the liberties their schoolmates were taking and by the general lack of structure.

A girl at Gandhi High told about some of the problems they had there:

Those that started out had this beautiful idea of this Summerhill-type school, including most of the teachers, and like we began to realize that it wasn't going to be that easy, and one teacher kept holding us down to the fact that this was school and that when the schools reopened we had to have something to show for it—or we'd just be laughed at.

To some people nakedness is embarrassing at first, even in the midst of the beloved community.

The students and the teachers were together talking and somehow it turned into a whole thing about the T groups, and most of them were really upset. We called a general meeting after school and there were people playing cards at the time and Tom [the teacher appointed as acting principal] got rather upset, like . . . I don't think he minded them playing cards so much but what he minded was little groups sprawled out all over the school. It turned into a really black and white issue, like, they said, "If they can have their T groups, and if they can bring guitars, why can't we play cards?" And there were always people walking into the school, like the head of the parents association and the district superintendent. And we never got together on anything. So it started splitting, and then by the time we were just getting unified again, the strike ended. And we made provisions for student union meetings after that.

The two things the students and teachers were seeking were new ways of relating as students and teachers without the old irrelevant, divisive status barriers, and areas of study that might seriously engage their interests. Time and privacy would have been needed to create a new educational process, and neither was granted. The intrusion of both the internalized inhibitions taught by school as it had always been and of the authority figures of school as it was going to be again, interfered with the first faltering steps of the young educational community. Still, after each day's fall, it came back to take new steps the next day—until the strike ended too soon. And the real teachers and students came back to play again their old roles. The somewhat anarchic experimentation which could have led to new forms of organization was put an end to as school became again "sensible and realistic"—in that school way of real-world lunacy.

Defenders In, Rebels Out

As the strike had provided the student rebels with the first step in their strategy for 1968-69, the strike settlement provided the second. Like the I.S. 201 governing board and parents, students throughout the city were enraged at the provision by which their holidays were to be sacrificed so the teachers could make up lost pay.

On a Wednesday toward the end of November, school—"real" school—opened. The students who, like Temma and her friend had delightedly wandered the city for three months and the students who, like the girls from Gandhi, had been trying out another kind of freedom inside the school buildings, came back to all the old insulting unfreedoms, plus the new injuries of the teacher-designed speedup to "help the students make up all they had missed"—which meant not only an extra forty-five minutes a day but the prospect of having to go to school on the day after Thanksgiving and the days between Christmas and New Year's. Temma cried in school that day, and her brother Kenny wandered through the school in a deliberate daze, but the rebels organized to fight back. At that moment, when the eyes of New York were turned toward

Ocean Hill-Brownsville to know in what way that community would bow to the imposed terms of the strike settlement, the revolutionary thrust passed from the parents to the children. Nobody was looking—neither the parents nor even the children quite noticed what was happening—when the students moved into the places of the fallen grownups. The students even traveled, physically, several hundreds of them, to the battleground of Ocean Hill-Brownsville in Brooklyn.

Especially the authorities charged with defending the system didn't notice. One wonders, whether if they had, they would have looked up from their adult preoccupations when the kids signaled. Because the kids did signal. On the day before Thanksgiving, after a week of discussions about tactics in individual schools, the rebels first surfaced. Three hundred of them demonstrated in front of City Hall against the extra forty-five minutes each day and the lost holidays. A small delegation was invited in to meet the Mayor's "cool-it squad," a very handsome young Puerto Rican man and a very Afro-looking young black man. These two issued a statement to the press that the students in the delegation "were not goons,"[6] a reassurance which the students couldn't have found very flattering, and which, stated like that, the public probably didn't believe. The two also said that they had told the students that "Mayor Lindsay had no control over school schedules, and suggested that they take their grievance to the board of education. Mr. Segarra [the handsome Puerto Rican] also said he had offered to try to arrange a meeting between representatives of the students and the board of education." Which statement demonstrates how little the men at the top had learned in all the years since the days before Stanley Lisser when other kindly intermediaries were *trying* to get somebody responsible to *meet* with the Harlem parents. The students may or may not have learned something from such past efforts. In any case they weren't having any of that game of patience—of waiting for meetings with officials who likely would turn out when they did meet to have either no power or no will to use it.

Then, on Friday, November 29, the day after Thanksgiving, on a block in east Harlem a confrontation was occurring in front of P.S. 39 which would lead to the destruction of community control in that school by the police and the UFT and to the destruction eventually of community control everywhere by legislative enactment, while in the rest of the city almost half the high school students stayed out in a boycott to protest the violation of their holiday. They were in an amiable holiday mood as they traveled about the late autumn city, 1,500 of them on their way to a mass demonstration at the United Nations Plaza, where they were addressed by Leslie Campbell and Albert Vann, black teachers from J.H.S. 271 in Ocean Hill-Brownsville and leaders of the Afro-American Teachers Association. Campbell said, "Do you know why we are here? To do as students what adults have not been able to do."

But the authorities were still not receiving the students' message, trying as they were to cope with what must have seemed the more serious problem of getting Rhody McCoy and the Reverend C. Herbert Oliver of Ocean Hill-Brownsville to bend to the yoke. Or else they had already decided to respond to the students' message with force.

On Monday, while Mayor John Lindsay was vacationing in Antigua (not knowing that his settling of the Great Strike was only another stage in rather than the end of his troubles with the school situation), the students continued and intensified their boycott. This day, after demonstrating at their individual schools and in Washington Square Park and sending small detachments to invade operating schools, a contingent of them, responding to Leslie Campbell's urging, moved through the city subways to Ocean Hill-Brownsville, where J.H.S. 271 had been ordered closed by the state Commissioner of Education, Dr. James E. Allen, for refusal to accept the strike settlement terms. They were met there by club-wielding police who chased them up and down the streets. On a day a few weeks later, when a group of parents whom the authorities had ordered to be kept out of the school, brushed by a police cordon and did enter, I heard one policeman say good-humoredly to another, "How were you gonna stop them?" They may have been respectful toward the adults, but the police knew very well how to stop the students: by the time the boycott was called off after five days, 126 persons (mostly students) were reported to have been arrested and untold heads and backs had been beaten, including at least one reporter's. For their part, the students during this period had rushed out of some schools, rushed into others, damaged one building slightly with a home-made bomb, ignited fires here and there, busted up some shop windows and subway cars, and started on its way a determined attack against their previous condition of servitude.[7]

Organizations and Aims

In January, 1969 the High School Principals Association, a constituent association of the Council of Supervisory Associations, issued a report on the high school crisis entitled "The Nature and Limits of Student Dissent and Participation." A few days later, columnist Joseph Alsop asked Abraham Lass, principal of Abraham Lincoln High School in Brooklyn and chairman of the committee that prepared the report, what was the report's "real meaning." Lass replied: "Kids all over the city don't do the same thing the same way at the same time without some organization somewhere; and that organization seems to us to be of a highly professional character."[8]

After several extended encounters with student rebels from a number of schools, I opine that not a resurrected Ché Guevara himself would be able to whip those students into an ordered, disciplined revolutionary army responding to commands from their general—nor Leon Trotsky nor George Washington either. The attitude of the students toward organization and toward adults is New Leftist, which means that they will accept help and even advice from adults they have come to trust, but never orders, and that each group is far less organized than its most organized member, although, with luck, somewhat more organized than its least organized member. Within each school, individual groups are suspicious of coalitions with other schools' groups and with other groups in their own school. Further, at the individual school level, and the interschool or supraschool level, white groups and black groups were beginning to come together only tentatively and on specific issues and actions and only toward the end of the school year 1968-69. What Messrs. Lass and Alsop did not see, because it was too close to them, was that from the very beginning it was similar conditions which provoked a similar pattern of rebellion throughout the city. It was the school establishment that had "an organization somewhere . . . of a highly professional character." It was representatives of the school establishment who responded on almost every single occasion with repressive action, born, no doubt, of inchoate anxiety over the challenging of their despotic rule. Actually, while students throughout the city responded to both their long-standing grievances and new repressions with similar tactics, they had a considerable repertory of such tactics, including publishing student papers, setting fires, signing petitions, mounting demonstrations, showing "revolutionary" movies, wearing prohibited costumes, trying in various ways to get rid of teachers they hated, and seeking, usually unsuccessfully, to negotiate with the principal. They employed one or another tactic freely according to their mood and their need. (It's called "doing your own thing.") And there was no controlling conspiratorial strategy.

There were, however, a few student organizations that sought to coordinate and encourage the students' uprisings and a number of adult organizations that sought to support them. Among the latter were the National Emergency Civil Liberties Committee and the New York Civil Liberties Union, which provided legal aid for students who were arrested or suspended or expelled without due process. These organizations also provided advice to students on their legal rights in general vis-à-vis the school system. To a system that had for decades been treating students quite without regard for their substantive and procedural rights, this intrusion of "outsiders" was indeed very threatening. Other adult organizations which actively or sentimentally supported the students included; the Metropolitan Applied Research Center, headed by State Education Regent Kenneth Clark, which successfully intervened against a mass expulsion of almost 700 students from Franklin K. Lane High School in Brooklyn; the Afro-American Teachers Association and the Black Panthers, which worked closely with some of the black students groups; some SDS students, who sought to work with some white groups but were usually not made too welcome; and a number of anti-UFT or anti-Shanker white teachers groups. In individual schools, school districts, and boroughs, various parents, teachers, and community rebels, sometimes formally organized, supported student rebels in their demands and their actions. All these organizations and individuals were hated and probably feared by representatives of the school establishment (including the teachers union), who usually saw them not as restless rebels tending to respond alike and so to come together, which they were, but as the serried ranks of a disciplined revolutionary army, which some of them would have liked to be.

There were three black and Puerto Rican coordinating student groups and one white one. All had few members and little formal organizational structure, and they consisted mainly of a few nonstudents, who worked more or less full time with individual student groups, plus activist students from various schools. The black and Puerto Rican student groups, often with overlapping personnel, tended to work in different boroughs—the High School Coalition in Manhattan, the Afro-American Students Association in Brooklyn, and the Black Student Union in the Bronx. The coordinating white group, the New York High School Student Union (HSSU), likewise with a handful of full-time personnel and a loose structure, considered itself citywide and published a student paper, the *New York High School Free Press,* which was circulated citywide among both black and white students. The *Free Press* says it sells for "5¢ in schools, 15¢ at the best newsstands, and 25¢ to UFT members," and it carried a few movie, record, and hippie-type retail store ads. It printed stories of actions at various schools, interviews with student rebels, analytical articles about the student movement and the school system, speeches by community-control leaders, and articles and statements from the enemy camp. It was sometimes rhetorical, sometimes obscene, sometimes funny, always informative and revealing.*

The predominantly white HSSU and the predominantly black and Puerto Rican groups operated independently throughout the 1968-69 school year,

* *Many of the dozen or so members of the* HSSU *in Manhattan lived in a commune (a living arrangement that has been gaining in popularity among students and others of the fifteen-to-thirty generation), some of them being supported by their parents, others by part-time jobs. Their irregularly published paper, the* High School Free Press, *was set by volunteer labor and received*

gradually moving toward mutual trust and common actions. When a Black Panther who had been organizing high school students was jailed, some white HSSU members moved in to continue his activities, although normally they confined themselves to organizing white students. Black and white groups together, after several months of scattered student actions thoughout the city, called for a special Spring Offensive to begin in April, 1969 and last for a month. The result of the call was a moderate increase in the number of acts of rebellion in the various schools, but nothing like the mass uprising that some of the rebel leaders were probably hoping for—another demonstration of the fact that most of the student actions were responses to local stimuli rather than to central direction.

The HSSU and the boroughwide black groups were not primarily interested in "reforming" the New York City high schools. They were radical revolutionaries who saw the system as repressive agents of a repressive society. For example:

In one issue of the *Free Press*, the entire center spread is devoted to an organizational chart demonstrating the corporate and organizational affiliations of a number of members of the then board of education and of the group of "prominent citizens"—the selection board—responsible for nominating board of education members under the appointment system that prevailed prior to May, 1969.

In another issue, an article entitled "Textbooks and Bullshit" contains the statement: "As might be expected of textbooks written for future managers of the [U.S.] Empire, these [books] reflect all the chauvinistic, anti-communist and counter-revolutionary assumptions which have underpinned American foreign policy for the past twenty years."

Another issue carries a favorable review of *Soul on Ice* by Eldridge Cleaver and also urges readers to attend the

some printing assistance from another "underground" paper. While our society generally considers it nobody's business how somebody earns his living, especially in the case of people of comfortable or more than comfortable means, I provide this information because of the excessive curiosity and suspiciousness there is about how these young people subsisted and put out a paper.

anti-Inaugural demonstration in Washington, D.C., sponsored by the National Mobilization Committee to End the War in Vietnam. The call says, in part: "We are planning an organized structured presence of anti-war, anti-racist, anti-poverty forces."[9]

An activist in the HSSU explained to me, "We are not about making better schools. We are about making a revolution, and the schools is where the people are. They [the school system] can't fulfill our demands the way the system is."

A participant-observer who worked closely with the High School Student Union explains its aims and strategy as follows. I have left unedited the writer's shifts between "we" and "they" to indicate the duality of the role he was playing.

> The position of the HSSU on the function of the public schools is essentially similar to the SDS position on the colleges. The schools serve to channel the students into the class role in society for which they were born. School is essentially an indoctrination center. It's just that we don't like the kind of indoctrination that's being given—hence the demands for black and PR studies and a history of the working class in America.
>
> They also perceive of the school struggle as part of a greater one; it cannot be won without radical changes in society. One of the Student Union's demands is for jobs and housing for everyone. They feel that the ruling class not only won't but in fact can't provide this. Thus the aim of their demands is not so much to win them as to build a revolutionary movement in the high schools. (And we can't win in the high schools without radical change anyway.)
>
> This is not to say that the Union is composed of idealist revolutionary dreamers. Like good radicals, they know that radical demands must be constantly pushed; as radical *unionists*, they know that a union is built (in part) on the bread and butter issues—the little day-to-day things. Thus their concern with suspensions, etc. An organization can't be built if its organizers are being constantly harassed. Hopefully, the union will become strong enough so that if any of us gets harassed, we can exert equal harassment on them. (I can see the day when every second year the Student Union contract comes up for renegotiation with

the board of ed, and, along with the teachers, sanitation men, and subway workers, the city has to count on a student strike every two years.)

And on curriculum content, he explained the HSSU's position as follows:

When [a community-control leader] spoke at City College, she said she wasn't talking about having her children learn what the kids in the suburbs are learning. She wants her kids to learn about themselves. The struggle is the struggle of the black and Puerto Rican communities to teach their children who they are, what their position is in society, and how to change it. Education can succeed with most black and Puerto Rican kids only when it is education for revolution. We have to use the schools for what *we* want *them* for, not let them use us for what *they* want *us* for.

In the April-May 1969 issue of the *Free Press,* both the union and the Black and Puerto Rican Citywide High School Council published their programs. I print the objectives of these programs as they appeared in that issue. The union had eleven demands: a number related to "student power" (namely improvement of school conditions), while others related directly to the students' eventual entry into a society which the union considers exploitative and repressive. The HSSU demands were:

1. *No suspensions, involuntary transfers, exclusion from classes, detention, harassment of students. Due process for students.*
2. *No cops in schools, no narcos, security guards, plainclothesmen, informers.*
3. *No program cards, hall checks, ID's, passes.*
4. *An end to commercial and general diplomas, one diploma for every student upon graduation.*
5. *Open admissions to colleges, a college education free for everyone that wants one.*
6. *Jobs and housing for every student who wants one on graduating, dropping out, or leaving home. The Army is not a decent job.*
7. *No military recruiting in schools, no military assemblies, literature, no sending names to draft boards or recruiters. An immediate end to the draft.*

8. *Black and Latin departments controlled by Black and Latin students.*
9. *Community control of the schools, and every other community facility. Students are part of the community.*
10. *POWER! Student control of curriculum, publications, assemblies, clubs, student government, dress, etc. The right to organize politically.*
11. *We support the 15 points of the Black and Puerto Rican Citywide HS Council.*

The fifteen demands of the Black and Puerto Rican Citywide High School Council were:

1. *No more automatic suspensions of* H.S. *students.*
2. *No more police and police aides inside* NYC *high schools.*
3. *Strict adherence to fire regulations—doors to schools must be left open.*
4. *Open the school daily to parent observation.*
5. *Community rehabilitation centers should be allowed to set up programs to treat known drug addicts.*
6. *Elimination of the general course of study [i.e., non-Academic track].*
7. *Because of the total chaos in education this year, the suspension of all Regents exams this June.*
8. *Recognition by all* NYC *schools of the two Black holidays, May 19th—Malcolm X Birthday, and January 15th—Dr. King's Birthday.*
9. *Immediate alteration of teaching population and examination to supply Black educators proportionate to the student population.*
10. *Complete examination of all books and educational supplies used by the schools.*
11. *The creation of school clubs along ethnic lines with facilities and funds from the school G.O.*
12. *Improved conditions for the students in school such as music in the lunchroom, more dances, improved athletic programs with rifle clubs and self-defense classes.*
13. *Teachers who are teaching a course should have a background related to the course.*
14. *Creation of Student-Faculty (equal-representation) Council in each school which will make binding*

decisions on the following matters: Curriculum, school staff, discipline, rules and regulations, etc.

15. *The reorganization of high school by September 1969, along community lines, so that black students will not be forced to go to hostile communities to seek an education.*[10]

The demands of the two groups can be summarized and rephrased as follows:

1. Establishment of a relevant curriculum (HSSU demands 8 and 10; Council demands 5, 10, 11, 12, 13, and 14).
2. An end to status arrangements in the school (HSSU demands 4 and 10; Council demands 6 and 14).
3. An end to security measures, harassment, and suspensions, and the institution of student participation in school control (HSSU demands 1, 2, 3, 10; Council demands 1, 2, 4, 14).
4. Establishment of community control of high schools (HSSU demand 9; Council demands 9 and 15).
5. A change in the relationship between the schools as a status-reinforcing institution and the political, economic, and military arrangements of the larger society (HSSU demands 5, 6, 7, 9—these demands embody its radical program).

While both groups supported a kind of separatism (HSSU demand 8; Council demands 11 and 15), it should be observed that the elimination of the General and Commercial courses of study (which both groups want) would end the kind of invidious status separatism which the school system now enforces, and also that among themselves the students were breaking down racial barriers in a way that conforming students cannot do.*

The basic, radical demands of both groups reflected their appraisal of the general faults—the repressiveness, the power arrangements, the status systems—of the school

**The following school year, 1969-70, the board of education announced that it was planning to terminate the issuance of different categories of high school diplomas. The projected single diploma, however, would list on its back the courses students had completed, to "aid colleges or prospective employers to evaluate better the students' talents" (New York* Times, *October 10, 1969).*

system and society. The form of the "student power" demands reflected the immediate situation in the high schools in that school year. They were the bread-and-butter issues, the "little day-to-day things" that the participant-observer had referred to—arbitrary disciplinary actions, suspensions, transfers, police in the schools, and so on.

In most of the city's individual high schools, and even in a few junior high schools, little groups of students, some associated with and some independent of the citywide coalitions, formulated their own demands. Generally these reflected the day-to-day concerns that make up a student's work life, as they do an adult's. Students demanded to be allowed to go out of the building during lunch ("with parents' permission," said the conservative radicals at the elite Bronx High School of Science); to have the locker rooms and showers open ("They won't let you shower after gym and then they have the nerve to tell you that you smell," said a junior high school girl); to be allowed to wear trunks in the pool, instead of swimming nude; to be allowed to go in and out the front door, as teachers and visitors did.

Students in many schools demanded a smoking lounge. Students are forbidden to smoke in school, although they do smoke secretly into milk cartons, in bathrooms, in stairwells. A good part of the cafeteria hassle and the bathroom hassle is really a smoking hassle. In addition, there is no place in school where a student can simply *be*—be a sociable human being with other human beings. Except in the cafeteria during lunch, free communication among students is almost as illicit as smoking. Therefore the demand for a student smoking lounge.

Many students demanded that the G.O. (General Organization, the student government apparatus) be made more democratic and more responsible. Most schools set high grade-average requirements for candidates for G.O. office (an analogue to property qualifications for political

Whether the homogeneous classes which currently fit into the system of different diplomas would also be eliminated the announcement did not say. It is hard to imagine how the proposed change might have any serious effect on academic and other status differences among students without a complete turning upside down of almost all other school arrangements.

office-holding), subject all G.O. decisions to faculty review, and do not provide a public accounting of the expenditure of G.O. funds, most of which are collected from student dues. The students demanded reform in all these matters.

Most lists of demands included: black studies in the curriculum, more black teachers and administrators, student participation in disciplinary procedures, and other student-power demands.

The students at Bronx Science made some serious curriculum demands—more electives, seminars conducted by visiting scholars, pass-fail system in minor subjects.

There were a host of free-speech demands and, as the year went on, demands for: removal of the police, return of suspended students, retention of transferred teacher sympathizers, and removal of unpopular ("racist") teachers or disciplinary personnel.

It was at the individual school level and over these little day-to-day things that the student rebels and the school personnel fought the battle of 1968-69.

3. COUNTER-RESISTANCE—AND OLD STANDARDS

Throughout the weeks of the Great Strike, observers and combatants alike frequently expressed anxiety about how the defenders of the system and the rebel teachers would be able to come back together again once the strike ended. My notes record a conversation with Mrs. Wilkinson, Benny's mother, who had supported a group of rebel teachers in their takeover of her younger daughter's junior high school.

Mrs. W. expecting the worst when the teachers finally return. Says, "It'll be a mess—all that hate." I sensed an undercurrent of how much she hates them [the striking teachers]. She seems emotionally unprepared to accept them back. Also, and especially, the principal, who simply stayed away the whole time.

At that school too, on one of the first days of the strike, I talked with some picketing teachers and school secretaries and sensed in them a gathering of anger that recalled to me retired Principal Edward Gottlieb's comment, "The whites don't know how much fury they have in them." One of those striking teachers, incidentally, directed her hostile feelings mainly against her principal, simply because of his general unkindness and incompetence as a boss. In many cases what the strike did was to mobilize and direct chronic discontents (*ressentiment*) into attack on the system or, alternatively, attack on the attackers, along more or less race-oriented lines.

As Mrs. Wilkinson feared, the angers were not played out by the end of the ten weeks, and the make-up pay clause in the settlement helped, as we have seen, to spread them more widely among the student population. However, the angers of the defenders were also not played out, and they were beset by an anxiety that even the victory of the strike settlement had not really secured the system against its attackers. This anxiety was immediately aggravated by the students' five-day boycott right after the settlement.

During the strike, the teachers had been in the forefront of the defense of the system, with help from the supervisors, the custodians, and the police. In the aftermath of the strike, throughout the academic year 1968-69, the chief defenders were the principals and the police with help from the teachers and support from the top levels of the city government and the media.

Throughout the city, the principals, their angers and their anxieties rearoused every day, overreacted to almost every evidence of student independence. I suspect that playing the role of despot produces in and of itself an abnormal degree of inner insecurity, rising in crises to something like paranoia. In addition, as we have seen, the system's customary response to infringement or challenging of the rules had always been a laying on of further, more restrictive rules. Meanwhile on their part, the rebelling students were emboldened by their successes in seizing the schools during the strike and by the open support of rebel teachers, parents, and organized adult groups. Thus they dared to challenge school rules and procedures which they had long felt to be repressive and unfair (and many of which were also illegal) but which they had never before had the courage to challenge. Every challenge seemed to create new anxieties in the principals, who reacted with ever greater repressiveness; and every act of repression intensified the resentments of the students, who became more and more determined, it seemed, to throw off the whole system. The principals, with the continuing erosion of their power, came to rely more and more on force —suspensions and police—and the consequent buildup of physical resentment among the students seemed to lead to more and more frequent acts of simple violence on their part—fights, fires, and assaults. The effect was seemingly to transform the whole high school system of New York City, once a fairly orderly arrangement of sterile but quiet John Brown junior highs, into one great "chaos system": where there had never been more than an occasional serious engagement of the minds, there was no longer even order.

The phenomena described occured in high schools in every borough of the city, with the possible exception of Staten Island, were there are few black and Puerto Rican students and also few white misfit students. There seemed to be relatively less trouble among the 40,000 students in vocational high schools than among the over 200,000 in academic high schools, suggesting perhaps that the curriculum in the former still maintained some legitimacy. There was less violence (fighting and fires) in the specialized (elite) high schools, but considerable student-civil-liberties-type agitation. Troubles were most acute at predominantly black and Puerto Rican and mixed schools.

We can break into the cycle of violence and force at any point in order to try to observe the process of escalation. Two of the issues that most exercised rebels and defenders were free speech and freedom from interference with their personal lives, as the former put it, or the limits of student dissent and proper attire, as the latter put it.

Edgar Friedenberg argues in an article, "Contemptuous Hairdressers: Ceremonies of Humiliation in School," that the schools' demand for conformity in dress "has evolved to meet society's demand for a docile and uncritical youth."[1] Ira Glasser of the New York Civil Liberties Union suggests that the item of dress that symbolizes noncomformity (the beard, the "shades," the bell-bottom pants) is the one that especially enrages school personnel.*

When Stokely Carmichael and Rap Brown appeared in public wearing shades, they were respecting not initiating a common style among black youth. It was and is a style that school people for some reason cannot stand. Schools for

* *The wording of the dress code of a California junior high school supports Glasser's and Friedenberg's interpretation: "Clothing symbolic of gangs or radical movements is not to be worn on campus. Hair styles symbolic of radical movements will not be worn." (Quoted in* No More Teachers' Dirty Looks! *published by the Bay Area Radical Teachers Organizing Committee, January, 1970.)*

long had rules that students were not allowed to wear dark glasses. Black students wore them anyway and claimed that they were their real glasses. Schools then made rules that if a student made such a claim he had to bring a note from the optometrist to back him up. I don't know if the style would have run down had it not driven the teachers up the wall. As it was, it really caught on. Dark glasses is one of those things that students and teachers fought about over the years to occupy the hours that they were mandated to spend in each other's presence. Beards on boys, hats worn while walking in the corridors, pants on girls, shirts worn outside the pants, length of skirts, blue jeans, and white jeans were others.

One would have thought that, with so much else for students and principals to fight about in 1968-69, the principals might sensibly have pulled in their horns on the dress issue, at least temporarily. However, acting under the old teacher principle that "if you want to keep control, you musn't let them get away with one little thing," they intensified the battle. Girl students were sent home for wearing slacks and black students were forbidden their shades.

In 1966, state Commissioner of Education Allen declared in two cases that a school principal could not dictate to a student what style of clothing he should wear, except if the clothing was dangerous or distracting.*[2]

During the school year 1967-68 the New York Civil Liberties Union distributed copies of Commissioner Allen's rulings to every high school principal in New York and made follow-up phone calls. Nevertheless principals continued to suspend students for dress-code violations until the National Emergency Civil Liberties Committee intervened in December, 1968 with Superintendent Donovan to insist on observance of Commissioner Allen's rulings. The co-director of the NECLC issued a statement to the press saying it was "a disgrace for principals in the City to have flouted the Commissioner of Education's 1966

* *The long-hair battle, closely related to the "radical" clothing battle, was also carried into federal courts in five states in 1969, with victories for the long-hairs in all cases. In Wisconsin the federal district court stated: "It is time to broaden the constitutional community by including within its protection younger people whose claim to dignity matches that of their elders." (Quoted in* Civil Liberties, *published by the American Civil Liberties Union, December, 1969.)*

ruling. They cannot expect obedience to authority when they themselves disobey the Commissioner's ruling."[3]

School principals do not normally consult either their consciences or the laws of the land in determining how to run their schools. They run their schools the way they have always run their schools except when they are specifically instructed to do otherwise by their supervisors, and even then they may balk some. Even the members of the board of education recognize how little authority the board has over principals, one member publicly expressing doubts about whether the principals would abide by the new guidelines on student conduct which the board issued in the fall of 1969: "If the board looks the other way as principals violate the Guidelines," he is quoted as having said, "the new policy will be a sham."[4]

The principals' defense of their enforcement of clothing conformity was that, for example, pants on girls was a violation of a school rule, so that, whatever their personal feelings, they could not in conscience allow students to violate the rules. (A similar response occurred when the Harlem parents of I.S. 201 were seeking to wrest powers over the schools from the board of education: We cannot allow you to do this because the rules—read laws—say that you are not allowed to do this.) What the principals were defending when they sent home the girls in pants was not so much decency of feminine attire as the right to make "school rules" in a power vacuum, beyond the control or even the scrutiny of those affected by the rules. Under pressure, they came to admit that perhaps some of the rules were outmoded and needed revising, but they said they alone were invested by law with responsibility for making or changing the rules. Sometimes they said, reasonably, that they were glad that some outmoded rules had been called to their attention and that they would give serious thought to changing them but that, of course, they deplored the vulgar, raucous ways the rebels had chosen to state their grievances. (They were referring to student demonstrations, demands for an immediate audience with the principal, and so on.)

That the principals were deaf to the students ("He tore up our petition. He shut the door in our face," said the boy under the elevated) until they became vulgar and raucous, the students knew but the public did not. In one specialized high school when the rebel students finally persuaded the principal to meet with them and hear their grievances, he captured the microphone (claiming laryngitis) and *he* lectured *them* for the duration of the meeting. Then, when he was finally pushed to putting their demands to a student plebiscite, he inserted an item in which the voters could indicate that they disapproved of the "methods" the student rebels had chosen to make known their demands.

In fact, probably the major substantive issue over which students and administrators battled at the individual school level was the free-speech issue. While the principals frequently made statements affirming the students' right to "responsible dissent," by and large they were in such a state of distress that they clamped down even on kinds of behavior that in previous years they had managed to not notice. Most principals banned distribution of the *Free Press* and of independent little student papers inside the schools, and many confiscated copies that they took from students' arms or lockers. In some schools the students hid away in secret unassigned lockers during the school hours papers that they wanted to distribute outside the school before and after the school day. In their response to these matters, the principals violated not only commonly accepted standards of fairness and "due process," and not only court-recognized rights of citizens, but also what, in the judgment of some "enlightened" school administrators, would have been the correct defensive strategy.

In November, 1968, the magazine *School Management*, a trade magazine whose name tells its audience, published a special report on "How Administrators Are Using Student Activism as a Force for Better Schools." In it, Dr. John P. Spiegel, director of the Lemberg Center for the Study of Violence, at Brandeis University, advised school administrators:

As soon as student demands or the possibility of student disorders come to the attention of school administrators, the administration contacts student leaders in order to hear their views and work out, through negotiation, some compromise solution to the issues at conflict.

The compromise should satisfy some of the demands or feelings of protest motivating the activists and, on the other hand, maintain the position of those in authority for the control of school processes and procedures in the best interests of the entire school community.

In most instances, this compromise solution, which requires a good deal of innovation and risk-taking, heads off more serious disorder.

Another article by Lawrence M. Brammer, a professor of educational psychology, in the September, 1968 issue of the *National Association of Secondary School Principals Bulletin* suggests that school personnel must help "youth face their intense private feelings" and "work out pilot models for including teen-agers in planning educational and social change."

But the Machiavellian principle that a despotism is easier sustained by manipulation than by repression was not the only principle violated by the schools' refusal to allow students to circulate their papers. In February, 1969, the Supreme Court of the United States handed down an opinion, in *Tinker* v. *Des Moines Independent School Community District,* immediately relevant to the issue of freedom of expression in the schools. The Court held that the principals of Des Moines, Iowa, could not constitutionally refuse to allow schoolchildren to wear black armbands to school to symbolize their opposition to the Vietnam War. The Court affirmed that the First Amendment right to freedom of speech extends to teachers and children: "It can hardly be argued that either students or teachers shed their consitutional rights to freedom of speech and expression at the schoolhouse gate." They noted that the school officials feared that the wearing of the armbands *might* cause a disturbance in the school: "But, in our system, undifferentiated fear or apprehension of disturbance is not enough to overcome the right to freedom of expression." The Court enunciated a broad interpretation of the school in society, saying "In our system, state-operated schools may not be enclaves of totalitarianism. [Students] may not be confined to the expression of those sentiments that are officially approved." And they recognized the importance of relationships and communications among students: "personal intercommunication among the students . . . is not only an inevitable part of the process of attending school. It is also an important part of the educational process. A student's rights, therefore, do not embrace merely the classroom hours. When he is in the cafeteria, or on the playing field, or on the campus during the authorized hours, he may express his opinions, even on controversial subjects . . ."[5]

The Tinker case, granting to students broad freedom of expression rights so long as the exercise of these rights did not disrupt classwork or involve substantial disorder or invasion of the rights of others, is in its way as significant a case as *Brown* v. *The Board of Education of Topeka* (which outlawed segregated school systems). But during the first few months of its existence the Tinker decision seemed, like that earlier decision, to have passed over the heads of the school officials for whom it was relevant. In general, they continued to prohibit the distribution of "unauthorized" printed material at any time or place in the school buildings.[6]

The ways in which shrewd strategy, a sense of fairness, a sense of humor, and obedience to the law of the land were all abandoned when the principals blew their cool are evident in the following different events.

A group of black students in one of the city's high schools stuck up the popular "ELDRIDGE CLEAVER WELCOME HERE" poster. An administrative officer immediately had it removed. Angered, a couple of hundred black students demanded a meeting with the principal. The principal locked his door and sent for the police.

At another school, an eleven-year-old junior high student who had attended school during the strike, Joshua Mamis, was so pleased with the rebel teacher who assumed the role of acting principal that when the strike was over and the real principal came back, he circulated among his fellow students a petition asking to have the rebel principal become the regular principal. The petition was taken out of circulation and Joshua forbidden to go on circulating it. He instituted a suit against the principal for denial of his First Amendment rights.

Joshua came from an activist family. His older brother published a small one-man student paper at one of the elite specialized high schools, and his mother was active in the community-control movement. Because there were many such families, in which rebels against the school system crossed the generation gap, many school administrators tended to see all children of activist parents as troublemakers and as being "put up to bad behavior" by their parents. Activist parents complained that their children were being harshly treated in school regardless of their behavior. What generally was happening in such cases was that the parents were withholding from the school the acquiescence necessary to sustain its despotism and to ensure among their children general behavioral conformity to the school's mandates. And without such acquiescence, the schools could not enforce the kind of conformity they had been accustomed to enforce.

This also happened in the black community. Ronald Dicks, a black high school student in the Bronx, is an example:

I was suspended from Taft for supposedly distributing unauthorized literature in school. I had some leaflets hanging out of my bag, and there was a lot of students passing me by, but I wasn't giving them anything. Now a girl I know came up and asked me for a leaflet, after she had given the proper introduction, and I gave her a leaflet. The UFT Chapter Chairman saw this, and he asked for one, and I gave him one. The third period they called me down to the office and told me to get out. I told them I wouldn't leave unless my parent was notified or I had a witness. They said no, get out now. This pig comes and takes my arm and drags me down the hall. He continues to touch me and we start pushing.

Dicks was within his rights when he insisted that his parent be sent for before he be sent out of the school, and as he insisted on his rights, even in the presence of the policeman, who was prepared to eject him from the building, his parent was sent for. He was then suspended, and a few days later a small group of adults and fellow students mounted a demonstration protesting his suspension in front of the school building. Dicks explains:

Remember the teachers strike—the UFT was permitted to picket on the same side of the street as the school [he was attending]. As a matter of fact, they stood at the school doors, inside the gates, and watched us walk between their lines into the school. We [the student and parent demonstrators] were not allowed to stand on the same side of the street as the UFT did. The police put up barricades. . . . Two boys pulled apart the barricades. The police . . . started beating the boys with their clubs. Screaming girls scattered . . . . Seven demonstrators were arrested and three were seriously injured.

Ron Dicks's parents attended a protest mass meeting several days later. "I think it's a beautiful thing," said the student who introduced them to the audience, "when one of the brothers get into trouble he has a mother and a father to stand behind him."[7]

Early in the academic year 1969-70, the board of education issued its new set of guidelines "Rights and Responsibilities for Senior High School Students," which brought official board rules more nearly into line with state and federal enacted and court law.[8] Thus students would be allowed to be represented by counsel at suspension hearings, to distribute literature outside school buildings without prior authorization, and to distribute leaflets and other (noncommercial) literature inside the schools *with prior authorization.* The last, and other, rights must not "interfere with the operations of the regular school program." In addition to the question, noted earlier, of whether school authorities would observe the new regulations, the matter of what is or is not disruptive of school operations would presumably be decided by school authorities themselves. An example: during that very autumn, several students were suspended for sitting quietly at their desks during the class recitation of the pledge to the flag, on the grounds that their refusing either to stand and pledge or to leave the room during the ceremony was disruptive of class procedure.[9] (Abstaining from the pledge to the flag has on several occasions been held by the courts to be protected by the First Amendment.) As requiring a student to leave the room and then recalling him is certainly more intrusive than ignoring his nonparticipation, it seems clear that what was at stake in these cases was student rebellion and nonconformity.

In any case, the new guidelines failed even to recognize the generally inhuman security regulations and physical conditions which had prevailed long before the demand for "student civil rights." (It would be hard to imagine the board of education's addressing itself to the problem of providing toilet paper, soap, and public telephones for student use, although its 1969 contract with the UFT did just that for teachers.) Perhaps a court suit under the "cruel and unusual punishment" clause of the Eighth Amendment would be the most appropriate manner of approaching these conditions.

Loss of Power: Use of Force

If the authority of a relevant curriculum had failed at least a generation before, the power of the laws of compulsory attendance and competitive accreditation, which had substituted for it (badly), failed in 1968-69. And the high school system had nothing left to sustain itself but naked force. It exercised this force in two ways: by throwing students out and by calling the police in.

The unsound premise that produced the UFT's disastrous "disruptive child" clause in 1967 produced the rash of suspensions throughout the school year during the school year 1968-69. Many of the suspensions were summary and in violation of the board of education's own rules or simply of fair procedures.* For example, students, even some below the high school level, were suspended and sent home in the middle of the school day with the message that their parents would receive a letter to report for a hearing; the rule requires that the parent come and get the suspended child or that the child be kept in school until the end of the day. As a good many school rules, such as those having to do with leaving school before the end of the school day, are grounded on the rationale that the school is responsible for the students' safety during

* *My sources for statements regarding suspensions of students and transfers of teachers are mainly firsthand: teachers, students or their parents, and community activists. In addition, the* Free Press, *local student papers, and various community-control-oriented newsletters reported these events. While I checked out only a very few of them by going to the persons involved, the number of reports of such events that flooded the city during that year was clear evidence that something untoward was going on. The daily press, which regularly reported student "violence," and also school drug traffic, did not cover the action on the other side of the guerrilla war.*

school hours, the schools' violation of board of education rules would seem also to have been a violation of prudence and consistency. Again, students were suspended for longer than the permitted short five days without a hearing at the district superintendent level. Students were brought to district level hearings but not allowed to confront and question the accusing faculty member. Students were transferred from one school to another with no hearing at all. (When I questioned UFT supporters about teachers' very strong feelings against being transferred from one school to another without procedures, they explained that teachers become attached to schools, to particular routines, and to their colleagues, and that they should not be transferred "punitively," even at year end, without an impartial hearing. I should think that this rationale would apply even more strongly to transferring a student in the middle of the school year, when not only his social attachments but his school work, about which the school is presumably primarily concerned, would suffer.) At Franklin K. Lane High School, as I have mentioned, almost 700 students were disposed of in one sweep without even a pretense of consulting them or their parents. When parents who felt that they were not well informed of their children's rights sought to bring to the hearings to which they were summoned community leaders who might provide support and help, the leaders were usually denied admittance, police sometimes being called to eject them. Exclusion of community leaders, sometimes district school board members, from suspension hearings was based on the then-standing board of education by-law prohibiting suspended students, or their parents, from bringing "counsel" to such hearings. Exclusion, and sometimes ejection from the building, of these would-be helpers (or troublemakers, depending on the point of view) was based on a clause in the settlement of the Great Strike which tightened considerably admission of outsiders to school premises. What was happening in such situations was that parents were beginning to question the right of the school personnel to make unilateral decisions regarding their children and the school personnel, which had always before made such decisions without being questioned, felt, correctly, that there was a general movement afoot to undermine their powers.

While parents and community members could be ignored or dealt with summarily, there was no way of silencing them. Rebel teachers, on the other hand, were far more vulnerable. In school after school, and district after district, principals were letting teachers go who had worked during the strike and continued to be sympathetic to rebellious students and parents after the strike ended. Most of the nonstriking teachers were young men and women closer in age and weltanschauung to their students than to their senior colleagues and not yet torn away from that generational sympathy by the despair, or the esprit de corps which alone can stave off the despair, of teaching non-college bound New York City students in the public high schools. Many of these young nonstriking teachers, who had braved the picket lines together with their students, continued to play an independent role after "real" school resumed. For their attitude during and after the strike, they were sensed to be—as indeed they were—hostile to the school establishment. As many of them were teaching under substitute licenses or, if under regular licenses, were still on probation, they did not have the rights to tenure and to procedures which tenured teachers have. Scores and perhaps hundreds (there is no count) were asked to leave their schools at the end of the first semester or at the end of the year. Distaste for the UFT and a feeling that in a way it was on behalf of the UFT that they were being dispensed with prevented them from bringing grievances to that agent. (The story of one of these teachers is told below.) But whereas in previous years, students and parents might simply mourn a popular young teacher mysteriously transferred out of their school, now many groups of parents and/or students began to raise sand on behalf of these transferred teachers, and on several occasions succeeded in persuading the principal that perhaps, after all, retaining the teacher would prove less gritty than letting him go.

The position of the teachers being disciplined was especially anomalous in that the strongest teachers union America had ever seen had just successfully concluded the longest teachers strike America had ever experienced ostensibly on behalf of due process for teachers. And that union was tolerating, if not collaborating in, the most extensive political purge of teachers the New York schools had ever conducted. In insisting on defending the Ocean

Hill-Brownsville Nineteen by striking the entire school system, the union leadership had taken the position: "If we can let it happen to one of us in one school or one district, it can happen to all of us all over the city. Not one of us will be safe in our jobs." Almost more than anything else, it was the specter of (black) community leaders firing teachers left and right that had rallied the teachers to the union call in September, 1968. And now it was mainly the young and the maverick who were experiencing just such a mass purge, not at the hands of students and community but for actions on behalf of them.

The UFT as a citywide body was relatively unconcerned about the violation of students' and teachers' procedural rights. At the individual school level, teachers, and especially UFT chapter chairmen, often took the lead in vigorous and aggressive counterattack against student, teacher, and parent rebels, without much regard for the niceties of due process. Their objects were those who had opposed them during the strike and continued to oppose them after it. The union's strategy all along had been that rules and procedures are worthless to protect teachers if there is no strong union to guarantee their enforcement. Now, if the union's strength was threatened by antiunion rebels, then they, not the union, must be sacrificed. The *United Teacher* published more or less straight factual accounts of student misbehaviors but nothing about the schools' attacks on students and their teacher supporters. In May, the union's Executive Board issued a position paper on student unrest which ascribed student unrest to school overcrowding, the need for remedial services, and the tide of unrest sweeping the country and the world. The paper called for more money and creative solutions to youth's discontent, and it scored (student) violence as undemocratic.[10] It did not repeat the resolution which the Delegate Assembly had adopted at the time of the Fucillo Affair supporting a fair hearing for student and parent grievances, although the position paper would certainly have been an appropriate occasion for such a rememberance. Under the heading "Viewpoints: Principals vs. Students," the *United Teacher* also published excerpts from a document issued by the High School Principals Association "Limits of Dissent" and next to that accounts of actions regarding student grievances in Grinnell, Iowa, Sylvester, Georgia, and Oakland, California (!).[11]

I think it must be acknowledged that the principals of the city schools were quite right to see a grave threat in all the little acts and symbols of rebellion – the long hair and the shades, the student papers with their dirty words and the pictures of Eldridge Cleaver, the students who insisted on going to school when the teachers said the schools must be closed and on staying out when the teachers said the schools were to be open. It was all very well for the lawyers to insist on the students' constitutional rights to freedom of costume and freedom of speech. But the principals recognized, if the lawyers did not, that, as in Czechoslovakia and elsewhere throughout the civilized and semicivilised world, little freedoms granted lead to big freedoms demanded. And the principals sensed, as I believe the lawyers did not, but as many students did, that the system, having so little legitimate authority left, could not survive a serious assault on its power.

The principals did not intend to preside over the dissolution of "their" school system. Accordingly they issued a manifesto seeking to put their plight before the public and enlist its support.

The report, "The Nature and Limits of Student Dissent and Participation" (January, 1969), continued the appeal to the backlash anxieties to which the Great Strike had given direction and purpose. "Disorders and fears of new and frightening dimensions stalk the corridors of many of our schools," the principals said, evoking images of dope pushers, rapists, and arson-minded mobs. The report pictured a few students as being manipulated by "small destructive groups [which] are a menace to their education and security" and which are "working to radicalize, subvert, and poison the minds of our students." (At Nat Turner High, when the first issues of a one-page mimeographed student paper began to appear, teachers called for an FBI investigation. What must have flipped them was one rhyming headline, "No One Can L--k Our D--k.") The principals' report aroused the older generation's sexual and social as well as political anxieties by referring to the student papers as "obscene, gamy . . . strident, belligerent, and arrogant" and by appealing to "community canons of good taste and good manners."

The principals, who had for so long been running their schools like autonomous spheres with almost no administrative control over anything but their paper procedures, now, when their powers were being challenged, were looking for an authority to take control. A member of a civil liberties organization who had called a principal's violation of law and administrative order to the attention of a high board of education official, had been told, "Well, it's his school." "But he's breaking the law." "Well, I can't tell a principal how to run his school." But in 1968-69, desperate in their impotence, the principals were pleading for someone to come in and take over for them.

The report began and ended with elegant political flourishes: "Pre-occupied with the dismantling of a school system it does not understand or care about, our Board of Education seems unable or unwilling to come to the defense of our beleaguered schools." The reference is to Mayor Lindsay's "pro-community-control" board of education (headed by John Doar). "No one appears to be in charge. No one appears to be listening." The coda of the report trumpets: "We call on our Mayor, our Board of Education, our Superintendent of Schools, to stop surrendering our schools piecemeal to the foundations, the opportunists, the extremists, the unrealists."

In their defense it must be pointed out that the principals really did not know how to go on doing the job that they had been entrusted by society to do. Their desperate appeal seemed to help arouse the Mayor to certain political realities in New York and to pave the way for his turn a few weeks later away from the black reformists toward the white liberals.

When he spoke to the Bronx mass meeting in March, Ron Dicks's father said:

I just heard over the radio that the High School Principals Association blames the high school disorders on a few adult agitators "who move from school to school." I *know* they can't be talking about me! [Laughter.] It's unfortunate that the Mayor has fallen in this trap. He was beautiful when he served on the Kerner Commission, and he said that white racism has caused the trouble in this country. I don't see how he could switch his position so fast!

Maybe it wasn't even fast enough. The Mayor was sitting in a hot seat. With the mayoralty primaries just around the corner, he was being blamed for everything that made New York an ever-more inelegant city, from the mountains of uncollected garbage sharing the sidewalks with the bumper-to-bumper pedestrians to a heavy snowstorm. If only somebody would make the kids shut up for a little while, maybe he could slide through the primaries in June.

Both the board and the Mayor made little gestures to a "progressive" approach to the high school students. The board's gesture was the appointment of a committee on student participation in high school affairs composed of principals, teachers, parents, students, a UFT representative, and two representatives of headquarters. Expectedly, the committee came up with a soft report containing recommendations mainly in the fringe area of student government. And even there, the recommendations (which no individual school principal was mandated to observe) did not meet conventional American standards of democracy and legality. For example, the report proposed lowering but not eliminating grade-average requirements for student government office. The report also suggested that students be allowed the "privilege of expressing opinions on the formation of codes of dress" (although codes of dress, except as to safety, were outlawed entirely by both the state commissioner of education and the city superintendent of schools).

The Mayor's gesture was the appointment of a Task Force on Student Unrest whose members sought to bring together administrators, parents, and student leaders at the individual school level. The Task Force's ineffectuality was assured by the activists' amused contempt for it and the school officials' resentment of it (that is, it lacked legitimacy in both camps, for opposite reasons). The real participants to the struggle knew that the conflict between a fundamental attack on the school system and a back-to-the-wall defense of it could not be turned into an amiable search for a compromise.

In any case, the main reliance of both board and Mayor was on force in the form of the police department.

In March, Lindsay involved the police department as a full-fledged partner in "solving" the high school problem and called for the arrest of student disrupters. His law-and-order position was echoed by "liberal" president of the board of education, John Doar, in a public statement emphasizing security and disciplinary procedures, and by Superintendent of Schools Bernard Donovan in a circular entitled "Student Participation and School Security."[12] The circular dealing almost entirely with security, very little with participation, provided official authorization for the repressive, illegal, undemocratic policies the principals had been employing for some months. It also provided for the establishment of what amounted to a "police school system" (to adapt the term "police state").

Meeting Force with Violence

The collaboration between school and police assayed tentatively in Ocean Hill-Brownsville, and then repeated over a longer period but still on a limited front at P.S. 39, was escalated into a way of life in many high schools beginning in the early spring of 1969. As the spark of revolt had passed from the grownups to the students, so also did the tactical maneuvers which the defenders had first tried out in earlier stages against the earlier rebels.

Although the law in New York State excludes police from schools except where a crime has been committed on school property or where the police have a warrant for arrest,[13] it had been common practice in many schools for one or two patrolmen to be stationed near the cafeteria in the middle of the day. But the new police presence was considerably more than that. Police were deployed in considerable numbers outside school buildings, and they patrolled the corridors as if they were public streets. They reinforced administrative orders by their presence as well as by their power to arrest. Perhaps to relieve the drain on police department resources, perhaps to reduce the provocative effect of armed police inside schools, in April a force of specially trained, unarmed "security guards" were assigned to the problem schools, with power to make arrests.

The police presence in heavily or predominantly nonwhite high schools and in many junior highs meant that in those schools there was a devaluation of the customary authority figures and an escalation of punishment. The seriousness of suspension, previously the supreme punishment, was reduced as suspensions throughout the system soared, and arrest took the place of suspension. In Franklin K. Lane High School, for example, where seven hundred students were summarily suspended by mass mail order, a student was arrested and held for days without notice to his family.

The Brownsville Community Council, checking a report from a member of the Lane Commission on Human Rights, discovered that a Lane [High School] student had been imprisoned for six days on Riker's Island after arrest and handcuffing at the school on Feb. 6. . . . His mother reported him missing to the police. Two days later she received a letter from the school . . . asking her to accompany her son to the school on Feb. 13. On Tuesday, Feb. 11, the boy's sister called the school . . . and learned that her brother was in jail.[14]

The police presence in the schools did not mean, of course, that many, or in some schools most, students did not continue to respond to the old disciplinary sanctions even while the police patrolled their corridors, or that police were present in all schools or at all times. It did mean that police rather than parent or dean or principal had been added as the ultimate in the conventional sequence of authorities. The addition of another rank at the top tends to devalue the ranks below it. Who is going to tremble before the threat of being sent to the principal's office when he knows the principal himself is so frightened that his only resort is to call the cops? One of the boys at the Turner High reflected something of the new situation in a comment about a previously much-feared dean who "was the one that was responsible for the Rap Brown incident": "He also got some of our members busted and bloodied up a lot by the police. He's afraid of us now. He'd better be. Because we're not afraid of him."

Newspaper headlines, media reports, and New Yorkers' general anxieties about their fellow citizens led to a general belief that the police had been called in to the schools to prevent dope taking and violence. While police did arrest people for possession of dope and did break up fights —there was, in fact, considerable violence in the schools—

the students felt that the quashing of dissent, not the matters of pushing or fighting, was the primary object of the police power:

On Friday, January 10, a student was taken to the hospital from Junior High School 22 after taking an overdose of drugs. On three separate occasions teachers have found male students shooting up drugs in the boys' toilets. On one occasion the pusher was also there, but when the teacher returned after going for help, the pusher had escaped. How is it that pushers can enter the school at will, but when a parent comes to see about the suspension of her child, policemen are called to remove her? *[Emphasis in original]*[15]

As we have seen, dope taking and pushing were tolerated in the high schools for many years (or anyway not dealt with), to the distress of many parents and students. Many rebel students, especially the black rebels, tended to frown on dope taking, saying, "The Man wants us to take dope." In at least one black group dope taking in any form at any time was grounds for expulsion. They believed that "going off and getting stoned is no solution to their problems," as a reporter wrote in the *Free Press*, adding that they also saw no solution in "setting themselves up in a confrontation with the pigs and getting massacred."[16]

The inverse relationship of dope taking (copping out) to protesting (fighting back) was also observed by defenders of the system. "H.S. CRISIS: 'MORE DRUGS, LESS VIOLENCE' " read the headline of a column by Joseph Alsop reprinted in the very conservative *New York Daily Column.*[17] The column quoted Elliott Shapiro, "one of this city's most humanely wise school superintendents" (and, it should also be said, one of the few former adult misfits who did not rise to the new situation by becoming a rebel): "More drugs, less violence; less drugs, more violence; that's about the size of it!" The columnist pointed to the relative calm at Hughes High School in Manhattan, where "40 per cent of the students have reached the stage of heroin use, or at least of heroin experiments." He compared this school with Franklin K. Lane High School, a school beset by more overt troubles not only then but for some years previous. Once, in a period when high school students only had trouble but didn't make much trouble, I had heard Shapiro lament that he could not get enough police assigned to Hughes to help him control the narcotics traffic there. At Lane, on the other hand, when the long endemic student violence began to be turned against the school, that is, began to be politicized, then police manpower was made available to help contain the situation.

The school violence which had become the object of so much concern tended to take three forms: fighting among students, the setting of fires, and attacks on teachers. All three were either unaffected or aggravated by the police presence.

Fights among students, usually in the cafeteria, seemed to increase in 1968-69 in both frequency and intensity. The press and school personnel commonly ascribed the student fighting to "overcrowding" and "racial tensions." The former can probably be discounted as a reason, the schools in which much fighting occurred not being the most overcrowded or any more overcrowded than they had been in previous years. But racial tensions were, indeed, higher, both throughout the city and often in the specific neighborhoods in which the troubled schools were located. Lane High School, for example, was located in a lower-middle-class and working-class white area, but its student body was composed not only of students from that area but of almost 50 percent black and Puerto Rican students, many from nearby Bedford-Stuyvesant and Ocean Hill-Brownsville, which neighborhoods had insufficient high school facilities of their own. This situation was repeated in many areas throughout the city, reflecting decades of the city's failure to provide high school facilities to meet the needs of its black and Puerto Rican communities. In these white neighborhoods, small shopkeepers and residents frequently complained of the daily "influx" of noisy and sometimes rude black and Puerto Rican teenagers. In the vicinity of Lane a right-wing, avowedly antiblack and anti-Puerto Rican political group sought the transfer of the nonwhite students from the school, and black students complained they were sometimes harassed on their way between busstop and school.* The radical black and Puerto

* *When, in June, the board of education sought to alleviate these pressures at Lane by transferring some of the nonwhite students to more heavily white schools even further away from their homes, the*

Rican student groups responded to this general situation by including in their demands neighborhood high schools for black and Puerto Rican students. But inside the troubled schools the familiar phenomenon of resonance produced among individual students, white and black alike, an increase in fighting, or "chaos schools, high school division." The student response was undoubtedly aggravated by the decline in adult authority and the provocative presence of the police.

Willie Gallagher, who had some dealings with radical black students in this time, commented on the fights: "They was always fights in cafeterias. There ain't no more now. Only thing is, teacher use to come say, 'Break it up,' they break it up. Now they don't listen no more."

And Jerry Connelly, a white student from a school similar to Lane, said: "The police are here and it just increases all the tension in the place. It makes people feel like we can't take this shit. When the police are here, the black guy looks at the the white guy and says, 'Wow, the police are here to stop us from fighting, so let's have a fight.' It just increases tension."

The setting of fires, like the fighting, was a "chaos school" symptom. It was also for some radical students a deliberate expression of their conscious hostility to school as an institution. However much it risks damaging the arsonist himself, setting fires is a common enough symptom of personal or group rebelliousness. Witness the disturbed-child arsonist; the vast fires, in which they burned their own harvests, set by French peasants throughout the countryside in the summer of 1789; and the setting of fires by blacks in the urban uprising in the last years. The police did not seem to have been at all effective in curbing this symptom, nor to my knowledge were any of the arsonists ever apprehended.

Physical attacks by students on teachers was another form of what we may call violent acts of rebellion. Student assaults on teachers—at least by teenagers—are almost

white residents of those neighborhoods complained bitterly, and the Mayor, now sensitive to his image among the white voters, reproached the board of education for having produced the transfer plan without consulting him. The entire exchange produced the uncomfortable impression that the authorities had more black and Puerto Rican students than they liked or knew what to do with.

always in response to hostile verbal or physical acts committed by the teachers against the students, or series of such acts. I personally was a strict and controlling teacher in a "bad" high school. I had a physical encounter with a student only once, when I made the mistake of trying physically to restrain a very angry girl from leaving a room. Even then she merely tried to shake off the restraint and did not actually strike at me. I came in that encounter, however, to understand the way in which merely touching an agitated student arouses intense feelings of hostility in both teacher and student and makes them want to strike at each other. An enormous degree of self-control is required to prevent oneself from doing so.

In the school year 1968-69, the most dangerous and widely publicized attack on a teacher occurred in Franklin K. Lane High School, where Frank Siracusa, a white science teacher, was sprayed with lighter fluid and then ignited by three young black men. The attackers were not inhibited, identified, or even apprehended *although uniformed patrolmen were deployed both inside and outside the building at the time of the attack*. Siracusa escaped without serious injuries.

The attack came in the wake of strike-aggravated hostilities, including painting of swastikas, flying the Confederate flag, a couple of harsh police attacks on students, and fights between black and white students. Siracusa was considered to be a Wallace supporter and party to general anti-Negro sentiment in the neighborhood and in the school, sentiment which expressed itself at one point in a teacher's telling a newspaper reporter, "Well, we're not going to live with fear. I think if the black people don't get into line, then we'll either have to annihilate them or neutralize them. That's not as harsh as it sounds. It has happened in other societies. It may be the only way of dealing with this."[18] One radical white student reported about Siracusa: "He has a long history of harrassing students. He used to just walk up and down the cafeteria and he would bust a lot of people for one reason or another. He would just go up to you and harass you—yell at you—take you to the dean. Students don't just indiscriminately pick out teachers and beat on them. They do have reasons."

The Siracusa attack was not, strictly speaking, in the

category of impulse acts of rebellion, but rather a part of a general campaign on the part of Lane's black student rebels to get rid of teachers they felt to be racists. "We all came to a conclusion," a student said in an interview about the situation, "that we have to get them sooner or later in any way possible."

The attack on Siracusa, the fighting, and the fires may be regarded as analogous to the terrorist acts of a people controlled by the force of an authority whose legitimacy they do not recognize. In a relationship of increasing brutality, each hostile group loses sight of individuals in the other group and attacks only representatives of the enemy, using the weapons of attack at their disposal. Thus the mass suspension of black students from Lane was a solution by power without concern for the record or fate of the individuals suspended. A subsequent police attack on protesting students in the street was conducted without regard for the specific behavior of the individuals being attacked, demonstrating that it is the situation, and not the difference between a Mayor Daley and a Mayor Lindsay, that prevails. The students' violent responses to their long-term grievances as well as to the more immediate acts of counter-resistance by the schools' defenders were usually made without a nice concern for the individual responsibility of the individuals who might be damaged. However, the school defenders and in general the public did not see the two hostile groups as equally immoral, so to speak, in their use of force, but tended to justify such violent acts of the defenders as they knew about as necessary for the protection of a legitimate institution, and to condemn the acts of the rebels as violent and destructive.

4. THE END OF INNOCENCE

In the climax to an English film (Lindsay Anderson's *If . . .*) that was very popular with teenagers and young adults, especially men, in the early months of 1969, a progressive-minded, boyish headmaster of a harshly despotic boys prep school has a rendezvous with violent death. A fierce guerrilla battle, with machine guns, rifles, and hand grenades, is in progress between four rebellious students and a girl positioned on a roof and. below them in the landscaped courtyard, the rest of the students along with the staff and elegant guests, who have been driven out of a chapel ceremony by a fire which the rebels have set. Alone and unarmed, the comradely headmaster suddenly rises from among the crouching defenders and with soft authority stills their fire. Then he calls to the rebels on the roof, firm benevolence in his voice, "Boys, boys, I understand you." Plunk! a ball makes a neat round hole right between his eyes, and grimacing moronically he sinks out of sight.

So did Mayor John Lindsay and the liberals of New York City get plunked between the eyes in the mayoralty primaries of June, 1969, and Lindsay's playing of the role of understanding headmaster was largely responsible.

Winner of the race for the Republican nomination against liberal John Lindsay was John Marchi, very conservative state senator from the very conservative borough of Staten Island, who had been catapulted to such citywide and statewide prominence as he attained by the United Federation of Teachers, when he shared with them the authorship and the sponsorship of both the 1968 and the 1969 anticommunity "decentralization" bills passed by the state legislature in Albany. In his campaign for mayor, he proclaimed himself to be " 'very, very hawkish' toward crime and civil disorder"; he saw the police as almost the only possible instruments of restoring " 'some kind of tranquillity in the life of the people' "; and he said of the Kerner Commission report on civil disorder, " 'The Kerner Commission didn't develop anything that wasn't known to us already, though I don't always agree with its conclusions. There problems were not that massive 20 or 30 years ago when everyone had his place' " (a condition of society that might be restored, one might infer, by judicious police action).[1]

Winner of the Democratic primary (against trade-union-oriented Robert Wagner and liberal Herman Badillo) was equally conservative Mario Procaccino, the city comptroller whose action in releasing the teachers' salary checks for a number of weeks during which they were on strike earned him extravagant praise from the UFT plus three articles in one issue of the *United Teacher*, including two photographs evidencing another facet of New York's ecumenical trend – one of Procaccino and his family having an audience with Pope Paul, and one of Procaccino, yarmulke on head, at the Wailing Wall in Israel.[2]

The ecumenical trend which in the camp of the city's defenders was beginning to render indistinguishable Jew and Gentile, conservative and liberal, policeman and teacher, in the camp of the rebels was beginning to unite black and white, teacher and student, parent and child, Honors student and General student. And in both camps individuals were beginning to perceive more clearly the roles and the status the system assigned them. In other words, they were beginning to get themselves "together."

Getting together inevitably involves some loss of innocence. The high school principals warned in one document ("Confrontation and Response," prepared primarily for the group's own consumption) that the "corrupt fringe" of the radicals must not be allowed to "seduce the innocent." Indeed many New Yorkers began to lose their innocence in that year after the Great Strike, but not to seducers. Some black Honors students, who had before always been "good Negroes" (in the words of one), lost their innocence when they passed between the hostile pickets to open their school. A white working-class General student lost his simple "antinigger" innocence when he began to see in what ways he and the "niggers" were in the same boat. An idealistic young teacher who had planned to become a principal because he thought the way to have better schools would be in his words "to have nice people" running them, lost his innocence as he kept bumping into ordinary nice people doing some not very nice things. And the principals themselves lost their innocence when they came to see that in their struggles with the children their own survival as a power group was at stake.

Three black students, Karen Butler, Naomi Carnes, and Jackie Glover were college-bound seniors at Taft High School in the Bronx, the school from which Ronald Dicks had been suspended for "passing out" unauthorized literature. Interviewed by Julius Lester over a New York listener-sponsored radio station (WBAI) in February and March 1969, the three girls said:

Naomi: *I had a run-in with a teacher when he realized that I was in support of some black militant students. . . He said: "I've never felt any animosity from you. How can you back up what these fellows have to say?" I answered: "It's very simple. We're all black. We all have the same goals. We might not all be following the same route, but we intend on getting to the same place." I found the same attitude in many of the teachers after the UFT strike. They are constantly trying to cut me off from the rest of the black students by telling me, "Naomi, you're an intelligent student, and you want to go to college." . . . There's always this kind of undertone. You always feel like you're being plucked—like a petal from a flower.*

Karen: *I was really a good Negro for three years in that school. I was in the honor school and I was a perfect Negro.*

But with the strike everything changed. "Karen, you're a intelligent student" and "Karen, I don't understand." What they were really . . . saying was that I was being influenced. Of course I'm being influenced; a lot of things came to me and made a lot of sense. I can get a lot of places by acting quite well and capitalizing on my honor school, but at the same time I realize it was only by accident that I happened to be in honor school. Most black kids are not.

Jackie: *Everything was fine before the strike. But once they were on the picket line we could see what was going on. We saw hatred in the teachers' eyes. Like we had 10 teachers who came into the school and helped us to open it. They told us they had been threatened; their time cards were destroyed; very malicious comments were made from the picket line. Now while I was out there I saw all this, so when I came back I had a different attitude altogether. When I came back the teacher said: "You don't smile anymore." Now here I was out of school for 10 weeks because of the teachers' strike, and they want me to smile! . . . And then they said: "Well, Jackie, your attitude has changed. You used to be a nice, sweet girl." I'm not sweet anymore because I saw for the first time what was really going on in that school.*[3]

There is some confusion here about whether Jackie was in a "liberated" Taft High School with the strike-breaking teachers during the strike, or whether she stayed out of school. Despite this confusion and despite the occasional rhetoric in which the three girls express their sentiments, I think the strike must, indeed, have been, as they say, a shocking and reorienting experience for them.

The "conversion" of Jerry Connelly, one of the white boys under the elevated and a senior in the General course at Bartolomeo Vanzetti High School, is described by the interviewer who became his friend during the year of the rebellious flareups following the Great Strike. The interviewer went to Vanzetti High at first because the troubles in that school had been officially described as arising out of racial hostilities between black and white (working-class) students. He wanted to find out how the white students viewed themselves not only in relation to the black students but also in relation to the school administrators and teachers. Their hostilities, their feelings of powerlessness, their alienation from school are reflected in the initial interview with them reported in earlier portions of this section of the book. At the end of the school year, the interviewer wrote a report of Jerry's education during his last semester before graduating from Vanzetti High.

When I first went out to Vanzetti [the interviewer writes], I dressed kind of straight: after all, working class kids don't like hippies and do love the flag. The day I went was Black Monday—so-called by the black students—and there was supposed to be some sort of happening there, put on by the blacks. So there were lots of cops, and groups of kids standing idly around. I was suprised to see that there were no white working-class kids though. I did notice a few groups of whites, but they looked like hippies—bell-bottoms, long hair, etc. So they must have been middle class. On the other hand, they were hanging out like lower-class kids do. I mean just standing around—watching things—not talking much. I don't know what it is, but hanging out is not a middle-class pasttime. Later I came to realize that these fellows were lower class and dressed like hippies as a sign of rebellion, the same as some middle-class kids do, and that they regard straight kids (like one who plans to be a cop) as punks. One of the kids later told me that he thought I was a detective. And for a long time Jerry was always suspecting that I would betray him.

These students tended to be morbidly suspicious of anyone who looked square to them. On one occasion, when the interviewer was ill and could not keep an appointment with them, I went in his stead. Although by this time the interviewer more or less had their confidence and although they knew that he was working for a lady writer, during the whole time I was with them, I felt that they were looking at me from under lowered lids. Actually they were ambivalent in a way that touched me and helped me overcome my initial shock at their naked racism. There was a kind of reaching out for the satisfaction of being listened to seriously by an adult who knew the school situation in which they lived. And that made them want to talk endlessly. On the other hand, surges of prudence kept warning them that I might well be a clever agent from the enemy camp, and they would suddenly clam up on a quite trivial matter. When they met the interviewer again the next time, they told him that they had suspected that he had been arrested and that I was actually a lady detective, not an altogether unrealistic suspicion in view of the fact that some of them had been "busted" on a couple of occasions.

Jerry had been an activist before I met him. He said that the school was like a concentration camp and the 45 minutes extra was just to make up for the teachers' lost time, so why should the students have to pay for their lost time, right? During the first student boycott (against the extra 45 minutes) he and some friends had joined the black students in rioting in the cafeteria, protesting in the street, and going down to Washington Square. When the black students moved on out to Ocean Hill-Brownsville, they split. Another white student, who was close to the blacks' group, once described to me how one of the days of the boycott, these armies of cops just started marching down on the students, how the students got scared and started to run, and that was a signal for the cops to run after them, to beat them, club them, knock them down. Jerry used the word "pig" for the cops, just like the black kids and the radical white kids, even though some of his friends' fathers are cops.

But still he had a dual alliance: one was to anyone who was an enemy of the authorities (especially of the cops and the school administrators); the other was to white people. He used "nigger," and seemed to both hate and be jealous of blacks. I think he sensed somehow that they were more together than he was, and since he considered them inferior to him, he hated them for that. All the fellows were pro-war, but of course none of them wanted to go. Still, they said that draft-card burning and peace demonstrations made the United States look like punks to the rest of the world.

All the fellows were racists. But still they were all willing to argue and listen to me. Once I was having a discussion with a guy who's a cousin to some Mafiamen, and after ten minutes, he turned to the others and said, "Hey, somebody come help me, because I'm losing this argument." Jerry, who was the most racist of all, was at the same time talking with some of the black leaders at Vanzetti. The first action Jerry and his frinds planned was for Thursday before the Monday that was to set off the students' spring offensive. On Wednesday, they handed out leaflets saying, "The time will come soon for student power. Are you ready?" Also that day, Jerry approached Tito, a black leader, for support in his (Jerry's) demonstration. Tito said, "What's the demonstration about?" And Jerry responded, "We're supporting the ten demands." Tito almost fell over he was so surprised. Tito apparently understood Jerry to mean that he was supporting the demands that the black students had made on the principal, whereas Jerry meant the [white] High School Student Union demands. Actually, it made little difference: they both knew that both sets of demands were essentially the same.

But the same time that he was working with them, he still was always suspecting that the blacks would betray him. "They can talk friendly to me, but I know what they really think," he would say.

Sometime later Jerry was describing how this "nigger" stood up to the dean, and he was laughing when he told it, out of enjoyment at seeing the dean told off. Clearly, he was on the side of the "nigger." He was beginning to see that the black students really get it just as rough as he does, and he was going on talking with the black student leaders. All that had more of an effect than anything I could say.

*Memorial Day weekend he and I hitched out to Rockaway Beach. One of the rides we caught was with a couple of white guys who started talking about "the niggers." Jerry and I were sitting in the back. We looked at each other, and he was laughing—*at them.

He seemed to be saying, "What can you do? They don't know any better."

While the adult defenders of the system were coalescing in a way that blurred the distinctions between liberal and conservative by pushing the former toward the latter, the young rebels were beginning to cross the age-old American color barrier. Jerry Connelly was the son of the kind of people who, if they were Republicans, supported "law and order" Marchi or, if they were Democrats, "law and order" Procaccino. In another period he would likely have been a law-and-order man himself. In this period he seemed to be moving away from the use of police force toward the use of people force. Somewhere long ago and far away a great-grandparent of his might have heard southern Populist Tom Watson say, "You are kept apart that you may be separately fleeced . . . You are made to hate each other because upon that hatred is rested the keystone of the arch of . . . despotism which enslaves you both. You are deceived and blinded that you may not see how this race antagonism perpetuates a . . . system which beggars both."[4]

But when the interviewer last saw him, Jerry had not gone beyond the point of no return. Once, one of his black fellow students had said to him, "You know damn well you ain't going to be out there with me and try to stop a tank when you can get *in* one." Who knows? Maybe the black fellow student knew the later history of Tom Watson and was right about Jerry.

James Horelick, a young high school English teacher, lost his innocence (although not his good humor or his charm) perhaps because he had too much of it. Product of a Connecticut farm family and Amherst College, he was spiritually not prepared for New York's smart cynicism and clever manipulativeness when he came there to teach in 1966. Not a trade unionist, not interested in politics, in effect unworldly, he took people and events at face value—as he expected to be taken at face value—and was outraged when he found himself betrayed.

He said about the Great Strike: "Well, the big cry in the strike was 'due process,' and I must say frankly I didn't even know what due process was. I suppose I sound kind of simple—like I don't know anything, but I am really pretty sharp. I'm just not interested in politics."

His first assignment for the year 1966-67, was in a predominantly black and Puerto Rican high school, where his students were reading two and three years below grade level and the only books he had to give them were battered twenty-year-old hand-me-downs containing teenage tales illustrated with white faces and 1940-vintage cars and styles. He hated the school bureaucracy, which he felt was designed to "relieve you of any contact with human beings," and began to take courses in school administration, "because it seemed to me the way to have better schools was to have nice people running the schools."

He describes his department chairman as a "little old maid who hated men" and systematically sought replacements for any men teachers she was forced to take on. But he quickly became fond of his students (his subsequent career shows him to be a man who cares for teenagers in a simple, direct way and aims to do them good), so when his chairman used a flimsy pretext for writing a bad report about him and then having him transferred out, he protested to the principal and the UFT chapter chairman. The department chairman said he hadn't had a lesson plan for a lesson she had observed. "I was a very conscientious teacher," he explained, "and I used to spend all my evenings typing up my lesson plans, so I was insulted by what she said in the write-up, and I wouldn't sign it." The principal told him he would give him a fine reference if he would go along quietly. And the UFT chapter chairman patted him paternally on the back and said, "You're young and it's all in the game. This is the way the board of education works. You're going to a new school, and it's going to be a better school, and you're going to make the same pay. So why the fuss?" Up to that point he'd been thinking about joining the UFT, but he decided against it when the chapter chairman advised him firmly to go along with the deal.

To the principal and the chapter chairman he must have seemed, as in a sense he was, young and simple-minded. In a few years he would come to understand how the system works and settle down to working with it. He did come to understand how the system works; he did not settle down to working with it.

He was serving his probationary period at Washington Irving High School, a predominantly nonwhite all-girls school in Manhattan, when the UFT went out on strike in 1967. He helped man the picket line for several days until he began to think that the UFT slogan "TEACHERS WANT WHAT CHILDREN NEED" did not represent what the strike was about. "I told the chapter chairman that if I could have a sign that said 'GIVE ME MORE MONEY,' I would go on picketing. But he told me that would be unprofessional. So I thought 'That's enough of that,' and the next day, I went to work."

When the UFT again struck the schools in 1968, Horelick was ambivalent. On the one hand, the Ocean Hill-Brownsville people were being arbitrarily transferred—*just as he had been*—and not even at the end of the term. On the other hand, he felt that the transferred nineteen were really opposed to the community-control idea even if, as Rhody McCoy claimed, they weren't actively sabotaging it, so it seemed right for McCoy to want to transfer them. "It seemed like the principle they were working on—to have some sort of community or parent or people's say in the school—was the right principle. So I decided that balancing the pros and the cons, I wanted *not* to be on the UFT side."

While he was still balancing the pros and cons, he attended a meeting of his union chapter, and, telling about it later, he recalled two speakers whose remarks must have influenced his decision:

There was one lady there whom I admired very much. Kind of an elderly lady who went down to march in Martin Luther King's funeral procession. You know then there were rumors of all kinds—riots and violence—and I thought she was pretty great for that. She got up and said, "What are we striking against? Are we striking against the board of education? What is the point in it?" And nobody wanted to listen to her. A man got up and said, "Just remember what we are striking against! If we don't strike, we are going to be teaching on our knees while the Rap Browns come in and tell us what to teach." A very hysterical meeting.

We have a school with a lot of nonunion members and a lot of frightened old lady teachers who last year [1967] didn't go on strike at all. And I was really embarrassed to join them. But they all wound up going on strike even though they are not union members.

Before the Council of Supervisory Associations and the custodians union formally announced support for the strike, Horelick along with a handful of rebel students and other rebel teachers crossed the picket line, first in a neighboring high school and then in his own Washington Irving.

It was really a bad scene going through the picket lines [at the neighboring high school]. They were shouting at the kids, and they followed us in and started to give the kids a really hard time and some of [the kids] started crying. And the janitor or somebody began to play loud music over the PA system and ring the fire bells. And a guy came in who was some sort of connection with the union and began to berate the teacher in charge.

Eventually a tiny group of Washington Irving students and teachers, made plans to recruit more students, open the lunchroom, and run a meaningful all-day program. It was just at that point that the CSA and the janitors really closed down and locked up the schools. Aroused rather than beaten by being balked, Horelick's group along with some parents sought a court order against the principal of Washington Irving to force him to let them in to their school.

We got all excited. We were going to have our day in court, and we were going to get the school open. We were about 20 or 30 kids and 10 teachers and parents. There was a lawyer for Landman [the acting district superintendent] and a lawyer for the principal and a lawyer for the janitor. And they all got up and said something like, "There is no point to this action. It is being settled elsewhere." And the judge just slapped his gavel on the table and said, "Postponed to November 1st." So that was our day in court.

They then went to the office of the district superintendent and finally secured a letter authorizing them to keep school at Washington Irving.

And we were all elated again and we expected that after trying and trying, we were finally going to get in. So we went to the janitor and showed him the letter and he looked at the letter, and he turned it over, and he said "This is no letter. How do I know this is the real signature?" And gosh! you just begin to get the picture after so many things happen to you, like gosh, really everybody wanted that strike to keep going, except us. And all the kids were so mad! By then we had about 50 girls from our school and 50 boys from Stuyvesant. And they were really mad and the boys just wanted to break into the school. So I went out and bought some crowbars to open the doors—I and another teacher. We figured the kids were just going to break in by themselves and we should not stand by and let them do it, we should be the ones to do it and take the responsibility for doing it. The janitors were running around nailing the windows shut, But I found one window in the basement that was not only unlocked but wide open, and it had a gate over it and the gate was ajar. So, I figured the boys and I would go in the window, and then open the door and let all the other kids in. This, by the way, was happening all over the city, people were breaking into the schools. And I went in the window and turned around—and no kids in back of me! I ran up the staircase and I opened the door and ran right into the janitor who was coming down the stairs, so he called the cops who were in the school. And the cops just grabbed me. And they beat me up.

They put handcuffs on me and took me to the front lobby of the school. There is a desk there and they said to me something like "Sit down!" or "Get out your wallet" or some such thing. I just felt cantankerous and I said "No!" So this cop grabbed me and laid me down on the desk and he began to choke me with his nightstick. I began to swear at him through my gasps, and all of his friends came over—about seven or eight cops. They grabbed me by the arms and legs and dragged me out of sight of the glass doors of the lobby. They do it very cleverly. As they drag you, they bounce your arms and legs up and down on the floor—a very hard marble floor—and it is really kind of painful. And one of them—and this is when I *really* got scared—one of them grabbed my head and lifted it up about a foot from the floor and was going to smash it down on the floor, and that's when I felt like that's good-by, but one of the other cops said, "Hey! You better lay off." And they stopped doing everything and they stood me against the wall and the custodian came over and he said he wanted me arrested for burglary, and breaking and entering, and trespassing.

When we came out to the police car, the police had me by the arms, and the people have since told me that when I came out I had my jacket under my arm, and my shirt was all ripped. And I was all dazed and really horrible looking. So they got all excited and started mobbing the patrol car and beating on the roof. The cops pushed me into the car and one of the teachers said she wanted to go, too. Like trying to say, "He's not the only guilty one. We are all equally responsible." So they took her along and one of the kids. At the station house, they let the kid go. They charged me with trespassing and resisting arrest. And they charged her with nothing but resisting arrest. That's all.

You know we didn't try to break into the school until we had this letter of authorization [from the district superintendent], and all these other pronouncements from John Doar [the president of the board of education] saying we are supposed to be in the school. And the janitor and the DA won't drop the charges. For three years I was never absent from school. And now I have to take one day a week off to go to court, we had to go six or seven times. We are still trying to get the charges dismissed.

In November, John Doar announced that wherever teachers and students were prepared to attend schools, the schools must be opened, and a phone number was provided of a board of education official who would aid parents, students, and teachers gain access to their schools.

So then we not only called, we went to visit the guy, I don't remember his name, his office was where the big executives have their offices. He was about 50 years old, with this thick gray hair, very gentle and smiling type, gold spectacles, just as nice as he could be. It said on the front page of the New York *Times* call this man if you have trouble getting into your school. And we sat down and asked him, "Can you do anything to help us get our school open?" And he said, "Well, you know the legislature is doing a lot with decentralization now, and we don't exactly know what powers we have and what powers we don't have. And if Mr. Landman [the district superintendent] takes these actions, I'm afraid that we can't really interfere." And I kept saying, "You mean you won't do it? You mean you don't have the power to overrule Mr. Landman?" I mean *he was the man in charge of getting the schools open!*

The group finally did get into their school. Their struggle was the beginning of a collaboration among a few Washington Irving girls, a few Stuyvesant boys, and Jim Horelick which lasted the whole school year and produced, in addition to whatever spiritual changes various individuals experienced, one of the most charming and least rhetorical radical student papers of the 1968-69 student movement. *The Weakly Reader,* the kind of paper that, in another time, would have been considered "good, clean fun," carried irreverent spoofs on the school establishment, but no "gamy language" and no harsh, *ad personam* attacks. Horelick says it was deliberately not pornographic and not militant.

Horelick says he's a good teacher. The students say so, too. But on March 25 his principal sent him a registered letter charging him with distributing for sale copies of an unauthorized publication, *The Weakly Reader,* for which he was deemed "guilty of conduct unbecoming a teacher and prejudicial to the good order, efficiency and discipline of the service." If the charge were upheld, he would lose his teachers license. Adding to the gravity of the charges was the fact that the principal had previously inserted into Horelick's file a "letter of reprimand" in respect to a confused and unsubstantiated charge of inducing truancy—Horelick, the man who had been beaten up and arrested for trying to bring students *into* school!

Jim Horelick, teacher, was not a New Leftist, not a radical, not even interested in politics. He was a farm boy and an Amherst boy who had brought to adulthood and to his teaching career a fast-disappearing but most appealing strain of the American character—a belief in the essential goodness of America's institutions and an expectation of forthright and honest treatment from their representatives. One by one, the representatives he met betrayed his belief and expectations—his first principal and his first chapter chairman, both of whom said, in effect, "Grow up and learn to play the game by the real rules, not the published rules"; the judge who postponed his case and the janitor who refused to honor a perfectly valid official letter;

the cops who barely restrained themselves from pounding his head into the marble floor; and the gentle, gray-haired, gold-spectacled gentleman who somehow couldn't do what the highest education official in the city of New York had publicly announced he was specifically charged with doing. The high school principals had warned that the "corrupt fringe" must not be allowed to "seduce the innocent." And, indeed, Jim Horelick was, in his own way, so innocent that all the forces of law and order in New York could not shake him from his simple belief that his competence and conscientiousness as a teacher should be the determinants of his retaining his teaching license. He continued to observe all the published rules of the game, including the rule enjoining courtesy and good taste, while again and again breaking the unwritten rules according to which the game is really played. But he was not yet out of his twenties. Perhaps the corrupting forces would still succeed in teaching him to play by the real rules.

The high school principals, too, lost some of their innocence, not by seduction, but by a clearer perception of the struggle in which they were engaged and the "perilous equilibrium" of the despotism over which they presided. The despotism had, indeed, lost its stability and its prestige. It was being openly challenged as to its techniques of self-maintenance not only by parents but also by teachers, by lawyers, and even by some educators. And the children were suddenly not at all the most tractable members of the community.

Between "The Nature and Limits of Student Dissent and Participation," which the High School Principals Association released to the press in January, 1969, and a document that they circulated privately among themselves some time later that school year, "Confrontation and Response," the principals' vision sharpened and their tactic toughened in a way that made them more nearly equal to the rebel forces in perception and strategic finesse. The contents of this document I think make it clear why the principals did not publicly release it. In it, the principals honestly acknowledged how beleaguered and vulnerable they were and also made clear that they themselves, not a board of laymen, made policy for the high schools.

Both these revelations are at variance with the principals' and the board's public stance. A copy of the document fell into the hands of the United Bronx Parents, however, which published it "as a service to the public," and it was subsequently republished by the student paper which was the result of a merger between the *Weakly Reader* and Toby Mamis's *Herald Tribune.*[5]

The essential message of the principals' earlier and public paper, "Student Dissent and Participation"—that the rebellion must be put down—had been swathed in thick layers of soft "educationist" language:

We are deeply committed to insuring and protecting the rights of all students to responsible dissent. . . .

We are aware that some of the present student discontent has its roots in very real defects and inadequacies in our educational system.

We are encouraged by our students' active interest and concern about their education and about the times they live in. We take their efforts to bring things "nearer the heart's desire" as a heartening sign of their growing maturity.

Some of [the official, school] student organizations are not as alert, as concerned, or as effective as we or our students would like them to be.

. . . the unequivocal recognition that students have a right to speak and to be heard . . . youth's essentially idealistic impulses . . . students' right to examine the content of their educational program and to make specific recommendations designed to improve them . . .

The potential danger for its authors of wrapping a message in this kind of language is that the unwary or the innocent reading it might mistake the package for the contents and be led to risk the security of the despotism to the needs of remedying real defects. In fact, as I have suggested, "Student Dissent and Participation" was less a position paper to help principals themselves defend the schools than it was an appeal to the public and its official agents to throw their weight into defending the schools. And as such, it served: the mayor, the media, the police, and the state legislature did what they could. (And if what they could should turn out to have been not enough, the

National Guard and the FBI had not yet been sent for.) Since the report served more or less effectively as a public relations document, it is not necessary to ask whether the principals were actually or only apparently innocent when they prepared it. In any case, their mental set was far less innocent when, probably soon afterwards, they produced a document intended only for themselves—in recognition of the reality that (given the school system as it is now organized) the principal's power within each school is by tacit consent immune from interference from the prevailing power groups of the larger community.

From among the twelve members of the Committee on Student unrest that produced the earlier document, there was appointed a five-man Subcommittee on Confrontation and Response. "Confrontation and Response" is a hard-nosed strategy statement which contains only a minimum of educational rhetoric; provides a fairly realistic picture of the rebel leadership; assesses coolly the cadres within the school community that principals can draw upon for defense; suggests a number of delaying or evasive tactics that can be employed when delay and evasion still seem possible; and makes no concession whatsoever to student wants or needs except insofar as and in such a way as concession may be tactically useful. The statement makes no reference to addiction and pushing, reflecting the fact that the principals' primary concern is with students who dissent not with those who cop out. It makes scant reference to violence to property or person, except as a tactic of "trained extremists."

Referring to the rebels as "the New Left," the document acknowledges nonetheless that they are a diverse group, some independent, some with ties to college or community militants. "If it [the antagonistic student group] seems unified at the moment of confrontation," the writers point out, "the unity is deceptive. With time and under pressure, cracks will appear and caucuses surface."

The "unfolding of a confrontation," along with student discontent, faculty anxiety, erosion of discipline, and administrative temporizing, is described in a series of three short sections labeled "A. The Pre-Confrontation Milieu" ("student unrest virulent" and "vague dissatisfactions among the staff"), "B. The Catalyst" ("a dramatic event" such as college riots or the "death" of Martin Luther King, a situation with "cutting uncontrolled" or when an "administration deceives itself with an illusory peace"), and "C. The Confrontation Proper" (student demands are a "mix of the reasonable and unreasonable" and "new issues appear daily"). Then the "unfolding" climaxes: "For a school, this is the moment of truth."

The guidelines suggest the following for dealing with such an unfolding:

—Call on all groups possible for support: students, parents, community leaders, especially faculty.

—Delay and evade where possible: "Claims of censorship of the student newspaper should be referred to the faculty advisor"—that is, to the chief censor; a request for a bulletin board may be referred to a "student cabinet" or the fine arts department.

—Defuse where possible: "A coke machine eliminates complaints about restricted offerings in the cafeteria." [If only the dentists and nutritionists could hear that!]

—Divide where possible: "Use trusted staff to subdivide [large hostile mobs] into smaller, identifiable, more rational groups." "Isolate the radical leadership from their followers." Also meet with rebel students, rebel parents, and rebel teachers separately, never all together.

—Use force where necessary: "Request standby police." "Arrest trespassers and law breakers." "Publicize the nature and inevitability of the punishment."

—Appear reasonable: "Adopt a reasonable and liberal stance . . . ." The "silent majority will be less ready for radicalization if negotiable requests receive serious consideration." In meetings with rebel leaders (if such meetings are absolutely necessary), "display a reasonable and responsive attitude and conspicuous good manners. Insist on similar manners by the students." "A flexible, reasonable, and liberal posture creates a climate of opinion that prevents the radicalization of the moderates."*

—As a last resort, meet with the rebels, but concede nothing: "All attempts to resolve the problem having

* *A foreshadowing of Richard Nixon's use of the term by several months.*

failed, student clamor for an immediate hearing must be granted." But "the nature of the demands . . . and the manner of their presentation . . . allow only one response: denial, simple, clear, and unequivocal. Discussion, perhaps. Negotiation, no."

But the framers of the paper were not at all confident that their shrewd strategy would either prevent confrontations or ensure an effective put down of them if they occurred. "A school may die," they write. "We know only that we cannot be sanguine." "Our future is uncertain . . . The problem will not disappear."

Indeed, the problem will not disappear. Nor can either society or the principals as its representatives even begin to cope with the problem until they state it accurately.

The problem in the nation today is not urban riots or social discontent. The problem is social and economic injustice. Urban riots and other expressions of social discontent may conceivably be put down by intensified national repression. But they will not be put down by a liberal "line." Two national civil rights acts, the presence for three years of a President and a brace of brothers more beloved by the bulk of the black population than any since Lincoln, and Lyndon Johnson's stirring "We shall overcome!" speech at Howard University were followed by the fiery summer of 1967.

Similarly, the problem in the schools today—in New York and the United States—is not the confrontation and radicalizing tactics of an "elite corps of left fascism," "masters of organized disruption," and "trained extremists" (as the principals believe). The problem is an entire school operation which for most students is irrelevant, humiliating, repressive, and, if willingly endured, corrupting. Much greater repressiveness might conceivably put an end to the student rebellion. While police busts have been frequent, serious jail (or reform school) sentences have not yet been employed. And while a few individual leaders have been threatened with bad references to college admissions officers, college and employment blacklists on a large scale have not been used. But a liberal "posture" or "stance" will have less effect on the student movement than did a liberal politicians or liberal laws on the oppressed population nationwide. It is a few years and one big teachers strike later, and the students are that much more "together." They are far less likely than were their parents throughout the nation only a short time ago to mistake "a responsive attitude and good manners" for serious redress of serious grievances. The time for a responsive attitude and good manners was always. Now is the time for confronting the problem in the schools, as the problem is experienced by the students.

"Confrontation and Response" is a considerably more sophisticated document than "Student Dissent and Participation." It even proclaims: "A new sophistication is needed to understand and contain them." But the only discernable antecedent of "them" is "the new left leadership." And such an assessment shows that the principals' sophistication has not yet gone far enough to produce either radical change or radical repression. It goes only so far into the students' ranks as to appraise those students whom the writers consider their "enemy," but not at all those students whom they consider their subjects. The sophistication goes only so far into the past as to appraise the "pre-confrontation milieu," but not the decades' long despotic milieu from which arises, finally, the desperate push to confrontation. It goes so far as to recognize that a confrontation is likely to be immediately stimulated by a climactic event outside the immediate environment, like "riots at Columbia, demonstrations in Ocean Hill-Brownsville, the death of Martin Luther King," but not that the principals themselves and their fellow defenders might provide the catalyst, as they did in the Great Strike. It goes so far as to recognize that the rebel leaders search for issues that will arouse the majority to act on their own behalf—the principal's "insensitivity," the "white, middle-class teachers," the irrelevant courses, the boring assemblies, the dropout rate, the inedible cafeteria food—but not that the issues are nevertheless only too real and were created not by the rebels but by the system against which they rebel. It goes so far as to recognize that demonstrations are likely to be accompanied by violence but not that the police whom the principals call are frequently greater instigators and perpetrators of violence than are the demonstrators.* And

* *The violence of the schools' critics "may assume the form of picketing and demonstrations outside the building," the report says.*

it goes so far as to recognize that students are being "radicalized" at an accelerating rate, but not that it is the system's stubborn defenders more than the reckless rebels who have been the chief agents of that process.

The rebels are searching, not only, as the principals say, for "an issue," but for understanding. They may arrive at it and begin to achieve that consistency of words and action, that wholeness or unity within themselves that is being "together," more or less in a moment, as Jackie Glover did when she passed through her furious teachers' picket line. Or they may arrive at it more slowly by a combination of approaching warily those whom they have been taught to believe were their inferiors and trying on new attitudes and so new views of the world, as Jerry Connelly and Temma Fields were trying to do. Or they may arrive at it, as Jim Horelick did, by stubbornly refusing to relinquish a faith that school and society ought to be what in America we say they are, institutions intended to benefit individuals.

With the despotism being attacked by individuals and groups who are seeking to understand its nature and dynamics, the defenders, too, must try to understand what previously they could contain without understanding. Recognizing the need for a "new sophistication," they are still far behind the attackers in perception of the system and of the various roles in it, including their own. A good and innocent posture will not serve, or not for long. Plunk! went the bullet between the eyes of the kindly headmaster of the brutal boys school. The defenders are beginning to know this—that innocence, real, or self-protective, or disingenuous is not enough—and to talk

At UFT headquarters, I passed through an entirely orderly picket line of community-control advocates on the day after President Albert Shanker's 1968 legislative campaign for defeat of decentralization had produced the delaying bill of that year. A young lady with whom I ascended in the freight elevator explained that the front elevators were by-passing the UFT floor "because of those rioters outside." "They're not rioters," I said, still the English teacher, "they're picketers." "Rioters, picketers, what's the difference, it's all the same thing," she answered. When the UFT mounted picket lines outside the schools of New York City for ten weeks, that was a respectable labor union strike in a just cause. When the students or the community-control parents mount picket lines outside the schools or outside the UFT headquarters, they are rioters engaged in violence.

about it among themselves. They sense that they are engaged in a desperate power struggle. But they seem still to believe that the antagonists are a handful of committed revolutionaries, on the one hand, and a beneficent institution, on the other. However, the institution which they are defending is not only not beneficent, it is no longer even functionally legitimate, in the sense of efficiently training people to perform those tasks which society has decreed they are to perform. What they are defending then is itself an empty system of power arrangements and their own status within that system.

The defenders began, especially during the Great Strike and the subsequent mayoralty contest, to close the gap between liberals and conservatives, demonstrating that the issue was power, not ideology. They have not gone all the way. In New York City many of the law-and-order constituents were distressed when they succeeded in producing two law-and-order mayoralty candidates. In the nation, a law-and-order President is weekly confronted with dissidence in his own ranks. And in the schools, the principals still declare themselves to be "spokesmen in the great libertarian tradition," a tradition that has run a course in New York and in America parallel to other, less beautiful, traditions. So long as these defenders of New York's and America's school and social systems say they believe in our liberation traditions, and so long as they are ambivalent about their repressive roles, there will still be room for the rebels to maneuver and to challenge. And still a chance that the issue of the confrontation between challengers and defenders will be fruitful rather than disastrous.

Postlude

The School Fix, USA

"When James Bevel . . . asked a class of student leaders at Washington Junior High School [in Seattle, Washington] to whom the school belonged," a recent article reports, "they cited the principal, the public, the taxpayers, and the parents before they got to themselves . . ."*

It appears that the students failed to mention the teachers at all, even last.

Throughout the United States, it is universally agreed that neither the students nor the teachers "own," i.e., are responsible for, either the physical place in which they work–school–or the interpersonal and subjective processes that compose their work–education. If, as Karl Marx wrote, the workers, not owning the means of production or the product, are alienated from their work, students and teachers too, meeting in a place which is not theirs and caught in a process over which they have no control, are

* *Barbara Caley, "How a School Fails,"* Integrated Education, *September-October 1969. The Reverend James Bevel was one of the closest associates of Martin Luther King, Jr., from the early days of the Southern Christian Leadership Conference.*

alienated from teaching and learning. Today, throughout the land, the settled and presumably nonalienated old are experiencing terrible uneasiness in respect to the wandering, alienated young. But how early the alienation begins and how society and schools support and demand—and need—this alienation are barely appreciated.

Miss White's or Miss Jersild's students are not peculiar to them, or to Harlem, or to New York, or to big cities. The alienation of children from their impulses, their creativity, their language, their bodies is a regular function of public schools everywhere, with some limited variation as to the means and the harshness by which it is accomplished. For example:

Item. In rural and urban counties of the Southwest where Mexican-Americans constitute sometimes a large minority, sometimes a majority, of the population, Spanish-speaking first graders are not only not taught to read their mother tongue, they are penalized, sometimes cruelly, for even speaking it. Denied, from their first contact with school, the use of man's most distinctive skill, language, they shuffle through to high school where they may finally be taught "real" Spanish—by a teacher from the Argentine, or from Cuba, whose accent is quite different from theirs, and out of books written perhaps a half-century ago by Spaniards whose vocabularly is archaic and foreign. So, generation after generation of native-born Americans, who might be enriched and enrich America by command of two languages, graduate from or drop out of high school barely literate in either.

Item. In San Francisco, several times a week I pass a schoolyard at a recess time when it swirls with bodies and balls in motion. One day, passing at an unaccustomed hour, I saw one teacher and her class of ten or eleven year olds engaged in what I presume was "physical education." The children were arranged in facing lines, wriggling only a little in the chill and their immobility, while the teacher, clipboard in hand, flew back and forth from line to line and child to child, counting, organizing, checking off. Eventually began a fatuous little game in which two children at a time picked up balls and tried to make a basket, while the remaining twenty-eight watched and fidgeted. And, unlike the Mexican-American children, these children were not even sullen.

Item. "In the dormitories [of a Navajo boarding school] in Tuba City I found cold, really inhumane structures for these children, some of whom are 5 years old. There were no pictures on the wall, no paintings, and only two people monitoring dormitories of 100 or 130 people [children]." And a letter from a Mesquakie mother about her young son: "He doesn't *care* to go [to school] . . . Once he came home–sat around the house–kept going from his Dad and [*sic*] me, saying nothing significant. I knew he wanted to talk–so we sat with him and talked. His question was 'Why do we have to be Indians!?!' I knew this was coming one time or another . . . He will have to get used to it . . . Even (another son) comes home (from kindergarten) and tells us things like 'dumb Indian' . . . "[1]

And while everywhere in the country teachers are engaged, sometimes energetically, sometimes lethargically, sometimes cruelly, in teaching the children their place, they themselves are treated as mere mechanical contrivances in the educational process–without responsibility and without dignity. And everywhere, too, within the status-reinforcing institution that serves a status-bound society, parents are scorned; children, classes, schools, communities, whole populations are designated "bad" and "good," whether covertly or brazenly; minority-group members are systematically excluded from school staffs, or from the professional categories of the staffs, or from the higher reaches of the professional staffs; educational hardware and research and administration are valued over human beings and experiences and learning; and fatuous or paranoiac excuses are offered for lunatic rituals or for revolts against them.

An example of a fatuous excuse: In a special creative-arts school for Indian students from all over the country, the halls and workshops and publications and studios are thick with glorious weaving, metalwork, poetry, sculpture, dance, all representing the best of two cultures. But in one darkened room, young men and women from many tribes sit languidly watching an educational film about Shakespeare. Their teacher extracts from the desiccated husks of the moldy educationists' larder the explanation that "Like so many of our–uh–rural disadvantaged, if you'll forgive the term, these youngsters–uh–lack cultural enrichment."

An example of a paranoiac excuse: Adolph A. Berle Jr., professor emeritus of law at Columbia University and one of the most respected senior statesmen of the nation, explained student unrest to a conference of school superintendents: "Forces of student unrest probably originated in the political and propaganda warfare set up by the Chinese Communist Government six or eight years ago . . . "[2]

The excuses may be fatuous, but for most Americans they continue to justify the rituals; and the rituals may be mad, but their prevalence and persistence suggest that as with most manias, they serve a function.

Schooling in America, while it is ever less personally fulfilling, continues to some extent to be socially useful. Lacking an openly hereditary class system, our hierarchical, status-concerned society uses schooling to fix the young of the various population groups into their proper places. And if, as one consequence of this social function performed by the schools, more and more people must spend more and more years in school, that, too, is not without benefit to society. Of the 15 million persons added to the laboring population, ages 18 to 64, between 1950 and 1965, there were 3.68 million more students, and 3.19 million more persons in educational employment; in other words, a total of 7.87 million, or 45 percent of the possible slack in employment, was taken up by the blowing up of the education sector of the economy.[3]

To the extent that the teaching, the learning, and the administering which proceed in our schools are humiliating, constraining, and counterproductive, the individuals involved tend to substitute status gratifications for the gratifications of truly productive work. And to the extent that the individuals are caught in these emotional binds, they become ever more anxious about and fearful of freedom–their own and others'. So it is that the defensive needs of individuals at all levels of the hierachy– from the littlest child to the superintendent of schools, from the illiterate truant to the Westinghouse scholar–support school arrangements that in turn support society's grosser ranking system.

But as the nation's school system helps to absorb some of the shock of the larger society's internal contradictions, greater and greater stress is produced by its own internal contradictions—status reinforcement which supersedes education, administration which holds priority over teaching, professionalism which denies common sense, order which precludes growth, and a student ranking system which requires failures.

New York's hopes and agonies, which I have told about here, are merely exemplary, not unique.

In St. Paul, Minnesota, the black student body of one high school, in collaboration with civic groups and black community groups, issued a seven-point manifesto which opened with: "WE WANT FREEDOM. WE WANT POWER TO DETERMINE THE DESTINY OF OUR SCHOOL." In Alburquerque, New Mexico, the governors of five Indian pueblos filed suit against federal, state, and county officials, charging discrimination against Indian children, against the hiring of Indian professionals, and in the use of federal funds for education. In Detroit, Chicago, Philadelphia, San Francisco; in Cedarhurst, Long Island; Montgomery County, Maryland; Ossining, New York; in a half-dozen communities in New Jersey; in Abingdon, Pennsylvania; Joliet, Illinois; Kansas City, Missouri; Wilmington, Delaware; and Cordele, Georgia—in hundreds if not thousands of communities, large and small, throughout the nation, high school and junior high school students have been disobeying, petitioning, protesting, demonstrating, disrupting, and in many of these communities they have been subdued only with the aid of the school systems' new arm, the police force. In some communities, black students were battling the administrations for dignity and equality, in others white students were protesting that the administrations were "knuckling under to the blacks," in others black and white students together were seeking to break the hold of the school despotism.

In the very well-to-do and "liberal" New York City suburb of Great Neck, on Long Island, while a group of middle-class students operated a "free" school inside the high school, with the permission of their principal, their parents were locked in fierce dispute over whether 260 "disadvantaged" Negro students from the slums of New York City should be brought in to share the "quality education" of the system's 9,400 white students and 400 local Negro students. At the same time, paradoxically, in the not at all liberal community of Delano, California, middle-class parents and farm-worker parents; Mexican-American parents, Anglo parents, black parents, and Filipino parents; parents who were members of Cesar Chavez' grape-pickers' union (the United Farm Workers Organizing Committee) and parents who were members of bitter anti-UFWOC groups—all joined forces in an uprising against a despotic school board and administration, the uprising having been triggered by a disciplinary action imposed on a popular young student named Freddy Chavez (no relation to Cesar).

In Ohio, the educational inflation that keeps demanding more and more schools and higher and higher school salaries encountered the resistance of taxpayers whose family budgets were strained to meet the ordinary cost-of-living inflation, and in several districts, the schools closed down entirely for weeks at a time when their boards of education ran out of money to pay salaries. And in two semirural, semi-industrial districts of Long Island, New York, middle-class Negro families who had moved there from New York City some years before to obtain better housing and better schooling, voted down school tax increases which they felt would go mainly to support remedial programs for the children of poor welfare families.

The ironic internal contradictions of public education in America are so glaring that even the public institutions that are the natural allies of the schools and are dependent on them to contain America's youth until they can be absorbed into the work force sometimes turn against the schools. The probation department of Mendocino County, California, advertised recently in a "free-school" exchange newsletter for a place in a non-institutionalized school which would offer close relationships and tolerance to a fifteen-year-old ward of the juvenile court, thereby acknowledging that while the police and the courts may sometimes have to serve as arms of the public schools, the public schools are losing their ability to serve as arms of the police and the courts.[4]

The Mendocino County probation officer simply gave up on the public schools, at least as a place for his "intelligent, sensitive" charge. So did the school psychologist of the New York City high school when he counseled parents of "sensitive" students to take their children out of the public school with its harsh antitoilet, antismoking, antihuman school rules and send them to private schools. So, in the last year or so, have the numbers of teachers and students (or parents) who have founded "free schools" outside the public school system, to enable pupils and teachers to interact and grow as human beings. But when all those who can escape have escaped, there will still be some 45 million American children and some 2 million American adults fixed in their places in the American public school system, and—for one reason or another—hundreds of thousands of us are concerned about their fate and about the centuries-old American institution of public education.

Our solutions for the educational crisis which, however different the focus of our concerns, we all recognize, lie along a continuum:

Return to the fundamentals: Tighten up on discipline—give more tests, return to the old rigorous standards—stop coddling them—either shape up or ship out—eliminate the frills.

Be scientific: Buy teaching machines, programed books, Montessori materials—use the Bereiter-Engelmann method—punish them for wrong answers, give them cookies for right—put an overhead projector, a TV set, individual tape-recorder booths in every classroom—test and evaluate every method, every teacher, every child.

Be humanistic: Make the classes smaller—fill the school with paraprofessionals, mothers, master teachers, tutors, guidance counselors, reading specialists—institute remedial programs, after-school tutorial programs, cultural-enrichment programs, trips to the zoo—hire more men teachers, black teachers, Indian teachers, bilingual teachers—organize a student court for offenders, an advisory committe of parents, a student government council on dress codes, a teacher-parent-student consultative assembly—introduce "relevant" electives, controversial assembly speakers, a paperback reading program.

There is no one of these educational solutions and no combination of them, that, if seriously pursued, will not have some immediate effect on the educational atmosphere of any school. Almost any method that a teacher really believes in will work, so long as she also believes in herself and in her students. *And there is no one solution, and no combination of them, that, if instituted as an isolated educational solution, will have any long-term effect.*

Because so long as the power and status functions of the public schools remain fundamentally unchanged, most teachers cannot for long believe in themselves or in the spontaneous will to learn of all their students and the ability to learn of their discriminated-against minority students. And so long as the power and status functions of the public schools remain fundamentally unchanged, most students, and especially most low-status students, cannot believe in themselves or trust their teachers.

The interactions of our society's dependence on the schools' status-reinforcing functions and of school people's need to defend their souls against failure and its attendant distresses, have again and again defeated promising and apparently sound educational programs—and will continue to do so. All the plans and programs of scientists and scholars, educators and administrators, all the public and foundation monies (most of which, instead of trickling down to the clients, pours out through the leaks in the educational vessel), are going to produce no significant educational change in our public schools. All touch only the surface of the ugliness, the superficial ways in which the system manifests its systemic disorders. Because the system is not about educating children as human beings. It is about fixing them in their correct places in the school and the adult societies. And it is about holding all the adults in the school—including the parents—in their correct places. And only direct attacks on that central function can produce significant change. Thus, until power and status in the schools have been dislodged and relocated—or abolished—the appropriate educational question is not "What kinds of educational programs shall we institute to make the schools more harmonious and fruitful institutions?" but "What are the terms and strategy of the struggle to dislodge power and status in the school system?"

In New York the defensive strategies of administrative evasions and liberal doubletalk obscured the essence of the struggle for almost everyone at the beginning, and for some observers and participants, they continue to obscure it to this day. So that even after the massive putdown of the parents and students and even in the midst of the continuing erosion of faith in schools and schooling, some of the defenders still believe that educational change can be effected by administrative fiat.

We must, indeed, think about educational change, but we must think about it in the context of political change. If we do not, whatever educational change we succeed in making will be sterile. Thus, in a high school in White Plains, a large-city suburb of New York City, a social studies elective in Afro-Asian history was instituted, but until a militant action by the school's black students changed the entrance requirements for the course, the class's roster included only upper-level academic white students. The popular cry for relevant course material was met—but was subverted by the school's status system until that system was specifically challenged by the school's lowest-status students.

But if we make educational change with the intent of challenging power and status, then we are likely to set in motion a train of moves and counter-moves that will carry us deep into the interior of the schools' dilemmas. In a school in northern California, Jane Goldman, a teacher of a "bad" sixth-grade class of children from white and Mexican-American working-class families, allowed her students to get up to sharpen their pencils without permission, to call out answers without raising their hands, and so on. She also conducted a daily current-events discussion dealing with such matters of local interest as the grape pickers strike, the Indian occupation of Alcatraz, and the bust of the Black Panther Los Angeles headquarters. A bulletin board display on racism elicited from her supervisor a request that her bulletin boards deal with "instructional matters," and she was also admonished to keep her class in better order. She explained to the children and in a letter to their parents that she believed both classroom freedom and serious discussion of serious issues are necessary to the education of American citizens. For her clearly disloyal maneuver of seeking to enlist the children's and their parents' interest on behalf of the children's education and in opposition to the administration, she was threatened with transfer out of the school. The children, informed of this, spontaneously organized a letter-writing campaign and a picket-line against the threatened transfer. They said: "But we like her. When she gives us work she tell us real nicely how to do it." "In the morning we discuss what is going to happen in the world." "Me and Larry don't care if we get suspended [for the picket line]. It's for our teacher and we care who teaches us and how we get our education."

The teacher's educational method had provided her students with a sense of people's rights and with ideas about instruments that might be used to defend these rights. Eventually bringing a First Amendment suit against the transfer, the teacher chose to defend herself not conventionally by denial of the typically trivial charges made by her supervisors but by an affirmation of an antistatus philosophy of education: ". . . if children are always told what to do, they begin to feel that they couldn't know what to do if given the chance. Once they lose confidence in their abilities, they truly can't solve problems any more . . . I don't feel that any authority has the right to remain unquestioned."[5]

The shifting or eliminating of power and status in the public schools is at once a function of change in other sectors of society and the responsibility of those in the schools who are most powerless. That means the students (in the case of young children, the parents) and the teachers. More and more children, parents, and teachers throughout the country will undoubtedly indulge in audacious individual or small-group acts of defiance of authority, eliciting, like Miss Goldman's defiance, a chain of retribution and perhaps also of support. However, the possibility for effecting deep change in the system of power and status over a wider area than one classroom or one school will probably rest on teachers and students (or parents) acting in concert. In New York City, as we have seen, parents and teachers blew the chance for together effecting change by a mutual suspiciousness amounting almost to paranoia, by the parents' tendency to ascribe to teachers an evil which is systemic rather than personal, by the teachers' hysterical defense of a wretched mess of two-penny status advantages, and perhaps by something like pure historical chance.

In New York, the teachers, through their union, were already well on their way to prying loose some power for themselves when the parents and students began to move. In most other communities, the gathering force of the two movements is far less disparate, with the teachers' movement for tenure and rights and, invariably, higher salaries barely in advance of the students' and parents' movement for dignity and power and respect. So, whereas in New York the teachers' slight edge seemed to have diminished the chances of collaboration between the two groups, and the crushing of the students' and parents' movement to have strengthened both the established powers and the teachers union, in other communities the fact that the two groups are at roughly the same stage in their demand for power may facilitate collaboration between them.

In some cities, some militant students have joined teachers' picket lines, as—it seems so long ago—they did in New York City, when they thought they and the teachers union had a common grievance against the distant administrators. In other cities, teachers—sometimes black teachers, sometimes young teachers—have incorporated community control and cooperation with community and student groups in their organizing philosophy and tactics.

On the other hand, the very weaknesses of the teachers' situation in most communities in the country, the want of tenure, the want of procedural protection, the absence of a defending and militant organization, may well undercut the will of all but the most courageous teachers to assert their own and their students' rights. It may be, especially in the face of a looser labor market for teachers and a generally more repressive political atmosphere, that teachers will give up the struggle for their own rights, or else, as in New York, defend their own at the expense of their students'. So that, as in New York, there will not be no struggle, but a struggle so structured that the relatively powerless brutalize one another and dehumanize themselves—teachers against students, black students against white students, middle-class black and white families against welfare black and white families, Mexicanos against Indians, and so on, and so on.

Meanwhile the plans for the improvement of our schools will proliferate. But the solemn tones of scholars and scientists proclaiming new methods and new findings, or the swelling chorus of sweet voices that sing of love and creativity should not delude us into believing that America is about to set its children free. It is too long that we have woven unfreedom into every strand of the cords that bind school and society, children and adults, whites and nonwhites, well-to-do and poor. Scientists and scholars and poets, outside the struggle as they are, are not the ones to free us. Which does not mean that the scientists and scholars and poets are of no use to the struggle. They can show us how the knots are tied and envision how freedom might feel and work, trying it out perhaps in such little islands as the new free and community schools.

But the advice of men of good will, while it may support, will not produce freedom. Only those who are tied can loosen the bonds, by straining against them. And if it is the most unfree—teachers and low-status students and parents—who will seek to free themselves, in doing so, they will release also the rest of us. For if the status and power arrangements fix the teacher into a posture of humility, they also fix her principal into a posture of arrogance. If they alienate Miss White's children from their living language and their vigorous bodies, they also alienate Miss White from her ability to understand and her power to love. And if they need an agonizing Willie Gallagher, always reaching out for the beautiful world which always eludes him, they also need a resigned and joyless Temma Fields, who senses that she is being trained to accept a world in which soon there will be nothing worth reaching out for.

There is always the possibility that straining against the bonds will merely tighten them—painfully. But I suspect that in many communities in America more and more people are going to take that risk and try anyway.

NOTES

Part I. Power and Status in the Schools

THE APPETITE FOR ADVANTAGEOUS EDUCATION

1. A sociological analysis of the original Jackson Heights-Corona controversy is offered by two participants Kurt Lang and Gladys Engel Lang in "Resistance to School Desegregation: A Case Study of Backlash Among Jews," *Sociological Inquiry*, Winter 1965. A study of the entire desegregation controversy in New York City, with emphasis on the role of school officials and bureaucracy, is offered in David Rogers, *110 Livingston Street* (New York: Random House, 1968).

2. Public hearings on high school rezoning at John Bowne High School (New York City), February 26, 1968, taped by the author.

3. Metropolitan Applied Research Center, "Fact Sheet: School Crisis at Franklin K. Lane and Canarsie High Schools" (New York: the Center, March 1969).

4. Lang and Lang, "Resistance to School Desegregation."

EDUCATIONAL INPUTS AND OUTPUTS–CONVENTIONAL MEASURES

1. Robert H. Wiebe, "The Social Functions of Public Education," *American Quarterly*, Summer 1969. See also Arthur W. Calhoun, *A Social History of the American Family* (New York: Barnes & Noble, 1945).

2. See, for example, U.S. Department of Health, Education, and Welfare, *White-Nonwhite Differentials in Health, Education and Welfare,* 1965; National Education Association, *Wilcox County, Alabama: A Study of Social, Economic, and Educational Bankruptcy*(Washington, D.C.: the Association, June 1967); and James S. Coleman, et al., *Equality of Educational Opportunity* (U.S. Department of Education, 1966). There are merely three items from a wealth of material in support of this point.

3. For an analysis of the declining tax base of central cities and the effect on education, see "Education in the Ghetto," *Saturday Review*, 11 January 1969. Also see Arthur E. Wise, *Rich Schools, Poor Schools* (University of Chicago Press, 1968).

4. 394 U.S. 322 (1969).

5. United Bronx Parents, "Training for Local Control: Expenditures per Pupil in the Bronx Schools," mimeographed, n.d.

6. Queens College Institute for Community Studies, *New York City School Fact Book* (Flushing, New York: the Institute, n.d.).

7. United Bronx Parents, "Distribution of Educational Resources Among the Bronx Public Schools," mimeographed, April 1968.

8. Robert E. Herriott and Nancy Hoyt St. John, *Social Class and the Urban School* (New York: John Wiley, 1966).

9. Miriam Wasserman, "Planting Pansies on the Roof: A Critique of How New York City Tests Reading," *The Urban Review*, January 1969.

10. Abundant illustrations of this generalization from the experiences of large employers are provided in Ivar Berg, "Rich Man's Qualifications for Poor Man's Jobs," *IRCD Bulletin*, March 1969.

11. Harlem Youth Opportunities Unlimited, Inc., *Youth in the Ghetto* (New York: HARYOU, 1964).

12. Metropolitan Applied Research Center, "10.5% Increase in New York City Pupils Critically Below Grade Level in Reading," 15 March 1969.

13. Sidney Schwager, "An Analysis of the Evaluation of the More Effective Schools Program Conducted by the Center for Urban Education" (New York: United Federation of Teachers, 1967).

14. HARYOU, *Youth in the Ghetto.* The data cover the year 1962.

15. United Bronx Parents, "Do Black and Puerto Rican Students Get the Same Opportunities as White Students Get in the New York City Public Schools?" Figures given are for 1967.

ORDERING THE ADULTS

1. Annual meeting of the local school boards of the city of New York, 16 March 1968, taped by the author.

2. The story comes from Edward Gottlieb known throughout the New York school world for his unconventionality, which consisted largely of an uncommon warmth and a lack of concern for status.

3. Quotation from *The United Teacher*, 7 September 1969.

4. See Rogers, *110 Livingston Street.*

5. See, for example, Joan C. Baratz and Roger W. Shuy, *Teaching Black Children to Read* (Washington, D.C.: Center for Applied Linguistics, 1969); William A. Stewart, *Non-Standard Speech and the Teaching of English* (Washington, D.C.: Center for Applied Linguistics, 1964); *Improving English Skills of Culturally Different Youth in Large Cities,* (U.S. Department of Health, Education and Welfare, 1962); and Roger W. Shuy, *Social Dialects and Language Learning* (Champaign. Illinois: National Council of Teachers of English, 1964).

6. Daniel E. Griffiths et al., *Teacher Mobility in New York City: A Study of the Recruitment, Selection, Appointment and Promotion of Teachers* (New York University, 1963).

7. Data from ibid.; United Bronx Parents, "Selection of Personnel," 1969; and Board of Education of the City of New York, "Special School Censuses," *New York Times,* 6 November 1969.

8. For a description of how "plugging" worked in some community-control crises, see "Final Report of the Advisory Committee on Decentralization" ["The Neimeyer Report"], (Board of Education of the City of New York, July 1968).

GROUPING PUPILS TO SERVE THE STATUS SYSTEM

1. Quoted in Christina Tree, "Grouping Pupils in New York City," *The Urban Review,* September 1968.

2. Board of Education of the City of New York, Office of Elementary Schools Circular E.P. 16, 1966-67.

3. See Joseph Lederer, "The Scope of the Practice," and Tree, "Grouping Pupils," in *The Urban Review*, September 1968. Also Alfred Yates, ed., *Grouping in Education* (New York: John Wiley, 1966).

4. Tree, "Grouping Pupils."

5. See Board of Education of the City of New York, Elementary Schools Memorandum 4, 1968-69.

6. The concept of *ressentiment*, a psychosocial phenomenon especially prevalent in the teaching profession, is developed in Carl Nordstrom et al., *Society's Children* (New York: Random House, 1967). The authors maintain that it is the basis for certain schoolteacherish behavior toward students.

7. Robert Rosenthal and Lenore Jacobson, *Pygmalion in the Classroom* (New York: Holt, Rinehart, and Winston, 1968).

8. Some questions regarding the validity of their findings are raised in Harris Dienstfrey, "Outside the Expected," *The Urban Review*, September 1968.

9. A. Harry Passow, "The Maze of Research on Ability Grouping," in Yates, ed., *Grouping in Education.* Also, Jane Franseth and Rose Koury, *Survey of Research on Grouping as Related to Pupil Learning* (U.S. Department of Health, Education, and Welfare, 1966). Also James S. Coleman et al., *Equality of Educational Opportunity* (U.S. Department of Health, Education, and Welfare, Office of Education, 1966), especially Table 3.23.1, which suggests that low-status children are more affected by the attitudes and aptitudes of their fellow students than are high-status children.

10. Aaron Lipton, "Classroom Grouping and Integration," in Meyer Weinberg, ed., *Integrated Education* (Beverly Hills: The Glencoe Press, 1968).

BLOWING THE CURVE AT THE BOTTOM

1. See Nat Hentoff, *Our Children Are Dying* (New York: Viking, 1966).

2. In "Ghetto Education," *Center Magazine,* November 1968.

3. Coleman et al., *Equality of Educational Opportunity.*

4. For a beautiful appreciation of strengths and resources developed by poor and oppressed families, the reader is referred to the writings of the Boston psychiatrist and writer Robert Coles, especially *Children of Crisis* (Boston: Little, Brown, 1967).

5. The concept of "cultural deprivation" was first popularized by Frank Riessman in *The Culturally Deprived Child* (New York: Harper & Row, 1962), and Benjamin Bloom et al., in *Compensatory Education for Cultural Deprivation* (New York: Holt, Rinehart, and Winston, 1965). A critique of the concept is provided in Yetta Tractman Goodman, "The Culturally Deprived Child: A study in Stereotyping," *Integrated Education,* July-August 1969.

6. Emmett Albert Betts, *Foundations of Reading Instruction* (New York: American Book Company, 1946).

7. Edward Sapir, *Language, An Introduction to the Study of Speech* (New York: Harcourt, Brace, 1921).

8. Examples given are from the Metropolitan Achievement Tests in reading, published by Harcourt, Brace & World. These are the tests most used in New York City to test elementary school children's reading level. They do not differ substantially from most of the other reading achievement tests which are commercially available. All are commonly used throughout the country.

9. Morris Gross, *Learning Readiness in Two Jewish Groups* (New York: Center for Urban Education, 1967).

10. For a report of a Mississippi tutoring program see Miriam Wasserman, "The Loud, Proud Black Kids," *The Progressive*, April 1968; a report on the Urban League street academy in New York and on a similar program in Chicago is contained in the *Carnegie Quarterly*, Fall 1968.

11. Rosalie H. Wax, "The Warrior Dropouts," *Trans-action,* May 1967.

12. Wilfred Pelletier, "Childhood in an Indian Village," *This Magazine is about Schools,* Spring 1969.

13. Murray Wax and Rosalie Wax, "Great Tradition, Little Tradition, and Formal Education," to be published in a forthcoming book edited by Murray Wax et al., *Anthropological Perspectives on Education* (New York: Basic Books).

14. *San Francisco Chronicle*, October 17, 1969.

15. Jules Henry, *Culture Against Man* (New York: Random House, 1963).

LORETTA TUBMAN: "BEING A SECRETARY JUST ISN'T ME."

1. *The United Teacher,* 8 January 1969.

2. "The Clash of Cultures in the Classroom," *Integrated Education*, August 1963.

MILES RANDOLPH: "I COULD PLAY BASKETBALL. I COULD STUDY. I WAS A JIVE CAT."

1. For a scholar's confirmation of Miles's point about black culture heroes, the pimp and the hustler—also, and most especially, the blues man—I recommend the very informative and sensible *Urban Blues*, by Charles Keil (University of Chicago Press, 1966). Also see *The Autobiography of Malcolm X* (New York: Grove Press, 1966).

CHAOS SCHOOLS AND THREE VETERANS

1. In the order given: *New York Times*, 8 May 1968; *The Jewish Press*, 27 September and 3 October 1969; High School Principals Association statement, "The Nature and Limits of Student Dissent and Participation, January 16, 1969"; and Board of Education of the City of New York, Special Circular No. 77, 22 March 1969. The *Amsterdam News*, a weekly with distribution limited almost entirely to black readers, saw the situation slightly differently: "COPS SWARM CANARSIE HIGH" read a headline of 8 March 1969.
2. *Community Attitudes in Bedford-Stuyvesant: An Area Study* (New York: Center for Urban Education, 1967).
3. From an untitled mimeographed report by the Harlem Education Project, 1963–64.
4. *Amsterdam News*, 19 April 1969 and 3 May 1969.

Part II. The Struggle for Power and Status

INTRODUCTION

1. Murray L. Wax et al., *Formal Education in an American Indian Community*, Supplement to *Social Problems*, Society for the Study of Social Problems, Spring 1964, pp. 4–5.
2. For an example of the debate between those who advocated improvement through desegregation and those who advocated improvement through compensatory education, see *Ghetto Schools: Problems and Panaceas*, A *New Republic* Pamphlet, 1967.
3. "The Education of Minority Group Children in the New York City Public Schools," mimeographed (Harlem Parents Committee, 1965).

4. An account of the role of the board of education and school personnel in impeding desegregation can be found in David Rogers, *110 Livingston Street*. An excellent account of the desegregation conflict from the point of view of some participants is contained in Estelle Fuchs, *Pickets at the Gates* (New York: The Free Press, 1966). A good capsule review of both the failure of desegregation and of the various compensatory programs of the board is contained in the report of the Harlem Parents Committee listed in the previous note.

RATIONALE FOR CHANGE: DECENTRALIZATION AND COMMUNITY CONTROL·

1. *The United Teacher*, 6 December 1967.
2. Marilyn Gittell, *Participants and Participation* (New York: Frederick A. Praeger, 1967).
3. The speech was published by the Ford Foundation as a pamphlet entitled "Making Education Relevant."
4. Among the many statements of this general thesis, one of the most temperate and least rhetorical is contained in "A Proposal for an Independent Board of Education for Harlem," mimeographed (New York-Harlem CORE, 1 March 1967).
5. Both quotations from "Minutes of a Meeting of the I.S. 201 Complex Governing Board with Unit Administrator designee Charles Wilson," mimeographed, 16 February 1968.
6. Meeting on the "Disruptive Child," Manhattan District 5, 29 January 1968, taped by the author.
7. For Clark's position, see *An Intensive Program for the Attainment of Educational Achievement in Deprived Area Schools of New York City* (New York: Metropolitan Applied Research Center, March 1968); and "Ghetto Education," *The Center Magazine*, November 1968.
8. "The Controversy Over I.S. 201: One View and a Proposal," *The Urban Review*, July 1966.
9. Frederick Douglass, 4 August 1857; quoted in Preston Wilcox, "The Meaning of Community Control," mimeographed, 2 December 1968.

THE 201 STORY

1. New York State Education Commissioner's Advisory Committee on Human Relations and Community Tensions, with the assistance of The Institute of Urban Studies, Teachers College, Columbia University, *Desegregating the Public Schools of New*

York City (a report prepared for the Board of Education of the City of New York, 12 May 1964).

2. Wilcox, "The Controversy Over I.S. 201."

3. Dorothy Jones, "The Issues at I.S. 201: A View from the Parents' Committee," *Integrated Education,* October-November 1966.

4. *The United Teacher*, Special Issue on 201, October 1966.

5. Board of Education of the City of New York, "Decentralization, Statement of Policy" (adopted at a Public Meeting, 19 April 1967).

6. Quoted from "Proposals for Improving Education in Schools in Disadvantaged Areas," as excerpted in the *New York Times,* 20 October 1966.

7. *The United Teacher*, 23 September 1966.

8. WINS news conference, (transcript 7 October 1966, 10:30 p.m.).

9. Personal communication from a teacher-participant to the author.

10. Personal communication from a UFT official to the author.

11. *New York Times* and Ford Foundation press release, both 6 July 1967.

12. Ford Foundation press release, 6 July 1967.

13. Friedenberg's comments are quoted in one of the few honest education journals I know, *This Magazine Is About Schools*, Winter 1969.

14. Martin Mayer, "The Full and Sometimes Very Surprising Story of Ocean Hill, the Teachers' Union and the Teacher Strikes of 1968," *New York Times Magazine*, 2 February 1968.

15. Both quotations by David Spencer from "A Harlem Parent Speaks Out," *NEA Journal*, March 1968.

16. Ibid.

17. Board of Education of the City of New York, "Proposals for Improving Education in Schools in Disadvantaged Areas," 19 October 1966.

18. For a discussion of the CSA (and UFT) board suit and an excellent analysis of the role of the courts in power struggles see Joseph S. Lobenthal, "Educational Experimentation and "The Merit System,' " *The Center Forum,* 28 June 1968.

19. *African-American Teachers Forum*, November–December 1967.

20. *Amsterdam News*, 2 March 1968.

21. *New York Times*, 1 March 1968.

22. Ibid., 26 February 1969.

23. *201 Newsletter*, 27 January 1969.

24. For analyses of press and media reactions to other, related events, see Gladys Engel Lang, "The 1967 Teachers' Strike: A Comparison of TV and Newspaper Coverage"; Barbara Carter, "The Press Coverage of the Ocean Hill-Brownsville School Dispute: A Case History"; and George Barner, "The Ocean Hill-Brownsville Community Views: The News Coverage" —Urban Reporting Project, New School For Social Research. Mimeographed, n.d.

25. Board of Education of the City of New York and I.S. 201 Governing Board, typed minutes of meeting held at 110 Livingston Street, 1 March 1968, 10:30 p.m.

26. A good description of the method, its premises, and its initiation at P.S. 133 is provided in A. J. Tobier, "P.S. 133: A Catcher in the Rye," *The Center Forum*, 15 May 1969. Possible use via TV of the reading method used in this program is discussed in Caleb Gattegno, *Towards a Visual Culture* (New York: Outerbridge & Dienstfrey, 1969).

THE UFT: DEFENDERS OF THE FAITH

1. *The United Teacher*, 4 December 1968 and 7 October 1968 respectively.

2. The first quote is from *The United Teacher*, 13 May 1965; the second from the issue of 4 September 1968; the third from a letter to the *New York Times*, 2 May 1968.

3. See Thomas R. Brooks, *Towards Dignity: A Brief History of the United Federation of Teachers* (New York: United Federation of Teachers, 1967).

4. Interview with Albert Shanker, 1 August 1968, taped by the author.

5. Mary Reichsman, "School Suspension at the District Level in One Manhattan School District," mimeographed (Community Service Society of New York, June 1969).

6. See George Forlano and Jack Abramson, *Measuring Pupil Growth in Reading in the More Effective Schools* (Board of Education of the City of New York, April 1968); David J. Fox, *Expansion of the More Effective Schools Program* (New York: Center for Urban Education, September 1967); and Sidney Schwager, "An Analysis of the Evaluation of the More Effective Schools."

7. *The United Teacher,* 6 January 1967.

8. For a good generally prounion view of the 1967 strike, see Deborah Meier, "The New York Teachers' Strike," *Midstream*, December 1967, and reprinted in *The United Teacher,* 24 January 1968.

9. As quoted in "Reconnection for Learning: A Community School System for New York" ["Bundy Report"], Mayor's Advisory Panel on Decentralization of the New York City Schools, November 1967.

10. *New York Times*, 25 January 1968.

11. *New York Post*, 23 January 1968.

12. *New York Times*, 23 January 1968.

13. Meeting of the UFT Delegate Assembly, 6 February 1968, taped by the author.

14. From "Draft Guidelines for a Demonstration Project," 26 March 1968, in *Confrontation at Ocean Hill-Brownsville*, by Maurice R. Berube and Marilyn Gittell (New York: Federick A. Praeger, 1969).

15. Administrative Hearing into Complaints of Rhody A. McCoy, Unit Administrator of Ocean Hill-Brownsville, Requesting Transfer of Teachers, "Report and Recommendations of Francis E. Rivers, Esq. Special Trial Examiner," 26 August 1968.

16. *New York Times*, 13 June 1968, and 26 May 1968, respectively.

17. Ibid., 28 May 1968.

18. Howard I. Kalodner, "Analysis of Marchi Legislation on School Decentralization as it Affects Demonstration Decentralization Projects and Other Local School Boards," prepared at request of Marilyn Gittell for the Queen's College Institute for Community Studies. (Flushing, New York: the Institute, 1 August 1969).

19. John O'Neill, Letter to the *New York Times* in response to Martin Mayer's article, "The Full and Sometimes Very Surprising Story." Reprinted by the New York Civil Liberties Union, March 1969.

20. See "Ghetto Schools Need Black Power. Part Two: Nothing is as simple as it seems," *WIN Magazine*, 15 November 1968.

21. Steve Zeluck, "The UFT Strike," *New Politics,* Winter 1968.

22. *New York Times,* 21 October 1968.

1. *The United Teacher*, 18 December 1968.
2. Quoted in Ibid., 30 March 1969.
3. Quoted from a 201 Complex press release, 12 December 1968.
4. The following were useful in analyzing the decentralization act of 1969: *Community*, published by the Queens College Institute for Community Studies, May 1969; *Summary of New York City Community School District System*, distributed by John H. Lotz, member of the board of education of the city of New York, 8 May 1969; memorandum on the foregoing by David N. Barus, Metropolitan Applied Research Center, 15 May 1969; *A Summary of the 1969 School Decentralization Law for New York City*, New York City Office of Education Affairs, n.d.
5. "The Teachers' Contract: It Doesn't Seem Right!" *The Village Voice,* 3 July 1969.
6. *The United Teacher,* 29 June 1969.

PART III. The Struggle Against Power and Status

THE SCHOOLS AS DESPOTISM

1. For a contemporary account of the school's despotic maneuvers, the reader is referred to the happily vulgar "The Student as Nigger," by Jerry Farber *This Magazine Is About Schools,* Winter 1968.
2. In the spring of 1969 a student who had been committed to a special school (once designated by the number "600") designed for boys not susceptible to normal school discipline instituted a suit challenging the constitutionality of the New York State Compulsory Education Law. His lawyer explained: "Our claim of unconstitutionality is grounded in the contention that the schools are destructive. The challenge relies on the constitutional doctrine that the State cannot infringe on individual liberty without proof of substantial benefit. We are going to argue that P.S. 58 and most of the former '600' schools are essentially custodial, not educational. That the function of the '600' schools, and the whole system, is to train kids for mediocrity and obedience. And that the schools have an adverse impact on creativity, intelligence, and future possibilities." Quoted in *The Village Voice*, 13 March 1969.
3. U.S. Department of Labor, Bureau of Labor Statistics, Special Labor Force, *Employment of High School Graduates and Dropouts in 1967*, Report No. 100.

4. *The New York Post*, 7 May 1969.
5. An extensive survey of the ignorance and arrogance purveyed by standard textbooks may be found in Jules Henry, "Education for Stupidity," *The New York Review of Books*, 9 May 1968.
6. *The New York Review of Books*, 8 May 1969.
7. See the *New York Times*, 11 April, 12 April, and 7 December 1967.
8. *New York Times*, 22 October, and 24 October 1969.
9. For a discussion of aggression and empathy, see Christine Olden, "On Adult Empathy with Children," *Psychoanalytic Study of the Child,* Volume VIII (New York: International Universities Press, 1953).

RESISTANCE–AND NEW DIALOGUES

1. *New York Times,* 7 November 1969.
2. *New York Times*, 20 February 1969.
3. "Statement of the Special Committee on Racial and Religious Prejudice," The Honorable Bernard Botein, Chairman, mimeographed, n.d.
4. SCOPE Bulletin, mimeographed, September 1968.
5. *New York High School Free Press*, no. 6 (February-March 1969).
6. *New York Times,* 28 November 1969.
7. Sources for my account of the events of Monday, December 2, 1968, are the *New York Times,* the *New York Post,* and an illustrated article in the *Village Voice,* December 5, 1968, by a reporter who wrote that he was himself clubbed by police in Ocean Hill-Brownsville during the police charge there.
8. Quoted in the *New York High School Free Press*, no. 6 (February-March 1969).
9. Ibid., no. 8 (April-May, 1969), no. 2 (Halloween, 1968), and no. 5 (15–29 January 1969).
10. Both sets of demands as published in ibid., no. 8 (April-May 1969).

COUNTER-RESISTANCE–AND OLD STANDARDS

1. Edgar Friedenberg, "Contemptuous Hairdressers," *This Magazine Is About Schools,* August 1966.

2. The University of the State of New York, the State Department of Education, appeal in the matter of Dalyrymple, no. 7594 (14 March 1966), and appeal in the matter of McQuade, no. 7683 (30 September 1966).

3. NECLC press release, mimeographed, 30 December 1968.

4. *New York Times*, 31 October 1969.

5. *Tinker* v. *Des Moines Independent Community School District*, no. 21, October Terms, 1968, 24 February, 1969.

6. In New York's neighboring state, New Jersey, cognizance was taken of the Tinker ruling by the state education commissioner when he overruled, as an improper encroachment on freedom of expression, a school's ban on distribution of printed materials by students. *New York Times*, 24 June 1969.

7. Sources are: for the Cleaver incident, interview with Ira Glasser of the New York Civil Liberties Union; for the Mamis incident, the press and interview with the Mamis family; for the Dick's incident, mass meeting of Bronx high school students and parents, daily press, and *NYHS Free Press,* no. 7.

8. *New York Times*, 30 October 1969.

9. Ibid., 8 October, 10 October, 28 October, and 1 November 1969.

10. *United Teacher*, vol. 10, no. 26 (25 May 1969).

11. Ibid., no. 15 (5 March 1969).

12. The report of the Committee on Student Participation in High School Affairs, the statement by John Doar, and the circular by Bernard Donovan are printed in Board of Education of the City of New York Special Circular no. 77, 1968–1969 (24 March 1969).

13. Division of Law of the New York State Department of Education, Formal Opinion of Counsel no. 67, contained in Item 2 of General Circular no. 13 for 1967–68 (8 February 1969).

14. Metropolitan Applied Research Center, "Fact Sheet: School Crisis at Franklin K. Lane and Canarsie High Schools," mimeographed (18 March 1969).

15. Newsletter, "Things in School that Parents Don't Know About!", District 1 Community School Council, vol. 1, no. 1 (27 January 1969).

16. Miriam Bokser, "Free the Panther 21!" *NYHS Free Press,* no. 8 (April-May 1969).

17. *New York Daily Column*, 3 April 1969.
18. In addition to newspaper accounts of this incident, I have drawn for my explanation of it on interviews with black and white students, the *United Teacher*, the Metropolitan Applied Research Council's "Fact Sheet: School Crisis at Franklin L. Lane and Canarsie High Schools," and an article "F - - k Lane," *NYHS Free Press*, no. 6.

THE END OF INNOCENCE

1. *New York Times*, 14 May 1969.
2. *United Teacher*, vol. 10, no. 10 (8 January 1969).
3. Transcript of the interview published in *Levathian*, vol. 1, no. 3 (June 1969).
4. Quoted in C. Vann Woodward, *Tom Watson, Agrarian Rebel* (New York: Oxford, 1963).
5. *New York Herald Tribune*, September 1969.

Postlude

THE SCHOOL FIX, USA

1. Hearings before the Senate Subcommittee on Indian Education, 91st Congress, Ist sess., Part 1, p. 303, and Appendix, Part II, p. 783.
2. *New York Times,* 17 July 1969.
3. The figures are cited in John Rowntree and Margaret Rowntree, *The Political Economy of Youth* (Ann Arbor, Michigan: the Radical Education Project, n.d.). The pamphlet provides an interesting analysis of the class role of youth in America.
4. *New Schools Exchange Newsletter,* 25 October 1969.
5. Jane Goldman, "Rebuttal to Teacher Evaluation." Unpublished document (Fremont, California, 1970).

BIBLIOGRAPHY

Alsop, Joseph. "H.S. CRISIS: 'MORE DRUGS, LESS VIOLENCE.' " *New York Daily Column,* 3 April 1969.

The Autobiography of Malcolm X. New York: Grove Press, 1966.

Baratz, Joan C., and Shuy, Roger W. *Teaching Black Children to Read.* Washington, D.C.: Center for Applied Linguistics, 1969.

Barus, David N. "1969 School Decentralization Law for New York City." Memorandum. New York: Metropolitan Applied Research Center, 15 May 1969.

Betts, Emmett Albert. *Foundations of Reading Instruction.* New York: American Book Company, 1946.

Berg, Ivar. "Rich Man's Qualifications for Poor Man's Jobs." *IRCD Bulletin,* March 1969.

Berube, Maurice R., and Gittell, Marilyn, eds. *Confrontation at Ocean Hill-Brownsville.* New York: Frederick A. Praeger, 1969.

Bloom, Benjamin, et al. *Compensatory Education for Cultural Deprivation.* New York: Holt, Rinehart and Winston., 1965.

Board of Education of the City of New York. "Administrative Hearing into Complaints of Rhody A. McCoy, Unit Administrator of Ocean Hill-Brownsville, Requesting Transfer of Teachers, Report and Recommendations of Francis E. Rivers, Esq." New York: the Board: 26 August 1968.

———. "Elementary Schools Memorandum 4, 1968–69." New York: the Board.

———. *Final Report of the Advisory Committee on Decentralization* ("Niemeyer Report"). New York: the Board, July 1968.

———. Office of Elementary Schools Circular E.P. 16, 1966–67.

———. "Proposals for Improving Education in Schools in Disadvantaged Areas." New York: the Board, 19 October 1966.

———. Special Circular No. 77, 22 March 1969.

———. Staff Bulletin.

———. "Special Census of School Population," issued annually.

———. "Statement of Policy on Decentralization." New York: the Board, 19 April 1967.

———. "Summary of Citywide Reading Test Results," issued annually.

Bokser, Miriam. "Free the Panther 21!" *New York High School Free Press* 1969, no. 8.

Brammer, Lawrence M. "The Coming Revolt of High School Students." *National Association of Secondary School Principals Bulletin*, September 1968.

Brooklyn Education Task Force. "Academic High Schools – Brooklyn, or Why Children Fail." Mimeographed,

Brooks, Thomas R. *Towards Dignity: A Brief History of the United Federation of Teachers.* New York: United Federation of Teachers, 1967.

———. "Tragedy at Ocean Hill," *Dissent,* January-February 1969.

Caley, Barbara. "How a School Fails. *Integrated Education.* September-October 1969.

Calhoun, Arthur W. *A Social History of the American Family.* New York: Barnes & Noble, 1945.

Carmichael, Stokely, and Hamilton, Charles V. *Black Power: The Politics of Liberation in America.* New York: Random House, 1968

Carnegie Quarterly, Fall 1968.

Center for the Study of Democratic Institutions. "Ghetto Education." Supplement to *Center Magazine,* November 1968.

Center for Urban Education. *Community Attitudes in Bedford-Stuyvesant: An Area Study.* New York: the Center, 1967.

Clark, Kenneth. "The Clash of Cultures in the Classroom." *Integrated Education,* August 1963.

Cleaver, Eldridge, *Soul on Ice.* New York: McGraw-Hill, 1968.

Coleman, James S., et al. *Equality of Educational Opportunity.* U.S. Department of Health, Education, and Welfare, Office of Education. Washington, D.C.: Government Printing Office, 1966.

Coles, Robert. *Children of Crisis.* Boston: Little, Brown, 1967.

Conant, James Bryant. *Slums and Suburbs, A Commentary on Schools in Metropolitan Areas.* New York: McGraw-Hill, 1961.

CORE. "A Proposal for an Independent Board of Education for Harlem." Mimeographed. New York-Harlem CORE, 1 March 1967.

Dienstfrey, Harris. "Outside the Expected." *The Urban Review,* September 1968.

Erikson, Erik H. *Childhood and Society.* New York: W. W. Norton, 1963.

———. *Identity: Youth and Crisis.* New York: W. W. Norton, 1968.

Erikson, Kai. *Wayward Puritans.* New York: John Wiley, 1966.

Fanon, Frantz. *Wretched of the Earth.* New York: Grove Press, 1963.

Farber, Jerry. "The Student as Nigger." *This Magazine Is About Schools,* Winter 1968.

Feldman, Marvin J. "Making Education Relevant." Speech published as a pamphlet. New York: the Ford Foundation, 1966.

Focus. New York: I.S. 201.

Ford Foundation. Press release, 6 July 1967.

Forlano, George, and Abramson, Jack. *Measuring Pupil Growth in Reading in the More Effective Schools.* New York: Bureau of Educational Research, Board of Education, April 1968.

Fox, David J. *Expansion of the More Effective Schools Program.* New York: Center for Urban Education, September 1967.

Franseth, Jane, and Koury, Rose. *Survey of Research on Grouping as Related to Pupil Learning.* U.S. Department of Health, Education, and Welfare, Office of Education. Washington, D. C.: Government Printing Office, 1966.

Friedenberg, Edgar. "Contemptuous Hairdressers," *This Magazine Is About Schools,* August 1966.

———. "What Do Schools Do?" *This Magazine Is About Schools,* Winter 1969.

———"What Do Schools Do?" *This Magazine Is About Schools,* Winter 1969.

Fuchs, Estelle. *Pickets at the Gates.* New York: The Free Press, 1966.

Gattegno, Caleb. *Towards a Visual Culture.* New York: Outerbridge & Dienstfrey, 1969.

Ghetto Schools: Problems and Panaceas. A *New Republic* Pamphlet, 1967.

Gittell, Marilyn. *Participants and Participation.* New York: Frederick A. Praeger, 1967.

Goodman, Yetta Trachtman. "The Culturally Deprived Child: A Study in Stereotyping." *Integrated Education,* July–August 1969.

Goldman, Jane. "Rebuttal to Teacher Evaluation." Unpublished document. Fremont, California, 1970.

Gottlieb, Edward P. "Ghetto Schools Need Black Power." *WIN Magazine,* 1 November, 15 November, and December 1968.

Griffiths, Daniel E., et al. *Teacher Mobility in New York City: A Study of the Recruitment, Selection, Appointment,and Promotion of Teachers in the New York City Public Schools.* New York: New York University, 1963.

Gross, Morris. *Learning Readiness in Two Jewish Groups.* New York: Center for Urban Education, 1967.

Hall, Edward T. *The Silent Language.* New York: Doubleday, 1959.

Harlem Education Project. No title. Mimeographed report, 1963–64.

Harlem Parents Committee. "The Education of Minority Group Children in the New York City Public Schools." Mimeographed. New York: the Committee, 1965.

Harlem Youth Opportunities Unlimited, Inc. *Youth in the Ghetto: A Study of the Consequences of Powerlessness and a Blueprint for Change.* New York: HARYOU, 1964.

Hatchett, John F. "The Phenomenon of the Anti-Black Jews and the Black Anglo-Saxon: A Study in Educational Perfidy." *The African-American Teachers Forum,* December 1968.

Hearings before the Senate Subcommittee on Indian Education, 91st Congress, 1st sess. Washington, D.C.: U.S. Government Printing Office, 1969.

Henry, Jules. *Culture Against Man.* New York: Random House, 1963.

———. "Education for Stupidity." *The New York Review of Books,* 9 May 1968.

Hentoff, Nat. *Our Children Are Dying.* New York: Viking, 1966.

Herndon, James. *The Way It Spozed To Be.* New York. Simon and Schuster, 1968.

Herriott, Robert E., and St. John, Nancy Hoyt. *Social Class and the Urban School.* New York: John Wiley, 1966.

High School Principals Association. "The Nature and Limits of Student Dissent and Participation, January 16, 1969." New York: the Association.

Hollingshead, August B. *Elmtown's Youth: The Impact of Social Classes on Adolescents.* New York: John Wiley, 1949.

———. "Confrontation and Response." Published in the *New York Herald Tribune,* September 1969.

IRCD Bulletin, Winter 1966–67.

The I.S. 201 Complex Community Information Manual. New York: I. S. Complex District Office, Fall 1968.

I.S. 201 Complex press release, 12 December 1968.

I.S. 201 Negotiating Committee. "Sequence of Events Surrounding Community Involvement with Public School 201." Mimeographed, Period covered, 1958–September 1966.

I.S. 201 Newsletter.

Jones, Dorothy S. "The Issues at I.S. 201: A View from the Parents' Committee." *Integrated Education,* October–November 1966.

Kalodner, Howard I. "Analysis of Marchi Legislation on School Decentralization as it Affects Demonstration Decentralization Projects and Other Local School Boards." Flushing, New York: Queens College Institute for Community Studies, 1 August 1969.

Keil, Charles. *Urban Blues.* Chicago: University of Chicago Press, 1966.

Kemble, Eugenia. "I.S. 201 and the First Days of the Bundy Report." *The United Teacher,* 22 November 1967.

Kohl, Herbert. *Thirty-six children.* New York: New American Library, 1967.

Kozol, Jonathan. *Death at an Early Age.* Boston: Houghton Mifflin, 1967.

Lang, Kurt, and Lang, Gladys Engel. "Resistance to School Desegregation: A Case Study of Backlash Among Jews." *Sociological Inquiry,* Winter 1965.

Larner, Jeremy. "I.S. 201: Disaster in the Schools." *Dissent,* January–February 1967.

Lederer, Joseph. "The Scope of the Practice." *The Urban Review,* September 1968.

Lobenthal, Joseph S. "Educational Experimentation and 'The Merit System.'" *The Center Forum,* 28 June 1968.

"The Mason-Dixon Line Moves to New York." *I.F. Stone's Weekly*, 4 November 1968.

Mayer, Martin. "The Full and Sometimes Very Surprising Story of Ocean Hill, the Teachers' Union and the Teacher Strikes of 1968." *New York Times Magazine*, 2 February 1968.

———. *The Teachers Strike, New York, 1968.* New York: Harper & Row, 1968.

McCandless, Boyd R. *Children: Behavior and Development.* 2nd ed. New York: Holt, Rinehart and Winston, 1967.

McInnis V. Ogilvie, 394 U.S. 322. 1969.

Meier, Deborah. "The New York Teachers' Strike." *Midstream*, December 1967.

Metropolitan Achievement Tests. New York: Harcourt, Brace and World.

Metropolitan Applied Research Center. "Fact Sheet: School Crisis at Franklin K. Lane and Canarsie High Schools." Mimeographed. New York: the Center, March 1969.

———. *An Intensive Program for the Attainment of Educational Achievement in Deprived Area Schools of New York City.* New York: the Center, March 1968.

———. "10.5% Increase in New York City Pupils Critically Below Grade Level in Reading." Press release, 15 March 1969.

———. Vertical File on I.S. 201.

Minter, Thomas K. *Intermediate School 201, Manhattan: Center of Controversy.* Cambridge, Massachusetts: 2 June 1967.

"Minutes of a Meeting of the I.S. 201 Complex Governing Board with Unit Administration designee Charles Wilson." Mimeographed, 16 February 1968.

National Education Association. *Wilcox County, Alabama: A Study of Social, Economic, and Educational Bankruptcy.* New York: the Association, June 1967.

New School for Social Research, Urban Reporting Project. "The Ocean Hill-Brownsville Community Views: The News Coverage," by George Barner; "The Press Coverage of the Ocean Hill-Brownsville School Dispute: A Case History," by Barbara Carter; and "The 1968 Teachers' Strike: A Comparison of TV and Newspaper Coverage," by Gladys Engel Lang. New York: the New School, October 1968.

New Schools Exchange Newsletter. Santa Barbara, California, 1969.

New York, City. Commission on Human Rights. *Education in Crisis: A Report on Decentralization, Teacher Training, and Curriculum in the New York City Public Schools.* New York: the Commission, December 1968.

———. *Report on Three Demonstration Districts.* New York: the Commission, February–March 1968.

New York, City. Office of Education. *A Summary of the 1969 School Decentralization Law for New York City.* New York: the Office, 1969.

New York, State. Education Commissioner's Advisory Committee on Human Relations and Community Tensions, with the assistance of The Institute of Urban Studies, Teachers College, Columbia University. *Desegregating the Public Schools of New York City.* Report prepared for the Board of Education of the City of New York, 12 May 1964.

Nordstrom, Carl, et al. *Society's Children,* New York: Random House, 1967.

Olden, Christine. "On Adult Empathy with Children," *Psychoanalytic Study of the Child,* vol. 8. New York: International Universities Press, 1953.

O'Neill, John. Letter to the *New York Times.* Reprinted by the New York Civil Liberties Union, March 1969.

———"The Teachers' Contract: It Doesn't Seem Right!" The Village Voice, 3 July 1969.

Pelletier, Wilfred. "Childhood in an Indian Village." *This Magazine Is About Schools,* Spring 1969.

Queens College Institute for Community Studies. *Community.* Flushing, New York: the Institute, May 1969.

———. *New York City School Fact Book.* Flushing, New York: the Institute, n.d.

Rainwater, Lee. "The Revolt of the Dirty Workers," *Trans-action,* November 1967.

Reconnection for Learning: A Community School System for New York ("Bundy Report"). Mayor Lindsay's Advisory Plan on Decentralization of the New York City Schools, November 1967.

Reichsman, Mary. "School Suspension at the District Leval in One Manhattan School District." Mimeographed. New York: Community Service Society of New York, June 1969.

Riessman, Frank. *The Culturally Deprived Child.* New York: Harper & Row, 1962.

Rogers, David. *110 Livingston Street.* New York: Random House, 1968.

Rosenthal, Robert, and Jacobson, Lenore. *Pygmalion in the Classroom.* New York: Holt, Rinehart and Winston, 1968.

Rowntree, John, and Rowntree, Margaret. *The Political Economy of Youth.* Ann Arbor, Michigan: the Radical Education Project, n.d.

Sapir, Edward. *Language, An Introduction to the Study of Speech.* New York: Harcourt, Brace & Co., 1921.

Schwager, Sidney. "An Analysis of the Evaluation of the More Effective Schools Program Conducted by the Center for Urban Education." Mimeographed. New York: United Federation of Teachers, 1967.

Sexton, Patricia Cayo. *The American School.* Englewood Cliffs: Prentice-Hall, 1967.

———. *Education and Income: Inequalities in Our Public Schools.* New York: Viking, 1964.

Shuy, Roger W. *Social Dialects and Language Learning.* Champaign, Illinois: National Council of Teachers of English, 1964.

Spencer, David. "A Harlem Parent Speaks Out." *NEA Journal,* March 1968.

Spiegel, John P. "How Administrators Are Using Student Activism as a Force for Better Schools." *School Management,* November 1968.

Steel, Lewis M. *Community Control and the Courts.* Flushing, New York: Queens College Institute for Community Studies, March 1969.

Stewart, William A. *Non-Standard Speech and the Teaching of English.* Washington, D.C.: Center for Applied Linguistics, 1964.

"Summary of New York City Community School District System." John H. Lotz, distributor, member of the Board of Education of the City of New York, 8 May 1969.

Tinker v. Des Moines Independent Community School District, no. 21, October Terms, 24 February 1969.

Tobier, A. J. "P.S. 133: A Catcher in the Rye." *The Center Forum,* 15 May 1969.

Tree, Christina. "Grouping Pupils in New York City." *The Urban Review,* September 1968.

Tressler, J. C. and Shelmadine, Marguerite B. *Junior English in Action,* book 1. Boston: D. C. Heath and Co., 1966.

United Bronx Parents. "Do Black and Puerto Rican Students Get the Same Opportunities as White Students Get in the New York City Public Schools?" Mimeographed, n.d.

"Distribution of Educational Resources Among the Bronx Public Schools." Mimeographed, April 1968.

———. "Training for Local Control: Expenditures per Pupil in the Bronx Schools. Mimeographed, n.d.

United States Department of Health, Education, and Welfare. *Improving English Skills of Culturally Different Youth in Large Cities.* Washington, D.C.: Government Printing Office, 1962.

———. *White-Nonwhite Differentials in Health, Education and Welfare.* Washington, D.C.: Government Printing Office, 1965.

United States Department of Labor, Bureau of Labor Statistics, Special Labor Force. *Employment of High School Graduates and Dropouts in 1967.* Report No. 100. Washington, D.C.: Government Printing Office,

Ward, Agee. "Ocean Hill: Education, Community, Power, and the Media." *The Center Forum,* 13 November 1968.

Wasserman, Miriam. "The Loud, Proud Black Kids." *The Progressive,* April 1968.

———. "Planting Pansies on the Roof: A Critique of How New York City Tests Reading." *The Urban Review,* January 1969.

Wax, Murray, et al., eds. *Anthropological Perspectives on Education.* New York: Basic Books, forthcoming.

———. *Formal Education in an American Indian Community.* Supplement to *Social Problems.* Society for the Study of Social Problems, Spring 1964.

Wax, Rosalie H. "The Warrior Dropouts." *Trans-action*, May 1967.

Weinberg, Meyer, ed. *Integrated Education.* Beverly Hills: The Glencoe Press, 1968.

Wiebe, Robert H. "The Social Functions of Public Education." *American Quarterly,* Summer 1969.

Wielk, Carol A. *The Ocean Hill-Brownsville School Project: A Profile.* Flushing, New York: Queens College Institute for Community Studies, February 1969.

Wilcox, Preston. "The Controversy Over I.S. 201: One View and a Proposal." *The Urban Review,* July 1966.

———. "The Meaning of Community Control," Mimeographed, 2 December 1968.

Wilson, Charles, and Spencer, David. "The Case for Community Control." In *Community and Racial Crisis,* ed., Barbara Flicker. New York: Practicing Law Institute, 1969.

WINS news conference. Transcript, 7 October 1966, 10:30 p.m.

Wise, Arthur E. *Rich Schools, Poor Schools: The Promise of Equal Educational Opportunity.* Chicago: University of Chicago Press, 1968.

Woodward, C. Vann. *Tom Watson, Agrarian Rebel.* New York: Oxford University Press, 1963.

Work Projects Administration. "Negroes in the New York City Public Schools." Unpublished file, Schomburg Library, New York City.

Yates, Alfred, ed. *Grouping in Education.* New York: John Wiley, 1966.

Zeluck, Steve. "The UFT Strike: A Blow Against Teacher Unionism." *New Politics,* Winter 1968.

INDEX

Fictitious names are indexed under the first name in the case of students, and under Miss, Mrs., or Mr. in the case of teachers.

232, 278, 440-442